Special Responsibilities

D1216071

The language of special responsibilities
with policy-makers and commentators alike speaking
particular states have, or ought to have, unique obligations in managing
global problems. Surprisingly, scholars are yet to provide any in-depth analysis of this fascinating aspect of world politics. This path-breaking study
examines the nature of special responsibilities, the complex politics that
surround them and how they condition international social power. The
argument is illustrated with detailed case studies of nuclear proliferation,
climate change and global finance. All three problems have been addressed
by an allocation of special responsibilities, but while this has structured
politics in these areas, it has also been the subject of ongoing contestation.
With a focus on the United States, this book argues that power must be
understood as a social phenomenon, and that American power varies
significantly across security, economic and environmental domains.

MLADA BUKOVANSKY is Professor of Government at Smith College,
Northampton, Massachusetts. She is the author of *Legitimacy and Power
Politics: the American and French Revolutions in International Political
Culture* (2002).

IAN CLARK is E. H. Carr Professor of International Politics at Aberystwyth
University. He is the author of many books, most recently a three-volume
study of international legitimacy – *Legitimacy in International Society*
(2005), *International Legitimacy and World Society* (2007) and *Hegemony in
International Society* (2011).

ROBYN ECKERSLEY is Professor of Political Science in the School of
Social and Political Sciences and Program Director of the Master of
International Relations Program at the University of Melbourne. She is
author of *The Green State: Rethinking Democracy and Sovereignty* (2004) and
editor (with J. Barry) of *The State and the Global Ecological Crisis* (2005)
and (with A. Dobson) *Political Theory and the Ecological Challenge* (2006).

RICHARD PRICE is a Professor in the Department of Political Science,
University of British Columbia. He is author of *The Chemical Weapons
Taboo* (1997), co-editor with Mark W. Zacher of *The United Nations and
Global Security* (2004) and editor of *Moral Limit and Possibility in World
Politics* (2008).

CHRISTIAN REUS-SMIT holds the Chair in International Relations
at the European University Institute in Florence. He is the author of
American Power and World Order (2004) and *The Moral Purpose of the State*
(1999), editor of *The Politics of International Law* (2004) and co-editor with
Duncan Snidal of *The Oxford Handbook of International Relations* (2008).

NICHOLAS J. WHEELER is Director of the Institute for Conflict,
Cooperation, and Security at the University of Birmingham. He is the
author of *Saving Strangers: Humanitarian Intervention in International
Society* (2000), co-author (with Ken Booth) of *The Security Dilemma: Fear,
Cooperation and Trust in World Politics* (2007) and co-editor (with Tim
Dunne) of *Human Rights in Global Politics* (2000).

Special responsibilities

Global Problems and American Power

Mlada Bukovansky, Ian Clark, Robyn Eckersley,
Richard Price, Christian Reus-Smit and
Nicholas J. Wheeler

CAMBRIDGE
UNIVERSITY PRESS

CAMBRIDGE UNIVERSITY PRESS
Cambridge, New York, Melbourne, Madrid, Cape Town,
Singapore, São Paulo, Delhi, Mexico City

Cambridge University Press
The Edinburgh Building, Cambridge CB2 8RU, UK

Published in the United States of America by Cambridge University Press,
New York

www.cambridge.org
Information on this title: www.cambridge.org/9781107691698

First published 2012

Printed in the United Kingdom at the University Press, Cambridge

A catalogue record for this publication is available from the British Library

Library of Congress Cataloguing in Publication data
Bukovansky, Mlada, 1962–
    Special responsibilities : global problems and American power /
    Mlada Bukovansky, Ian Clark, Robyn Eckersley, Richard Price,
    Christian Reus-Smit, Nicholas J. Wheeler.
        pages   cm
    Includes bibliographical references and index.
    ISBN 978-1-107-02135-8 (hardback) – ISBN 978-1-107-69169-8
    (paperback)
    1. International relations–Moral and ethical aspects.   2. United States–
    Foreign relations–Moral and ethical aspects.   3. Responsibility–Political
    aspects.   I. Clark, Ian, 1949–   II. Eckersley, Robyn, 1958–
    III. Price, Richard M. (Richard MacKay), 1964–   IV. Reus-Smit,
    Christian, 1961–   V. Wheeler, Nicholas J.   VI. Title.
    JZ1306.B85 2012
    327.73–dc23   2012008286

ISBN 978-1-107-02135-8 Hardback
ISBN 978-1-107-69169-8 Paperback

Contents

Preface

Some members of this team of authors have occasionally collaborated together over the years and decades. Collectively, we all came together for the first time in 2004, as part of a larger group working on a project on 'Resolving International Crises of Legitimacy', funded by the British Academy. That project was born of our shared interest in issues of international legitimacy, and how this interacted with 'power' in world politics. The specific legacy of that undertaking was a special issue of the journal *International Politics*, 44 (2/3) 2007. The broader legacy was the immense intellectual stimulus of working together as a group, and when the opportunity arose to resume this collaboration, it was immediately seized. This opportunity was created in 2007 by a funding award from the UK Economic and Social Research Council (ESRC) that included a collaborative dimension, and we all gratefully acknowledge this generous support. Given that throughout we have been variously based in Australia, Canada, Italy, the UK and the US, the award enabled periodic workshops that brought us together, and without which this book would not have been possible.

The award covered a generic project on the social bases of American power. In part, this represented a carry-over from the previous study: if an institution were to suffer a 'crisis' of legitimacy, how might this be resolved? What role should the United States specifically play in bringing about this resolution? These questions appeared to become even more pertinent with the election of the Barack Obama administration. Our initial intention was to approach this under the rubric of 'hegemony', as this was already the principal element of the cognate research being undertaken by Ian Clark as part of his individual role in the overall ESRC project. However, in the course of our meetings, it gradually became clear that what was routinely expected of hegemons was that they would bear special responsibilities for contributing to the solution of global problems. Slowly, the main focus on hegemony diminished and was replaced by that on special responsibilities. We wanted to emphasise that our theory of special responsibilities was one specific way of elaborating our general approach to the social constitution of power. This also justified the focus on the US as it offered a useful framework for disaggregating US power in particular. This concept, of which we became increasingly confident, fully encapsulated all the important elements that we wished to discuss – power, legitimacy and the normative dimensions that fused the two. This allowed us to develop our earlier work on legitimacy, while closely scrutinising a term that has long become part of the everyday vocabulary of international politics, but which nobody has so far taken the time to explore in detail.

In bringing this study to fruition, we have incurred a substantial number of debts. Principal amongst these is to Dr Rachel Owen. Rachel served as the research assistant for the project, and in this capacity she organised our various workshops (travel, hospitality and programmes), as well as managing the informational infrastructure of our collaboration. She did this with the greatest of efficiency, and with unfailing good humour. We were all delighted to have Rachel as part of our team, and we thank her for her major contribution to the successful completion of this undertaking.

A number of institutions served as hosts for our various meetings and provided important logistical support. In particular, we wish to thank Amy Gurowitz and the Institute of International Studies, University of California, Berkeley for hosting the first workshop of the project (29 March–1 April 2008); the European University Institute for twice hosting our meetings (30 March–1 April 2009, 12–13 May 2011); the Department of International Relations, Australian National University, for its support of our workshop (16–19 March 2010); and the Department of International Politics, Aberystwyth University (19–21 July 2010). At the Aberystwyth workshop, we invited a number of distinguished discussants to comment on the draft of our work. All eagerly accepted our invitation, and made heroic contributions over the three-day period. This greatly enhanced the way we approached our final draft, and so we are pleased to thank profusely the following: Campbell Craig, Tim Dunne, Kimberley Hutchings, Justin Morris, Matthew Paterson, Duncan Snidal, Andrew Walter and William Wohlforth. The book is all the better for their insights and telling reflections (but with the usual caveats).

In addition, the authors – individually or jointly – have given many presentations on the themes of the book at various institutions: Johns Hopkins University, Bologna Centre, Italy; Chuo University and Hitotsobashi University, Tokyo; School of Political Science and International Relations, University of Queensland; Oxford Institute for Ethics, Law and Armed Conflict, University of Oxford; Department of International Relations, London School of Economics; Department of Political Science, University of Western Washington; International Relations Colloquium, University of British Columbia; and the Munk School of Global Affairs, University of Toronto. We are happy to acknowledge all the constructive feedback we received at these venues.

We also wish to express our thanks to John Haslam for his support of our project, and to the Cambridge University Press team for the book's efficient production. In the final stage, the entire script was read by a professional copy-editor to iron out stylistic inconsistencies. For agreeing to undertake this major task, we are deeply indebted to Mary-Louise Hickey of the Australian National University.

So comfortable had we become in working together as a team that we set ourselves the additional challenge of making this a jointly authored, rather than edited, volume. Although individuals were assigned 'special responsibilities' for first drafts of specific sections, the text as a whole has been worked through by the entire team, and is collectively owned.

Abbreviations

AOSIS	Alliance of Small Island States
APP	Asia-Pacific Partnership on Clean Development and Climate
BASIC	Brazil, South Africa, India and China
CBDR	common but differentiated responsibilities
CDM	clean development mechanism
COP	Conferences of the Parties
CTBT	Comprehensive Nuclear-Test-Ban Treaty
EC	European Community
EPA	Environmental Protection Agency
EU	European Union
FMCT	Fissile Material Cut-Off Treaty
FSF	Financial Stability Forum
GATT	General Agreement on Tariffs and Trade
GHG	greenhouse gas
IAEA	International Atomic Energy Agency
ICJ	International Court of Justice
IMF	International Monetary Fund
IPCC	Intergovernmental Panel on Climate Change
IR	International Relations
MRV	measurable, reportable and verifiable
NAMA	nationally appropriate mitigation action
NATO	North Atlantic Treaty Organisation
NGO	non-governmental organisation
NNWS	non-nuclear weapon state
NPT	Nuclear Non-Proliferation Treaty
NRSRO	nationally recognized statistical ratings organization
NSG	Nuclear Suppliers Group
NWS	nuclear weapon state
OECD	Organisation for Economic Co-operation and Development
PPP	polluter pays principle
SALT	Strategic Arms Limitations Talks

SORT	Strategic Offensive Reductions Treaty
START	Strategic Arms Reduction Talks
UN	United Nations
UNFCCC	United Nations Framework Convention on Climate Change
WMD	weapons of mass destruction

Introduction

During his visit to China in November 2009, US President Barack Obama gave a joint press conference along with China's President Hu Jintao. In his statement, Obama identified three major global problems: nuclear proliferation, climate change and economic recovery from the global financial crisis. Their common feature, he insisted, was that none could be solved by either state acting alone. He therefore welcomed China's greater role, 'a role in which a growing economy is joined by growing responsibilities'.[1] This emphasised the seeming proportionality between the material resources enjoyed by a state, and the scale of responsibilities it was required to shoulder. It explicitly brought together one view of international politics, as rooted in material resources, with an importantly different view, as rooted in social responsibilities.

There are four interesting dimensions to this statement. First it specified those key global problems in particular. Second it attempted to address them by an explicit appeal to responsibility. Third it assumed that increased responsibilities flow from greater material resources. Fourth it attempted to (re)allocate these responsibilities to reflect those new material distributions.

This was no isolated pronouncement. The language of world politics has become thoroughly suffused with responsibility talk: states are deemed not merely actors in some quasi-mechanical international system, but also as the bearers of responsibilities in an international society. Their interests and their ability to realise them are shaped as much by the latter as by the former. Moreover, some actors are widely claimed to carry special responsibilities that set them apart. Such notions can be found even at a popular level. When asked in a survey conducted at the end of 2010 if the United States had a 'special responsibility to be the leading nation in world affairs', 66 per cent of Americans polled

---

[1] 'President Obama delivers joint press statement with President Hu Jintao of China', *Washington Post*, 17 November 2009, www.washingtonpost.com/wp-dyn/content/article/2009/11/17/AR2009111701090.html?sid=ST2009111700768 (accessed 27 July 2011).

answered in the affirmative.[2] In order to establish immediately the importance of this topic, let us briefly eavesdrop on this responsibility talk, as drawn from the discussion of those three global problems identified by Obama.

The topic of nuclear proliferation has long been dominated by special responsibility talk. A distinctive responsibility in this area has been widely accepted by various US administrations in the past, although often said to be shared with Russia, or with the other nuclear weapon states (NWSs) more generally. Thomas D'Agostino, Administrator of the US National Nuclear Security Administration under President George W. Bush, had already attested that 'the US has a special responsibility in advancing nonproliferation and nuclear security globally', even if it could not deliver these goals on its own.[3] Commonly, Russia has been identified as sharing this responsibility. In 2008, Republican presidential candidate John McCain argued that '[a]s our two countries possess the overwhelming majority of the world's nuclear weapons, we have a special responsibility to reduce their number'.[4] This view was confirmed by US Secretary of State Hillary Clinton on the signing of the latest Strategic Arms Reduction Treaty agreement with Russia in April 2010 which, she said, reflected the 'special responsibilities that the United States and Russia bear as the two largest nuclear powers'.[5] Susan F. Burk, the administration's ambassador for non-proliferation, allocates this 'special responsibility for pursuing nuclear disarmament' to the NWSs generally, but insists also that the 'non-nuclear weapons states share this responsibility under Article VI'.[6] In what sense the NWSs can have a *special* responsibility, but one that is at the same time *shared* with the non-nuclear weapon states (NNWSs), is itself an intriguing question.

Likewise, the policy issue of climate change has for many years been powerfully organised by a discourse about the allocation of

---

[2] J. M. Jones, 'Americans see US as exceptional; 37% doubt Obama does', Gallup, 22 December 2010, www.gallup.com/poll/145358 (accessed 27 July 2011).

[3] T. D'Agostino, 'Reducing the global nuclear threat: nuclear non-proliferation and the role of the international community', presentation to the Center for Strategic and International Studies, Washington, DC, 18 September 2008, www.nti.org/e_research/source_docs/us/department_energy/national_nuclear_security_administration/10.pdf (accessed 27 July 2011).

[4] J. McCain, 'Remarks at the University of Denver', Denver, 27 May 2008, www.presidency.ucsb.edu/ws/index.php?pid=77369#axzz1TGGuqlhn (accessed 27 July 2011).

[5] H. Clinton, 'Implementing a nuclear arms strategy for the 21st century', 7 April 2010, malta.usembassy.gov/arms.html (accessed 27 July 2011).

[6] S. Burk, 'Toward a successful NPT Review Conference', Carnegie Endowment for International Peace, Washington, DC, 31 March 2010, carnegieendowment.org/events/?fa=eventDetail&id=2841&solr_hilite=Burk+Susan (accessed 27 July 2011).

responsibilities. The principles underpinning this were set out in the United Nations Framework Convention on Climate Change and its related Kyoto Protocol. However, with the adoption of a more activist policy under the Obama administration, there has been a renewed acceptance of responsibilities by the United States, even if these are not to be singularly borne. Shortly after being appointed as Obama's special envoy on climate change, Todd Stern affirmed that the 'United States recognizes our unique responsibility' on this issue, and attributed its source both to America's record as 'the largest historic emitter of greenhouse gases', and also on account of America's endowment 'with important human, financial, and technological capabilities and resources'.[7] US Secretary of Commerce, Gary Locke, when speaking in China in the company of the US Secretary of Energy, Steven Chu, likewise acknowledged that 'as the two biggest emitters of carbon dioxide, the United States and China have a special responsibility to take action'.[8] Unsurprisingly, the official website of Friends of the Earth concurred:

We believe that as the world's biggest historical global warming polluter, and as a wealthy nation with considerable resources, the United States has a special responsibility to lead the world in finding equitable solutions to the climate crisis.[9]

What is so striking about all this talk is its explicit adoption of the language of special responsibilities, as well as its various attributions, assignments and acceptance of these responsibilities by a surprisingly diverse range of actors. Notable also are the range of reasons asserted for those special responsibilities, as well as their profoundly differing implications for the onus of undertaking future action. Do responsibilities arise because of retrospective contributions to the problem, or because of prospective resources for finding a solution?

This very same language is readily discernible in discussions about global finance. As might be expected, the recent global financial crisis has evinced a plethora of responsibility talk, within which some special responsibilities have roundly been assigned to the United States. For example, in one unusually blunt statement, the European Commission called upon the United States to 'take responsibility'. By way of

---

[7] T. Stern quoted in 'New day dawns for US global warming', *Environment News Service*, 30 March 2009, www.ens-newswire.com/ens/mar2009/2009-03-30-01.asp (accessed 27 July 2011).

[8] G. Locke quoted in 'US commerce, energy secretaries highlight cooperation with China on climate change', Xinhua News Agency, 6 July 2009, www.china.org.cn/environment/news/2009-07/16/content_18146470.htm (accessed 27 July 2011).

[9] Friends of the Earth, www.foe.org/international-work (accessed 27 July 2011).

explanation, it suggested that the 'turmoil we are facing has originated in the United States. It has become a global problem. The US has a special responsibility in this situation.'[10] Elsewhere, US Secretary of the Treasury, Timothy Geithner, has admitted to the need for US action to maintain the value of the US dollar, on account of its 'special responsibility for being a source of stability and strength in the global economy',[11] while President Obama acknowledged the somewhat different 'special responsibility' held by the US 'as one of the world's financial centers, to work with partners around the globe to reform a failed regulatory system'.[12] On this latter theme, Geithner and European Union Commissioner for Internal Market and Services, Michel Barnier, were subsequently able to agree that 'the United States and the European Union, as the world's two largest economies and financial systems, have a special responsibility to promote and implement stronger global financial standards'.[13] Once again, the substance, sources and allocation of responsibilities were central to the post-financial crisis diagnosis of what needs to be done to fix the global system.

What is the significance of all this responsibility talk? Is it no more than a rhetorical adornment to conceal the naked power politics underneath? Is the stated allocation of those responsibilities simply a reflection of the existing distribution of material power, and intended as one way of reproducing it? Are reallocations of special responsibilities little more than an acknowledgement of ongoing changes in that distribution? Alternatively, could it be that this language of responsibility actually helps to shape a distribution of power in a more fundamentally social sense?

This book enters upon the first explicit and sustained engagement with the notion of special responsibilities in world politics. It is, however, much more than a work of conceptual clarification: it also offers a

[10] Quoted in L. Phillips, 'US must take responsibility for global crisis, Brussels says', *euobserver.com*, 30 September 2008, euobserver.com/9/26835 (accessed 27 July 2011).

[11] T. Geithner quoted in G. Somerville, 'Geithner stresses strong dollar's global role', Reuters, 12 November 2009, www.reuters.com/article/2009/11/12/us-apec-idUSTRE5AA0IB20091112 (accessed 27 July 2011).

[12] 'Video and transcript: President Obama's remarks at the Summit of the Americas (17 April)', *EAWorldView*, 20 April 2009, www.enduringamerica.com/april-2009/2009/4/20/video-and-transcript-president-obamas-remarks-at-the-summit.html (accessed 27 July 2011).

[13] 'Joint statement by US Treasury Secretary Timothy Geithner and EU Commissioner Michel Barnier on the financial reform agenda', EU/NR 22/10, 12 May 2010, www.eurunion.org/eu/2010-News-Releases/JOINT-STATEMENT-BY-UNITED-STATES-TREASURY-SECRETARY-TIMOTHY-GEITHNER-AND-EUROPEAN-UNION-COMMISSIONER-MICHEL-BARNIER-ON-THE-FINANCIAL-REFORM-AGENDA.html (accessed 27 July 2011).

key insight into one important facet of those politics. Although the language of special responsibilities has become pervasive, both in practitioner and theoretical accounts, it has nowhere previously been subject to systematic examination and explication. As a group of scholars with a continuing interest in the role of international legitimacy, we saw the opportunity to develop our general understanding of legitimacy, and of the social power to which it gives rise, by a specific discussion of this concept.[14] Accordingly, our treatment of special responsibilities arises as one instance of international legitimacy more generally, insofar as they represent one variant form through which legitimacy comes to be practised. Just as international legitimacy is generally affected by material power relations, but manages still to serve as an autonomous influence on agent behaviour, so it will be argued that special responsibilities reflect existing distributions of material power, while at the same time also reconfiguring the social relations of power within its sundry policy domains. In this way, the contestation over special responsibilities represents one particularly good illustration of the contestation over principles of legitimacy more generally, and serves to track their historical evolution. The allocation of special responsibilities operates in this way, above all, through its unique compromise between the principles of equality and differentiation, and by its ongoing negotiation between the two.

Equality and differentiation

Every dimension of international politics – political, legal and moral – faces the challenge of reconciling the two principles of equality and differentiation. The first articulates a claim to equality, and stresses what all states share in common, including enjoyment of the same rights and responsibilities within the existing international order. This idea is most clearly captured in the modern doctrine of sovereignty, especially in the sovereign equality that it is thought necessarily to entail: it is in the very identity of their legal capacity that the equality of all states resides. The second articulates instead a principle of differentiated status, adopted to enhance the efficient working of international order, but often at the

---

[14] M. Bukovansky, *Legitimacy and power politics: The American and French revolutions in international political culture* (Princeton, NJ: Princeton University Press, 2002); I. Clark, *Legitimacy in international society* (Oxford: Oxford University Press, 2005); I. Clark, *Hegemony in international society* (Oxford: Oxford University Press, 2011); I. Clark and C. Reus-Smit (eds.), 'Resolving international crises of legitimacy', *International Politics*, 44(2/3) 2007, 153–339; C. Reus-Smit, *American power and world order* (Cambridge: Polity Press, 2004).

behest of the strongest parties to entrench their own position.[15] This is best demonstrated in the acknowledgement of the differential legal and practical entitlements to which unequal capabilities have given rise. As one powerful example reveals, the United Nations Charter was itself a 'compromise between ... the "special responsibility" of the Great Powers ... and the juridical commitment to equality'.[16] This is a characteristic of special responsibilities across the board.

Special responsibilities come to the fore in a world characterised by two opposed sets of conditions. These range along a spectrum bounded by the normative structure of sovereign equality at one end, and the pure play of inequalities of material power at the other. Special responsibilities are therefore one potential political modality, set against what would otherwise likely happen at these two extremes. The first is characterised by formal sovereign equality, a form of legal egalitarianism central to the post-1945 international institutional order. This modality is often cast as essential to alleviating several of the more pronounced challenges to international cooperation, and it is deeply embedded in contemporary forms of multilateralism. The second is characterised by the free play of power politics, depicting a classic 'realist' world, driven wholly by inequalities in material power. Special responsibilities occupy the broad middle ground of the spectrum insofar as they attempt to mediate between the more thorough-going social condition of sovereign equality at one end, and raw material hierarchies at the other.

There are therefore two distinct senses in which 'differentiation' comes into play in this book. In the first, it simply denotes the inequalities in material power. Second, however, it maps the allocation of social roles, and a central point of the analysis is how these two senses of differentiation are related to each other. Towards the pole of sovereign equality, special responsibilities can be allocated on a wide range of social and normative principles, going well beyond considerations of the distribution of material power alone. Towards the pole of material power politics (as in the position of Kenneth Waltz outlined below), the differentiation in power becomes identical to the differentiation in role. In practice, special responsibilities have been elaborated and allocated in a world that reflects both of those competing pulls, resulting

---

[15] A good discussion of this dynamic tension can be found in N. Krisch, 'More equal than the rest? Hierarchy, equality and US predominance in international law', in M. Byers and G. Nolte (eds.), *United States hegemony and the foundations of international law* (Cambridge: Cambridge University Press, 2003), pp. 135–75.

[16] G. Simpson, *Great powers and outlaw states: Unequal sovereigns in the international legal order* (Cambridge: Cambridge University Press, 2004), p. 167.

in considerable divergence between the two types of differentiation at one end of the spectrum (sovereign equality), but a total convergence between them at the other (material inequality).

Neither of the alternative modalities at the two extremes has proved sufficiently robust for actually dealing with global problems. This is because sovereign equality finds it hard to articulate the sense in which any states are 'special', whereas material inequality struggles to give meaningful content to the notion of 'responsibilities'. As such, the tendency instead has been to look for some middle position: special responsibilities occupy that ground, but continue always to experience strong pulls towards one pole or the other. A central contention we make is that ideas and practices of special responsibilities come to the fore, and assume particular political importance, in international orders where either sovereign equality or material power politics, each on its own, provides an inadequate basis on which to address challenges of coexistence and cooperation. So special responsibilities arise when unilateral imposition of material power fails, but so too does bargaining amongst formal equals, leading instead to a search for a hierarchical but socially grounded politics of responsibility.

It is this generic dialogue between principles of equality, on the one hand, and principles of differentiation, on the other, that is so central to the talk about responsibilities in world politics, and to the special responsibilities that are thought to attach to particular actors. These have become international society's preferred way of attempting to navigate between the two competing principles. In order to promote multilateralism and cooperation between states, it has been necessary to adopt the formal device of equality, thereby to confirm that all participants stand on an equal footing. At the same time, in the face of bitter experience, it has long been understood that those states most capable of obstructing international cooperation are exactly those that wield the most material power. In consequence, the search for effective international organisation has pushed towards increasingly formal acknowledgement of the different contributions that various states might make. These twin elements constantly recur in the diverse discussions of the balance of power (and the particular role assigned within it to the great powers), in international legal theory, in the practical construction of various international organisations and also in normative debates about the perceived tensions between 'cosmopolitan' egalitarianism and 'communitarian' special responsibilities.[17]

[17] A. Abizadeh and P. Gilabert, 'Is there a genuine tension between cosmopolitan egalitarianism and special responsibilities?', *Philosophical Studies*, 138(3) 2008, 349–65.

It is with a sharp focus on this tension that special responsibilities are best approached, as they immediately begin to pull in those two opposing directions. This can be clearly illustrated with reference to international law. In this context, the idea of responsibility above all emphasises equality, since all states are thought to be equally responsible, in the sense of answerable, for their international legal commitments and obligations. Indeed, without some assumption of the responsibility of all states, it is hard to see how any concept of international law could pertain at all. According to international legal authorities, responsibility is a 'necessary corollary' of the equality of states: state equality is constituted by this common responsibility, insofar as all are equally answerable and accountable under the law.[18] In that sense, responsibility equates directly with the principle of sovereign equality.

In contrast, however, major works of International Relations (IR) theory regard special responsibilities as a kind of differentiation, rooted in profound material inequalities. The classical statement of this has been provided by Waltz: '[I]n any realm populated by units that are functionally similar but of different capability', he tells us, 'those of greatest capability take on special responsibilities.'[19] Waltz is famously reticent about the degree of differentiation and specialisation that occurs in international politics. It is one essential feature of anarchy, as an organising principle, that it is applicable to like units: their 'sameness' is bound up with the fact that they are 'not formally differentiated by the functions they perform'.[20] On the face of it, such a notion contradicts any allocation of special responsibilities. At the same time, Waltz clearly recognises that units are not alike in all respects, since some are manifestly more capable than others. Accordingly, he readily accepts that in a self-help system, '[g]reat tasks can be accomplished only by agents of great capability'.[21] As a result, the units are not 'identical', and some 'specialization by function' develops, issuing in a basic 'division of labor'.[22] For Waltz, then, special responsibilities simply capture this division of labour, and roles are arrogated on the basis of the existing distribution of material capabilities: this distribution necessarily exists independently of, and precedes, the resulting division of labour. There is absolutely no suggestion here that special responsibilities are allocated on any other principle, nor, in turn, are they considered to be

---

[18] A. Pellet, 'The definition of responsibility in international law', in J. Crawford, A. Pellet and S. Olleson (eds.), *The law of international responsibility* (Oxford: Oxford University Press, 2010), p. 4.

[19] K. N. Waltz, *Theory of international politics* (Reading, MA: Addison-Wesley, 1979), p. 198.

[20] *Ibid.*, p. 93.   [21] *Ibid.*, p. 109.   [22] *Ibid.*, pp. 114, 105.

a potential source of the (re)distribution of power. Even more fundamentally, the very notion of 'responsibilities' is itself vacuous, since it
employs a social concept to refer to an inherently asocial condition.

However, if it is true – as international lawyers commonly attest –
that 'no responsibility, no law', then at least from the eighteenth century onwards international politics was coming to be regarded also as
a game of responsibility, and not exclusively as one of capability. This
raised further issues of whether this responsibility could be differentially allocated, and if so, on which principles this might appropriately
be done. The result of this evolution was a progressive movement away
from assigning roles to various actors, merely in accordance with their
existing material capabilities, and towards a new outcome in which this
allocation became an important source of social power in its own right.
By this we mean that the distribution of responsibilities (and not just
the distribution of material capabilities) is constitutive of structures of
political power.

In one such elaboration of the role played by responsibility in the
international legal order, it is said that 'responsibility is at the heart of
international law ... [I]t constitutes an essential part of what may be
considered the constitution of the international community'.[23] Within
such a world of equality, all states share the very same responsibility,
and this is what makes it possible to refer to them collectively as com-
posing an international community in the first place. In Waltz's world,
in contrast, the condition of material inequality results in a differentiation of responsibilities: however, those that are special are simply
'taken on' by those of greatest capability, not socially conferred: there is
no suggestion that they are recognised by anyone else. In sum, we are
then presented with one view of responsibility that is socially derived,
but also with another in which special responsibilities are rooted in
material capabilities alone.

It is this seeming tension that lies at the heart of the following study:
on the one hand is the formal recognition of the equal status of all state
actors, while on the other is the practical acknowledgement of the differentiation that results from varying capabilities. In this volume, we
therefore present special responsibilities as a *via media* between those
balance-of-power understandings, on the one hand, and those sovereign-
equality understandings, on the other, neither of which accurately
describes how international society has responded historically to the
global problems it has faced: the former wholly neglects the manifest
politics of special responsibilities, and the latter the significant impact

---

[23] Pellet, 'The definition of responsibility', p. 3.

of inequalities of material power. Accordingly, we emphasise a middle way that relies upon a hierarchical approach to tackling global problems, but in which a differentiation of responsibilities is not simply a byproduct of the existing differentiation in material power.

This development can be illustrated, for example, in the evolution of the very idea of sovereignty. If its initial emphasis was entirely upon sovereign equality, then there has more recently been a pronounced – if deeply contested – trend towards the more textured idea of sovereignty as responsibility.[24] While formal equality recognised the importance of responsibility, it was ill-equipped to provide a convincing principle for its differential allocation. Differentiation in social roles, in contrast, is much more conducive to the allocation of *special* responsibilities, and to a more complex elaboration of their nature. In turn, of course, it gives rise also to competing accounts of which principles of differentiation are most appropriate.

To this extent, our study draws upon general tenets of constructivist IR.[25] Specifically, it shares the commitment to the importance of the 'distribution of ideas' in the system.[26] In important ways, this provides the 'constitution of international society', and above all represents 'a set of norms, mutually agreed upon by polities who are members of the society, that define the holders of authority and their prerogatives'.[27] Special responsibilities have been one principal instrumentality for conferring that authority, and the prerogatives associated with it. International society has sought to allocate special responsibilities to enhance predictability about behaviour, and so contribute to international order.[28] In doing so, it has elaborated a structure of ideas, the most important characteristic of which is that it generates 'differential capacities'.[29] As such, it is a source of social power.

Already we have the beginnings of two radically different mappings of special responsibilities, and our task is to develop a sensible integration

---

[24] F. M. Deng et al., *Sovereignty as responsibility: Conflict management in Africa.* (Washington, DC: Brookings Institution, 1996); B. Jones, C. Pascual and S. J. Stedman, *Power and responsibility: Building international order in an era of transnational threats* (Washington, DC: Brookings Institution, 2009).

[25] See I. Hurd, 'Constructivism', in C. Reus-Smit and D. Snidal (eds.), *The Oxford handbook of international relations* (Oxford: Oxford University Press, 2008), pp. 298–316.

[26] A. Wendt, *Social theory of international politics* (Cambridge: Cambridge University Press, 1999), p. 96.

[27] D. Philpott, *Revolutions in sovereignty: How ideas shaped modern international relations* (Princeton, NJ: Princeton University Press, 2001), pp. 11–12.

[28] T. Hopf, 'The promise of constructivism in international relations theory', *International Security*, 23(1) 1998, 178.

[29] M. Barnett and R. Duvall, 'Power in global governance', in M. Barnett and R. Duvall (eds.), *Power in global governance* (Cambridge: Cambridge University Press, 2005), p. 18.

between them. Each gives rise to its own set of questions about the terminology of special responsibilities. The first asks what meaning *special* might have in a world that assumes equality for all those meeting the same basic threshold of legal capacity; the latter asks how *responsibilities* might arise at all in a political world characterised by differential capabilities. When these are juxtaposed, the teasing question is whether it is possible to construct some new synthesis that adequately captures this important facet of world politics. This needs to be sensitive both to the social construction of a particular role, and to the material differences that also exist. It is our claim in this book that special responsibilities best capture the historical practice of dealing with major global problems, and add to our understanding of the 'power' that is created in this context. As such, they are pivotal mechanisms that not only structure and define a particular issue area, but at the same time constitute the distribution of legitimate power within its domain. It is for this reason that special responsibilities have become such a recurrent feature of international behaviour in those areas, and why it is that they are a principal site of contestation over their source and allocation.

The United States, special responsibilities and IR theory

This book addresses a large number of concerns that are fundamental to IR theory, but it is principally located in two bodies of literature. First is that on international legitimacy, the nature of power and the associated idea of hierarchy; second is the international politics of power concentrations.[30] Our idea of special responsibilities makes a distinctive contribution to both. To the former, it offers a specific elaboration of the workings of international legitimacy, and of the disaggregated power that is constructed within particular policy areas: special responsibilities present a quintessentially social account of authority and power. To the latter, it adds some significant case studies of how special responsibilities not only mirror, but also shape and constrain, these material power concentrations. In doing so, it challenges the claim that 'the unprecedented concentration of power resources in the United States generally renders inoperative the constraining effects of the systemic properties' set out in the mainstream IR literature.[31]

---

[30] S. G. Brooks and W. C. Wohlforth, *World out of balance: International relations and the challenge of American primacy* (Princeton, NJ: Princeton University Press, 2008).
[31] *Ibid.*, p. 3.

Although presented as a study of special responsibilities generally, this is a book also about the United States specifically. We want to emphasise that our approach to special responsibilities is a particular way of elaborating our previously expressed view of the role of legitimacy in the social constitution of power. This also justifies the focus on the US, as it offers a framework for disaggregating US power in particular: special responsibilities map out a distinctive view of world politics, broken down by domain, and of the forms of power that are displayed within each.

There are many compelling reasons for this focus upon the United States. Since the 1990s, there has been an extended and voluble debate about US primacy. What many participants have largely neglected, however, is the need to locate this primacy within a context of social power, and hence of legitimacy.[32] For that reason, and as our subtitle conveys, this is equally a study of American power. It seeks to demonstrate how that power is contingent upon its international social acceptance, and how it varies from one issue area to another. In that way, it dissents from those materialistic accounts that treat US power in the abstract, as merely the measure of various capabilities, divorced from how they actually play out in the social world of international politics. In this way, it endorses the alternative claim that '[a]nalysis of power, then, also must include a consideration of the normative structures and discourses that generate differential social capacities for actors to define and pursue their interests and ideals'.[33]

This addresses concerns held in common with the recent work of John Ikenberry.[34] His principal interest lies in the nature of the current disturbance, not to the fundamentally 'liberal' principles of international order as such, but rather to the erstwhile bargains that have been struck around the strategies of rule of the dominant states, especially the United States. He does not directly allude to special responsibilities. Nonetheless, his account of the current crisis is largely compatible with the notion that we set out below about the contestation over roles and responsibilities. Notably, his 'constitutional' view of international order allows for 'special rights and exemptions to the leading state', and what is currently at stake

---

[32] Clark, *Hegemony in international society*, pp. 1–11.

[33] Barnett and Duvall, 'Power in global governance', p. 3. See also the discussion of the relationship between norms and the behaviour of China and the United States in R. Foot and A. Walter, *China, the United States, and global order* (Cambridge: Cambridge University Press, 2011).

[34] G. J. Ikenberry, *Liberal leviathan: The origins, crisis, and transformation of the American world order* (Princeton, NJ: Princeton University Press, 2011), especially chapter 3.

is the existing bargain about those allocations, resulting in a crisis of authority.[35] Nonetheless, his account remains more explicitly instrumentalist than ours, particularly as he assigns more agency than we do to the leading state. That said, Ikenberry's notion of 'liberal hegemonic order' could certainly incorporate the exercise of special responsibilities, and his core idea points to one important constraint on the dominant state's power.

Accordingly, and as implied in the earlier discussion of equality and differentiation, our work is located also in the general literature on hierarchy. The fullest recent statement of this theme has been provided by David Lake.[36] There is again common ground between our book and Lake's with respect to the role of legitimacy, and the forms of power. Lake accepts that authority is 'a form of international power', and that it 'does not exist absent the legitimacy conferred by subordinates'.[37] For that reason, authority is 'distinct from coercion and the material capabilities that give rise to forcible influence'.[38] On all this we strongly concur. But significant differences between our positions nonetheless remain. As Lake himself concedes, his theory is less 'social' than some critics, including ourselves, could readily accept.[39] It is in this respect that we offer a thicker account of authority, and of the social power on which it is grounded. For all his emphasis on legitimacy as the source of authority, Lake's analysis remains strategic and rationalist, and detached from social norms. Actors behave instrumentally, and his notion of legitimacy is likewise reductionist. In his view, 'authority rests on the largely material exchange of order for compliance and legitimacy', and 'international hierarchy exists largely despite, not because of, transnational ideas and norms'.[40] This renders legitimacy the product of a rational transaction, and no more. On the contrary, we maintain that special responsibilities, as the embodiment of a type of hierarchy, are incomprehensible without this architecture of ideas and norms. This will be illustrated in detail within our three selected case studies. These demonstrate that, even if there is some exchange of 'order' for 'legitimacy', this is far from purely material, and is instead mediated through the relevant norms and ideas. This can be supported by appeal to Charles Kindleberger's original account of what was to become the basis of hegemonic stability theory. In Kindleberger's version, the most

---

[35] *Ibid.*, p. 83.
[36] D. A. Lake, *Hierarchy in international relations* (Ithaca, NY: Cornell University Press, 2009).
[37] *Ibid.*, p. x.   [38] *Ibid.*, p. 62.
[39] *Ibid.*, p. xi.   [40] *Ibid.*

important public good provided by the leader was a 'public good of responsibility':

if leadership is thought of as the provision of the public good of responsibility, rather than the exploitation of followers or the private good of prestige, it remains a positive idea.[41]

This raises two problems for Lake's account of authority. The first is whether it can be adequately understood when reduced to rational instrumentalism in this way: the public good is simply a transaction between leader and followers. As others have objected, 'this language of responsibility is hard to reconcile with rational actor analyses where the basic premise is that parties are motivated by self-interest'.[42] Second, and stressing Kindleberger's version, we need to recall that the public goods provided are not themselves narrowly material, nor simply matters of self-interest. In his emphasis on a public good of *responsibility*, Kindleberger places norms and ideas at the centre of his analysis. Although Lake takes an instrumentalist approach to institutions, he nevertheless recognises their importance in constraining US authority.[43] It is a small but critical step to move beyond this recognition and to acknowledge that institutions do not simply mediate, but actually constitute, authority. They do so not because they are instrumental, but because they embody ideas of what responsibility, and hence authority, mean.

This raises complex and controversial issues, and we do not assert any straightforward dichotomy between 'socially constructed roles' on the one hand and 'strategic behaviour' on the other. Indeed, the relationship between these has been hotly contested in recent years. On balance, such consensus as presently exists calls into question any sharp polarity of this kind, insofar as the 'social construction of actors may well create instrumental, goal-seeking agents'.[44] Even so, there are important remaining differences, arising from the causal/constitutive distinction, that continue to be reflected in the contrasting findings of constructivists, as against rationalists, and this is demonstrated in the position that we take on special responsibilities.[45]

---

[41] C. P. Kindleberger, *The world in depression, 1929–1939*, rev. edn (Berkeley, CA: University of California Press, 1986), p. 304.

[42] C. Norrlof, *America's global advantage: US hegemony and international cooperation* (Cambridge: Cambridge University Press, 2010), pp. 13–14.

[43] D. Lake, 'Making America safe for the world: Multilateralism and the rehabilitation of US authority', *Global Governance*, 16(4) 2010, 471–84.

[44] Hurd, 'Constructivism', p. 310.

[45] *Ibid.*, pp. 310–12; Wendt, *Social theory*, pp. 165–6; Barnett and Duval, 'Power in global governance', pp. 9–10.

The book also addresses the literature on power concentrations. As will be shown below, special responsibilities have historically attached to the great powers collectively. Our book explores how those that were assigned to the collective of great powers might apply equally to a sole great power. At least since 1945, and even more so after 1990, there has been a widely held view that, if there were special responsibilities, they bore especially upon the United States. This was in no small measure a result of the unusual preponderance of material capabilities enjoyed by the United States at the end of the Second World War, and again in the aftermath of the Cold War. In this latter case, the key question was whether the special responsibilities of the great powers could be made relevant to a sole great power world, and if so what would be the appropriate theoretical frame of reference for making this allocation.

However, IR theory has been generally reluctant to accept any application of special responsibilities to the single great power.[46] In response to these objections, this book develops a more nuanced position. There are two good reasons to be wary of any dismissal of special responsibilities in the context of a sole great power world. First, the pervasive language of special responsibilities today – much of it directed towards the United States alone – suggests that in practice this idea is still considered relevant. Second, this book is sceptical of any claim to a single objectively existing concentration of power *per se*. The very language of special responsibilities suggests that the degree of concentration of social power is more variable, across issue areas, and with respect to the allocation of roles across a number of actors. What makes us so sceptical of any claim of the irrelevance of special responsibilities to a single great power world is that we question such a reified concentration across the board in the first place.

The main theoretical claims

In summary, we start with four propositions that collectively spell out the main theoretical claims, and demonstrate their significance and applicability:

(1) Neither balance of power nor sovereign equality, on its own, has supplied a convincing modality for responding to global problems. In practice, these have been managed through regimes of special responsibilities that have, in turn, generated a distinctive politics of responsibility.

---

[46] See Clark, *Hegemony in international society*, especially chapter 1.

(2) It is the distribution of responsibilities that structures legitimate political action within any of the individual policy domains that we study. Within this, there may then be a further allocation of special responsibilities that constitutes differential power. In this way, special responsibilities both enable and constrain the various agents that act within the regime, and so both harness (variably) and constitute the different capacities of the agents.

(3) The degree to which specific allocations of special responsibilities come to be accepted is itself variable, both within individual regimes and across time. This is largely a function of the various types of responsibility that are to be distributed, and the different rights attached to each in turn. Even when any particular distribution achieves a point of temporary equilibrium, it is likely to be sub-optimal (as explained below), and this gives rise to renewed contestation, as different understandings of capacities, fairness and vulnerability come back into play. This encourages attempts to reinterpret the meaning of existing special responsibilities. We are especially interested in those conditions that lead to the re-emergence of this contestation.

(4) These claims allow us to deploy an importantly different understanding of American power in relation to our set of global problems. Theories of unipolarity or hegemonic stability theory do not adequately explain the US's role on these issues, as they largely assume a world of (US) free choice.[47] Instead, as demonstrated in the following cases, US control over these issues has, in fact, been both variable and disaggregated. In all, however, it still remains key to any successful allocation of current special responsibilities, and hence to any resolution of these problems.

Accordingly, our working definition includes two elements, denoting both what special responsibilities *are* and what they *do*: *special responsibilities are a differentiated set of obligations, the allocation of which is collectively agreed, and they provide a principle of social differentiation for managing collective problems in a world characterised by both formal equality and inequality of material capability.*

The book unfolds also as a set of ethical claims, and this dimension is critical at several levels in the following analysis. The issue of recurrent contestation, arising out of the sub-optimality of the existing allocation, can plausibly be understood to have both normative and empirical elements. The sub-optimality could result from its normative deficits,

---

[47] Brooks and Wohlforth, *World out of balance*, p. 19.

in that the allocation is perceived to be unfair or unjust. Alternatively, it may originate in a perceived clash between what is deemed right and proper, on the one hand, and what is needed for regime effectiveness, on the other: what is fair may not 'work'. Yet again, what is considered effective in the short term, if resting on unstable normative foundations, may lack durability in the longer term. In that sense, any equilibrium point in the allocation of responsibilities is necessarily related to normative assessments, as is the subsequent revival of the politics of responsibility. This normative dynamic is conspicuous in all three of our cases.

It is particularly prominent with respect to the categories of states or actors between which the original distributions of responsibilities have been made, and as such raises the question of the ethical stability of those categories themselves. In the case of nuclear proliferation, responsibilities were differentially allocated between NWSs and NNWSs. These categories have remained stable only insofar as no obvious replacement categories have been proposed (even if the recent treatment of India might be seen as a partial attempt to blur the division). However, they are fundamentally unstable in that the categories are regarded by the NNWSs as temporary only. In the case of climate change, it is precisely the fundamental categories of developed and developing states that are now being challenged by those who make both an 'effectiveness' and an 'ethical' case for replacing them instead with the responsibilities of large emitters (regardless of whether developed or not). In finance, this issue is even less clear: for example, it is not the categories of surplus and deficit countries that have been in dispute, but the consequences for the allocation of responsibilities of the movement of particular states from the one category to the other. Nowhere has this been more marked than in the historical shift by the United States from the category of major surplus state to that of conspicuous deficit country: part of the contestation has been driven by the concern that the allocation of its responsibilities has not sufficiently closely tracked this migration. There can (legally) be no such movement under the terms of the Nuclear Non-Proliferation Treaty (NPT), but in climate change it is the potential re-categorisation of states like China that has become such a major feature of the ongoing contestation.

The cases

Briefly, there are three reasons for the selection of nuclear proliferation, climate change and global finance as our cases. First, all provide excellent illustrations of the disaggregated, and ambiguous, nature of

American power. Second, this project is interested in how individual and collective power can be mobilised to address major global problems. This selection does not reflect any arbitrary set of policy issues, but three pressing global problems where the issues of power and ethics are manifest. Third, all three problem areas are already structured in terms of an understanding of responsibilities, and their differential allocation. It is this that effectively defines the existing distribution of social power within them.

There were other possible cases that could have been selected to make the same argument. For instance, notions of responsibility have been widespread in the humanitarian area, leading historically to claims about special responsibilities to undertake intervention where large-scale abuses have occurred. It was in the context of the debate about humanitarian interventionism in the 1990s that the link between responsibilities, and the rights needed to implement them, was most powerfully asserted.[48] Accordingly, the US sought exemptions from the jurisdiction of the rulings of the emergent International Criminal Court on the grounds that its own military were more likely to be involved in operations of this kind on behalf of the international community, and therefore should not be subject to the same rules as the rest: special responsibilities entailed special rights for their implementation. By the turn of the millennium, the issue had largely transformed from one of a 'right' of intervention to one of a 'duty' of protection; it was now increasingly configured by the notion of a 'responsibility to protect'.[49] The question that this immediately prompted, of course, was the locus of any such responsibility. Some writers have already begun to set out, in a theoretical way, how this international responsibility might be allocated as individual special responsibilities. Standard considerations in this regard have been, for instance, the capacity to intervene, geographical proximity, or cultural affinity, amongst others.[50] However, in its adoption by the UN General Assembly – and contrary to the tone

---

[48] N. J. Wheeler, *Saving strangers: Humanitarian intervention in international society* (Oxford: Oxford University Press, 2002).

[49] See International Commission on Intervention and State Sovereignty, *The responsibility to protect: The report of the International Commission on Intervention and State Sovereignty* (Ottawa: International Development Research Centre, 2001); A. J. Bellamy, *Responsibility to protect: The global effort to end mass atrocities* (Cambridge: Polity Press, 2009).

[50] See D. Miller, 'Distributing responsibilities', *Journal of Political Philosophy*, 9(4) 2001, 453–71; D. Miller, 'The responsibility to protect human rights', Working Paper SJ0007 (Oxford: Department of Politics and International Relations and Centre for the Study of Social Justice, Oxford University, May 2007); A. Buchanan and R. O. Keohane, 'Precommitment regimes for intervention: Supplementing the Security Council', *Ethics and International Affairs*, 25(1) 2011, 41–63.

of the original International Commission on Intervention and State Sovereignty report – it was emphasised that this responsibility lay initially, and primarily, with the affected state itself. The international responsibility is subsidiary, and is to provide a safety net only in the event of 'manifest' failure of that first line of protection.[51]

To this extent, the delegation of special responsibilities in this area has been principally towards domestic jurisdiction, and only secondarily to the UN Security Council. Such international responsibility as there is has been couched (at the level of principle) as a responsibility that is shared by the 'international community' as a whole, rather than as a responsibility that is special to particular members of it. So far then this has not reached a stage that goes much beyond the assignment of this general responsibility. Hence, as a policy debate about the responsibility to protect, and unlike our other cases, there has been less overt discussion of any specific international distribution, either to the US or otherwise. Moreover, this is still a recently emerging norm, and the situation remains too fluid to pin much down as yet. Our three case studies have been drawn from longer histories, which give us more to say about how special responsibilities have evolved over time, and about the high levels of contestation to which they have been subject. Although this case is not included in our study, its implications are certainly important to the argument as a whole.

The existing international politics of nuclear weapons proliferation, climate change and global finance do not take place in a 'natural' or 'original' condition, but are already configured by embedded conceptions of responsibilities, and how these should be allocated. Our starting point is that each of these issue areas is manifestly already structured by the language of responsibilities, and by a putative distribution of them. In that way, the cases operate in the shadow of a counterfactual ('the original position') that indicates how different the actual framing of the issue has already become.

Given these theoretical propositions, each of the cases is organised into three sections:

(1) First, what was the initial framing of the issue, and how did this arise? This investigates the origins of the respective regimes, primarily through the NPT, the Earth Summit at Rio de Janeiro and Bretton Woods. How did responsibility talk come to define the possible courses of action within each of these particular issue areas,

---

[51] United Nations General Assembly, 'Resolution adopted by the General Assembly, 60/1. 2005 World Summit outcome', A/RES/60/1, 16 September 2005, paras. 138–9.

and how were responsibilities differentially allocated? What were the prevailing categories for making this allocation, and what enabled the achievement of such an equilibrium point?

(2) The second section maps out the contestation and the attempts to re-allocate responsibilities within the regime, and traces the dynamic of this reallocation. This includes efforts to redefine the meaning of existing special responsibilities in order to legitimate actions previously excluded. The specific language of special responsibilities in each case then becomes the site of political contestation and argumentation. The form these arguments take shapes, in turn, what counts as the legitimate exercise of specific capacities. In particular, each case identifies the particular concepts and concerns (such as capability, fairness and vulnerability) that have informed the language of special responsibilities, and their evolution.

(3) Since achievement of an equilibrium point between the allocation of special responsibilities and their acceptance has been variable, what then are the conditions that appear to have facilitated this equilibrium? On the other side, it is certainly not implied that special responsibilities have devised the perfect solution to these problems of collective action. On the contrary, special responsibilities have often produced sub-optimal courses of action. In turn, then, what are the negative consequences of any framing of the issue in those terms?

In our final comparative reflections, we explore the relationship between responsibilities in the different domains, and any spillover that occurs between them. Do actors appeal to their bearing of special responsibilities in one domain that might, in consequence, constrain what they should accept within any other? Are there trade-offs in play, such that the bearing of special responsibilities in one domain serves as a claim to specific rights with regard to another? In short, while our method is to disaggregate the topic of special responsibilities into its separate issue areas, at the end it is necessary to put the elements back together again, in order to see the full composite picture.

Organisation

The book advances in a number of stages. In Chapter 1, the broad contours of the history of special responsibilities, both as an international practice and as an element in IR theory, are established. This relationship is depicted as an extant practice in search of a viable explanatory theory. Chapter 2 then sets out a detailed conceptual overview, as well as the theoretical framework to be applied in the remainder of this study. It does so by building from the ground up, starting from the basic notion of responsibility as accountability: in a particular domain, and in relation to a specific constituency, a subset of actors is answerable for the discharge of the role assigned to it. It is for that reason that special responsibilities are quintessentially social. With respect to international relations, the chapter sets out the central arguments about the nature of special responsibilities and the role they play in anarchic orders, about their importance in the constitution of social power, and why the structure of 'power' is not monolithic across domains, but specific to each. The chapter also considers the relationship between leadership and special responsibilities.[52]

This is followed, in Chapters 3, 4 and 5, by the substantial case studies of the responsibility talk in the three global problem areas already identified by Obama: nuclear proliferation, climate change and global finance. Although the resolution of these major global problems requires collective action, how exactly are they being approached? Is the international response simply a continuation of great power management, as characterised in the nineteenth and twentieth centuries, and in which the idea of special responsibilities was first formally developed? Or should this international response now be conceived in the distinctively new terms of global governance?[53] If such a transition from great power management to global governance is accepted, what are the wider imports for the nature of special responsibilities? While special responsibilities are inherently social in nature, it is appropriate to ask searching questions about the changing nature of the international society of which they are a part.

In Chapter 6, the book confronts the ethics of special responsibilities. Stepping outside a mainly empirical account of legitimacy, it asks fundamental normative questions about the ethical bases of special responsibilities, and how particular allocations of them might come to be justified. This approach allows a deeper engagement between power and ethics, as through E. H. Carr's ideas. Carr had famously suggested that 'every effective demand for change … is compounded of power and

---

[52] H. Shue, 'Face reality? After you! – A call for leadership on climate change', *Ethics and International Affairs*, 25(1) 2011, 17–26. See I. Hurd, 'Breaking and making norms: American revisionism and crises of legitimacy', in Clark and Reus-Smit (eds.), 'Resolving international crises', 194–213.

[53] K. J. Holsti, 'Governance without government: Polyarchy in nineteenth-century European international politics', in J. N. Rosenau and E.-O. Czempiel (eds.), *Governance without government: Order and change in world politics* (Cambridge: Cambridge University Press, 1992), pp. 30–57.

morality'.[54] In their unique blend of social power and the language of morality, special responsibilities open a unique window onto his claim. This helps bring together the various dimensions of change: changing distributions of material power, changing norms, changing expectations and the changing locus of agency. At the same time, this entails an expansion in the moral purpose of special responsibilities, beyond order as preventing great power war and managing international security, to include other ends (such as forestalling climate change and underwriting financial stability), and also brings in a wider array of actors as their potential bearers.

In sum, the book seeks to shed an original light on the social nature of American power, and how it comes to be variably instantiated in attempts to address key global problems. At the same time, it explores those three issue areas, not just from the perspective of the interplay of material capabilities, but also through the lens of how special responsibilities both enable and constrain the choices of all the actors, including those of the United States. Global problem-solving has succeeded neither through the modality of sovereign equality, nor through that of the unbridled imposition of material power differentials. Special responsibilities are the device that has been adopted by international society to negotiate between those two extremes, and it is this social strategy that has become so prominent in its search for solutions to major global problems. These investigations will hopefully position us to engage the question of which claims to special responsibilities are good ones: which ought to be accepted, if any, and on what basis? In turn, this will help us to move beyond the study of special responsibilities merely as a historical practice, and towards an appreciation of them as a fundamental dimension of normative IR theory.

---

[54] E. H. Carr, *The twenty years' crisis, 1919–1939: An introduction to the study of international relations* (London: Macmillan, 1939), p. 265.

Part I

Theoretical framework

1   A practice in search of a theory

'The grading of powers is a matter of theory', Martin Wight once remarked, whereas the 'managerial function of the great powers is a matter of practice'.[1] Special responsibilities erode this distinction: they are about the grading of powers, as well as their managerial functions. Accordingly, this chapter traces how special responsibilities came to be developed in both theory and practice. At its heart is to be found the complex interplay between the category deemed to be special, and the nature of the responsibility that is as a result attached to it. Special responsibilities first arose within a traditional and European-centred states system. In that context, it was the seemingly fixed category of the special that attracted attention; subsequently, a more reflexive understanding of responsibility has led to a more fluid understanding of those who are to be considered special, and for what specific purpose. This fluidity has tracked the more complex global system that has evolved in the meantime.

This chapter clearly demonstrates that there was a practice of special responsibilities long before there developed any coherent 'theory' to account for it. When a theory began to emerge, it was one that largely emphasised a responsibility attaching to a pre-existing group of states, namely the great powers. That the explanation and justification took this particular form, rather than something else, meant there were a number of significant consequences. Any attempt to make sense of special responsibilities must therefore begin with a brief history of its practice, and how this subsequently came to be engaged in the International Relations (IR) theory literature.

That is the scope of this chapter, and it is undertaken in three stages. First, it traces the practice of special responsibilities: in particular, it constructs for the first time an outline history of its emergence in

---

[1] M. Wight, *Systems of states*, ed. H. Bull (Leicester: Leicester University Press, 1977), p. 136.

international diplomacy, and how it became established as a 'social fact'.[2] Second, it examines how the notion of special responsibilities has developed within IR theory, and how that literature has sought to establish its own connection between the special and the responsible. Finally, the chapter identifies major gaps in existing accounts, and so stakes out the importance of the task for this volume. Its message, in brief, is that there is a sharp contrast between the deep entrenchment of special responsibilities in international practice, and its relatively superficial engagement by IR theory. Correcting this imbalance, both by broadening the theoretical underpinnings of the concept, and also by a fuller analysis of how they have operated in practice, is the main objective of the remainder of this book.

The historical practice of special responsibilities

Historically, this practice arose as one way of affirming what was special about the great powers, singly and collectively, and what was entailed by their specialness. This initially concentrated upon the 'rights' of these powers. 'The status of great nation confers certain rights', Raymond Aron pointed out, since 'no matter of importance can be treated in a system without all the great nations being consulted'.[3] However, as this category became more formalised during the early nineteenth century, it was necessary also to provide an explicit rationale for this arrangement. Moreover, this had to be done in a way that avoided overt violation of the principle of sovereign equality. The solution adopted was to present it as a matter of responsibilities, not just of rights. What made this possible, in turn, was the simultaneous emergence of a more formal category of great powers, as the putative bearers of these responsibilities. Bestowal of this status at once reinforced the specialness of the great powers, while also justifying this arrangement by appeal to the distinctive responsibilities they bore.

There is substantial consensus that a clear practice along those lines first appeared in 1814–15, in the lead up to the Congress of Vienna, and during the subsequent Concert system. It was then, and especially at meetings held in September 1814, that the notion

---

[2] J. G. Ruggie, *Constructing the world polity: Essays on international institutionalization* (London: Routledge, 1998), p. 12.

[3] R. Aron, *Peace and war: A theory of international relations* (London: Weidenfeld and Nicolson, 1966), p. 58. Some nineteenth-century legal theorists believed of 'stronger states' that 'custom has given them what can hardly be distinguished from a legal right to settle certain questions as they please'. T. J. Lawrence, as quoted in B. Kingsbury, 'Sovereignty and inequality', *European Journal of International Law*, 9(4) 1998, 604.

of the great powers, as denoting a special category, was first clearly articulated. That there had always been differences in the material resources possessed by states, and in their resultant hierarchical ordering, is not in question. The novel development of this time was acceptance of the great powers, not only as materially special, but as having a *recognised status* as a group. We have been told that this emerged specifically at meetings in the second half of September 1814.[4] 'The great-power principle', it has been suggested, 'provided the missing concept needed to stabilize the system.' Moreover, relative to past practice, this was 'totally new'.[5]

At the same time, this institutionalisation of the great powers demanded an acceptable justificatory doctrine. Accordingly, it was accompanied by a fuller expression of the role to be played by these great powers, not just in terms of their special rights, but also of their unique responsibilities. With regard to the Concert, these related both to maintaining the territorial settlement of 1815 specifically, and to managing the international order more generally.[6] In the Concert, it has been suggested, 'each state had responsibilities as well as rights', but, in addition, 'the Great Powers had more responsibilities and more rights than the other states'.[7] As part of its working, the great powers 'acted on the principle that they had special responsibilities for the smooth functioning of international society – that great power brought with it great responsibilities'.[8] This amounted to an implicit contract between the great and small: 'just as the great powers claimed special rights for themselves, so the small states claimed that the great had special responsibilities for their well-being'.[9] That relationship, over time, became more formally inscribed into international law.[10] This does not suggest that the great powers lived up to those special responsibilities. On the contrary, their disregard for them often became the

[4] H. Nicolson, *The Congress of Vienna: A study in allied unity, 1812–1822* (London: Constable, 1946), p. 137; G. Peterson, 'II: Political inequality at the Congress of Vienna', *Political Science Quarterly*, 60(4) 1945, 534; C. K. Webster (ed.), *The Congress of Vienna, 1814–15*, 2nd edn (London: Bell, 1945), p. 61. See I. Clark, *Legitimacy in international society* (Oxford: Oxford University Press, 2005), pp. 97–8.

[5] A. Osiander, *The states system of Europe 1640–1990: Peacemaking and the condition of international stability* (Oxford: Oxford University Press, 1994), p. 234.

[6] F. H. Hinsley, *Power and the pursuit of peace* (London: Cambridge University Press, 1963), p. 225.

[7] *Ibid.*, p. 234; C. Brown, 'Do great powers have great responsibilities? Great powers and moral agency', *Global Society*, 18(1) 2004, 7.

[8] Brown, 'Do great powers have great responsibilities?', 6.

[9] F. R. Bridge and R. Bullen, *The great powers and the European states system 1814–1914*, 2nd edn (Harlow: Pearson Longman, 2005), p. 2.

[10] Wight, *Systems of states*, p. 42.

overarching problem of international order, rather than part of its solution.[11] Nonetheless, that their contribution to order came to be framed by this idea of responsibility was important, and had a variety of long-term effects.

One good example was the convening of the powers in response to the crisis over Belgian independence in 1830–1. The documentation surrounding this episode drew particular attention to that sense of 'ownership' of the problem, and of its resolution, that belonged specifically to the great powers. However, those powers were deemed special not just on account of their rights, but importantly also because of the duty that this placed upon them. Accordingly, the Protocol of a meeting held at the Foreign Office in London, on 19 February 1831, recorded these agreed sentiments:

> It did not belong to the Powers to judge of the causes which severed the ties which they had formed … It belonged to them to secure, by means of new combinations, that tranquillity of Europe … To this duty the Powers were imperiously called. They had the right, and events rendered it their duty, to prevent the Belgian provinces, become independent, from disturbing the general security and the balance of power in Europe.[12]

The precise language of special responsibilities did not make any direct appearance, as far as can be told, during the remainder of the nineteenth century. That said, ideas about the 'specialness' of the great powers, and the responsibilities that they owed – commensurate with their special rights – were certainly articulated in a broad sense. The terminology remained likewise implicit during the debates framing the League of Nations at the end of the First World War. President Woodrow Wilson had come to Paris expressing marked diffidence about the role traditionally played by the great powers in European diplomacy: international salvation was not, ostensibly, to be found at the hands of these erstwhile great powers. Nonetheless, he had come around to the realisation that 'it was crucial to endow the more powerful states with special responsibilities', on the grounds he set out in September 1919, that 'only the power of the strong can maintain the right of the weak'.[13] This

[11] K. J. Holsti, *Taming the sovereigns: Institutional change in international politics* (Cambridge: Cambridge University Press, 2004), pp. 25–6.

[12] R. Albrecht-Carrié, *The concert of Europe 1815–1914* (New York: Harper and Row, 1968), p. 72.

[13] P. O. Cohrs, *The unfinished peace after World War I: America, Britain and the stabilisation of Europe 1919–1932* (Cambridge: Cambridge University Press, 2006), pp. 35–6. This basic idea is adapted from Jean-Jacques Rousseau. See W. Bain, *Between anarchy and society: Trusteeship and the obligations of power* (Oxford: Oxford University Press, 2003), p. 19.

was, in any event, reflected in the directorial role asserted by the 'Big Three' during the conference proceedings. The great powers may have been special because of their material power, but they were responsible because of the obligation this imposed upon them for the welfare of international society as a whole, including the protection of the weak and vulnerable.

This terminology then became increasingly prominent during the interwar period, and its first employment in diplomatic documents appears to date from this time. One early example was its formal adoption in the Four Power Pact, signed in Rome on 7 June 1933, by Britain, France, Germany and Italy. Its preamble declared the signatories to be 'conscious of the special responsibilities, incumbent on them as possessing permanent representation on the Council of the League of Nations ... and of the responsibilities resulting from their common signature of the Locarno agreements'.[14] These states were held to be special in the double sense, first, of their membership of the League Council and, second, in upholding the specific settlement that they had signed at Locarno in 1925: each, in turn, gave rise to special responsibilities. It scarcely needs further comment that an affirmation of special responsibilities by those four powers in particular, and during the 1930s, should make us very wary of accepting this language at face value.

The concept, however, had reached its fullest expression by the time of the Second World War. After the Moscow Conference of 1943, British Foreign Secretary, Anthony Eden, informed the House of Commons that the Big Three had no intention of forming any international dictatorship. He insisted, nonetheless, that 'special responsibilities do rest on our three powers and we did at Moscow try to devise machinery and agree on a policy that would enable us to give full expression to that sense of our responsibility'.[15] This sentiment was evidently shared by President Franklin D. Roosevelt who, in a statement of 15 June 1944, stressed the importance for future order of states 'large and small, bearing responsibility commensurate with their individual capacities'.[16]

This emerged candidly in Britain's proposals for the new world organisation to be considered at the Dumbarton Oaks conference in 1944.

---

[14] United States Congress, *Events leading up to World War II: Chronological history of certain major international events leading up to and during World War II with the ostensible reasons advanced for their occurrence, 1931–1944* (Washington, DC: US GPO, 1944), www.ibiblio.org/pha/events/1933.html (accessed 28 July 2011).

[15] Quoted in G. Simpson, *Great powers and outlaw states: Unequal sovereigns in the international legal order* (Cambridge: Cambridge University Press, 2004), pp. 170–1.

[16] Quoted in I. L. Claude, *Swords into plowshares: The problems and progress of international organization* (London: University of London Press, 1965), p. 63.

In a paper for the War Cabinet, Foreign Secretary Eden insisted with respect to the (then) Four Powers that the 'machinery of the organisation should make it possible for them to carry out the responsibilities which they will have agreed to undertake', and for that reason, 'they must be given ... a special position in the organisation'.[17]

Such ideas became notably conspicuous in the framing of the United Nations (UN) Charter, which included provisions 'elaborately setting forth special responsibilities and privileges for the Big Five'.[18] The issues this raised were to become highly contentious, but mostly concerned the detailed implementation of special responsibilities, rather than any objection to the basic principle itself. For instance, in the draft Staff Charter, Article 4 described the four main powers as having 'exceptional responsibilities for the maintenance of international security'.[19] At San Francisco, this language was found on everyone's lips. President Harold S. Truman, addressing the conference on 25 April 1945, attested of the victorious powers that 'these great states have a special responsibility to enforce the peace'.[20] The following day, Eden confirmed that, while the Dumbarton Oaks proposals placed obligations on all states, nonetheless 'a special responsibility lies on the great powers'.[21] In his report to the Senate after San Francisco, US Senator Arthur Vandenberg, speaking with reference to the veto, insisted that the 'so-called "special privilege" of the great powers is matched by its equivalent in "special responsibilities"'. For the UN to work, he added, 'the Great Powers must assume special and particular responsibilities'.[22]

---

[17] Memorandum by Secretary of State for Foreign Affairs on 'Future world organisation', W. P. (44) 370, 3 July 1944, National Archives CAB/66/52/20, para. 15. We are very much indebted to Justin Morris for bringing this document to our attention.

[18] Claude, *Swords into plowshares*, p. 65.

[19] R. B. Russell, *A history of the United Nations Charter: The role of the United States 1940–1945* (Washington, DC: Brookings Institution, 1958), p. 241. Hans Kelsen noted, however, that it was the Security Council as a whole that was charged with special responsibility for international security, and not just its permanent members. See H. Kelsen, *The law of the United Nations: A critical analysis of its fundamental problems* (Clark, NJ: The Lawbook Exchange, 2000), pp. 272–3.

[20] H. S. Truman, 'Address to the United Nations Conference in San Francisco', 25 April 1945, www.presidency.ucsb.edu/ws/index.php?pid=12391 (accessed 10 August 2011).

[21] A. Eden, 'Secretary of State for Foreign Affairs of Great Britain, Anthony Eden's address at first plenary session of San Francisco conference', 26 April 1945, www.ibiblio.org/pha/policy/1945/450426d.html (accessed 28 July 2011).

[22] A. Vandenberg, 'Senator Vandenberg's report to the Senate on the San Francisco conference', 29 June 1945, www.ibiblio.org/pha/policy/1945/450629a.html (accessed 28 July 2011). For a dissenting account, see K. Mahbubani, 'Permanent and elected council members', in D. Malone (ed.), *The UN Security Council: From the cold war to the 21st century* (Boulder, CO: Lynne Rienner, 2004), p. 262.

Gerry Simpson refers to this as the creation of a 'legalised hegemony', as formulated by the Charter. In doing so, he accentuates the previously highlighted tension generated between legal equality, on the one hand, and the 'special responsibility' of the great powers, on the other.[23] The British paper for Dumbarton Oaks had stressed the compromise that this necessitated: '[t]hough the status of all members is equal and all will enjoy the same rights and undertake the corresponding obligations, their differences in power make necessary some recognition of differences in function'.[24] Simpson notes, however, that while this language was widely deployed as one of the rationales for the great power role, the 'Great Powers did not wish to have this justification articulated in the UN Charter itself',[25] and so the terminology of special responsibilities makes no direct appearance in the Charter. It did, however, very much colour the background discussions.

As we shall see, these debates rested on various assumptions about what it was that made the great powers special, and what in particular it then was that gave rise to their resulting responsibilities. In effect, these amounted to a conflation of a number of slightly different arguments: that the specialness of the great powers derived from their part in the victory in the recent war; from the sacrifices that they had made in effecting this outcome; and, finally, also from their capacity to manage the future international order in conformity with the Charter design. In whichever precise form, however, what made the great powers special was their aggregate capability to act on behalf of the new organisation. To ensure that they would remain committed to the United Nations, this principle was acknowledged also by the conferral of the veto, to prevent collective action being taken against any one of them that dissented.

It was precisely this linkage between capability and responsibility that was considered so central in the provisions specifically pertaining to the Security Council. Britain's Dumbarton Oaks paper accordingly suggested that 'the more power and responsibility can be made to correspond, the more likely it is that the machinery will be able to fulfil its functions'.[26] There was a widely expressed need for a 'definite relationship between the obligations imposed on certain states and their capacity to influence the decisions of the Organization'. In short, 'power and responsibility should be joined together'.[27] This echoed sentiments

---

[23] Simpson, *Great powers and outlaw states*, p. 167.
[24] Memorandum, 'Future world organisation', para. 15.
[25] Simpson, *Great powers and outlaw states*, pp. 170–1.
[26] Memorandum, 'Future world organisation', para. 15.
[27] L. M. Goodrich and E. Hambro, *Charter of the United Nations* (London: Stevens and Sons, 1949), p. 199.

previously expressed about the League of Nations, that it 'is better to allow responsibility to rest with power than to attempt to divorce power from responsibility'.[28] The great virtue of the Charter, William T. R. Fox explained at the time, was exactly this fusion between the Permanent Five's possession of the 'greatest share in the making of decisions', and their 'gravest responsibilities for their execution'.[29] Such a conception had been explicitly advanced by US Secretary of State, George C. Marshall, in the proposals he placed before the UN General Assembly on 17 September 1947: 'the Great Powers bear special responsibilities', he averred, 'because of their strength and resources'.[30] Accordingly, it was their strength and resources that marked these great powers out as special, and in turn was the source of their responsibility. It remained to be seen if this was the only way in which responsibility could be explained, and whether it must necessarily adhere to the great powers alone.

In those Charter debates, special responsibilities were set out as part of an implicit contract which, while acknowledging the special entitlements of the great powers, also sought to set specified limits to them. This was very clearly articulated in the protests issued by one small power, Australia, at the end of the war. Australia had robustly challenged any overly broad scope for the special responsibilities of the great powers at San Francisco, particularly in connection with the right of veto.[31] In the aftermath, the Australian Department of External Affairs protested to its UN delegation that it had nonetheless allowed the United States and the USSR, in the absence of Australia, to discuss the future of the Japanese Mandates in the Pacific. It had been wrong to do so, it asserted, because Australia had a 'special interest' in their fate, both on account of its 'geographical position' and its 'war effort'. In contrast, 'the Great Powers have no special responsibility in matter of future disposal of Japanese Mandates'.[32] In a related use of the idiom, Australian Foreign Minister Herbert Evatt was further to complain in 1947 to his British and American counterparts about the format of the German

---

[28] F. Williams, *Some aspects of the covenant of the League of Nations* (London: Oxford University Press, 1934), p. 87.

[29] W. T. R. Fox, 'Collective enforcement of peace and security', *American Political Science Review*, 39(5) 1945, 980.

[30] United Nations General Assembly, *Official Records*, Second Session, Vol. I (New York: United Nations, 1947), pp. 19–35.

[31] D. L. Bosco, *Five to rule them all: The UN Security Council and the making of the modern world* (New York: Oxford University Press, 2009), p. 36.

[32] '289 Department of External Affairs to Australian Delegation, United Nations', Cablegram UNY468 Canberra, 8 December 1946, www.info.dfat.gov.au/info/historical/HistDocs.nsf/10~289 (accessed 10 August 2011).

settlement, and to point out that 'there has been a misinterpretation of the special responsibilities of the four powers in regard to the German Settlement'. These applied, he insisted, only to its 'preparation', and not to the final substance of the peace.[33] These views were conveyed to US Secretary of State, George C. Marshall.[34] Clearly, at this juncture, the attribution of special responsibilities had become part of the wider political dispute between the great and small powers, and was deployed especially to encourage the idea that they entailed restrictions, not just permissions, on the scope of great power action.

All such usages related to the special responsibilities of the great powers collectively, rather than to those of any one great power acting alone. At the same time, however, this alternative sense – that one power alone might be special, and hence bear special responsibilities as an *individual* great power – was also creeping into the language of diplomacy. It did so most directly via the Mandates system established under the League of Nations, as this charged the separate mandatory powers with special responsibilities for the administration of former colonial territories, and for which they were now deemed accountable to the Mandates Commission.[35] Accordingly, as early as 1931, Quincy Wright asked questions about the conditions under which Britain's special responsibilities for Iraq might come to be discharged.[36] In an interesting adaptation, since it had been assigned such responsibilities over former German possessions in the Pacific, Japan asserted by the mid-1930s that it also held 'special responsibilities for East Asia' more generally, and used this claim to underwrite its new order for the region.[37] During April 1934, newspapers carried a Japanese foreign ministry statement to the effect that 'Japan is called upon to exert the utmost effort in carrying out her mission and fulfilling her special responsibilities in East Asia.'[38]

---

[33] '266 Evatt to Deschamps for Marshall', Cablegram 69 Canberra, 20 April 1947, 9.15 p.m., www.info.dfat.gov.au/info/historical/HistDocs.nsf/12~266 (accessed 10 August 2011).

[34] 'Deschamps to Marshall, 21 April 1947', in United States Department of State, *Foreign relations of the United States, 1947. Council of Foreign Ministers; Germany and Austria*, Vol. II (Washington, DC: US Government Printing Office, 1947), pp. 499–500.

[35] Bain, *Between anarchy and society*, p. 102. In this sense, special responsibilities can be understood as the near cousin of international 'trusteeship'.

[36] Q. Wright, 'The proposed termination of the Iraq mandate', *American Journal of International Law*, 25(3) 1931, 444.

[37] G. D. Hook *et al.*, *Japan's international relations: Politics, economics, and security*, 2nd edn (Abingdon: Routledge, 2005), p. 30.

[38] A. Trotter, *Britain and East Asia, 1933–1937* (London: Cambridge University Press, 1975), p. 72.

As another illustration, Truman hinted after the war at a concept that applied specifically, and exceptionally, to the United States. This has marked relevance for this study, given that after 1945 any attribution of special responsibilities to a single state has most often occurred with the United States in mind. Speaking in New York at the opening session of the UN General Assembly on 23 October 1946, Truman made the following observations:

> The course of history has made us one of the stronger nations of the world. It has therefore placed upon us special responsibilities to conserve our strength and to use it rightly in a world so interdependent as our world today.
> The American people recognize these special responsibilities. We shall do our best to meet them, both in the making of the peace settlements and in the fulfilment of the long-range tasks of the United Nations.[39]

At this point, the prospective tension between special responsibilities as a *collective* responsibility of the great powers, and claims to their individual exercise by a *single* great power, was already surfacing. Nonetheless, a strong case can be made that the international legal recognition of the special – understood as the group of great powers – reached its apogee in 1945. Since then, international law has tended to move in the opposite direction, and 'legal doctrines of the special status of great powers have been in the descendant since 1945'.[40] This, however, has not led to any abandonment of special responsibilities in practice. Instead, it has contributed to a shift in emphasis away from the special, taken to be a predefined category, and towards a more nuanced and complex contestation around the scope of this category. In turn, this has required a closer scrutiny of the nature of responsibility. It is in this area that IR theory has sought to make its own distinctive contribution.

Theories of special responsibilities

Such practice, and the understandings on which it has rested, came slowly to be absorbed also into IR theory, although it is quite difficult to trace this transference with any great precision. The twin challenge IR theory has faced is to locate the source of this responsibility, and to specify any principle for its differential allocation. To date, it has fallen short of providing a persuasive account of these issues.

---

[39] H. S. Truman, 'Address in New York City at the opening session of the United Nations General Assembly', 23 October 1946, http://trumanlibrary.org/publicpapers/viewpapers.php?pid=914 (accessed 28 July 2011).
[40] Kingsbury, 'Sovereignty and inequality', 600.

The most common theoretical point of departure has reflected its genesis in historical practice. 'The bearing of international responsibility', Inis Claude roundly noted, 'is expected of great powers.'[41] In this way, most IR discussions have concurred on the attribution of special responsibilities to the great powers, and in their assumed plurality. In his prescient book of 1944, famous for introducing the language of 'super-powers', Fox foresaw a future international order resting precariously on the joint collaboration of three powers (the United States, the Soviet Union and Britain), operating within the framework of an international organisation. In combination, he insisted, these would 'provide a supra-national justification for assumption of special responsibilities by the great powers which the smaller states could accept with no sense of derogation of status'.[42] In support of this blueprint, he quoted the representative of one small state, Norway, who had written in 1944 that:

in any universal organization ... a few great countries will have to bear the burden of carrying out the ultimate decisions of the world authority, and to those countries must be given, constitutionally, the formal power corresponding to their real and factual responsibility.[43]

This formulation is crucial because it distinguishes between the 'real and factual' elements of material power, on the one hand, and the 'constitutional' and 'formal' expression of it, on the other. It is this relationship between the 'natural' and the 'social' that is so important to an understanding of special responsibilities, as they evidently entail some combination of both elements. This is especially so in those international-society accounts, commonly associated with an 'institutional' view of the role of the great powers, and especially as developed by the English School. The status accorded to the great powers is to be regarded, not just as some material reality found in a state of nature, but as part of international society's political artifice to mitigate that condition. Most prominently, Hedley Bull highlighted 'the assumption by great powers of special rights and responsibilities',[44] understood in this specific institutional sense.

Accordingly, our initial focus needs to be upon the adoption of the language of responsibility in IR theory. The archaeology of this particular concept is intriguing, if still partly elusive. Generally, it is true that

---

[41] I. L. Claude, 'The common defense and great-power responsibilities', *Political Science Quarterly*, 101(5) 1986, 724.

[42] W. T. R. Fox, *The super-powers: The United States, Britain, and the Soviet Union – Their responsibility for peace* (New York: Harcourt, Brace & Co.: 1944), pp. 153–4.

[43] *Ibid.*, p. 143.

[44] H. Bull, *The anarchical society: A study of order in world politics* (London: Macmillan, 1977'), pp. 73–4.

IR has been much beholden to the Weberian notion of responsibility.[45] Otherwise, in the specifically English School version, it is certainly traceable back to Alfred Zimmern, the first Woodrow Wilson Professor at Aberystwyth University, and subsequently Montague Burton Professor at the University of Oxford. Zimmern suggested in his study of the League of Nations that its future success would require 'a transformation of Power-politics into Responsibility-politics'.[46] In amplification, he had explained that power could not be eliminated, but might be transformed by 'moral responsibility', such that there would 'no longer be *Great Powers*. There would only be *Great Responsibles*.'[47] In a subsequent 1947 manuscript, Zimmern had echoed this same theme of a move to 'responsibility politics' within the United Nations Security Council, by the great powers acting 'with a common sense of their responsibility to provide the world with a framework of law'.[48]

Zimmern's account has been particularly influential within the English School. Wight subsequently recollected it,[49] and it is quite probable that this topic came up in the discussions of the British Committee on the Theory of International Politics. Herbert Butterfield was likewise convinced that maintenance of international order was not just an interest, but indeed a responsibility, of the great powers.[50] 'To speak of great powers', Bull (another British Committee participant) had concluded, 'is already to presuppose the existence of an international society in which these states are "great responsibles".'[51] This was evidently a direct allusion to Zimmern, as also was the title of Bull's subsequent article on the 'great irresponsibles'.[52] This lineage is further attested by the reference to the 'great responsibles' found in the work of Bull's student, John Vincent.[53]

---

[45] D. Warner, *An ethic of responsibility in international relations* (Boulder, CO: Lynne Rienner, 1991).

[46] A. Zimmern, *The League of Nations and the rule of law 1918–1935* (London: Macmillan, 1936), p. 285; D. J. Markwell, 'Sir Alfred Zimmern revisited: Fifty years on', *Review of International Studies*, 12(4) 1986, 282.

[47] Zimmern, *League of Nations*, pp. 83–4, emphasis in original.

[48] P. Rich, 'Reinventing peace: David Davies, Alfred Zimmern and liberal internationalism in interwar Britain', *International Relations*, 16(1) 2002, 126.

[49] Wight, *Systems of states*, p. 42.

[50] A. R. Coll, *The wisdom of statecraft: Sir Herbert Butterfield and the philosophy of international politics* (Durham, NC: Duke University Press, 1985), pp. 93, 104–5.

[51] H. Bull, 'World order and the super powers', in C. Holbraad (ed.), *The super powers and world order* (Canberra: ANU Press, 1971), p. 143.

[52] H. Bull, 'The great irresponsibles? The United States, the Soviet Union, and world order', *International Journal*, 35(3) 1980, 437–47.

[53] R. J. Vincent, 'Order in international politics', in J. D. B. Miller and R. J. Vincent (eds.), *Order and violence: Hedley Bull and international relations* (Oxford: Oxford University Press, 1990), p. 46.

Special responsibilities, however, have by no means been the exclusive intellectual property of English School scholars. These themes of responsibility, and of the special responsibilities attaching to the great powers, have insinuated themselves into other surprisingly diverse schools. They have made even guest appearances in the most unlikely of theoretical settings. Chris Brown makes the commonsense observation that ideas of this kind are unlikely to be adopted by realist thinkers. To realists, 'the idea that Great Powers have special responsibilities to international society as a whole makes little sense, because the notion of international society itself ... makes little sense'.[54] Paradoxically, however, there have been striking exceptions to this general rule, and Hans Morgenthau was one of the earliest. He expressed a view of the great powers that, in important respects, exactly prefigured that institutional interpretation later favoured by English School writers. While acknowledging the distinction between great and small powers as 'one of the elemental experiences of international politics', he nonetheless went on to describe it in importantly different terms as 'an institution of international politics', and as carrying with it 'differences in legal status'.[55] He also proceeded to give an account of the European Concert virtually identical to that recorded above. Within this framework, he noted, 'the great powers continued to assume responsibility for the settlement of political issues', and in a number of nineteenth-century conferences there was demonstrated 'that responsibility of the great powers for the peace of the world'.[56] Contrary to Brown's intuition, we then find that it is a text on realism that highlights this institution of the great powers 'which allocates special rights and responsibilities to leading states'.[57]

According to IR theory, what is it that gives rise to special responsibilities? Do they attach directly to great capabilities, and, if so, how does a material capability transmute into a social responsibility of this kind? Are these responsibilities moral or legal,[58] or else more loosely political? Are special responsibilities a function of the spread of interests, such that great powers have a larger stake in the system as a whole, and the

---

[54] Brown, 'Do great powers have great responsibilities?', 11.
[55] Ibid., 11.
[56] H. J. Morgenthau, Politics among nations: The struggle for power and peace (New York: Knopf, 1948), pp. 367–8.
[57] J. Donnelly, Realism and international relations (Cambridge: Cambridge University Press, 2000), p. 97.
[58] J. Feinberg, Doing and deserving: Essays in the theory of responsibility (Princeton, NJ: Princeton University Press, 1970); T. Erskine, 'Introduction', in T. Erskine (ed.), Can institutions have responsibilities?: Collective moral agency and international relations (Basingstoke: Palgrave Macmillan, 2003), p. 7.

'specialness' of their responsibilities is commensurate with the broad extent of those interests? Otherwise, is it the special attributes of leadership that gives rise to them, and not simply a great power's material resources, narrowly conceived? Max Weber famously described an 'ethic of responsibility' as resting upon the leader, and much realist theory has frequently adopted one version that emphasises the need for due consideration (and allowance) of the consequences of the leader's actions.[59] Is there some covert domestic analogy at work here, as between the national leader, on the one hand, and the leading states, on the other: the responsibilities of both might be considered special because of the potentially fateful consequences of their actions? Moreover, are special responsibilities self-identified by the individual state, or part of a social and intersubjective condition, giving rise not just to *claims* on the part of leading states, but also to *demands* for their exercise arising from others? In that sense, are they simply part of the dense network of rights and responsibilities, characteristic of any conception of international society more generally? Finally, how many great powers must there be for special responsibilities to be assigned to them, and is it possible that these could reduce to one great power acting on its own? These are some of the principal questions that underlie IR's theoretical limited engagement with special responsibilities. How, and how satisfactorily, has IR so far responded to them?

Evidently, several potentially discordant interpretations have competed for attention in our overall understanding. The 'answerability' of the great powers might be thought to derive from their disproportionate historical agency, and so from the salient impact of their actions in the preceding causal story. This has certainly been so with respect to the great peace settlements wherein the great powers have asserted their responsibility for the peace (and justified their directorial role within it), on the basis of their having won the preceding war: their past causal efficacy, and associated sacrifice, have, from this point of view, given rise to a new entitlement to manage the ensuing peace. In close proximity, but divergent in interesting ways, is the ascription of responsibilities on the basis of an assumed future capability to maintain international order. This became especially prevalent with the adoption of ideas of collective security, and it is unsurprising that it was during the period 1919–45 that the language of special responsibilities became so widespread: the more formally international security was to be organised, the more pointed was the question of responsibility for its provision. In

---

[59] Warner, *Ethic of responsibility*; M. C. Williams, *The realist tradition and the limits of international relations* (Cambridge: Cambridge University Press, 2005), chapter 5.

these various ways, frameworks have been constructed around notions of widespread interests, effective capabilities or resources to lead – each conveying subtle, but important, differences about the source and nature of these responsibilities, and about our expectations of what needs to be done to live up to them.

Of these various possibilities, a direct correlation between special responsibilities and material capability is the one most commonly found amongst an assortment of realist theorists. This follows from the logical connection made between 'power' and the ability to manage international affairs. 'To internationalise government in any real sense', E. H. Carr had asserted, 'means to internationalise power', and, to that extent, 'international government is, in effect, government by that state which supplies the power necessary for the purpose of governing.'[60] This same tone was adopted by Morgenthau as well: 'the United States holds a position of predominant power', he declared, 'and hence of foremost responsibility'.[61] This was a direct continuation of the role played by the European great powers in the Concert, where they had 'assumed responsibility', and exercised it through various conferences.[62] However, this role was rooted in the 'fact' of their preponderance, he suggested, and no 'legal arrangement nor organizational device, short of destroying that preponderance of power itself, can undo the consequences of that disparity of power'.[63] This remark seems at odds with the 'institutional' version he had acknowledged elsewhere. Aron likewise located the responsibility of the powers in their factual capability.[64] Kenneth Waltz concurred, since '[g]reat tasks can be accomplished only by agents of great capability'.[65] The great powers act in this way, above all, because they can.[66] Even Bull reminds us that international society is not the sole element in international politics, and it is therefore misleading to imagine that the great powers act only as 'great responsibles': at other times they behave as great predators.[67] If they sometimes undertake the former role, because they can, they sometimes do the latter, again because they can.

---

[60] E. H. Carr, *The twenty years' crisis, 1919–1939: An introduction to the study of international relations* (London: Macmillan, 1939), p. 137.

[61] Morgenthau, *Politics among nations*, p. 8. Reinhold Niebuhr also spoke of the US exercising 'the global responsibilities concomitant with its vast power'. See his 'Foreword', in A. Wolfers, *Discord and collaboration: Essays on international politics* (Baltimore, MD: Johns Hopkins Press, 1962), p. vii.

[62] Morgenthau, *Politics among nations*, p. 367.

[63] *Ibid.*, p. 370.   [64] Aron, *Peace and war*, p. 58.

[65] K. N. Waltz, *Theory of international politics* (Reading, MA: Addison-Wesley, 1979), p. 109.

[66] *Ibid.*, p. 198.   [67] Bull, *Anarchical society*, p. 51.

This is to acknowledge that mere possession of great capabilities does not, by itself, necessarily result in 'responsible' behaviour, and this has itself become an important theme of discussion. It has been especially evident in the nuclear sphere, and in the contrary logics at work in this area. Is possession of nuclear weapons in itself transformative, so that states act more responsibly in consequence of their acquisition? Or, conversely, is there some otherwise pre-defined category of responsible states, and only its members are fit to possess nuclear weapons? In this case, which is chicken and which is egg? This same general issue recurs in debates about the membership of the UN Security Council, and its possible expansion. 'Seats in the Security Council', we are told, 'should not simply be a reflection of power, but an inducement towards responsibility.'[68] What this seems to assume is that responsibility is a quality or attribute of behaviour, not in itself guaranteed by capability: the latter may be a necessary precondition, but is not sufficient on its own to ensure responsible behaviour.

This captures the general logic of any self-help system. In the case of Waltz, it should be emphasised that, even when he introduced the extra element of 'authority' into this role, it was never far removed from this existential capability. 'Whatever elements of authority emerge internationally', he insisted, 'are barely once removed from the capability that provides the foundation for the appearance of those elements.'[69] For that reason, there is little additional social purchase in Waltz's account of authority. As he elaborates elsewhere, the 'power of the strong may deter the weak from asserting their claims, not because the weak recognize a kind of rightfulness of rule on the part of the strong, but simply because it is not sensible to tangle with them'.[70] If special responsibilities do no more than demarcate the terrain within which it is not sensible for the weak to tangle with the strong, they would be of peripheral interest for our account of international legitimacy, scarcely going beyond what the concept of material capability already provides: responsibility becomes superfluous in this perspective.

Other theorists, even when writing from an English School point of view, have nonetheless just as clearly sourced the responsibilities of great powers directly in their great capabilities. Nowhere is this better illustrated than in the work of Robert Jackson, and in his explanation about why great powers enjoy a 'special joint responsibility':

---

[68] B. Jones, C. Pascual and S. J. Stedman, *Power and responsibility: Building international order in an era of transnational threats* (Washington, DC: Brookings Institution, 2009), p. 58.

[69] Waltz, *Theory of international politics*, p. 88.

[70] *Ibid.*, p. 113.

Great Power brings greater responsibility: great powers can justifiably be
called upon to maintain or restore international peace and security or to
uphold or repair the world economy ... [G]reat powers have greater ability
to act and thus they can be said to have greater responsibilities ... So differentiated responsibilities are particularly evident in world politics because
countries differ enormously in the weight of their organized power.[71]

This direct correlation between capability and special responsibilities has appeared in a variety of more subtle forms, and in a diversity
of theoretical accounts, ranging from hegemonic stability theory, to
moral arguments for humanitarian intervention. What unifies these
sundry claims is the expressed need – to ensure the supply of important public goods – for agents able to act in the 'last resort'. This is
most familiar in the economic context, as in the version of 'lender of
last resort'.[72] More recently, this role has sometimes been recast for
the US to act as the 'consumer of last resort', to sustain growth in the
global economy. In the specific context of humanitarian intervention,
it is presumably a similar conception that underpins Michael Walzer's
'agents-of-last-resort':[73] in all these versions, special responsibilities
fall to the materially powerful, not necessarily because they have any
greater responsibility for causing the problem, nor any greater moral
responsibility for redressing it, but rather as the 'default agents simply
because they alone enjoy the capacities and conditions necessary to
act'.[74] The important question here is how material capabilities come
to be associated with an ethical duty. In specific moral theories, those
capable of acting are said to have a special responsibility to protect
the vulnerable. This, for example, is Robert Goodin's argument, as he
applies it in the inter-personal context: 'others are depending on us.
They are particularly vulnerable to our actions and choices. That, I
argue, is the true source of all the standard special responsibilities that
we so readily acknowledge.'[75]

A second cut at the problem has been to redefine the source of
responsibility in terms not just of raw power, but of the great powers'
considerable spread of interests in the system. It has been commonplace to do so, as much amongst practitioners as amongst theorists. For

[71] R. Jackson, *The global covenant: Human conduct in a world of states* (Oxford: Oxford
University Press, 2000), pp. 139–40, 142.
[72] C. P. Kindleberger, *The world in depression, 1929–1939*, rev. edn (Berkeley, CA:
University of California Press, 1986).
[73] M. Walzer, 'The politics of rescue', *Social Research*, 62(1) 1995, 64
[74] T. Erskine, 'Assigning responsibilities to institutional moral agents: The case of states
and "quasi-states"', in Erskine (ed.), *Can institutions have responsibilities?*, p. 36.
[75] R. E. Goodin, *Protecting the vulnerable: A reanalysis of our social responsibilities* (Chicago,
IL: University of Chicago Press, 1985), p. 11.

example, at Vienna in 1815, 'the Great Powers were said to have wider interests in European security … Only the Great Powers had interests transcending geography.'[76] Relatively, they have a 'big stake in the system', or, otherwise expressed, have a greater appetite for 'consumption of collective goods'.[77] Bull agreed, with specific reference to the superpowers after 1945, which he described as having a 'special stake in the system'.[78] From this perspective, special responsibilities continue to be related to capabilities, but more indirectly so. The immediate source, for these great powers, is instead the extent of their stake in the system as a whole, and hence their interest in making a distinctive contribution towards its form of order.

There is one particular issue that has exercised IR theory's engagement with special responsibilities. It follows from past claims that a single great power might bear special responsibilities, as in Morgenthau's assignment of them on the basis of US predominance after the Second World War. Given the very substantial consensus that special responsibilities are borne (only) by the great powers, the related question is how many states are needed for this status to be conferred, and before responsibilities can be assigned to them? In other words, in which capacity do great powers bear special responsibilities: do they do so jointly, as members of the collective of great powers, or is it possible that such an 'institutional' role might yet devolve to a single great power acting on its own? 'Singly and jointly', Claude once remarked, 'the great powers are responsible for managing the international system.'[79] If literally so, this opens the prospect of the sole great power continuing to bear special responsibilities in its own right. How readily has IR theory taken this additional step away from responsibilities, borne and exercised by the great powers collectively, and towards their falling upon one great power only? In the case of the 'lone superpower', it has been suggested, 'the particular responsibilities and duties that a power in the position of the United States may be considered to exercise is a fascinating question'.[80] Despite this fascination, theorists have displayed a manifest reluctance to take it up. The wide consensus on the existence of special responsibilities for the great powers collectively – found across the theoretical spectrum – is mirrored exactly in the almost universal disinclination to countenance their exercise by one great power acting on its own.

---

[76] Simpson, *Great powers and outlaw states*, p. 108.
[77] Waltz, *Theory of international politics*, pp. 195, 208.
[78] Bull, 'World order and the super powers', p. 154.
[79] Claude, 'The common defense', 727, emphasis added.
[80] Brown, 'Do great powers have great responsibilities?', 6.

It may be objected, of course, that this diffidence reflects a profoundly Eurocentric view of the history of state practice, and does not
draw sufficiently on historical experience elsewhere. For example, in
the context of East Asia, there is a different story to tell. This emphasises acceptance of an explicit hierarchy that is the exact opposite of
experience in Europe. David Kang, for example, has drawn attention to
this distinctive aspect of East Asian politics: its 'international relations
have historically been hierarchic, more peaceful, and more stable than
that of the west'.[81] Accordingly, he draws the highly revealing contrast
between Asia and Europe:

> The European order consisted of formal equality of sovereign states combined
> with informal hierarchy since the largest powers have disproportionate influ-
> ence in the system. In Asia the hierarchy consisted of formal hierarchy and
> informal equality.[82]

This suggests that the formal and informal principles upon which
allocations of responsibility were made have been inverted in the two
regions: the formal principle in one has been the informal principle
in the other, and vice versa. In short, East Asian international relations have developed a different accommodation between the principles
of equality and differentiation, as discussed in the Introduction. It is
from the European states system that the particular distrust of the sole
great power is largely derived, and if other regional histories are taken
into account, a quite different impression may emerge. Histories of the
states system in Asia, and particularly of China's role, readily illustrate
this possibility of one dominant state exercising special responsibilities
within the system, in a way that is acceded to by neighbouring states.
While this is certainly true, the qualification may be less compelling
than it appears, insofar as China's role was developed within an avow-
edly hierarchical or suzerain system, rather than in one of (formally)
sovereign equals.[83]

Mainstream IR accounts have otherwise been highly sceptical of the
exercise of special responsibilities on the part of a single great power.
One standard objection, for example, can be found in Waltz's influential

---

[81] D. C. Kang, 'Hierarchy and stability in Asian international relations', in G. J. Ikenberry
and M. Mastanduno (eds.), *International relations theory and the Asia-Pacific* (New York:
Columbia University Press, 2003), p. 164.

[82] *Ibid.*, p. 169.

[83] See, for example, D. C. Kang, 'Getting Asia wrong: The need for new analytical
frameworks', *International Security*, 27(4) (2003), 57–85; D. C. Kang, *China rising:
Peace, power, and order in East Asia* (New York: Columbia University Press, 2007);
A. Watson, *The evolution of international society* (London: Routledge, 1992); Wight,
Systems of states.

account. As already noted, this provides a clear example of special responsibilities sourced in material capabilities.[84] Of greater interest to the present point, however, is Waltz's view of the minimum number of powers thought able to shoulder those responsibilities:

> [t]he smaller the number of great powers, and the wider the disparities between the few most powerful states and the many others, the more likely the former are to act for the sake of the system and to participate in the management of, or interfere in the affairs of, lesser states. The likelihood that great powers will try to manage the system is greatest when their number reduces to two.[85]

Notably, in Waltz's formulation, this logic apparently cuts out at that point, and does not apply below two.

The English School had reached very similar conclusions. Not only could one great power not bear special responsibilities but, even more fundamentally, there could be no such thing as a sole great power in the first place: '[t]hus there could not be simply one great power', and, by way of illustration, Bull concluded that 'if the United States were indeed a single dominant power, it could no longer rightly be called a great power or super power'.[86] His reasoning is instructive: by the term 'we imply ... that there are two or more powers that are comparable in status; we imply ... the existence of a club with a rule of membership'.[87] The great powers exist, therefore, only in a plurality, and to suggest that there might be one only is contradictory. In sum, what both those theories suggest is that a single preponderant state cannot be the bearer of special responsibilities.

How valid is this assumption, and why should a single great power be considered so problematic? Is there something inherent in a single great power that makes this arrangement unworkable, or have we simply experienced so many unfortunate precedents as to put in question the category as a whole? For instance, that such a role was actually played by the United States in the early 2000s has been explicitly denied: 'the unilateralist and frequent norm-violating foreign policy of the United States during the George W. Bush administration is inconsistent with the idea of the great powers as having special responsibilities'.[88] However, even if so, was this because of the idiosyncratic qualities of that particular administration, or inherent in the relationship between special responsibilities and *any* single great power, regardless of which specific policies it pursued? The answer to this question has important

---

[84] Waltz, *Theory of international politics*, p. 198.
[85] *Ibid.*   [86] Bull, *Anarchical society*, pp. 200, 201.
[87] *Ibid.*, p. 200.   [88] Holsti, *Taming the sovereigns*, p. 26.

implications for our understanding of the recent and present role of the United States.

One main reason why it is believed special responsibilities cannot be exercised by one great power is that the responsibility is owed, not just to the remainder of international society, but specifically also to other great power peers: in the absence of other great powers, this part of the relationship breaks down. This objection is closely aligned with the perceived necessity for a balance of power. As Richard Little reminds us, from Bull's perspective, a balance of power is integral to the very conception of a great power.[89] That is, if reciprocity is fundamental to viable special responsibilities, so is the existence of a peer constituency from which the responsibilities are partly derived, and to which they are in part owed. While special responsibilities map out a vertical social relationship between the great powers and the remainder of states, they depend equally upon a horizontal bond amongst the members of the great power club. This horizontal axis drops out altogether when there is but one putative great power.

In summary, it is already clear that there are at least two broadly contrasting theoretical conceptions of special responsibilities. The first comes by the Waltzian route, and is derived directly from the exceptional capabilities possessed by the leading powers, such that they play a distinctive 'structural' role within the system. As noted in the Introduction, at this extreme point on the spectrum, the differentiation in material capability and the differentiation in social role converge completely. However, there is a second position. If the bearing or exercising of special responsibilities is regarded as a 'role', then it is surely necessary to inject one further component: '[r]oles are structural positions', Alexander Wendt avers, 'not actor beliefs'.[90] This introduces a critical distinction. Wendt continues: '[r]ole-identities are subjective self-understandings; roles are the objective, collectively constituted positions that give meaning to those understandings'.[91] This opens up a second account of special responsibilities in which they are not simply reflections of capabilities, but instead positions 'collectively constituted', such as to render them socially legitimate. It is appropriate to think of special responsibilities in the context of those roles, rather than just as role-identities: this stresses the social order as a whole, and not

---

[89] R. Little, *The balance of power in international relations: metaphors, myths and models* (Cambridge: Cambridge University Press, 2007), p. 155.

[90] A. Wendt, *Social theory of international politics* (Cambridge: Cambridge University Press, 1999), p. 258.

[91] *Ibid.*, p. 259.

simply the self-understandings of a specific state, or group of states, within it.[92]

Towards a praxis of special responsibilities

From the above, it is obvious that IR's existing engagement with special responsibilities remains both limited and inconclusive: while the notion of special responsibility emerged as part of a developing diplomatic practice, IR theory has thus far been unable to make much sense of it. Accordingly, this final section briefly outlines those principal gaps in the IR theoretical account, as a way of shaping an agenda of what still remains to be done. This identifies five main areas in need of refinement: our basic understanding of responsibility, in general, and of special responsibilities, in particular; the circumscribed scope of the agents capable of bearing special responsibilities; the restricted substance of those responsibilities with regard to management of international security; the prevalent assumption that their assignment reflects a monolithic international system across a number of policy domains; and a limited sense of the moral purpose of special responsibilities.

First, despite the longevity of appeals to 'responsibility' in IR, one critic laments our 'often cavalier treatment of the concept'.[93] In most versions, responsibility has been derived, directly or indirectly, from material capabilities. Elsewhere, it has been linked to past causal agency, to the capacity to lead in brokering solutions, or to act in the last resort. There is much more, however, to be said about the importance of the allocation of responsibilities in the constitution of social orders. This deficiency is further exacerbated with reference to special responsibilities: the emergence of a common language of special responsibilities has not yet been accompanied by any one single and coherent account of their substance and source, nor of their importance in IR theory and practice.

Second, it is abundantly clear from this survey that special responsibilities have been uniquely assigned to the great powers: the traditional practice worked on this assumption that they alone were special, and responsibilities should be distributed on that basis alone. This point can be made inversely by reference to many contemporary discussions of the role of China. Their common motif is the 'test' imposed on

---

[92] See I. Clark, *Hegemony in international society* (Oxford: Oxford University Press, 2011), chapter 2.

[93] T. Erskine, 'Locating responsibility: The problem of moral agency in international relations', in C. Reus-Smit and D. Snidal (eds.), *The Oxford handbook of international relations* (Oxford: Oxford University Press, 2008), p. 706.

China to accept the 'responsibilities' that accompany its newly found capabilities, as part of its exercise of a great power role.[94] What would make it a great power, on this reckoning, is not simply its increased material resources, but its acknowledgement of the responsibilities that they bring, and its willingness to act in accordance with them. In that sense, the symbiotic relationship between special responsibilities, and the existential nature of great power, is firmly established. For the most part, special responsibilities have been restricted to this class of great powers, normally understood to exist in a plurality. Largely excluded from any such understanding is the notion that, within a hierarchical distribution of power, and one marked by social stratification, a number of different agents may bear special responsibilities that are uniquely attributable to their distinctive social roles: for specific purposes, various categories of actors might be deemed special. For example, as will be discussed later in this volume, the Nuclear Non-Proliferation Treaty assigns responsibilities that are 'special' also to the non-nuclear weapon states, as well as to the nuclear weapon states, just as the Kyoto Protocol assigned 'differentiated' responsibilities to the developing countries, as well as to the developed states. Distinctive responsibilities attach to each separate class, and each is thought special in its own way. In other words, to fully unpack the meaning of responsibility, we need to establish the sense in which any category is thought to be special.

Third, those special responsibilities that have been attached to the great powers in the past have been narrowly focused upon managing the security aspects of international order. This is fully encapsulated in the special responsibilities assigned by the UN Charter to the Security Council in the sphere of international security, in return for which the permanent members are granted special privileges within its voting system. One of the pronounced trends of security analysis in recent decades has been its attempt to broaden the security agenda, either by 'securitising' other policy domains (such as the environment), or by reorienting the subject away from state-based conceptions of security, and towards conceptions of human security. These have direct implications: not only are special responsibilities borne by a variety of agents, and recognised within a wider social sphere, but their substantive content may be

---

[94] S. Breslin, 'Understanding China's regional rise: Interpretations, identities and implications', *International Affairs*, 85(4) 2009, 822; Y. Zhang, 'Understanding Chinese views of the emerging global order', in G. Wang and Y. Zheng (eds.), *China and the new international order* (London: Routledge, 2008), pp. 149–67; Li Hongmei, 'Reflect on China's responsibility', *People's Daily Online*, 23 March 2009, english.peopledaily. com.cn/90002/96417/6619895.html (accessed 28 July 2011).

understood to have deepened as well.[95] While the case study of nuclear weapons below perhaps reflects the more traditional version of special responsibilities, within a familiar international society, the other cases of climate and finance point to examples of this substantive deepening, as well as of a more complex 'social' framing.

Fourth, prevailing accounts of special responsibilities are firmly anchored in analysis of the distribution of material power. It is only within such an intellectual scheme that the notion of the great powers bearing special responsibilities makes any sense at all. As we have seen, predominant views about the source of those responsibilities are tied to the 'capabilities' of the great powers, or to the spread of their interests. It is assumed that special responsibilities, in some fundamental way, are significant only if they are associated with a commensurate capacity to act. Unfortunately, at the same time, this has contributed to a simplification and reification of the distribution of power, treating it as monolithic in this regard. While it has been commonplace for IR theory to attempt to disaggregate the distribution of power into a number of discrete functional games or chessboards, or into distinct regional settings, this disaggregation has not carried across into the discussion of special responsibilities. As a result, the great powers have been considered, indiscriminately, to bear responsibilities across the board. One of the objectives of this volume is to refine our grasp of special responsibilities by locating them within specific functional and policy domains, allowing for a more nuanced and textured discussion of their content and distribution.

Finally, there is the issue of the moral purpose of special responsibilities. Relating them solely to the extent of capabilities, or to the spread of interests, might be thought to yield an ethically impoverished understanding. To employ English School language, this might serve to locate special responsibilities in a context of 'order', but only at the expense of any relationship to a more demanding concept of 'justice'. For this reason, the additional suggestion has been made that ideas of justice are not simply some optional add-on to a concept of responsibility, but are instead an integral aspect of its deeper social meaning: 'there is an intimate, reciprocal relationship', insists Matt Matravers, 'between our ideas of fairness and of responsibility'.[96] How does this contribute to an expanded notion of special responsibilities, and one that mediates between a rudimentary capacity to act, on the one hand,

---

[95] See S. Bernstein, 'Legitimacy in intergovernmental and non-state global governance', *Review of International Political Economy*, 18(1) 2011, 17–51.

[96] M. Matravers, *Responsibility and justice* (Cambridge: Polity Press, 2007), p. 64.

as against a more ethically informed capacity to act fairly, on the other? For example, it might be perfectly possible for the United States and China to seize the international initiative in responding to climate change, but in ways that would not necessarily guarantee any kind of climate justice. Would such action then amount to the exercise of special responsibilities? This brings out the essential normativity of the concept.

The first four of the above listed issues will be elaborated in Chapter 2, and the fifth in Chapter 6. However, one theme running through all those shortcomings has been the general failure to establish a coherent theoretical relationship between special responsibilities and 'power'. The claim set out above is that its distribution has been treated as simplified and reified, rather than broken down into its specific manifestations within discrete domains. However, a more fundamental point can also be made. It is implicit in the above history that special responsibilities have been generated by the exercise of forms of material power: the practice of the special demanded a rationalisation provided in terms of the responsible. It followed from this logic that the allocation of special responsibilities should be viewed as little more than a social mapping of an already existing material distribution of power: the pattern of responsibilities takes the form that it does because of a distribution of material power that is already in place.

'Power' is assuredly implicated in special responsibilities, but in a much more profound sense than this might suggest. The development of special responsibilities within the states system has been but one manifestation of the general tendency to exploit existing inequalities as the basis of order, and to do so through 'institutionalized forms of hierarchy'.[97] On this reading, it is indeed material power that determines special responsibilities, and structures their allocation. However, an alternative reading of the above history points to a more complex, and interactive, development. As the practice of special responsibilities went in search of a supporting theory, it evoked a theory of the responsible that, in turn, has been able to redefine the identity of the special: this need no longer be the great powers alone, but could include various other categories of actors with distinctive attributes. Moreover, the substance of the responsible found itself subject to deeper and more complex demands, extending well beyond that of traditional military security. Even where a military role is still potentially envisaged – such

---

[97] A. Hurrell, 'Power, institutions, and the production of inequality', in M. Barnett and R. Duval (eds.), *Power in Global Governance* (Cambridge: Cambridge University Press, 2005), p. 53.

as in a responsibility to protect – this responsibility has now been cast widely to include protection in areas beyond the state's national security, and national interest, as traditionally understood.

This has resulted in a process of ongoing contestation, and has created varying degrees of social entrapment. In this respect, responsibility has proved to be a particularly sticky norm. It may be true that there has been a decline in international law's recognition of the special status of the great powers.[98] However, there has been no comparable decline in the social scripting around special responsibilities, only a shift of emphasis towards more elaborate and complex concepts of responsibility, and its allocation. All this has contributed to a new distribution of power in which special responsibilities have played a formative role. Thus viewed, special responsibilities do not just reflect an already existing distribution of material power, but actively reshape it in important ways. This is a function of their social power, and their potential to create new social facts on the ground. A praxis of special responsibilities is thus inescapably about 'power', but is as much about the power generated by special responsibilities, as it is about the material power that establishes them in the first place.

In summary, over the past two centuries, there has developed a distinctive practice of special responsibilities within which that specific language has become increasingly idiomatic. Those responsibilities designated within this practice have been assigned predominantly to the great powers as a category, assumed to exist in a plurality. IR theory has largely adopted these core assumptions. Possibly even more so than in the practice, it has been deeply resistant to the idea that special responsibilities can be borne and exercised by a single great power. There remains a dissonance, however, between this pervasive practice, and the relatively slight nature of IR theory's attempted explication of it. Special responsibilities offer the potential to shed considerable light on the management of individual global problems, and the distribution of power pertinent to each. Accordingly, this concept deserves a much richer treatment at the hands of IR theorists. Specifically, in those areas identified above as the most notable omissions, there is scope for a much fuller engagement. This is the task undertaken in the remainder of this volume.

---

[98] Kingsbury, 'Sovereignty and inequality', 600.

2 Special responsibilities in world politics

As we saw in the preceding chapter, the practice of claiming, ascribing and distributing special responsibilities has been a prominent and persistent feature of world politics for at least the last two centuries. Furthermore, International Relations (IR) scholars of diverse theoretical persuasions talk as though such responsibilities do exist, and fall disproportionately on the shoulders of some states. Yet we struggle to find within IR much in the way of sustained theoretical reflection on the nature, function and significance of special responsibilities in world politics. The nature of responsibility itself has gone largely unexplored, as have the particular characteristics of 'special' responsibilities. Very little has been written on the relationship between the definition and distribution of responsibilities and the constitution of international social orders, and discussions of the relationship between responsibilities and political power seldom amount to more than an equation of great capability with great responsibility. More specifically, as the previous chapter explained, the existing literature on special responsibilities in world politics suffers from five principal weaknesses: (1) a conceptual shallowness, apparent in a general failure to probe the nature of responsibility in general and special responsibilities in particular; (2) an unnecessarily narrow conception of agency, in which special responsibilities are the preserve of great powers, but it is consistently denied that a single superpower could have or uphold them; (3) the restriction of special responsibilities to the maintenance of international order, narrowly defined; (4) a monolithic conception of the international system, in which there is one, central distribution of special responsibilities spanning the full range of diverse social domains (security, economic and environmental); and (5) a failure to grapple with the complex ethical issues raised by practices of special responsibilities (addressed in Chapter 6).

This chapter lays the conceptual and theoretical foundations for the remainder of the book, overcoming, we hope, a number of the existing literature's gaps and limitations. Our approach is to work from the ground up. We begin with the nature of responsibility itself, and then consider several key conceptual distinctions – most notably between 'general' and 'special' responsibilities. Having laid these foundations, we address the social nature of responsibility; not only the way in which arguments and judgements about responsibility are made with reference to prevailing social and legal norms, but how the allocation of responsibilities shapes the contours of social orders – constituting role identities, affecting the distribution of legitimate social powers and conditioning the prevailing moral grammar. After considering the issue of whether states, as institutional entities, can bear special responsibilities, we step up to the international level, advancing the three core arguments of the book. The first is a claim about the functional role that special responsibilities play in anarchic international orders in which neither sovereign equality nor the free play of great power politics provides adequate solutions to problems of cooperation and coexistence. The second is an argument about the relationship between the politics of special responsibilities and the constitution of social power. The distribution of such responsibilities, we contend, conditions legitimate political agency and action, thus affecting the distribution of power. Because of this, special responsibilities are a site of recurrent political struggle. Our third, and final, contention is that the present international system cannot be viewed in unitary or monolithic terms – in complex systems such as this, the definition and distribution of special responsibilities varies from one social (or 'issue') domain to another.

As will already be clear, our focus in this chapter is on the 'social theory' of special responsibilities: on their nature as normative precepts, and on how they function in world politics. This is but the first instalment, however, in our theoretical engagement with this issue. Special responsibilities are not just sociological phenomena; they are principles about how the social powers of actors *ought* to be exercised. There are a complex set of moral and ethical issues, therefore, that accompany the politics of special responsibilities: for whom or what should special responsibilities be exercised in world politics? Which actors ought to be the bearers of special responsibilities? And how should special responsibilities be fulfilled? These questions have particular salience with regard to the United States, the material capacities of which are important to harness in addressing key issues of global governance. We take up this second category of 'normative-theoretic' issues in Chapter 6.

Responsibility

Contemporary social and political discourse is saturated with responsibility talk. We talk about the responsibility of parents for the care of their children, the responsibility of children for keeping their rooms tidy, the responsibility of government ministers for their portfolios, the responsibility of citizens for executing their civic duties, the responsibility of corporations for the pollution they generate, the responsibility of all living humans for the environment they bequeath to future generations, the responsibility of individuals for their own well-being, the responsibility of societies for the disadvantaged, the responsibility of governments for the human rights of their citizens and the responsibility of the international community to protect those who their governments fail or abuse.

The ubiquity of such talk is a modern phenomenon, however, something that came to the fore only in the last three to four centuries. Philosophical considerations of the subject existed before, Aristotle's discussion being one of the earliest known.[1] But as other scholars have observed, earlier societies privileged different moral languages and attendant meanings to apportion and evaluate social and political action.[2] Here is not the place to explore this in detail, but the rise in responsibility talk corresponds with the advent of modern individualism, and it may well be that the two are closely connected, with the idea of individuals as atomistic and self-interested demanding a new moral architecture for the rightful allocation of social tasks. It is not surprising, then, that the discourse of responsibility is generally paired with that of rights: the latter being a modern discourse of entitlements, the former of obligations. It is also unsurprising that the idea that great powers have special responsibilities in international relations emerges in the same modern period. As we shall see, the 'absolute individuation' of sovereign states demanded a new moral architecture for the allocation of international social tasks.

Responsibility is a quality we ascribe to actors. While we commonly refer to earthquakes being responsible for countless deaths, greenhouse gas emissions for global warming, faulty brakes for car accidents, visual media for the decline in teenage literacy, and so on, we miss the fact that 'responsible' is not a synonym for 'caused'. For an earthquake to be responsible for countless deaths, it would need not only to have caused those deaths, it would have to be answerable or accountable for them. Hence the etymology of the term – 'responsible' comes from the Latin *respondeo*, to answer.[3] The term is correctly applied to actors only, to those capable of answering or accounting for the things they do or fail to do. Parents are not responsible for the care of their children simply

---

[1] Aristotle, *Nicomachean ethics* (New York: Bobbs-Merrill, 1962), Book 3, Chapter 5.
[2] J. R. Lucas, *Responsibility* (Oxford: Oxford University Press, 1993), p. 5.
[3] *Ibid.*

because they can affect their well-being, but because most societies deem them answerable and accountable for that well-being. The same is true of children and their rooms, government ministers and their portfolios, citizens and their civic duties, and so on. In each case it is not solely the capacity of these actors to causally affect or not affect something that makes them responsible; it is the fact that they are answerable or accountable for those effects, or lack thereof. Earthquakes and Nazis have killed countless humans, but only the latter are properly deemed 'responsible' for such deaths.

Saying that an actor is *responsible* for something is thus to say that they are accountable for it; that they are answerable for its performance or non-performance, occurrence or non-occurrence. *Responsibilities*, it follows, are those things for which an actor is accountable. We often describe certain actors as 'responsible', by which we mean that over time they have shown themselves to be reliable in the performance of their responsibilities. Similarly, 'responsibility' is a characteristic we ascribe to certain model categories of actors. Responsibility is a quality of the ideal parent just as bravery is a quality of the ideal soldier.

Because responsibility is tied to accountability, it is commonly seen as dependent upon free will. An actor is thought to be responsible for acting, or for failing to act, when he or she could have chosen otherwise. Indeed, many scholars see this as the essence of responsibility. In a classic statement of this position, Aristotle wrote that 'if a man harms another by choice, he acts unjustly, and it is this kind of unjust act which makes the agent an unjust man'.[4] Voluntarism is thus considered central to the concept of responsibility. Two things are considered important here. First, for an actor to be considered responsible for an action, he or she must have had the capacity to have acted differently. Actors who are coerced out of fear of death to perform certain actions are not considered answerable for those actions in the same way as those who do these things out of choice. Similarly, actors are commonly held responsible for failing to perform certain tasks only if they had the capacity to do them. While we hold the great powers responsible for failing to prevent the Rwandan genocide, we ascribe no such responsibilities to small Pacific island nations (or no more responsibility than we might ascribe to humanity in general). Second, the notion that actors are responsible for actions only when they had a modicum of choice implies intentionality as well as capacity. Actors who act out of ignorance are not considered responsible in the same way as those who act

---

[4] Aristotle, *Nicomachean ethics*, Book 5, Chapter 8.

with an understanding of the nature and implications of their actions. In this respect, when we hold an actor responsible for something, we are holding them accountable or answerable for 'the rational and moral exercise of discretionary power'.[5]

There are, of course, notable exceptions that reintroduce the issue of causality. Take the case of global climate change abatement. The earth is now experiencing accelerated global warming, a product in large measure of two centuries of industrial development, starting first in the industrialised West and spreading across the globe. If the adverse consequences of such warming are to be contained, even reversed, somebody needs to take responsibility. But who? Under the principle of 'common but differentiated responsibilities', which until now has framed the development of global climate change norms, it is the developed world that has special responsibilities. This is a case, however, in which the actors who caused much of the global accumulation of greenhouse emissions were not, at the time, aware that their actions would have such consequences. Yet this lack of intentionality is not considered a valid reason for developed countries to shrug off their special responsibilities. Having caused the problem is taken to be sufficient reason for the allocation of responsibility. This shows us two things. First, while intentionality may often be central to how we allocate responsibilities, it is not always so. Second, while causality and responsibility are not synonyms, causality is not irrelevant to many of our judgements about responsibility. This is especially true in cases where remedial action is needed to address problems that evolved as a consequence of human actions, but where these consequences were unintentional.

Responsibility takes *positive* and *negative* forms. We can be responsible for performing certain actions (positive responsibility) and for refraining from others (negative responsibility), a distinction similar to that between positive and negative rights.[6] For instance, under the Convention on the Prevention and Punishment of the Crime of

---

[5] J. R. Pennock, 'The problem of responsibility', in C. J. Friedrich (ed.), *Responsibility* (New York: The Liberal Arts Press, 1960), p. 13.

[6] The distinction between positive and negative rights has been subjected to far-reaching criticisms, and many of these apply equally to any distinction between positive and negative responsibilities. For example, it is often pointed out that a classic negative right such as the right to physical security requires more than other actors refraining from aggressive or predatory actions; it requires the development of an institutional order that keeps security threats to a minimum: it requires positive actions for its fulfilment. Similarly, the negative responsibility of states not to commit acts of aggression may well depend, for its fulfilment, on the development of domestic institutions that minimise such impulses, and participation in international initiatives that ameliorate the security dilemma.

Genocide, all persons have a negative responsibility not to commit genocide, but in addition to this, the Contracting Parties have a positive responsibility to 'prevent and punish' such crimes. Responsibility also takes *historical* and *prospective* forms. 'In a temporal sense', as Peter Cane observes, 'responsibility looks in two directions.'[7] We are responsible for things that happened in the past – as Saddam Hussein was responsible for massacring Iraqi Kurds – and we are responsible for future eventualities – as Hedley Bull considered great powers responsible for the preservation of the general balance of power. Prospective responsibility, as Cane points out, subdivides into 'productive' and 'preventive' responsibilities: the former relating to the production of certain goods, the latter to the prevention of particular ills.[8] Cane argues that historical responsibility is about accountability, answerability and liability, whereas prospective responsibility is about roles and tasks. In reality, however, prospective responsibility is as much about answerability as historical responsibility – when a government minister is given responsibility for a portfolio, the implication is that he or she will be answerable for the satisfactory performance of its attendant tasks.

It is commonplace to distinguish between *moral* and *legal* responsibility. This distinction is mired in controversies over the nature of both morality and law. Here is not the place to detail such controversies or attempt their resolution. We will confine ourselves to two observations. First, to be legally responsible is to be answerable for one's actions, or lack thereof, in relation 'to the purposes and values of a particular legal system'.[9] In contrast, to be morally responsible is to be answerable in relation to broader social norms about what it means to be 'good' and to act 'appropriately'. It is this distinction that Joel Feinberg alludes to when he says that 'a stubborn feeling persists even after legal responsibility has been decided that there is still a problem – albeit not a legal problem – left over: namely, is the defendant *really* responsible (as opposed to "responsible in law") for the harm?'[10] Second, to be legally responsible is to be liable to official, authoritative sanctions. But to be morally responsible is to be liable 'to credits and charges on some ideal record, liability to credit or blame'.[11] We can see these differences between legal and moral responsibility at work in international debates over the Rwandan genocide. Leading members of the Security Council

---

[7] P. Cane, *Responsibility in law and morality* (Oxford: Hart Publishing, 2002), p. 31.
[8] *Ibid.*
[9] J. Feinberg, *Doing and deserving: Essays in the theory of responsibility* (Princeton, NJ: Princeton University Press, 1970), p. 30.
[10] *Ibid.*   [11] *Ibid.*

denied that the massacring constituted 'genocide', thus seeking to avoid any legal responsibility to intervene to prevent the killing. In failing to act, however, they were subsequently judged to have been, at the very least, morally responsible for allowing the slaughter to escalate.

This brings us to the crucial distinction of the book: between *general* and *special* responsibilities. It is important to note at the outset that this distinction works at two levels – at the level of agency and the level of value. With regard to the first of these, the difference between general and special responsibilities rests on which agents hold them. A general responsibility is one held by all members of a particular social order (the modern international system, for example), or when we disaggregate such orders, by all parties to a particular regime of social cooperation (the nuclear non-proliferation regime, for instance).[12] All members of Australian society have a general responsibility not to take another's life or to illegally appropriate their property. At the international level, all sovereign states are said to have a general responsibility not to commit aggression or violate the territorial integrity of other states. A special responsibility, in contrast, is one that only particular members of a social order or particular parties to a given regime of social cooperation, have. Parents have special responsibility for the care of their children, doctors for the health of their patients, and so on. Internationally, as we saw in the last chapter, it is commonplace to attribute special responsibilities to the great powers.

The distinction between general and special responsibilities does not rest solely, however, on whether they are held by all members of society (or regime of cooperation) or a particular subset. We also differentiate them on the basis of value. The special responsibilities of the doctor or the government minister are 'special' because society values them highly, and this is why social roles with special responsibilities often carry high social status. This is not always the case, though. India's Harijans ('Untouchables') traditionally had special responsibilities for the daily removal of household excrement, but neither their role nor attendant responsibilities were valued highly, even if society depended on their services. What matters here are the rights that special responsibilities bring. The special responsibilities of the doctor and Harijan

[12] General responsibilities are not the same as 'normal' responsibilities. The term 'normal' implies what is usual, not out of the ordinary, or persistent over time. Sometimes general responsibilities are normal. For instance, the general responsibility of states not to intervene in other states is normal (*qua* usual). Often, however, general responsibilities are not normal, particularly when a regime of cooperation is emergent. For example, when the Nuclear Non-Proliferation Treaty (NPT) was first negotiated, it imposed certain general responsibilities on all parties. These were abnormal, though; they were new and utterly novel.

carry with them special rights, entitlements they both need in order to fulfil their respective responsibilities. But the rights the doctor acquires are qualitatively different to those of the Harijan. Doctors have rights to prescribe medicines, conduct surgery and make critical decisions in life and death situations, whereas Harijans had little more than the right to enter the rear of houses at discrete times of the day. These are not just different rights; they generate different social powers. The doctor's special responsibilities convey special rights that enable forms of social action that the Harijan's did not. In sum, when special responsibilities bring with them rights that are significantly empowering, societies tend to value them highly, to see them as 'special' in our second sense.

This connection between special responsibilities and the rights they may or may not confer has a significant impact on the attractiveness of such responsibilities, on the willingness of actors to assume and fulfil them. Special responsibilities that entail empowering rights are likely to be more attractive than those that bring burdens only. Taking this one step further, positive special responsibilities that entail few if any worthwhile rights may be harder to allocate than negative responsibilities that carry desirable rights. Two examples illustrate this kind of variation. As we shall see in Chapter 4, the special responsibilities needed to address climate change are positive as well as negative, yet they bring few if any desirable rights. Current demands for reform of the United Nations Security Council reveal the opposite tendency. Permanent membership carries with it certain positive special responsibilities, but also status and rights, making it attractive to aspirant states.

Special responsibilities come in two forms. The first is what we might term 'universal' special responsibilities. Here the sub-group of actors who bear these responsibilities is, at least theoretically, an open category, such as great powers or developed states. The particular actors that populate these categories are not pre-ordained; membership may vary, and any actors who satisfy the relevant criteria (such as 'greatness' or 'developed') can claim, or be allocated, the attendant special responsibilities. We see this in the case of climate change – the sub-group of 'developed' states is an open one, and at some point China will enter that category and be expected to bear whatever responsibilities attend membership. The second type of special responsibilities are 'non-universal', in the sense that the sub-group in question is not an open category. Only actors with certain integral characteristics are included; characteristics other actors may admire, but which they cannot acquire or develop. A classic example here is the sub-group of 'civilised nations' who, during the eighteenth and nineteenth centuries, ordained themselves with special responsibilities for the rule of 'barbarian' and 'savage' peoples. While 'civilised' can be read as an open category – a measure of social and cultural achievement – it was not in this case, so bound up was the concept with ideas of racial superiority. Africans, Indians and Chinese could develop all manner of social and institutional habits and practices, but they would never be white. More significantly, because they weren't white their prospect of achieving these qualities was considered remote. The Nuclear Non-Proliferation Treaty (NPT) provides another example, this time closer to our central concerns. Under the treaty, the category of nuclear weapon states (NWSs) is non-universal. Even if a state manages to acquire nuclear weapons, it cannot enter the select club of recognised NWSs under the treaty: this is a closed category.

It is important to recognise that general and special responsibilities are often in tension with one another. Most of the time they are not – the special responsibilities that come with most people's jobs don't conflict with their general responsibilities as law-abiding citizens, for example. But in notable cases they do. Police officers have the same general responsibility that we all have not to kill, but because they have a special responsibility to uphold law and order, they may in certain circumstances have to act in ways that contradict this general responsibility. Social orders deal with such tensions by establishing institutional mechanisms that do two things. First, they evolve rules that specify when actors with special responsibilities may act in ways that conflict with their general responsibilities, and often attach sanctions to violations of these rules. In most liberal democracies, for instance, police shootings are meant to be followed by inquiries to determine whether rules governing the lethal use of force have been observed. Second, societies develop norms that preserve the multiple role identities of actors with special as well as general responsibilities, and intersubjective understandings about when these actors are assuming particular roles with particular responsibilities. Doctors and police officers step between their special and common roles and attendant responsibilities, and when they have stepped out of their special roles, societies consider it inappropriate for them to exercise the rights that come with their special responsibilities, bar in emergency situations.

Special responsibilities, like all responsibilities, can be formal or informal, codified or embedded in more diffuse social understandings. This is apparent in two of our cases. With nuclear proliferation, the special responsibilities of both NWSs and non-nuclear weapon states (NNWSs) are formally set out in the NPT, and the often heated debate that surrounds these contrasting responsibilities takes place with reference to the terms of the treaty itself. The situation with global finance is quite different. Any special responsibilities that the United States has in this area are less clearly defined and are codified in scattered fragments. Moreover, understanding of what these responsibilities might be has changed over the past seven decades, and is under considerable debate today. This case also shows the importance of practices in both the development and reproduction of norms concerning special responsibilities. Norms are not always conscious constructions, intersubjective meanings argued out by knowledgeable actors seeking to condition human behaviour in particular ways. Rather, they are often the product of practice, of 'doing' rather than 'designing' or 'deliberating'.[13] Jutta Brunnee and Stephen Toope argue, for example, that states develop feelings of legal obligation by engaging in legal practices.[14] We can see this connection between practices and understandings at work in the international politics of special responsibilities. Again, the finance case is illustrative. What are now commonly regarded as the special responsibilities of the United States for global financial stability only partially developed through conscious design: key responsibilities emerged first as practices that only later came to be understood, by the wider community of states, as the United States' special responsibilities.

Before proceeding a word is needed on the relationship between special responsibilities and leadership. The two concepts are often conjoined, as though one necessarily entails the other. Frequently this is indeed the case – we often think of our leaders as having special responsibilities, and say that certain actors have a special responsibility to lead (the United States, for example). But while the two are, in many cases, closely connected this is not always so. Let us take a purely abstract example. A group of ten friends like to socialise with one another, but they all have busy lives and finding times that fit everyone's diaries is difficult. For years, though, they manage to meet regularly, keeping their friendships strong. The only reason this happens, however, is that one of the friends, Julie, takes it upon herself to organise get-togethers. In other words, she takes on a leadership role, one recognised as legitimate by the other friends. The question is, however, whether Julie's leadership entails special responsibilities. As explained above, one is responsible for something when one is accountable for its performance or non-performance. Imagine that after some years Julie gets tired of organising social events and gets caught up in other aspects of her life.

---

[13] See V. Pouliot, *International security in practice* (Cambridge: Cambridge University Press, 2010); and E. Adler and V. Pouliot (eds.), *The practice turn in international relations* (Cambridge: Cambridge University Press, forthcoming).

[14] J. Brunnee and S. Toope, *Legitimacy and legality in international law: An interactional account* (Cambridge: Cambridge University Press, 2010).

As a consequence, the friends fall further and further out of touch. Would it be reasonable for the friends to criticise Julie for failing to bring them together; for them to hold her accountable for her failure of leadership? We think not. Indeed, if she was criticised in this way, Julie would surely respond: 'I did this for years, but ultimately it's not my responsibility.' We do not have to search hard to find similar examples in international relations: Norway's leadership in past Middle-East peace initiatives is a case in point, as is Australia's role in the establishment of the Asia-Pacific Economic Cooperation grouping. Both involved leadership that was not anchored in, or flowing from, special responsibilities. The reverse, of course, also occurs – actors can have special responsibilities that do not entail leadership. For example, Julie's social group might have given one friend, Manuel, special responsibility for buying wine for their get-togethers, but this responsibility would not, in all likelihood, have involved any form of leadership. In international relations, NNWSs under the NPT have special responsibilities to not acquire nuclear weapons, to open their nuclear facilities to International Atomic Energy Agency inspections, and to not transfer nuclear materials illegally. Yet none of these responsibilities entail leadership. What this discussion shows is that while leadership and special responsibilities are frequently connected, they must be treated as analytically distinct and their particular conjunctions understood.

Responsibility and the constitution of society

If to be 'responsible' means to be answerable, then the concept is an inherently social one. To be responsible for something, is to be accountable to others, to be subject to their judgements and resulting actions. Responsibility is not just social in the sense of involving other people, though. When we judge an individual to be responsible for something, we do so in relation to pre-existing expectations about what constitutes appropriate conduct for a person in that social role in that kind of situation. When we judge a teacher responsible for something that occurred in her classroom, we do so with reference to established understandings of what being a teacher means and what kinds of behaviour this demands of those performing such a role in particular contexts. We do so, therefore, in relation to prevailing intersubjective understandings. These understandings can be informal or formal, moral or legal. They can also be society-wide, embedded in the belief systems of sub-cultural groupings, or shared only between particular individuals or groups of individuals (between couples or within families, for example). As Kelly Shaver and Deborah Schutte observe, responsibility is conditioned by 'informal understandings of the expectations of a culture, societal norms about appropriate conduct, legal requirements for behaviour, and individual-level conceptions about the relationships among people'.[15]

Yet in a classic example of the mutual constitution of agents and structures, the intersubjective understandings that shape our judgements about responsibility are themselves the products of human innovation, negotiation and reproduction. Like Alexander Wendt, our position here is one of 'moderate holism', in that we see intersubjective understandings about responsibility as producing broad modes of social behaviour. Like all cultural norms, these understandings confront 'actors as an objective social fact that constrains and enables action in systematic ways, and as such generate distinct patterns'.[16] Yet, as Wendt insists, these structural understandings only persist because of the routinised practices of social agents. Norms about the responsibilities of teachers endure because they themselves engage in norm-conforming behaviour, students pattern their conduct around expectations of their teachers' responsibilities, and parents and principals challenge teachers who step out of line. But understandings about responsibility, like all social norms, change over time, and these structural changes are the product of social contestation, of actors' challenging and revising prevailing norms. There is now a considerable body of research on 'norm entrepreneurship', and here is not the place to review its insights. It is sufficient to note the five sources of cultural contestation identified by Wendt: the inherent contradictions between a society's many social norms, rules and institutions; the fact that individuals are never fully socialised and hold private beliefs that may lead them to seek social change; the way in which the unintended consequences of shared beliefs prompt actors to negotiate new norms; the impact of exogenous shocks on a social order; and the emergence of new ideas, the simple fact of creativity.[17]

The intersubjective understandings that define who has what responsibilities, and the discourses and practices that produce and reproduce them, shape social orders in profound ways. They are, in the first instance, critical in defining the multifarious social roles that characterise a society. Social roles are, in many respects, simply agglomerations of responsibilities (and rights). If we asked a doctor, teacher, plumber, cleaner, mother or a president to describe their social roles, they would

---

[15] K. G. Shaver and D. A. Schutte, 'Towards a broader psychological foundation for responsibilty: Who, what, how', in A. E. Auhagen and H.-W. Bierhoff (eds.), *Responsibility: The many faces of a social phenomenon* (London: Routledge, 2001), p. 36.

[16] A. Wendt, *Social theory of international politics* (Cambridge: Cambridge University Press, 1999), p. 184.

[17] *Ibid.*, p. 188.

in all likelihood do so with reference to their respective responsibilities. We see here an important difference between social roles and social identities, two things often conflated in the literature. In a modern setting in particular, it is difficult to see how one could define one's social role with reference to anything other than one's responsibilities. But it would be odd if we confined an account of our social identity to a list of our role responsibilities. If a social identity is a set 'of meanings that an actor attributes to itself while taking into account the perspective of others',[18] then those meanings would generally include not only responsibilities, but also qualities for which we are not answerable: just, loving, energetic, creative, engaging, funny, and so on.

In addition to defining the many roles that constitute a social order, understandings and practices of responsibility play a crucial role in distributing, constraining and licensing social power. Let us begin with a simple Weberian conception of power as 'the probability that one actor within a social relationship will be in a position to carry out his own will despite resistance, regardless of the basis on which this probability rests'.[19] In an imaginary world in which such power rested purely on the material resources that actors could mobilise, its distribution would match the distribution of such resources, and the only constraint on the exercise of power would be insufficient material resources or countervailing power. For 'really existing' societies to function, however, power needs to be disciplined and channelled, contained within socially acceptable bounds and harnessed to productive social ends. Intersubjective beliefs about responsibility, and their generative discourses and practices, help societies do this. Norms of negative responsibility constrain actors in the exercise of their capacities – 'responsible actors don't act that way, even if they have ability to do so' – while norms of positive responsibility demand that they employ their capacities in particular ways – 'you may not want to exercise your capacities in this way, but it is your responsibility'.

Seen from this angle, ideas about responsibility, and the norms and practices they engender, are invoked and enacted to contain, channel or harness the 'compulsory' power of actors, producing social outcomes that are not reducible to the material capacities of such actors. Seen from another angle, however, notions of responsibility also affect configurations of 'structural' power within a society. Such power, Michael

[18] A. Wendt, 'Collective identity formation and the international state', *American Political Science Review*, 88(2) 1994, 385.

[19] M. Weber, *The theory of social and economic organization* (New York: Free Press, 1964), p. 152.

Barnett and Raymond Duvall argue, 'produces the very social capacities of structural, or subject, positions in direct relation to one another, and the associated interests that underlie and dispose action'.[20] Once ideas about the nature and distribution of responsibilities are institutionalised – once they have been established as intersubjective social and legal norms – they assume a structural quality, confronting actors as social facts that condition their social identities and interests, by tying constellations of responsibilities to socially sanctioned roles, and shape their capacities by defining the terms of legitimate social and political action. More than this, though, intersubjective beliefs about the nature and distribution of special responsibilities constitute subject positions that stand in structural power relations to one another, the classic example being the master-slave relationship. Here 'the kinds of social beings that are mutually constituted are directly or internally related; that is, the social relational capacities, subjectivities, and interests of actors are directly shaped by the social positions that they occupy'.[21]

Because beliefs, discourses, norms and practices of responsibility play a key role in structuring social power, struggles over responsibility are an ever present feature of politics. Our understanding of politics extends beyond the commonly employed notion of strategic action, although it certainly encompasses this. Politics, for us, is about the negotiation of social identities, arguments about legitimate interests and social purposes, the formulation and execution of strategic practices, and struggles over the good and the just. Most importantly, it exists at the difficult intersection between each of these.[22] Ideas about responsibility are implicated in the constitution of social identities; they inform how actors conceive their interests and purposes, they serve as strategic resources in arguments over when actors should, or should not, act ('I must act in this way, it's my responsibility', or 'I cannot be expected to act, it's not my responsibility'), and they provide one of the principal moral grammars with which we argue about right conduct.

Can states have responsibilities?

So far we have confined our discussion to how responsibility functions within societies of individual human persons, peppered with occasional

---

[20] M. Barnett and R. Duvall, 'Power in global governance', in M. Barnett and R. Duvall (eds.), *Power in global governance* (Cambridge: Cambridge University Press, 2005), p. 18.
[21] *Ibid.*
[22] C. Reus-Smit, 'Politics and international legal obligation', *European Journal of International Relations*, 9(4) 2003, 591–625.

examples from international relations. This was an important first step, as it enabled us to deal with a number of key conceptual issues to do with the nature of responsibility often elided by studies that begin with responsibility in the international arena. But before we step from the domestic to the international, we need to address, however briefly, a key theoretical issue. Can sovereign states, as opposed to individual humans, have responsibilities? At one level, this is relatively straightforward: we speak and act as though states have responsibilities, and ideas of international legal personality give form and expression to this in the field of legal responsibility. At the same time, however, sovereign states are clearly not the same things as human individuals; they are political organisations, not corporeal beings, administrative and institutional entities that 'govern' societies and are populated by individuals, but are reducible to neither. Since we commonly assume that such entities have responsibilities, it makes little sense to deny this outright, particularly for a project such as this. A key question remains, however: in what sense do sovereign states have responsibilities?

Our argument here follows that of Toni Erskine, albeit with one minor if important modification. Like us, Erskine defines the state as an institution, and for her the key question is whether institutions are capable of bearing and fulfilling responsibilities. States are 'artificial' moral agents, she argues: 'They have a) identities different from the identities of their individual constituents, and b) the capacity for deliberation and decision-making.'[23] This means that they meet the first of two criteria for moral agency, the ability 'to understand and reflect on moral requirements'.[24] The second criterion is 'the capacity to then act in such a way as to conform to these requirements'.[25] Here Erskine correctly observes that different states have different capacities to act in response to their moral deliberations, to fulfil their responsibilities. Using the example of 'quasi-states', she shows how historical patterns of state formation have left some states with weakened internal capacities for deliberation and decision-making, and the external economic and political conditions in which they exist have limited their ability to act on their deliberations. Nevertheless, Erskine rightly shies away from the conclusion that some states can be considered moral agents and not others. Instead, she holds that all states are moral agents but

---

[23] T. Erskine, 'Assigning responsibilities to institutional moral agents: The case of states and "quasi-states"', in T. Erskine (ed.), *Can institutions have responsibilities?: Collective moral agency and international relations* (Basingstoke: Palgrave Macmillan, 2003), p. 27.
[24] *Ibid.*, p. 21.   [25] *Ibid.*

with varied capacities to meet responsibilities, something that needs to be taken into account when apportioning international responsibilities – some states are more appropriate bearers of responsibilities than others.[26]

Our minor departure from Erskine concerns her treatment of the relationship between states as institutions and collectivities. In her description of the state, she shifts between describing it as an institution and a collectivity. Indeed, at times she comes close to describing it primarily as the latter. In contrast to crowds and queues, the state is presented as a collectivity with certain characteristics – a separate identity from the individuals that comprise it, a capacity for deliberation and decision-making, and so on. But from this perspective, the state is only thinly institutional. More importantly, the implication, if not the intent, is that the collectivity in question is an 'agglomeration' of the individuals that fall within a state's territory. If this is the case, the boundaries between state and society blur. Our preference is for a thicker conception of the state as an institution, however. Not only do we believe that the state is, first and foremost, an institution, but this assumption is essential if we are to speak sensibly of states having responsibilities within international society, on the one hand, and domestic society, on the other. Erskine's contribution is to allow us to speak sensibly of the state as a moral agent in the first of these social realms, but her blurring of the distinction between state and society makes it harder for us to do the same for the second realm. We know, however, that a crucial aspect of the politics of responsibility in world politics is the tension between the international and domestic responsibilities of states, and the way in which particular states, in particular circumstances, manage this tension.

Responsibility under anarchy

The politics of special responsibilities among sovereign states takes place under conditions of anarchy, by which we mean nothing more than that the international system lacks a central authority. The behavioural implications of this are often over-stated. As commonly observed, there are different 'cultures' of anarchy, characterised by different intersubjective understandings and generating different kinds of international practices. And as we shall see, ideas about the nature and distribution of responsibilities occupy a central position within such understandings. The structural condition of anarchy does, however, have one important

[26] *Ibid.*, p. 34.

implication for the politics of responsibility. Within states, a central political and legal authority exists, one function of which is the authoritative definition, allocation and enforcement of social responsibilities. States not only allocate responsibilities to their own public agencies, but also to private actors; everything from the financial, labour and environmental responsibilities of corporations to the maintenance responsibilities of divorced parents. No such central authority exists in the international system, however densely institutionalised and marked by informal patterns of hierarchy it might be. For this reason, the international politics of special responsibilities assumes a decentralised form, characterised today by a broad range of state and non-state actors, more diffuse and variegated forms of allocation, and greater reliance on reputational techniques of enforcement.

Within anarchic international systems, states and peoples face a range of challenges, not merely those of coexistence, but also more complex problems of cooperation. It is useful here to distinguish between simple and complex systems. The former are characterised by relatively sparse structures of political agency (the terrain largely monopolised by sovereign states), lower levels of interdependence and dynamic density and a limited number of functional issues demanding attention. The latter are marked by the reverse: more dense structures of political agency, in which states share the stage with a myriad of other politically consequential actors; higher levels of interdependence and dynamic density; and a broader range of functional imperatives. In simpler anarchic systems, the challenges of coexistence and cooperation encountered by states are relatively few and dominated by fundamental issues of recognition and ameliorating the security dilemma, issues deeply entwined with one another. In more complex systems, of the kind we live in today, the challenges are multiple and diverse. Problems of recognition and security persist (even if they change in nature), but they coexist with a variety of other challenges, such as sustaining global economic growth and development and preserving the global environment. In addition to this difference in the number and variety of challenges that characterise simple and complex systems, they differ in another important respect: complex systems, in which there are multiple functional imperatives, develop multiple social and political domains (security, economic, environmental and so on), each manifesting a degree of relative autonomy.

To understand the role that the politics of special responsibilities play in anarchic international systems (both simple and complex), it is useful to consider two other political modalities in which functional imperatives might be addressed. The first is characterised by the free play of material power politics, a classic 'realist' world. The functional deficiencies of this mode of politics have long been noted: an unconstrained security dilemma leading to arms racing and repeated warfare, and chronic problems of collective action, leading to tragedies in multiple commons. The second political modality is one characterised by formal sovereign equality, a form of legal egalitarianism central to the post-1945 international institutional order. Built around the entwined norms of self-determination and non-intervention, this modality is often cast as essential to alleviating several of the more pronounced international challenges: reducing the security dilemma through robust norms of mutual recognition and non-aggression, and helping to overcome collective action problems by providing the normative foundation for the institutional practice of multilateralism. Yet, whatever benefits this modality may have over protean power politics, its deficiencies are clearly apparent. First, while the principle of sovereign equality allocates rights and obligations equally across states, addressing almost all of the functional challenges facing the international community today requires that states be treated differently, and that they assume different tasks with different responsibilities and attendant rights. Second, many of these challenges demand leadership in one form or another, but this again stands in tension with strict notions of sovereign equality. Finally, the present legal regime of sovereign equality coexists with significant differences of material capacity across states, and while the principle's attendant norms of non-intervention and non-aggression serve to constrain predations by the materially powerful, they do not, in themselves, provide any means by which differential capacities can be harnessed to meet global challenges.

A central contention of this book is that ideas and practices of special responsibilities come to the fore, and assume particular political importance in anarchic international systems where both material power politics and sovereign equality provide inadequate bases on which to address challenges of coexistence and cooperation. Like their domestic counterparts, international social orders need power to be disciplined and channelled, harnessed to productive social ends, especially if profound functional challenges are to be met. And just as in domestic societies, but with added imperative, the definition and distribution of general and special responsibilities help achieve this. The contestation and struggle that characterises the politics of responsibility is, of course, accentuated in international social orders, lacking as they do a central agency for the authoritative distribution of general and special responsibilities. The construction of international regimes of general and special responsibilities remains, however, an attractive response to functional challenges. For states well-endowed with material capacities, two enticements exist: assuming certain special responsibilities, such as mutual constraints on the use of force, can reduce the incidence of violent conflicts among great powers; and assuming responsibilities brings legitimacy. Exercising one's material capacities in the performance of a responsibility is to act rightfully; refraining from exercising such capacities in the name of one's responsibilities enhances one's standing as a legitimate actor. For states with limited material capacities – the ones empowered by the principle of sovereign equality – using regimes of general and special responsibilities to give states different tasks, with different benefits and burdens, is attractive because responsibility implies accountability, as we have seen. Allocating special responsibilities to particular actors gives other actors the right to hold the ordained answerable for the performance of those responsibilities, and the licence to 'account' is a form of social empowerment.

Distribution of power

Conventional realist accounts of international relations equate the distribution of material resources with the distribution of political power: the topography of one is the topography of the other. States are said to possess certain quantifiable material resources – guns, money, geographical position and so on – and these resources are assumed to translate, in some straightforward fashion, into compulsory power, the capacity to get other actors to behave according to one's will. This equation of resources with power is betrayed by the terminology employed in such accounts: that of capabilities. Correctly understood, this term means 'power of' or 'power to', and the sources of such power form no part of the definition. For realists, in contrast, the term refers simultaneously to 'power of' and 'power to' *and* material resources: any distinction between power and its sources is thus elided. From this perspective, the mapping of power in the international system is relatively simple and largely a quantitative exercise: assess the relative material resources of key states, and this yields a league table of relative power.

Elsewhere we have critiqued this understanding of power in international relations.[27] Not only does power take multiple forms – compulsory, institutional, structural and productive – it also has multiple sources. Even when understood in narrow compulsory terms, an actor's power is not just shaped by the material resources it can bring to bear,

---

[27] See the essays within I. Clark and C. Reus-Smit (eds.), 'Resolving international crises of legitimacy', *International Politics*, 44(2/3) 2007, 153–339.

but also by the legitimacy it commands. One commands legitimacy when others consider you, or what you want to do or achieve, rightful. As Mark Suchman explains, 'legitimacy is a generalized perception or assumption that the actions of an entity are desirable, proper, or appropriate within some socially constructed system of norms, values, beliefs, and definitions'.[28] Legitimacy contributes to compulsory power because it brings with it voluntary compliance; other actors help realise the 'powerful' actor's ends because they regard that actor or their ends to be rightful, not because they have been coerced or bribed. Bringing legitimacy into the equation reveals the social face of power. For realists, the power of one actor depends on the comparative capacities of others – it is 'relative'. Yet power is social in a deeper sense than this – it is 'relational'. Not only does a given actor's legitimacy depend on the perceptions of others; those perceptions are formed with reference to prevailing social norms, values and beliefs, all of which are intersubjective.

Understandings of responsibility, and of special responsibilities in particular, are key constellation points around which social and political power forms. As we have seen, special responsibilities are rightful powers. For those bearing them, they can be socially sanctioned licences to exercise one's capacities in particular ways, or to refrain from doing so. And for other social actors, they represent justified sites of critique; normative reference points against which those ordained with special responsibilities can be held to account. In short, the politics of special responsibilities is, in any social order, domestic or international, a principal locus of the politics of legitimacy, and hence a site for the constitution of social and political power. This means that the distribution of power within any given social order will be affected by the distribution of special responsibilities, and what those responsibilities are – who shoulders them, and how they are allocated – will be focal points of political struggle. Furthermore, because social roles are, in many respects, aggregations of special responsibilities, the construction of such roles is central to the power politics of responsibility. When former US Secretary of State Madeleine Albright described the United States as 'the indispensible nation', she was simultaneously seeking to construct a particular social identity for the US, tie this to notions of special responsibility and legitimise the US use of force abroad.[29]

---

[28] M. Suchman, 'Managing legitimacy: Strategic and institutional approaches', *Academy of Management Review*, 20(3) 1995, 574.

[29] United States State Department, 'Secretary of State Madeleine K. Albright, Interview on NBC-TV "The Today Show" with Matt Lauer', Columbus, Ohio, 19 February 1998, secretary.state.gov/www/statements/1998/980219a.html (accessed 29 July 2011).

In departing from the realist view of power as material capacity, we are not arguing that material capacities are irrelevant to the definition and allocation of special responsibilities or to the resulting distributions of social power. At the most general level, because we argue that the impulse to address global governance challenges through the allocation of special responsibilities emerges in the context of unequal material power and formal sovereign equality, we should not be at all surprised that regimes of special responsibilities are pushed and shoved by the play of material power politics – such is their fate as institutional *via media*. It is important to remember that once institutionalised, ideas about the nature and distribution of special responsibilities become social norms, and we should not expect them to have constitutive or constraining 'powers' beyond those of international norms in general. The fact is that materially well-endowed states that are prepared to bear significant reputational costs can shirk their responsibilities.

This having been said, though, regimes of special responsibilities have a significant effect on the social power of materially well-endowed states. Within a particular social domain, the allocation of responsibilities sets the terms of legitimate political agency and action, licensing and differentiating social roles, and prescribing or proscribing types of behaviour. In other words, regimes of responsibilities condition the field of legitimate politics. As our case studies show, once established these fields have proven difficult for even the United States to escape or manipulate. The NPT, for example, structures international nuclear politics, defining key social roles (NWSs and NNWSs) and their attendant special responsibilities. The politics of non-proliferation is played out within the frame of these roles and responsibilities, and the central political contests of this domain concern whether or not particular categories of states are meeting their obligations. As Chapter 3 explains, on a number of occasions Washington has sought to redefine both its special responsibilities as a NWS and the responsibilities of NNWSs. Its success, however, has been marginal at best, and international perceptions of its legitimacy as a NWS remain shaped by the responsibilities set down in the regime. The global finance and climate change cases display similar dynamics. This has important implications for how we think about the existence or non-existence of American hegemony today. A hegemon is conventionally understood as a state with sufficient power to define the rules of the international system, with the United States between 1945 and 1972 being the quintessential example. It is clear, however, that in none of our three cases did the United States define the original distribution of special responsibilities, and in none has it been able to unilaterally redefine or shake off these obligations – the games remain the same. The United States can, of course, fail to meet its special responsibilities, but changing the politics of legitimacy that surrounds such dereliction is considerably harder.

This argument runs directly counter to that advanced by Stephen Brooks and William Wohlforth.[30] In response to earlier work of ours, they develop a distinctive argument about unipolarity and legitimacy. We have argued elsewhere that the power of the United States – its ability to realise its interests and achieve intended rather than unintended outcomes – is conditioned by the legitimacy it commands internationally, and that judgements of American legitimacy are made with reference to international norms concerning legitimate agency and political action.[31] Brooks and Wohlforth challenge this argument, although not by making the standard move of denying that legitimacy matters in international relations. Rather, while acknowledging the importance of legitimacy, as well as its inherently social nature, they argue that the United States, as a unipolar power, has disproportionate capacities to manipulate the terms of its own legitimacy. If constructivists are correct that comparatively weak non-governmental actors can mobilise international norms to shape the domestic and international behaviour of states, then it is only reasonable, they contend, to attribute such capacities to the most 'powerful' state in the system. Yet a central argument of this book is that while the United States, like any actor, can influence perceptions of its legitimacy by how it manages its social identity and crafts and communicates its interests, its ability to manipulate the terms of its own legitimacy is far more circumscribed than Brooks and Wohlforth contend. In the three crucial areas of nuclear proliferation, climate change and global finance, these terms have been defined by distributions of special responsibilities that Washington has shirked and bucked against but has been unable to define away.

Two other observations are worth making about material capacities and special responsibilities. First, material capacities matter in the definition and allocation of special responsibilities: it makes no sense giving responsibilities to actors that do not have capacities, material or otherwise, to fulfil them. However, the kind of material capacities that matter for special

---

[30] S. G. Brooks and W. C. Wohlforth, *World out of balance: International relations and the challenge of American primacy* (Princeton, NJ: Princeton University Press, 2008), chapter 6.

[31] See C. Reus-Smit, *American power and world order* (Cambridge: Polity Press, 2004); I. Clark, *Legitimacy in international society* (Oxford: Oxford University Press, 2005); Clark and Reus-Smit (eds.), 'Resolving international crises of legitimacy'; and, more recently, I. Clark, *Hegemony in international society* (Oxford: Oxford University Press, 2011).

responsibilities varies from one social domain to another: in the nuclear area it is possession or non-possession of nuclear arms, or the nature of civil nuclear infrastructure; in the realm of climate change it is aggregate emissions and the economic and technological capacity to facilitate national and international adjustment. Second, the material capacities of states are socially constructed, not in the extreme sense that they have no existence independent of the interpretive frameworks through which we understand them, but in two other senses. To begin with, it is clear that actors attach different meanings to material capacities. For instance, ideas about different levels of economic and social development, and about historical contributions to present global warming, lead to different understandings of China's and the United States' aggregate emissions. In addition to this, states and peoples make choices about how to rank and deploy their material capacities, and these choices are informed by values about just levels of taxation, about the balance between military and social expenditure, about the appropriate use of human capital, and about the right balance between domestic and international use of material capacities. Material capacities are thus socially structured, and ideas about responsibility, national and international, play a role in this structuring.

Social domains and the distribution of responsibilities

In Hedley Bull's discussion of great powers and their attendant responsibilities, international society is treated as a unitary social structure with a single distribution of special responsibilities. At any particular moment in international history, the society of states comprises certain recognised states, consists of certain rules of coexistence and cooperation, and exhibits certain institutional norms and practices. And within this structure, special responsibilities are defined in a particular way and allocated to, or claimed by, particular great powers. This is the 'social' version of the traditional realist conception of the international system as a unitary political realm. Not only are international systems imagined as singular entities, but this is accentuated by two moves: the reduction of systemic politics to the politics of great powers, and the elevation of security as the primary issue area, a primacy based on the centrality of security to state interests, and on the purported fungibility of military strategic power. Other issue areas in world politics are acknowledged, but the politics of security supervenes on these, structuring them in ways that undercut their relative autonomy.

Conceiving international society in this unitary and singular fashion obscures the multifarious nature of the politics of special responsibilities in contemporary world politics. In reality, this politics varies from one domain of the global system to another, variation clearly apparent in the fields of nuclear proliferation, climate change and global finance. To capture this variation, we advance a disaggregated understanding of the global system. Our principal distinction is between different issue areas, a move akin to that made by Robert Keohane and Joseph Nye when they distinguish between different 'issue-structures'.[32] While acknowledging that politics in different issue areas is never hermetically sealed, as 'issue linkage' occurs all the time, we begin with the assumption that these can be treated as analytically distinct domains. And while different issue areas clearly affect one another, with the global economy and climate change being a case in point, these connections should be the subject of empirical exploration not *a priori* theoretical assumption. Within each of these domains we further differentiate between different levels of society. The politics of special responsibilities is not played out within a uniform social arena. Struggles over the nature and allocation of special responsibilities in any particular domain occur between states within 'international society', but they also occur within domestic society – particularly that of the United States – and in transnational society. Again, these levels are not hermetically sealed; domestic and transnational struggles blur into one another, for example. But as explained earlier when discussing Erskine's work, differentiating between these levels of society is analytically important, because in managing their international special responsibilities states are often caught between the conflicting demands of international, domestic and transnational societies.

Different domains of world politics have different structures, understood as sets of 'constraining conditions' that 'limit and mould agents and agencies and point them in ways that tend toward a common quality of outcomes even though the efforts and aims of agents and agencies vary'.[33] Keohane and Nye make this point when talking about issue-structures, hence the terminology: 'any given international system', Keohane writes, 'is likely to have several structures, differing by issue areas and according to the resources that can be used to affect outcomes'.[34] Within each domain, both material and institutional structures condition the politics of special responsibilities. Whether we are speaking about nuclear

---

[32] R. O. Keohane and J. Nye, *Power and interdependence* (Boston: Little Brown, 1977), chapters 3, 6.

[33] K. N. Waltz, *Theory of international politics* (Reading, MA: Addison-Wesley, 1979), pp. 73–4.

[34] R. O. Keohane, 'Theory of world politics: Structural realism and beyond', in R. O. Keohane (ed.), *Neorealism and its critics* (New York: Columbia University Press,

proliferation, climate change and global finance, arguments about the nature and allocation of such responsibilities take place within particular distributions of material capabilities and vulnerabilities. Possession or non-possession of nuclear weapons, the distribution of global carbon emissions and relative dependence on growth in the financial sector all affect how actors think about the appropriate distribution of responsibilities, although in different ways in each domain. These varied material structures exist within the context of distinctive institutions, sets of formal or informal norms, rules and principles that constitute actors' identities and regulate their behaviour. For instance, current debates over the allocation of responsibilities for climate change abatement take place within the normative framework established under the 1992 United Nations Framework Convention on Climate Change. Similarly, the politics of responsibility for nuclear non-proliferation is conditioned by the 1968 NPT. It is important to note, however, that relevant institutional structures exist not only at the international level, but also at the domestic level. The institutional structures of the American legal and political system, for example, have a significant impact on how successive administrations have approached the question of the United States' international special responsibilities.

While it is analytically useful to differentiate between material and institutional structures, these are often difficult to disentangle. First, while in some cases it is relatively easy to identify truly material structures, in others it is more difficult. The global distribution of military resources so emphasised by Kenneth Waltz is perhaps a good example of the former, as is the distribution of carbon emissions or nuclear weapons in our domains. What does one make, though, of relative national dependence on growth in the financial sector? At first blush this too appears essentially material, except that money is a social institution, and its price and movement is determined not only by markets but by regulatory frameworks. Second, as constructivists have long observed, institutional structures give meaning to material structures. The latter do have independent causal effects, defining 'the outer limits of feasible activity'.[35] At any given time, for example, the global distribution of military resources gives some states opportunities while imposing constraints on others. Yet, in reality, state behaviour rarely maps neatly onto these materially defined opportunities and constraints. How actors understand and respond to material structures is conditioned by the

1986), p. 184. Keohane's and Nye's original discussion of issue-structure is found in Keohane and Nye, *Power and interdependence*, pp. 50–1.

[35] Wendt, *Social theory*, p. 111.

intersubjective meanings in which those structures are embedded. As Marshall Sahlins has put it, 'material effects depend on their cultural encompassment'.[36]

Just as different domains have different structures, they also have different configurations of political agency. To begin with, no two domains exhibit the same number or variety of engaged actors. In the domains of nuclear weapons, climate change and finance, states, non-governmental organisations (NGOs) and international organisations are all implicated in the politics of special responsibilities. Yet different actors hold the stage in different domains: the NWSs, non-nuclear parties to the NPT, breakout nuclear powers and anti-nuclear civil society activists in the non-proliferation domain; key emitting states, international environmental and development agencies, vulnerable developing states and transnational environmental advocacy networks in the climate domain; and the G20 members, international financial institutions, corporations and leading developing countries in the financial domain.

In addition to this, the actors who populate different domains have different identities, or different conceptions of 'who they are'. When considering states, a crucial distinction lies between their corporate and social identities: the first involves the self-understandings of a state's members that constitute them as a corporate body or a polity; the second is the 'sets of meanings that an actor [a state in this case] attributes to itself while taking into account the perspective of others, that is, as a social object'.[37] Not only do different states have different corporate and social identities (compare those of the United States, Denmark and Iran), but for any given state these identities may be in tension. For instance, the United States' overarching social identity is that of a leading liberal democracy. But domestically these ideas are infused with notions of exceptionalism and manifest destiny, ideas that receive little recognition internationally. These tensions aside, it is important to note that actors' social identities can vary from one issue domain to another. This is not to say that the United States is considered a leading liberal democracy in some domains and not others. Rather, its overarching social identity can be 'compromised' by the reputation it gains for certain issue-specific practices. In the climate domain, for example, America's broader social identity has been compromised by its reputation as a 'laggard' not a 'lead' state.

---

[36] M. Sahlins, *Culture and practical reason* (Chicago, IL: University of Chicago Press, 1976), p. 194.
[37] Wendt, 'Collective identity formation', 385.

Finally, the actors within a particular issue domain vary according to their structural, material and idiographic power. The first refers to the capacities actors gain from their locations within particular material or institutional structures; the second to the material resources actors can mobilise to influence political outcomes; and the third to the moral suasion actors' can exercise by virtue of their socially sanctioned identities. The key thing is that the powers an actor enjoys vary from one domain to another: America's structural capacities are not the same in the nuclear proliferation, climate and finance domains, nor are the material resources it can mobilise or the moral suasion it can exercise. As explained above, when we make judgements about the nature and allocation of responsibilities (and special responsibilities in particular) we do so with reference to established social norms about who can, and should, bear these obligations. But because these norms, and the practices that sustain them, play such a crucial role in defining the many social roles that constitute a social order, and in distributing legitimate social powers, they are an enduring site of contestation. Indeed, struggles over the nature and allocation of responsibilities are a central feature of politics, and one of the principal mechanisms through which social and political change occurs.

Conclusion

We have now mapped out a conceptual and analytical framework for understanding the nature, dynamics and significance of special responsibilities in world politics. Special responsibilities appear in this framework as inextricably connected with accountability, making them inherently social, dependent as much on recognition as claiming. Discourses and practices of special responsibilities come to the fore in international relations under structural conditions of unequal material power and formal sovereign equality, where neither the pure play of material power politics nor cooperation among sovereign equals is an effective means of addressing problems of international governance. By constituting international social roles and defining the parameters of legitimate political action within given social domains, special responsibilities shape the nature and distribution of social power. Because of this, they constitute a key site of political contestation – it matters to states how special responsibilities are defined and allocated, and much of contemporary world politics is concerned with claiming, acknowledging, allocating, shirking and contesting who gets to be responsible for what, when and how. Importantly, though, this politics of special responsibilities varies from one social domain to another. In the next three chapters we examine this politics in the fields of nuclear proliferation, climate change and global finance. Not only are these among the most significant challenges of contemporary global governance, they also differ in their structural and agential characteristics. Nuclear non-proliferation is a classic statist domain. While a range of non-state actors and international organisations populate this field, the NPT defines a game in which states are the principal players and bearers of responsibilities. Global finance is at the other end of the spectrum. Not only have non-state actors and international organisations played a key role in this domain, but corporate actors are emerging as potentially significant bearers of special responsibilities. The climate change case stands somewhere between these extremes; it is a domain densely populated with NGOs and international organisations, yet the focus remains on distributing special responsibilities to states.

Part II

Three global problems

3   Nuclear proliferation

Our first case of nuclear weapons represents one that is predominantly state-centric, and is centred on core issues of international security. If there is one domain that approximates the Waltzian view of great powers taking on special responsibilities, this should be it: material capability and role converge to the point where there is no space left for any social idea of responsibility at all. In fact, as we will show, the nuclear domain has not simply followed this Waltzian dictum.

This chapter examines the nature and functioning of special responsibilities in relation to the development and possession of nuclear weapons, and it centres on an examination of the 1970 Nuclear Non-Proliferation Treaty (NPT). The reason for focusing on the NPT is that it established a legal categorisation between those that were recognised as nuclear weapon states (NWSs) and those non-nuclear weapon states (NNWSs) that consented, whilst parties to the treaty, to give up the right to acquire nuclear weapons. For our purposes, it is crucial that this categorisation became the focus of expectations (which pre-dated the treaty) regarding the special responsibilities of the nuclear and non-nuclear powers. We show how these special responsibilities have mediated between the principle of sovereign equality, on the one hand, and the stubborn fact of material inequality, on the other. Moreover, and contrary to the Waltzian argument, the chapter demonstrates how these special responsibilities constitute the possibilities of legitimate political action within this domain, supporting our cardinal claim in the book that special responsibilities cannot just be unilaterally asserted by powerful states, but have to be recognised as such by those to whom they are addressed.

The chapter is divided into two parts. First, we show how the signing of the NPT can be interpreted as an 'equilibrium point' regarding the allocation and acceptance of special responsibilities in the nuclear domain. The treaty emerged as an attempt to reconcile international society's commitment to the principle of sovereign equality with the inequalities of power which arose from the fact that when the treaty was signed in 1968, five of the most powerful states already possessed nuclear weapons (China, France, the United Kingdom, the United States and the Soviet Union).

The second and main part of the chapter then maps out the process of contestation which has taken place between the parties to the treaty over both the meaning to be given to the special responsibilities of the NWSs and the NNWSs, and how far they have lived up to the promises and expectations regarding the central bargain between disarmament and non-proliferation which has animated the treaty since its inception. We divide this into three phases. The first considers how the NNWSs, in the first three decades of the treaty, repeatedly invoked the terms of the original bargain (discussed in full below) to argue that the NWSs were failing to live up to their special responsibilities for nuclear arms control and disarmament. It is our contention that this process of contestation produced little change during the Cold War. However, in the changed geopolitical and normative context of the 1990s, there was growing pressure from states, and an increasingly active non-governmental organisation (NGO) community to revitalise the original NPT commitment to both non-proliferation and disarmament. This led to a new equilibrium point being reached between the allocation and acceptance of special responsibilities at the 1995 and especially the 2000 Review Conferences of the Parties to the Treaty on the Non-Proliferation of Nuclear Weapons (NPT Review Conferences).

This equilibrium point, however, proved to be short-lived and the chapter shows how the administration of President George W. Bush fundamentally challenged the fragile consensus which had been agreed at those meetings. The Bush administration viewed the NPT as yet another instrument in the battle against those so-called 'rogue' nuclear states which were seen as potential deadly threats to US security. A key consequence of this approach was that the US downgraded the importance it attached to the disarmament provisions of the treaty, and rejected key elements of the package which the NWSs had committed to in 2000. It is not surprising that these US moves were vigorously resisted by the vast majority of the NNWSs, but what is crucial for our purposes is that this attempt by the US to marginalise its special responsibility for nuclear disarmament was unsuccessful.

It fell to Bush's successor, President Barack Obama, to try and restore the consensus over the allocation and acceptance of special responsibilities in the nuclear non-proliferation regime. The Obama administration recognised the mutual security dependence between the NWSs and NNWSs which lies at the heart of the treaty. However, reflecting the increasing vulnerabilities which the US (and other members of the treaty) perceive from the risk that an increasing number of the NNWSs have acquired, or are in the process of acquiring, the technologies that make them latent or 'virtual'[1] NWSs, the Obama administration sought to reduce these risks and vulnerabilities by building a new consensus among the NNWSs. This would have seen them accept new special responsibilities in relation to International Atomic Energy Agency (IAEA) safeguards and the acquisition and development of proliferation sensitive fuel-cycle technologies. The chapter shows how, in this third phase of contestation, such moves have been resisted by a number of powerful non-aligned parties to the treaty. The latter could not accept what they viewed as a further erosion of the principle of sovereign equality, whilst the fundamental inequality of material power between the NWSs and the NNWSs remained unaddressed.

The evolution of special responsibilities

The nuclear domain is a textbook case of how special responsibilities emerge as a way of mediating between sovereign equality on the one hand, and recognition of the inequalities of material power on the other. The negotiations between the nuclear and non-nuclear powers which led to the signing of the NPT became the focal point for arguments over the allocation and acceptance of special responsibilities. The treaty can be viewed as steering a path between the alternative nuclear worlds that could be imagined at either of the two extreme poles of sovereign equality and material inequality. Turning to the former, it is possible to conceive of two diametrically opposed nuclear worlds if sovereign equality were to be the anchoring principle. The first would be one in which no state possessed nuclear weapons. Opinion has been fundamentally divided on whether a disarmed nuclear world would be a stable one. On the negative side, it has been argued that in the absence of high levels of trust, there would be the fear that others might be secretly hiding nuclear weapons, thereby encouraging others to hedge, bringing with it the danger that one or more states might break out of the agreement in the belief that others are about to. More positively, advocates of nuclear disarmament have argued that the dangers of nuclear breakout, and even use, in a disarmed world have to be set against the risks and costs of continuing with nuclear arsenals – even at low numbers – into perpetuity. We explore some of the ethical issues involved in these

---

[1] The term has been used by Mohamed ElBaradei. See J. Borger, 'Mohamed ElBaradei warns of new nuclear age', *Guardian*, 14 May 2009.

choices in Chapter 6, but schemes for radical nuclear disarmament are predicated on an elimination of the inequality which defines the current global nuclear order. As we discuss below, this commitment to replacing the existing hierarchical nuclear order with an egalitarian one dominates the political thinking and actions of many of the non-nuclear state parties to the treaty.

The other possible manifestation of the principle of sovereign equality is a world where all states had an internationally recognised right – a proliferation treaty as it were – to develop and possess nuclear weapons. Despite the claims of so-called 'proliferation optimists' like Kenneth Waltz that 'the measured spread of nuclear weapons is more to be welcomed than feared',[2] such a proposition has never secured wide acceptance by the society of states. Instead, increasing the number of fingers on the nuclear trigger has been seen as likely to lead to a weakening of the stigmatisation – Nina Tannenwald has gone as far as to call it a 'taboo' – against the use of nuclear weapons.[3]

If organising the global nuclear order on the basis of sovereign equality is either unworkable, or seen by at least some decisive players as too dangerous, what about allowing the unfettered exercise of material power to determine the politics of the nuclear domain? Even the most powerful nuclear-armed states in the international system have not relished this prospect, despite the fact that the nuclear great powers would be better placed to survive in such a world than other states. Instead, the dominant nuclear powers have recognised that if brute power were the only arbiter of politics within the nuclear domain, the only barrier to new states acquiring nuclear weapons would be a technological one. Although strategies of technological denial can work for a time, the story since 1945 has been one in which the capabilities to make nuclear weapons have spread to an increasing number of states. It has been estimated that some forty states are in varying degrees of 'latency' (the time it would take to convert a nuclear programme solely for civil purposes into one which could produce the nuclear fuel for a weapon) but all are capable of crossing the threshold, should a political decision be taken to do so.[4]

In a nuclear realm where the only currency is material power, it is highly likely that the world would have many more nuclear-armed states.

[2] K. N. Waltz, 'The spread of nuclear weapons: More may be better', *Adelphi Paper* 171 (London: International Institute for Strategic Studies, 1981), p. 30.
[3] N. Tannenwald, *The nuclear taboo: The United States and the non-use of nuclear weapons since 1945* (Cambridge: Cambridge University Press, 2007).
[4] United Nations, *A more secure world: Our shared responsibility: Report of the High-Level Panel on Threats, Challenges and Change* (New York: United Nations, 2004).

Weak and strong alike have viewed such a cascade of proliferation as a terrifying prospect, and it was this collective interest in preventing such an outcome which led to the creation through the NPT of a regime of special responsibilities. In short, establishing special responsibilities in the nuclear domain was better than either legalised or de facto proliferation.

The NNWSs assumed the greatest vulnerability in accepting the NPT. By forsaking the possibility of getting nuclear weapons, they exposed themselves to the risk of nuclear blackmail or even attack. This might lead to the conclusion that the NNWSs have less of an interest in the survival of the treaty than the NWSs. However, as we show below, despite decades of frustration and resentment with what has been seen as the failure of the NWSs to live up to their special responsibilities, the NNWSs have recognised a common interest with the NWSs in preventing the emergence of what Albert Wohlstetter and his co-workers once called 'a nuclear armed crowd'.[5] The three NWSs which signed the treaty in 1968 (the Soviet Union, the United Kingdom and the United States) undoubtedly accepted fewer restraints on their behaviour than did the NNWSs, but it is important to remember that the NWSs made themselves vulnerable in signing the treaty. By agreeing that all parties to the treaty have the right to obtain from other states the materials and technologies necessary for the development and operation of civil nuclear facilities, albeit subject to 'full-scope' IAEA safeguards, the NWSs accepted the potential vulnerability inherent in the possibility of a state mastering the fuel-cycle and thereby becoming a virtual NWS.

The NPT brought into existence that social categorisation of the nuclear domain which divides it in terms of the NWSs and the NNWSs.[6] The treaty defines 'a nuclear-weapon State [as] one which has manufactured and exploded a nuclear weapon or other nuclear explosive device prior to 1 January 1967'.[7] This ensured that forever thereafter (unless the treaty is amended) only five states could satisfy this criterion. China and France did not sign the treaty in 1968, but they had the right to do so as nuclear powers since both had conducted nuclear tests prior to the cut-off date. Thus, when both Paris and Beijing decided to sign and ratify the treaty in 1992, they could be admitted as NWSs. The political effect of this social categorisation is that aside from the five recognised

[5] The phrase was first coined by A. Wohlstetter, T. Brown, G. Jones, D. McGarvey, H. Rowen, V. Taylor and R. Wohlstetter in their 'Moving toward life in a nuclear armed crowd? ACDA/PAB-263, PH76-04-389-14, final report' (Los Angeles, CA: PAN Heuristics, 4 December 1975; revised 22 April 1976).

[6] Tannenwald, *The nuclear taboo*, p. 336.

[7] The Treaty on the Non-Proliferation of Nuclear Weapons (NPT), 1 July 1968, www. un.org/en/conf/npt/2005/npttreaty.html (accessed 27 July 2011), Article IX.

NWSs, all other states are categorised as NNWSs. Thus, when India and Pakistan declared themselves as nuclear-armed states (Israel has always maintained a position of nuclear opacity in this respect), they could not be admitted to the treaty as NWSs. This denial of status has proved irksome to Pakistan, and especially to India. Both remain determined to maintain their position as nuclear-armed states, and this, in turn, has created a major challenge in extending the non-proliferation status to states not party to the NPT.[8]

The NPT legalised the inequality of states in the nuclear sphere by prohibiting the NNWSs from developing and acquiring nuclear weapons.[9] Paradoxically, this unprecedented restriction by the NNWSs of the exercise of their sovereign rights in the military field only became possible because those states, in turn, exercised their sovereign rights in consenting to it. Article II of the treaty stipulates that:

[e]ach non-nuclear-weapon State Party to the Treaty undertakes not to receive the transfer from any transferor whatsoever of nuclear weapons or other nuclear explosive devices or of control over such weapons or explosive devices directly, or indirectly; not to manufacture or otherwise acquire nuclear weapons or other nuclear explosive devices; and not to seek or receive any assistance in the manufacture of nuclear weapons or other nuclear explosive devices.[10]

The acceptance by the NNWSs of a treaty which legalised inequality was the result of a bargaining process between them and the NWSs, and a key element of this was the inclusion of Article VI. The latter committed all parties to the treaty to 'pursue negotiations in good faith on effective measures relating to cessation of the nuclear arms race at an early date and to nuclear disarmament, and on a treaty on general and complete disarmament under strict and effective international control'.[11] Although this imposed a general responsibility on all parties to the treaty, logically only the nuclear powers could bring to an end the nuclear arms race. As Mohamed Shaker, a member of the Egyptian delegation when the treaty was being negotiated, reflected, 'the nature of the measures envisaged in the article left no doubt that the nuclear-weapon States were directly implicated by the obligation. Both the United States and Soviet Union admitted, in fact, their primary responsibility.'[12]

---

[8] W. Walker, *A perpetual menace: Nuclear weapons and international order* (London: Routledge, 2011), pp. 142–3.

[9] Tannenwald, *The nuclear taboo*, p. 336.

[10] The Treaty on the Non-Proliferation of Nuclear Weapons, Article II.

[11] *Ibid.*, Article VI.

[12] M. I. Shaker, *The Nuclear Non-Proliferation Treaty: Origin and implementation, 1959–1979*, 2 vols. (London: Oceana, 1980), Vol. II, p. 564. Such an interpretation has been

Securing recognition on the part of the nuclear powers that they had a special responsibility for arms control and disarmament had been a key demand of the non-nuclear powers in the Eighteen-Nation Disarmament Committee (which reported to the UN General Assembly). Without the inclusion of Article VI, the NNWSs would never have agreed to lock themselves into a position of nuclear inferiority.[13] The non-aligned caucus at the UN had used the vehicle of the First Committee of the UN General Assembly to call for a balance of responsibilities between the NWSs and NNWSs in relation to non-proliferation and disarmament. Specifically, Brazil and India argued that the 'commitment of non-nuclear weapon states to sign away the right to manufacture or otherwise to acquire those weapons must be coupled with a specific and binding agreement on the part of the nuclear powers to take concrete steps to halt the nuclear arms race'.[14] However, beyond a general commitment to negotiate in 'good faith' in relation to arms control and nuclear disarmament, the NWSs had resisted any language which specified limits on nuclear arms or a timetable for reductions. In an effort to bridge these competing positions, other NNWSs in the Eighteen-Nation Disarmament Committee, notably Sweden and Mexico, took a more moderate position, arguing that to press for binding measures within the text of the treaty would risk jeopardising agreement.[15] The final wording of Article VI reflected this compromise in so far as binding measures were omitted, but the NNWSs secured stronger language on the commitments than had been included in the earlier drafts of Article VI. Nevertheless, the NNWSs remained dissatisfied about Article VI[16] and to sweeten this bitter pill, the NWSs 'repeatedly

challenged by Christopher Ford who served, until 2008, as US Special Representative for Nuclear Non-Proliferation in the George W. Bush administration. Writing in November 2007, Ford argued that there was no legal obligation for the NWSs to pursue nuclear disarmament outside of negotiations 'pursuant (rather than prior) to a treaty on general and complete disarmament'. See C. A. Ford, 'Debating disarmament: Interpreting Article VI of the Treaty on the Non-Proliferation of Nuclear Weapons', *Nonproliferation Review*, 14(3) 2007, 404.

13 Shaker, *The Nuclear Non-Proliferation Treaty*, Vol. II, pp. 555–79; T. Price, 'Reconciling the irreconcilable? British nuclear weapons and the Non-Proliferation Treaty, 1997–2007', unpublished PhD thesis, Aberystwyth University, 2010, p. 60; D. H. Joyner, *Interpreting the Nuclear Non-Proliferation Treaty* (Oxford: Oxford University Press, 2011), pp. 18–19.

14 GOAR, A/C.I/22/PV.1551, 14 December 1967, cited in D. Bourantonis, 'The negotiation of the Non-Proliferation Treaty 1965–68', Discussion Papers in Diplomacy, No. 28 (The Hague: Netherlands Institute of International Relations 'Clingendael', April 1997), p. 6. We are grateful to Tristan Price for bringing this source to our attention. See also Ford, 'Debating disarmament', 406–7.

15 Shaker, *The Nuclear Non-Proliferation Treaty*, Vol. II, pp. 555–79; Price, 'Reconciling the irreconcilable?', pp. 51–2.

16 A further source of this dissatisfaction was the refusal of the NWSs to provide negative security assurances. The NNWSs had argued that if they were being asked to

reminded' the NNWSs of 'the origins of Article VIII-3 on review conferences, and its organic link with Article VI'.[17] As we will see, the NPT Review Conferences were to become a key mechanism by which the NNWSs would hold the NWSs accountable for implementing their special responsibilities for arms control and disarmament.

In the end, the NNWSs were not prepared to jeopardise the treaty because of the refusal of the NWSs to accept stronger responsibilities to limit their nuclear arms or provide negative security assurances. They wanted a treaty in which the NWSs recognised, to use William Walker's pithy phrase, that they 'were non-nuclear weapon states in waiting', and that the ultimate purpose of the NPT was to replace hierarchy with equality.[18] Mohamed ElBaradei, the former director-general of the IAEA, reflected in 2003 that 'in the climate of the mid-to-late 1960s in which the NPT negotiations took place, this bargain was the best that could be achieved. But the asymmetry it endorsed was never intended to be permanent.'[19] The NNWSs – especially those which wanted specific commitments on disarmament – recognised that if they pushed

give up the right to possess nuclear weapons, the NWSs should provide guarantees that they would not threaten or use nuclear weapons against them. However, incorporating such a commitment into the text of the treaty was resisted by the NWSs. The US, the Soviet Union and the UK argued that such negative security assurances, as well as positive security assurances (whereby other states would come to the aid of a NNWS if nuclear weapons were threatened or used against it) which the NNWSs were also requesting would be best provided through the framework of collective security in the United Nations Charter. The three depository states of the treaty were instrumental in securing United Nations Security Council Resolution 255 which was adopted on 19 June 1968. This recognised 'that aggression with nuclear weapons or the threat of such aggression against a non-nuclear-weapon State would create a situation in which the Security Council, and above all its nuclear-weapon State permanent members, would have to act immediately in accordance with their obligations under the United Nations Charter'. The resolution also welcomed 'the intention expressed by certain States [the UK, the US and the USSR] that they will provide or support immediate assistance, in accordance with the Charter, to any non-nuclear-weapon State Party to the Treaty on the Non-Proliferation of Nuclear Weapons that is a victim of an act or an object of a threat of aggression in which nuclear weapons are used'. The resolution was not legally binding as it was not adopted under Chapter VII of the Charter, and it fell far short of the type of assurances (positive and negative) which the NNWSs had been seeking, especially the non-aligned state parties to the treaty who lacked the shelter provided by the nuclear umbrellas of the Cold War alliance systems. See Shaker, *The Nuclear Non-Proliferation Treaty*, Vol. II, pp. 475–9, 523–32; G. Bunn and R. M. Timerbaev, 'Security assurances to non-nuclear weapon states', *Nonproliferation Review*, 2(1) 1993, 1–13; E. Bailey, 'The NPT and security guarantees', in D. Howlett and J. Simpson (eds.), *Nuclear non-proliferation: A reference handbook* (London: Longman, 1992), pp. 51–6; Tannenwald, *The nuclear taboo*, p. 247; Price, 'Reconciling the irreconcilable?', pp. 68–9.

[17] Shaker, *The Nuclear Non-Proliferation Treaty*, Vol. II, p. 578.
[18] Walker, *A perpetual menace*, pp. 141–2.
[19] Quoted in Joyner, *Interpreting the Nuclear Non-Proliferation Treaty*, p. 18, n. 40.

too hard, there might be no treaty at all. In the final analysis, it was an article of faith on the part of the NNWSs, as well as the NWSs, that increased proliferation was to be strongly avoided.

There was another key element to the bargain that the NWSs accepted in signing the treaty, and this went some way to compensating the NNWSs for agreeing to legitimise a discriminatory nuclear order. The NNWSs pressed for what became Article IV of the NPT which recognises the 'inalienable right of all the Parties to the Treaty to develop research, production and use of nuclear energy for peaceful purposes without discrimination'.[20] Thus, the legalised inequality at the heart of the treaty only applies to the military sector of the nuclear domain. As Tannenwald argues, '[w]ith regard to the peaceful uses of nuclear energy, the formal order of this system was still officially based on the formal equality of states'.[21] Article IV imposes on all signatories a general responsibility to 'facilitate … the fullest possible exchange of equipment, materials and scientific and technological information for the peaceful uses of nuclear energy'. Yet there is also wording in Article IV which suggests a special responsibility falls on those NPT parties in a position to do so (for example, those which have developed civil nuclear programmes) to:

co-operate in contributing alone or together with other States or international organizations to the further development of the applications of nuclear energy for peaceful purposes, especially in the territories of non-nuclear-weapon States Party to the Treaty, with due consideration for the needs of the developing areas of the world.[22]

This part of Article IV gives rise to a special responsibility on the part of some states because only those states which have mastery of the nuclear fuel-cycle have the technical capabilities to assist the NNWSs in benefiting from the peaceful uses of nuclear energy.

The right of the NNWSs to receive assistance in developing nuclear energy is conditional on their complying with Article II. To ensure that fissionable materials are only being used for peaceful purposes and not being diverted to military uses, the NNWSs agreed in Article III of the treaty to accept safeguards on all their nuclear facilities. These were subsequently administered and implemented by the IAEA which had been created in 1957 to facilitate and support the peaceful uses of atomic energy.

---

[20] Shaker, *The Nuclear Non-Proliferation Treaty*, Vol. I, pp. 274–5. See also Joyner, *Interpreting the Nuclear Non-Proliferation Treaty* p. 17.

[21] Tannenwald, *The nuclear taboo*, p. 335.

[22] The Treaty on the Non-Proliferation of Nuclear Weapons, Article IV.

A number of attributions of and claims for special responsibilities were made, recognised and contested in the formative period leading to the NPT, and the grounds for these were several. There were attributions of special responsibilities to the NWSs by the NNWSs to disarm that stemmed from vulnerability, claims by the NWSs to an associated right – issuing from capabilities – not to have to relinquish their nuclear weapons immediately given the absence of a perceived viable substitute to nuclear deterrence, and a recognition that the US and the Soviet Union, in particular, bore a special responsibility for maintaining the international nuclear order. The ethical bases of these claims and attributions of special responsibilities are explored further in Chapter 6.

That a capability-derived conception of special nuclear responsibilities influenced the thinking of both the NNWSs as well as the major NWSs, can be seen in the deliberations that took place in the Eighteen-Nation Disarmament Committee. Consider, for example, Romania's response in February 1964 to a disarmament proposal tabled by the Soviet Union. The Romanian delegate was emphatic in ascribing a 'special responsibility' to the 'great nuclear powers in connexion with the consolidation of peace and security, the accomplishment of nuclear disarmament, and the disarmament process in general'.[23] The NWSs did not deny that their nuclear capabilities imposed upon them a special responsibility, and recognition of this was eloquently expressed fifteen days after the signing of the NPT in a statement by US President Lyndon B. Johnson, which was read out by William Foster, head of the US Arms Control and Disarmament Agency, to his fellow delegates. Foster stated on behalf of the president that, 'the United States and the Soviet Union have a special responsibility to head off a strategic arms race. The fate of mankind could well depend on the manner in which our two nations discharge that responsibility.' Foster went on to claim that if the superpowers were successful in discharging this special responsibility, this would 'facilitate the achievement of various related measures of nuclear arms control and disarmament'.[24]

While capability set the US and the Soviet Union apart as prime bearers of special responsibilities, concerns of vulnerability interestingly and importantly facilitated a superpower concert between them. The cooperation of the US and the Soviet Union was critical to the striking of the bargain that made possible the NPT, and the impulse on

---

[23] Statement by Mr V. Dumitrescu of Romania to the 165th meeting of the Eighteen-Nation Committee on Disarmament, 11 February 1964, ENDC/PV.165, p. 31.

[24] Statement by Mr W. Foster of the United States to the 381st meeting of the Eighteen-Nation Disarmament Committee, 16 July 1968, ENDC/FPV.381.20, p. 20.

the part of Moscow and Washington to cooperate in this area stemmed from their shared perception of vulnerability to the increased spread of nuclear weapons.[25]

US thinking on the dangers of the spread of nuclear weapons was set out in the 1965 Gilpatric Committee's report (named after its chair the former Undersecretary of Defense, Roswell Gilpatric). This internal study was undertaken by the Johnson administration in the immediate aftermath of the Chinese nuclear test in 1964. It was feared in the administration that the Chinese nuclear test might trigger a cascade of proliferation in Asia and beyond.[26] The dangers of this were set out by the Gilpatric Committee a year later when it assessed that the spread of nuclear weapons would pose 'an increasingly grave threat to the security of the United States. New nuclear capabilities ... will add complexity and instability ... aggravate suspicions and hostility [and will] impede the vital task of controlling and reducing weapons around the world.'[27] What particularly concerned US officials was the prospect that if the nuclear club rapidly expanded after the Chinese test, West Germany would increasingly press for a national nuclear capability. The US knew that the Soviet Union would never accept West Germany as a nuclear power and this led the Gilpatric Committee (despite dissenting voices on the committee who felt the risks of proliferation should not be allowed to undermine key alliances of the US in Europe and Asia) to recommend that the Johnson administration make the control of proliferation a key foreign policy goal.[28]

President Johnson welcomed such a conclusion, recognising that securing Soviet cooperation was vital in the battle against proliferation. The president and his closest advisers also appreciated that this would only be achievable if Moscow was reassured that West Germany would not acquire, or be supported by the US in acquiring, an indigenous nuclear weapons capability. A key mechanism in achieving this reassurance was what became Article I of the NPT and which was only applicable to the NWSs. Article I prohibited the NWSs from transferring:

---

[25] Tannenwald, *The nuclear taboo*, p. 335; Price, 'Reconciling the irreconcilable?', pp. 40–1.

[26] F. J. Gavin, 'Blasts from the past: Proliferation lessons from the 1960s', *International Security*, 29(3) 2004/05, 104–6.

[27] Quoted in J. B. Wolfsthal, 'The next nuclear wave: Nonproliferation in a new world', *Foreign Affairs*, 84(1) 2005, 157. See also H. Brands, 'Rethinking non-proliferation: LBJ, the Gilpatric Committee and US national security policy', *Journal of Cold War Studies*, 8(2) 2006, 83–113.

[28] Gavin, 'Blasts from the past', 128–32.

to any recipient whatsoever nuclear weapons or other nuclear explosive devices
or control over such weapons or explosive devices directly, or indirectly; and
not in any way to assist, encourage, or induce any non-nuclear-weapon State to
manufacture or otherwise acquire nuclear weapons or other nuclear explosive
devices, or control over such weapons or explosive devices.[29]

The agreement of both superpowers to what became Article I of the
NPT reflected their growing commitment to securing a treaty that
would ban future proliferation, and this gave increasing momentum to
the negotiations taking place between the NWSs and NNWSs in the
Eighteen-Nation Disarmament Committee.

Johnson's personal commitment to achieving a treaty was critical to
the success of the negotiations.[30] Francis Gavin has argued that since
securing a treaty depended crucially on West Germany accepting a permanent position of nuclear inferiority, Johnson took a 'great risk', which
was not without 'political cost'.[31] He was rewarded when the treaty was
opened for signature on his presidential watch and West Germany
signed it (although it did not ratify it until 1975).

The NPT was a bargain, predicated on the assumption that the
NWSs and the NNWSs could trust each other to live up to the balance of responsibilities – special and general – between non-proliferation
and disarmament.[32] However, the ensuing decades witnessed each group
accusing the other of shirking their responsibilities. This led to processes of contestation as each grouping invoked the agreed language in
the treaty to press their claims. We divide this process of contestation
into three historical phases. The first centred on attempts by the NWSs
to deny the claims of the NNWSs that they were failing to live up to their
special responsibilities for arms control and disarmament, and the subsequent establishment of a new equilibrium point through the consensus
achieved at the 1995, and especially the 2000 NPT Review Conferences.
The second period of contestation developed out of the Bush administration's attempt to dismiss the special responsibility for nuclear disarmament the US had accepted in 2000. This attempt to marginalise the
disarmament pillar of the treaty failed, and it was in the third period of
contestation that President Obama worked towards establishing a new
consensus within the regime on the allocation and acceptance of special
responsibilities, giving rise to the third period of contestation.

---

[29] The Treaty on the Non-Proliferation of Nuclear Weapons, Article I.
[30] S. M. Keeny, 'The Non-Proliferation Treaty', memorandum, 24 December 1968,
NP01237, National Security Archive, Washington, DC.
[31] Gavin, 'Blasts from the past', 132.
[32] J. Ruzicka and N. J. Wheeler, 'The puzzle of trusting relationships in the Nuclear
Non-Proliferation Treaty', *International Affairs*, 86(1) 2010, 69–85.

Contestation from below

The NPT came into force on 5 March 1970 with forty states signing and ratifying the treaty, including the three NWSs (the UK, the US and the Soviet Union) who signed in 1968 and who are the depository states of the treaty. As noted above, the treaty establishes in Article VIII(3) a mechanism (subject to majority state approval) of five-yearly review conferences to report on progress in implementing the treaty. The exception was the first NPT Review Conference in 1975 which was mandated by the treaty, and which took place in Geneva in May of that year. This meeting witnessed the first of many such political confrontations to come between the NWSs and the NNWSs. Meeting against the backdrop of India's (a non-signatory of the NPT) decision to conduct a 'peaceful nuclear explosion', the three NWSs sought agreement from the NNWSs for tightened controls on the export of nuclear materials. Not surprisingly, this was viewed with suspicion by many of the NNWSs, especially the non-aligned state parties to the treaty who worried that the NWSs were trying to erode their sovereign rights under Article IV of the treaty. What particularly aggrieved these states was that non-signatories to the treaty, such as India, continued to be subject to less demanding safeguards on their nuclear activities than members of the treaty.[33]

These objections to how the NPT bargain was working out were amplified by the belief on the part of the NNWSs that the NWSs had failed to live up to the special responsibility they had accepted for pursuing arms control and nuclear disarmament. The problem was that the NNWSs and the NWSs were operating with very different expectations of what was meant by compliance with Article VI. The US and the other NWSs considered that Article VI imposed no more than a legal obligation on them to pursue negotiations in 'good faith'. Such reasoning was well-reflected in Gerard Smith's (the chief US negotiator of the Strategic Arms Limitation Talks SALT) testimony to the Senate Committee on Armed Services in February 1969 when he opined that Article VI 'does not require us to achieve any disarmament agreement, since it is obviously impossible to predict the exact nature and results of such negotiations'.[34] Moreover, the responsibility for arms control and disarmament was seen by the NWSs as a general one, which all parties shared given their commitment in both Article VI and the Preamble to

---

[33] W. Epstein, 'Failure at the NPT Review Conference', *Bulletin of the Atomic Scientists*, 31(7) 1975, 46–8.
[34] Quoted in Ford, 'Debating disarmament', 407.

achieving nuclear disarmament as part of a treaty on general and complete disarmament.[35] Certainly, US officials appear to have had little or no appreciation of how far they, and the other NWSs, would find themselves being beaten by the NNWSs with the stick of Article VI at successive NPT Review Conferences. Evidence for this lack of US awareness of how important Article VI was to the NNWSs, and how far it would come to be mobilised by them to leverage the NWSs on the question of disarmament, can be seen in a January 1969 memorandum on the NPT which was sent by Spurgeon Keeny of the National Security Council Staff to Henry Kissinger, President Richard Nixon's Assistant for National Security Affairs. In relation to Article VI, Keeny was emphatic that it would do little to constrain future US actions in the nuclear field, a proposition, which as we show in the remainder of this chapter, has proved to be anything but the case. As Keeny wrote, 'Article VI commits all parties to pursue negotiations in good faith relating to a cessation of the arms race and to nuclear disarmament. *This is an essentially hortatory statement and presents no problems.*'[36]

The US and the Soviet Union claimed at the 1975 NPT Review Conference that their signing of SALT I in 1972, and the Vladivostok Accords in 1974, showed that they were living up to their obligations under Article VI.[37] Despite Washington's and Moscow's claim that the SALT process showed that they were taking Article VI seriously, many of the NNWSs pointed out that the SALT process, far from leading to disarmament, was facilitating a major increase in both the quantitative, and crucially the qualitative character of both superpowers'

---

[35] *Ibid.*, 404.

[36] S. M. Keeny, National Security Council Staff, Memorandum to Henry Kissinger, 24 January 1969, National Archives, Nixon Presidential Materials, NSC Files, Box 366, Subject Files, Non-Proliferation Treaty through March 1969, emphasis added (we are grateful to Matthew Harries for providing us with a copy of this document and for sharing some of the ideas from his doctoral research).

[37] The significance of the SALT accords was that by agreeing to limit both offensive and defensive weapons, the superpowers apparently recognised that the pursuit of strategic superiority had no meaning in an age when both sides could wipe out each other's cities (even after suffering a surprise nuclear attack), and that plans to secure such an illusory advantage would be destabilising and dangerous. According to Smith, his Soviet counterpart Vladimir Semenov acknowledged that a 'situation of mutual deterrence existed' between the superpowers, and that 'solutions should be sought ... that would insure the security of each side equally rather than through efforts to obtain unilateral military advantages'. Quoted in P. J. Farley, 'Strategic arms control, 1967–87', in A. L. George, P. J. Farley and A. Dallin (eds.), *US–Soviet security cooperation: Achievements failures, lessons* (Oxford: Oxford University Press, 1988), p. 226. The shared understanding that neither side could gain politically or militarily from the use of strategic nuclear weapons represented an acknowledgement by both superpowers that they were, in Robert Oppenheimer's famous words, akin to 'two scorpions in a bottle, each capable of killing the other, but only at the

nuclear arsenals. More positively, the NNWSs tried in 1975 to get the superpowers to agree to deep reductions in their nuclear arsenals, end underground nuclear tests, and pledge not to use nuclear weapons against non-nuclear state parties to the treaty. All of these measures were rejected by the superpowers, and Moscow went so far as to warn the NNWSs not to meddle in the process of strategic nuclear arms control.[38]

The Soviet response to the criticisms of the NNWSs at the 1975 NPT Review Conference opened up the question of how to conceive the relationship between vertical and horizontal proliferation in the NPT. On the one hand, the treaty established a formal commitment on the part of the NWSs to sincerely negotiate arms control and disarmament agreements (although it says nothing about what those negotiations should entail or how they should be concluded). But on the other hand, it left the NWSs free to do this in a bilateral (as during the Cold War) or potentially in a multilateral manner, involving the other three recognised nuclear powers. The inclusion of Article VIII(3) (review conferences) in the treaty was a means of assessing progress on its objectives, particularly in the less well-defined areas such as Article VI and the arms control and disarmament paragraphs in the Preamble. And as we discussed earlier, the NWSs, particularly the UK, had emphasised to the NNWSs in the negotiations that led to the signing of the treaty the role that the review conferences could play in ensuring that progress on arms control and disarmament would be forthcoming.

Given the reassurance which had been given by the NWSs to the NNWSs on the potential for the NPT Review Conferences to serve as a mechanism of accountability in the sphere of arms control and disarmament, the Soviet Union's refusal at the first NPT Review Conference to accept the legitimacy of criticisms of the SALT process called into question the sincerity of this commitment, at least on the part of one of the superpowers. Indeed, as arms control negotiations stalled in the late 1970s (SALT II was signed but never ratified by the US), a casualty of the demise of the detente process between the superpowers, many states in the non-aligned movement, and some US allies and partners, began increasingly to view the NPT as an instrument of superpower hegemonism designed to freeze in place a two-tier nuclear world.[39]

---

risk of his own life'. J. R. Oppenheimer, 'Atomic weapons and American policy', *Foreign Affairs*, 31(4) 1953, 529.

[38] Epstein, 'Failure at the NPT Review Conference', 46.

[39] H. Bull, 'Rethinking non-proliferation', in *Hedley Bull on arms control*, sel. and intro. R. O'Neill and D. N. Schwartz (London: Macmillan in association with the International Institute for Strategic Studies, 1987), p. 220.

The 1980, 1985 and 1990 NPT Review Conferences did little to overcome the controversies between the NWSs and the NNWSs over the interpretation of Articles VI and IV of the treaty which had manifested themselves at the first NPT Review Conference. The refusal of the UK, US and the Soviet Union to sign a Comprehensive Nuclear-Test-Ban Treaty (CTBT), provide legally binding negative security assurances, including a commitment to no-first use of nuclear weapons, and commit to a wider programme of arms control and disarmament, prevented a final declaration being agreed in 1980.[40] The issue of the CTBT was particularly divisive with a majority of states calling for the setting up of a working group in the Conference on Disarmament to move forward negotiations on a test ban. The failure to reach agreement on these issues thwarted attempts to achieve a final declaration. The non-aligned parties to the treaty also made a statement at the conference calling for the NWSs to participate in an

ad hoc working group that would begin negotiations on the cessation of the qualitative improvement and development of nuclear weapons systems; the ending of the production of all types of nuclear weapons and their means of delivery, and the production of fissionable material for weapons manufacture; and the initiation of a comprehensive phased programme to reduce stockpiles of nuclear weapons and their means of delivery.[41]

However, these concrete proposals for advancing the goals of arms control and disarmament, and for increasing the accountability of the NWSs to the NNWSs for their performance in implementing Article VI were rejected by the NWSs.[42] Despite the fault-lines which had opened up between the NWSs and the NNWSs over who was living up to the original NPT bargain, and the disagreement over new accountability mechanisms, this did not translate into direct behavioural challenges by the NNWSs to abandon the regime.

Five years later, it was once again divisions over Article VI compliance which divided the 1985 NPT Review Conference. However, determined to avoid another conference where there was no agreed final declaration, the president of the conference produced a document

[40] Price, 'Reconciling the irreconcilable?', pp. 74–5.

[41] Acronym Institute, 'The Non-Proliferation Treaty: Challenging times', Acronym Report No. 13, February 2000, www.acronym.org.uk/acrorep/a13pt1.htm (accessed 27 July 2011).

[42] *Ibid.* See also B. Sanders, 'NPT Review Conferences and the role of consensus', *Programme for Promoting Nuclear Non-Proliferation Issue Review*, 4 (April) 1995, www.mcis.soton.ac.uk/PPNN/issue-reviews/ir04.pdf (accessed 27 July 2011); F. Barnaby, 'The NPT Review Conference – Much talk, few results', *Bulletin of the Atomic Scientists*, 36(9) 1980, 7; Tannenwald, *The nuclear taboo*, pp. 393–4.

which incorporated elements of both agreement and disagreement, and this compromise proved acceptable to the 128 state parties meeting in Geneva.[43] As Ben Sanders, a veteran observer of NPT Review Conferences later reflected: 'in that way, consensus was achieved on an agreement to disagree'.[44] Such a final declaration – even one that papered over the cracks – proved unachievable in 1990. Growing frustration on the part of some of the NNWSs that the NWSs could not agree on a CTBT and increased anxieties that the nuclear supplier states were trying to limit the entitlements of the NNWSs under Article IV prevented an agreement on this occasion.[45]

What is important about the process of contestation that takes place in the first twenty years of the treaty is that none of the participants fundamentally questioned the original NPT bargain. This verdict has to be qualified by remembering that for the vast majority of the NNWSs, especially the non-aligned grouping within the treaty, a condition of legalised nuclear inequality has always been seen as a transitional stage in the journey to a world free of nuclear weapons. However, there was sharp rhetorical disagreement on implementation, especially in relation to Article VI. Nevertheless, while many of the non-aligned state parties to the treaty might have viewed the bargain as increasingly one-sided, given what they perceived as the disarmament tokenism of the NWSs, at no point did any of these states seriously consider leaving the treaty.

The NPT undoubtedly served the superpowers' interest in maintaining their superiority over the nuclear have-nots, but as Hedley Bull argued, there was an alternative view of the treaty which conceived it as promoting both the interests and values of the wider international society. On this English School reading, despite the interpretive controversies over the meaning of the special responsibilities and whether they were being implemented, the parties to the treaty recognised a common interest, and perhaps a common value, in maintaining the treaty as a bulwark against the shared vulnerabilities that they feared increased proliferation would bring.[46] As a result, the NNWSs were

---

[43] Acronym Institute, 'The Non-Proliferation Treaty'; Sanders, 'NPT Review Conferences'.

[44] Sanders, 'NPT Review Conferences'.

[45] Acronym Institute, 'The Non-Proliferation Treaty'. The NWSs were actually divided on the CTBT – the Soviet Union under the new leadership of President Mikhail Gorbachev sided with the NNWSs against the US and the UK by supporting immediate negotiations on a CTBT.

[46] Bull, 'Rethinking non-proliferation', p. 222. Bull's verdict on the behaviour of the superpowers in the late 1970s and early 1980s suggested the limits of an English School reading of the treaty. He recognised that far from living up to their special responsibilities for arms control and disarmament which they themselves laid claim to, and which other states inside and outside the treaty ascribed to them, the

prepared to accept a position of inferiority in return for the security benefits which accrued from the treaty.[47] Nevertheless, as Tannenwald argues, the question is whether a point could arise where the NNWSs 'find the status inequality galling to the point that some of them [are] willing to risk abandoning the regime altogether'.[48]

The debate over whether to indefinitely extend the NPT at the 1995 NPT Review Conference provided a critical moment where the NNWSs had to weigh up these conflicting imperatives of security and status. The original treaty had a lifespan of twenty-five years, and then a conference was to be convened to decide whether it should continue indefinitely, or for an additional fixed period or periods. The Southern states in the non-aligned movement were determined to use the debate over extension to press for greater concessions from the now five NWSs, with China and France's accession to the treaty three years earlier.[49] The question, then, was whether the NWSs would be prepared to make the level of concessions necessary to secure a consensus for their preferred goal of indefinite extension. After some intense negotiations in which Mexico and especially South Africa played a key role, the latter capitalising on its decision in 1991 to renounce its nuclear capability, a compromise was agreed which allowed the treaty to be indefinitely extended by a decision of the 175 members of the 178 parties to the treaty.[50]

As the price for securing indefinite extension of the NPT, the nuclear powers agreed to three key 'decisions' as part of the overall 'package of decisions'. These established some clear benchmarks for disarmament and new mechanisms by which the NWSs could be held accountable for their performance of these commitments. Instead of just meeting every five years to review progress, it was agreed in Decision 1 that in the three years preceding each NPT Review Conference, there would be a full ten-day Preparatory Committee meeting. These meetings would

superpowers were in fact acting dismissively towards these. Bull wrote that neither of the superpowers could 'claim to be regarded as nuclear trustees for mankind', and went on to dub the superpowers 'the great irresponsibles'. He levelled this charge not only in relation to their failure to accept their special responsibilities under Article VI, but also in relation to their joint failure to manage their strategic relationship in ways that lessened rather than increased the risks of nuclear war. H. Bull, 'The great irresponsibles? The United States, the Soviet Union, and world order', *International Journal*, 35(3) 1980, 447.

[47] J. Simpson, 'The Non-Proliferation Treaty at its half-life', in I. Bellany, C. D. Blacker and J. Gallacher (eds.), *The Nuclear Non-Proliferation Treaty* (London: Frank Cass, 1985), p. 5; Price, 'Reconciling the irreconcilable?', p. 85.

[48] Tannenwald, *The nuclear taboo*, p. 342.

[49] *Ibid.*, p. 344.

[50] *Ibid.*, p. 345; Price, 'Reconciling the irreconcilable?', p. 90.

not only discuss the agenda of the next NPT Review Conference but also discuss substantive issues, including the principles and goals of nuclear non-proliferation and disarmament.[51]

A clear marker was put down in 1995 by the NNWSs as to what substantive issues they wanted to discuss at these preparatory meetings and subsequent NPT Review Conferences. Decision 2 set out the 'Principles and Objectives for Nuclear Non-Proliferation and Disarmament', and in a section on 'Nuclear Disarmament', the NWSs agreed to language which 'reaffirm[ed] their commitment, as stated in article VI, to pursue in good faith negotiations on effective measures relating to nuclear disarmament'.[52] Moreover, they also accepted for the first time that implementing Article VI required a programme of action. The NWSs committed themselves to the following goals:

(a) the completion by the Conference on Disarmament of the negotiations on a universal and internationally and effectively verifiable Comprehensive Nuclear-Test Ban Treaty no later than 1996. Pending the entry into force of a Comprehensive Test-Ban Treaty, the nuclear-weapon States should exercise utmost restraint; (b) the immediate commencement and early conclusion of negotiations on a non-discriminatory and universally applicable convention banning the production of fissile material for nuclear weapons or other nuclear explosive devices, in accordance with the statement of the Special Coordinator of the Conference on Disarmament and the mandate contained therein; (c) the determined pursuit by the nuclear-weapon States of systematic and progressive efforts to reduce nuclear weapons globally, with the ultimate goals of elimination those weapons, and by all States of general and complete disarmament under strict and effective international control.[53]

These promises on the part of the NWSs to implement Article VI were clearly very important to achieving a consensus in 1995. However, it has been questioned whether they would have been sufficient to secure agreement had there not been a resolution (Decision 4) which called upon all states to establish a Middle East Nuclear Weapon Free Zone. Jayantha Dhanapala, President of the 1995 NPT Review Conference, claimed that 'the indefinite extension of the NPT in 1995 became possible only with the adoption of a resolution on the Middle East'.[54] The resolution called upon all non-NPT signatories to join the treaty (Israel was the key state here), and stated that it was the responsibility of all

[51] Final Document of the 1995 Review and Extension Conference of the NPT, NPT/CONF.1995/32 (Part I), 11 May 1995, Decision 1.

[52] Ibid., Decision 2.   [53] Ibid., Decision 2, para. 4.

[54] J. Dhanapala, 'Evaluating the 2010 NPT Review Conference', Special Report 258 (Washington, DC: United States Institute of Peace, October 2010), p. 4. See also J. Dhanapala with R. Rydell, Multilateral diplomacy and the NPT: An insider's account (Geneva: UNIDIR, 2005), pp. 55–6.

NPT parties, especially the NWSs, to 'extend their cooperation and to exert their utmost efforts with a view to ensuring the early establishment by regional parties of a Middle East zone free of nuclear and all other weapons of mass destruction and their delivery systems'.[55] This was a goal which the Arab states had championed for many years, and this commitment ensured that Egypt – a key player in the non-aligned movement – was prepared to lend its support to an indefinite extension of the treaty.

Although the decision to give the treaty an indefinite life is legally binding (because it was required by the treaty) on the parties, the 'package of decisions' are not generally accepted by international lawyers as legally binding under international treaty law.[56] However, these decisions were solemn commitments which the NWSs accepted as necessary to maintain the continuing support of the NNWSs for the treaty. As such, the bargaining that made possible the indefinite extension of the treaty in 1995 revealed the mutual dependence between the NWSs and NNWSs which lies at the heart of the NPT.

The concrete steps towards the implementation of Article VI which the NWSs agreed to in 1995 represented acceptance on their part of a new set of special responsibilities in relation to arms control and disarmament. The original NPT bargain had not included any specific disarmament steps, and the inclusion of the latter in the 'package of decisions' agreed to in 1995 represents a new equilibrium point. Moreover, the consensus which made this possible was strengthened still further at the 2000 NPT Review Conference. The latter met against the backdrop of India's decision in May 1998, closely followed by Pakistan, to conduct a series of nuclear tests, thereby announcing their de facto entry into the nuclear club (although not as formally recognised nuclear powers given the definition of a NWS under the NPT). This threat to the non-proliferation norm from states outside the treaty was joined by growing concerns about the nuclear ambitions of Iraq and North Korea, two signatories of the NPT. These challenges to the treaty created a shared determination on the part of the NWSs and the NNWSs to reinforce the non-proliferation norm. A key result of this was the emergence within the NPT of the 'New Agenda Coalition', a small grouping of states from both the Western and non-aligned groups within the treaty, which was to play a

---

[55] Final Document of the 1995 Review and Extension Conference, Decision 4.

[56] Rebecca Johnson and Tariq Rauf argue that political declarations such as the 'package of decisions' can become legally binding under international customary law. See R. Johnson and T. Rauf, 'After the NPT's indefinite extension: The future of the global nonproliferation regime', *Nonproliferation Review*, 3(1) 1995, 34.

pivotal role in securing a strengthened NPT at the 2000 NPT Review Conference.

The eight-member New Agenda Coalition (Brazil, Egypt, Ireland, Mexico, New Zealand, Slovenia, South Africa and Sweden) was launched in June 1998. Its key purpose was to place nuclear disarmament at the heart of the NPT, considering that the lack of substantive progress in this sphere since the signing of the treaty demonstrated that the NWSs had failed to live up to their part of the original NPT bargain. The eight foreign ministers signed a declaration which included the statement that, 'we are deeply concerned at the persistent reluctance of the nuclear-weapon States to approach their Treaty obligations as an urgent commitment to the total elimination of their nuclear weapons'.[57] The capacity of the New Agenda Coalition to hold the NWSs accountable in this way was partly a function of the concessions which had been made by the NWSs at the 1995 NPT Review Conference, both procedurally and substantively. However, the NWSs found themselves even more exposed on their compliance with Article VI when the International Court of Justice (ICJ) issued its 1996 Advisory Opinion on the legality of nuclear weapons. The ICJ had stated that 'there exists an obligation to pursue in good faith and bring to a conclusion negotiations leading to nuclear disarmament in all its aspects under strict and effective international control'.[58] It was the question of whether the NWSs had been acting in 'good faith' which the New Agenda Coalition was determined to put under the spotlight.

Going into the 2000 NPT Review Conference, it became clear that a successful outcome would depend upon how responsive the NWSs were to the agenda promoted by the New Agenda Coalition. As Egyptian Ambassador, Fayza Aboul Naga, remarked at the beginning of the proceedings, without a successful outcome 'the NPT Regime could crumble'.[59] The UK delegation played a key role as a conduit between the New Agenda Coalition and the NWSs, and this facilitated the agreement that was reached between the 176 governments (of the then 187 parties to the treaty) meeting in New York on the thirteen 'practical steps' to implement Article VI.[60] The New Agenda

---

[57] 'A nuclear-weapons-free world: The need for a new agenda', Joint Declaration by the Ministers for Foreign Affairs of Brazil, Egypt, Ireland, Mexico, New Zealand, Slovenia, South Africa and Sweden, 9 June 1998, www.acronym.org.uk/27state.htm (accessed 27 July 2011).

[58] International Court of Justice, 'Legality of the Threat or Use of Nuclear Weapons', Advisory Opinion, 8 July 1996, para. 105(2)F, www.icj-cij.org/docket/index. php?p1=3&p2=4&k=e1&p3=4&case=95 (accessed 27 July 2011).

[59] Cited in Price, 'Reconciling the irreconcilable?', p. 124.

[60] Ibid., pp. 124–8.

Coalition secured a significant part of their agenda in that there were commitments to achieving a CTBT, a Fissile Material Cut-Off Treaty (FMCT), increased transparency, and measures towards de-alerting and reducing the salience of nuclear weapons in national security policy. A measure of how far the US and Russia had come in accepting the legitimacy of NPT oversight of their disarmament activity, as compared to their attitudes in 1975 at the first NPT Review Conference, can be seen in the fact that implementation of the Strategic Arms Reduction Treaties (II and III) was one of the practical steps to which the US and Russia agreed at the conference.[61]

These were significant achievements for those NNWSs who worried that the balance between the goals of disarmament and non-proliferation in the original treaty had tilted too far away from the former. The New Agenda Coalition had to compromise on its goal of securing from the NWSs a timetable for nuclear reductions and commitments to no-first use of nuclear weapons (China is the only member of the NWSs to have given such an undertaking). It was evident that concessions of this kind were red lines for the Western members of the NWSs, and the New Agenda Coalition wisely refrained from making the best the enemy of the good here. In this regard, it did not want to jeopardise its most significant political victory in the agreed final document, which was the sixth of the thirteen steps where the NWSs explicitly agreed for the first time that Article VI required an 'unequivocal undertaking by the nuclear weapon States to accomplish the total elimination of their nuclear arsenals leading to nuclear disarmament'.[62] The significance of this was that the NWSs accepted a special responsibility for nuclear disarmament separate from the general responsibility on all states for achieving 'general and complete disarmament'. The New Agenda Coalition and the other non-aligned state parties to the treaty, who were determined to hold the NWSs accountable under Article VI felt emboldened by the agreement on the thirteen 'practical steps'. This was reflected in the Mexican Ambassador's comments: 'today's events signify an important landmark on which to build a nuclear weapons-free world ... We leave this conference with greater faith in the prospects for nuclear disarmament.'[63]

However, as we discuss below, these expectations and hopes for nuclear disarmament on the part of the New Agenda Coalition, and

---

[61] Final Document of the 2000 Review Conference of the Parties to the Treaty on the Non-Proliferation of Nuclear Weapons, NPT/CONF.2000/28 (Parts I and II), 2000.

[62] *Ibid.*, p. 14; Price, 'Reconciling the irreconcilable?', p. 126.

[63] Quoted in Price, 'Reconciling the irreconcilable?', p. 126.

the wider NNWSs, proved premature. Bill Clinton's administration, which had been in office when the 2000 NPT Review Conference took place, was replaced by the Bush administration, which was determined not to be shackled by what it saw as a political declaration which was not suited to meeting the proliferation challenge in a post-11 September 2001 world. The result was a new process of contestation within the NPT over the balance to be struck between general and special responsibilities in the nuclear domain.

Contestation from above

The terror attacks of 11 September 2001 completed a revolution in the US approach to nuclear threats which had begun in the 1990s with the Clinton administration's growing preoccupation with the nuclear threat posed by so-called 'rogue states'. This led the US to develop a new militarised approach to non-proliferation, labelled 'counter-proliferation', which included a range of active measures such as the development of ballistic missile defences and plans for developing a generation of highly accurate nuclear weapons that could attack the weapons of mass destruction (WMD) capabilities of US adversaries.[64] The terrorist attacks of 11 September underlined for the Bush administration the possibility that the next attack against the US might be nuclear, perhaps supported by nuclear-armed rogue states. Moreover, in a radical move that went beyond the counter-proliferation policies of the Clinton administration, Bush espoused a doctrine of preventive war and regime change to remove at source these nuclear risks to the US homeland.

The Bush administration saw the US as uniquely imperilled in a post-11 September world, and this perception of extreme vulnerability led it to claim a special responsibility to lead the world in fighting this peril. The president and his inner circle believed that history and providence had at this moment of great danger bestowed upon the US a special responsibility to actively prevent its ideological enemies – by military force and regime change if necessary – from acquiring the capability to threaten the US and its allies with nuclear weapons. In his 2002 State of the Union Address, Bush described Iraq, Iran and North Korea as an 'axis of evil'.[65] Believing that the domestic nature of rogue states committed them to the export of aggression and terror,

---

[64] In 2004 the Bush administration sharply increased its funding of the Robust Nuclear Earth Penetrator as it proceeded beyond the study phase. See J. Medalia, 'Robust nuclear earth penetrator budget request and plan, FY2005-FY2009' (Washington, DC: Congressional Research Service, 24 March 2004).

[65] G. W. Bush, State of the Union Address, 29 January 2002.

and that there could be no long-term coexistence between the US and such regimes, the Bush administration defended a policy of preventive war and regime change. Bush warned, 'I will not wait on events, while dangers gather. I will not stand by, as peril draws closer and closer. The United States of America will not permit the world's most dangerous regimes to threaten us with the world's most destructive weapons.'[66]

The Bush administration named as rogue states those polities whose values and internal systems of government were fundamentally antithetical to that of the US. Moreover, it was reasoned that as long as such regimes remained in power, there was always the danger that they would develop or acquire nuclear weapons and their means of delivery. Equally frightening for US policy-makers was the prospect that through deliberate design or inadvertence, these regimes might serve as conduits for the transfer of radioactive material, or even nuclear weapons, to terrorist groups.[67]

In confronting the peril posed by rogue states, the Bush administration argued that nuclear deterrence was ineffective, because the regimes governing such states were extreme risk-takers, prepared to gamble all in the pursuit of their fanatical objectives. Thus, the 2002 National Security Strategy declared that 'deterrence based only upon the threat of retaliation is less likely to work against leaders of rogue states more willing to take risks, gambling with the lives of their people, and the wealth of their nations'.[68] In arguing that rogue states would view nuclear weapons as usable instruments of military and political intimidation, the Bush administration identified preventive military action against emerging nuclear threats and the development of national missile defences as critical components of its counter-proliferation strategy.[69]

The Bush administration viewed the challenge posed by Iraq's alleged WMD programmes in the early 2000s as a test case of both the limits of the NPT and the need for a new approach to proliferation that would address root causes. It showed the failure of the NPT, US decision-makers argued, because the rules and norms of the treaty – crucially the system of IAEA safeguards – had failed in the 1980s to

[66] *Ibid.*
[67] I. H. Daalder and J. M. Lindsay, *America unbound: The Bush revolution in foreign policy* (Washington, DC: Brookings Institution Press, 2003), pp. 182–5; M. O'Hanlon and M. Mochizuki, *Crisis on the Korean peninsula: How to deal with a nuclear North Korea* (New York: McGraw-Hill 2003), p. 34; G. T. Allison, *Nuclear terrorism: The ultimate preventable catastrophe* (New York: Times Books, 2004), p. 20.
[68] White House, 'The National Security Strategy of the United States' (Washington, DC: The White House, 20 September 2002), www.globalsecurity.org/military/library/policy/national/nss-020920.pdf (accessed 27 July 2011).
[69] See Bush's Foreword in White House, 'The National Security Strategy'.

detect Iraq's non-compliance which was only revealed after the first Gulf War (1990–1) when UN inspectors discovered the clandestine nuclear programme that Saddam Hussein had been operating.

Key policy-makers in the Bush administration had criticised the NPT in the 1980s and 1990s for failing to stop proliferation in the cases of Iran, Iraq and North Korea (all three then signatories of the treaty). But the new US response in the form of the Bush Doctrine and the invasion of Iraq proved no more effective in rolling back the nuclear capabilities of the remaining two members of the 'axis of evil'. Indeed, the war against Iraq arguably served to accelerate the nuclear programmes of both North Korea and Iran.

The Bush administration, however, rejected any suggestion that the US overthrow of Saddam Hussein had spurred the nuclear programmes in North Korea and Iran. It was an article of faith in the administration that only regime change in both countries would provide a long-term guarantee against either of them developing nuclear weapons. The fear that within the next ten to twenty years a nuclear-armed North Korea and Iran might be capable of launching nuclear strikes against US targets (initially US conventional forces deployed in the Middle East and Northeast Asia, but eventually including US cities) shaped the evolution of the Bush administration's nuclear strategy. To avoid a US president being self-deterred from employing US conventional forces by the risk that a potential adversary would escalate any conflict to the nuclear level, the Bush administration committed itself in its 2002 Nuclear Posture Review to the development and deployment of a full spectrum of nuclear and conventional forces. The Nuclear Posture Review, leaked to the *Los Angeles Times* and the *New York Times* in March of that year, caused a rupture in the NPT regime by suggesting a role for tactical and 'bunker-busting' nuclear weapons to nullify the WMD threat from rogue states.[70] Such a strategy meant that the US had to keep open the option of future nuclear testing, and so the administration abandoned the previous US commitment to a CTBT (the Clinton administration had failed to secure Senate ratification of the treaty in 1999).

[70] United States Department of Defense, 'Nuclear Posture Review [Excerpts]', Submitted to Congress on 31 December 2001, www.stanford.edu/class/polisci211z/2.6/NPR2001leaked.pdf (accessed 27 July 2011). For analysis of the 2002 Nuclear Posture Review, see J. du Preez, 'The impact of the Nuclear Posture Review on the international nuclear nonproliferation regime', *Nonproliferation Review*, 9(3) 2002, 67–81. See also M. Butcher, 'What wrongs our arms may do: The role of nuclear weapons in counterproliferation' (Washington, DC: Physicians for Social Responsibility, August 2003), pp. 57–69, action.psr.org/documents/psrwhatwrong03.pdf (accessed 27 July 2011).

The New Agenda Coalition and the non-aligned state parties to the NPT vigorously contested the Bush administration's nuclear policies at the 2002 and 2003 preparatory meetings for the 2005 NPT Review Conference. The increasing priority accorded nuclear weapons in US national security strategy was seen as a direct contravention of the commitments which the US had entered into in agreeing to the thirteen steps at the 2000 NPT Review Conference. For example, Mexican Ambassador Luis Alfonso de Alba declared that 'any plans or intentions ... by the nuclear-weapon States to develop new types of weapons or rationalizations for their use, contradict the spirit of the NPT and go against the agreement reached at the 2000 Review Conference for a diminishing role for nuclear weapons in security policies'.[71]

The very different meaning that the Bush administration gave to its special responsibilities for arms control and disarmament, compared to that of the Clinton administration, can be seen in the position it espoused at the 2004 preparatory meeting. Rejecting the interpretation which had been agreed at the 2000 NPT Review Conference as to what Article VI compliance required, the US tabled a working paper on the last day of the Preparatory Committee which stated that 'the United States ... does not support all 13 practical steps from the 2000 Final Document, and does not ... evaluate the NPT's operation mainly on the basis of Article VI'.[72] Moreover, in a statement that gave a very different meaning to the bargain between horizontal and vertical proliferation in the original NPT, US representative John Bolton had claimed in his opening address to the Preparatory Committee that 'the central bargain of the NPT is that if non-nuclear weapons states renounce the pursuit of nuclear weapons, they may gain assistance in developing civilian nuclear power'.[73] Such a claim ignored the special responsibilities which the NWSs had accepted in the field of arms control and disarmament, especially the concrete measures for implementing Article VI that they had committed to in 1995 and 2000.

[71] Statement by Ambassador Luis Alfonso de Alba on Behalf of the New Agenda Coalition at the General Debate of the Third Session of the Preparatory Committee of the 2005 NPT Review Conference, 26 April 2004, p. 3, www.reachingcriticalwill. org/legal/npt/prepcom04/mexiconac26.pdf (accessed 10 June 2010).

[72] 'US statement', working paper submitted to the Third Session of the Preparatory Committee for the 2005 Review Conference, 7 May 2004, NPT/Conf.2005/PC.III/ WP.28.

[73] J. R. Bolton, 'The NPT: a crisis of non-compliance', Statement by United States Under Secretary of State for Arms Control and International Security John R. Bolton to the Third Session of the Preparatory Committee for the 2005 Review Conference of the Treaty on the Non-Proliferation of Nuclear Weapons, 27 April 2004, p. 4, www.reachingcritical will.org/legal/npt/prepcom04/usa27.pdf (accessed 15 June 2011).

The Bush administration, operating with its ethos of exceptionalism, did not accept that the US should continue to be bound by these previous commitments. Bush considered that the thirteen steps lacked any firm basis in international law, and was no more than a collective agreement of governments at the 2000 NPT Review Conference as to what constituted steps towards the implementation of Article VI. Certainly, the Bush administration rejected the notion that its nuclear strategy – which it did not accept contravened Article VI – should be the subject of legitimate scrutiny and censure by other parties to the treaty.[74]

Despite the Bush administration's rejection of some of the thirteen steps the US had signed up to in 2000, it is important to recognise that at no point did it deny that it had a responsibility to pursue arms control and nuclear disarmament under Article VI. Nevertheless, the US clearly viewed this as a general and not a special responsibility, in so far as US negotiators emphasised the collective responsibility that fell on all parties to the treaty to take the steps and promote the conditions that would lead to global nuclear disarmament. At the same time, US officials claimed that the US had made, in Bolton's words, 'major contributions to the goals of Article VI'[75] by signing the 2002 Strategic Offensive Reductions Treaty (SORT). The latter committed the US and Russia to reduce their warheads to between 1,700 and 2,200 by 2012. However, such claims carried little weight with the New Agenda Coalition and other like-minded parties to the treaty. These states pointed to the prominent role which the Bush administration was according nuclear weapons in US national security policy, a development which was seen as in direct contradiction with the commitments the United Stated had entered into in 2000.

The US emphasis on the general responsibilities for non-proliferation and disarmament that fell on all parties to the treaty reflected the Bush administration's bedrock conviction that the value of the NPT resided in what it could contribute to the enforcement of the non-proliferation norm, especially in relation to the challenges posed by North Korea and Iran. The Bush administration refused to accept that the US had a special responsibility for arms control and disarmament, something the NNWSs were determined to pin on it, and this led the NNWSs to perceive in US actions a marginalisation of the disarmament goals of the NPT. Such a perception was fuelled by Bolton's inflammatory claim that the NNWSs should stop worrying about 'Article VI issues that do not exist', and instead invest their energies and commitments

---

[74] Ford, 'Debating disarmament', especially 411–13.
[75] Bolton, 'The NPT'.

in strengthening the enforcement capacities of the treaty against those members of the treaty who were in violation of its fundamental non-proliferation norm.[76] Although this was never stated explicitly by US officials or leaders, the clear implication was that some states could be trusted with nuclear weapons. And if some states could be trusted with nuclear weapons, then it was not necessary to worry about whether they were disarming or not.[77] This conception of the global nuclear weapons order fundamentally challenged the original NPT bargain which was predicated on the assumption that all proliferation was bad.

The Bush administration put this philosophy into practice with its 2005 deal with India. In a unilateral move, the US reversed the position which the Nuclear Suppliers Group (NSG) had adopted in 1992 that made nuclear cooperation with all NNWSs (India being treated by the NSG as a NNWS because of the definition of a NWS under Article IX of the NPT) conditional upon the acceptance of 'full-scope' IAEA safeguards.[78] Importantly, this move disturbed the categorisation between the NWSs and the NNWSs which lies at the heart of the treaty. The US categorised India as 'a responsible state with advanced nuclear technology', and pointed to its spotless record on non-proliferation.[79]

The proponents of the US–India deal have argued that it is a 'creative, outside-the-box' way of bringing India into the framework of the nuclear non-proliferation regime.[80] Critics of the deal, which include the vast majority of the NNWSs, have argued that it creates a dangerous precedent by conferring a set of advantages upon a state that did not accept to be bound by the treaty and its rules.[81] And in a direct assault on the universality of the non-proliferation norm, it appears that a key US criterion for privileging India in this way was that it was a democratic state.[82] The implicit assumption was that democratic states could be trusted with nuclear weapons and given exemptions from norms that the key nuclear supplier states had agreed outside of the treaty, even if

---

[76] *Ibid.*
[77] H. Müller, 'The 2005 NPT Review Conference: Reasons and consequences of failure and options for repair' (Stockholm: Weapons of Mass Destruction Commission, August 2005); R. Price, 'Nuclear weapons don't kill people, rogues do', *International Politics*, 44(2) 2007, 239–40.
[78] Three years later on 6 September 2008, this bilateral agreement received endorsement by the then forty-five members of the NSG.
[79] 'India–US Joint Statement', Washington, DC, 18 July 2005.
[80] See M. ElBaradei, 'Rethinking nuclear safeguards', *Washington Post*, 14 June 2006.
[81] J. Carter, 'India nuclear deal puts world at risk', *International Herald Tribune*, 11 September 2008.
[82] G. Perkovitch, '"Democratic bomb": Failed strategy', Policy Brief 49 (Washington, DC: Carnegie Endowment for International Peace, November 2006); Price, 'Nuclear weapons don't kill people', 243–5.

they could not be admitted to the NPT because of the latter's rules. The NSG guidelines agreed in 1992 were not formally part of the NPT, but they were aimed at strengthening the non-proliferation norm by restricting the benefits of nuclear commerce to those who were outside the treaty. The Bush administration's decision in 2005 to exempt India from the NSG guidelines complicated the insider-outsider distinction by giving India the status it had craved as a nuclear-armed power, but which hitherto it had been denied.

The Bush administration's approach to the NPT can, at best, be seen as an attempt to shift the priority away from the special responsibility for nuclear disarmament which it had accepted in 2000 towards the general responsibility of all parties to the treaty for promoting both non-proliferation and disarmament.[83] At worst, US repudiation of the thirteen steps amounted to an attempted deferral, if not explicit rejection, of the special responsibility for disarmament which it and the other NWSs had agreed to at the 2000 NPT Review Conference. The US was not alone in stepping back from the thirteen steps; France joined it, fearing that the commitments which the NWSs had made in 2000 went too far in weakening nuclear deterrence as the bedrock principle of French security.[84] However, Washington's and Paris's attempt to revise the original NPT bargain in this way challenged the equilibrium point which had been agreed at the 1995 and 2000 NPT Review Conferences, and such a move was strongly resisted by the other parties to the treaty. This was spectacularly seen in the collapse of the 2005 NPT Review Conference. The latter took place in the immediate aftermath of the US–India deal, and was another factor which prevented any agreement at the conference. According to Harald Müller, the 2005 NPT Review Conference was the worst in the history of the NPT. This was not so much because it ended without an agreed final

---

[83] Joyner, *Interpreting the Nuclear Non-Proliferation Treaty*, p. 40.

[84] On French attitudes to nuclear disarmament, see B. Tertrais, 'French perspectives on nuclear weapons and nuclear disarmament', in B. Blechman (ed.), *Unblocking the road to zero* (Washington, DC: Henry L. Stimson Center, 2009), pp. 1–22. On French nuclear strategy and doctrine after 2001, see D. Yost, 'France's evolving nuclear strategy', *Survival*, 47(3) 2005, 117–46. See also D. Yost, 'France's new nuclear doctrine', *International Affairs*, 82(4) 2006, 701–21. Shortly after the 2000 NPT Review Conference, the French government backtracked on its commitment to the 2000 NPT Review Conference Final Document and the thirteen steps. France refused to recognise that the thirteen steps agreement de-linked the unequivocal commitment to nuclear disarmament from the aspiration of general and complete disarmament. See R. Johnson, 'Incentives, obligations and enforcement: Does the NPT meet its states parties' needs?', *Disarmament Diplomacy*, 70 (March–April) 2003, 3–10; R. Johnson, 'Is the NPT up to the challenge of proliferation?', *Disarmament Forum*, (4) 2004, www.unidir.org/pdf/articles/pdf-art2186.pdf (accessed 27 July 2011).

document, but because 'there was disagreement among the parties across all frontlines'.[85]

At the 2005 NPT Review Conference, the Bush administration cherry-picked among the thirteen steps which it saw as standing in the way of its planned nuclear modernisation, while claiming that the latter was not a violation of its treaty obligations. The US did not deny that it had legal responsibilities under Article VI, but it argued that the qualitative improvements planned for the US nuclear arsenal were not in contravention of Article VI. In response to the criticism from the NNWSs (especially the non-aligned parties to the treaty) that US actions were a repudiation of the thirteen steps, Washington persisted with the claim that Article VI did not require it to fulfil the thirteen steps which had been agreed in 2000, including of course the 'unequivocal commitment to nuclear disarmament'.[86]

Legally, the US was probably on firm ground in making these claims, since the treaty language of Article VI has nothing to say about what is permitted in terms of numbers or types of nuclear weapons. The implication of the US position was that the thirteen steps (as against Article VI) were a political declaration and hence not legally binding. Christopher Ford, US Special Representative for Nuclear Non-Proliferation in 2007, argued that:

[s]tructurally, contextually, and grammatically, therefore, the 13 Steps amount to no more than any other political declaration by a convocation of national representatives ... There is nothing wrong with such statements, of course ... But one should not confuse such exhortations with legal obligations or mistake them for definitive treaty interpretive criteria.[87]

The problem was that legal scholastics of this kind were perceived by those NNWSs who had pressed for the thirteen steps as showing a cynical disregard for the promises which had been made in 2000.

In the eyes of the NNWSs, the significance of the thirteen steps was that the NWSs had accepted that there were limitations on what could be justified under Article VI, and by agreeing to measures like the CTBT and the FMCT, they were accepting that implementation of Article VI required concrete steps that went beyond the specific textual language of 'pursuing negotiations in good faith'. The concessions which the NNWSs had secured in 2000 were specifically aimed at constraining the qualitative improvement of nuclear arsenals, with a

[85] Müller, 'The 2005 NPT Review Conference', p. 1.
[86] Final Document of the 2000 Review Conference, p. 14.
[87] Ford, 'Debating disarmament', 413. See also Joyner, *Interpreting the Nuclear Non-Proliferation Treaty*, pp. 71–2.

view to marginalising the role of nuclear weapons in national security policy.

Not surprisingly, the US and French attempts to dismiss the thirteen steps were strongly contested, and such arguments failed to secure legitimacy among the wider NPT membership, including the other three NWSs who continued to recognise their special responsibilities under the thirteen steps. The US had failed under Bush to jettison the special responsibilities it had accepted in 1995 and 2000 for nuclear disarmament. The new Obama administration began a process aimed at building a new consensus which acknowledged that the US had special responsibilities (and not just general ones) in the nuclear domain. However, as we discuss below, this process of re-engagement with the NPT after the Bush years was also one in which the US sought to persuade the NNWSs to accept new special responsibilities in the nuclear domain, and this was to give rise to new contestations.

The search for a new equilibrium

As president-elect, Obama had emphasised that he would make the elimination of all nuclear weapons a key foreign policy goal. Less than three months after being sworn in as president, Obama gave a speech in Prague where he committed the US to lead the way towards nuclear abolition. The contrast between the Bush administration's belief in security through nuclear strength, and its successor's commitment (at least declaratory) to achieving security through nuclear disarmament, was starkly revealed when the president stated:

Just as we stood for freedom in the 20th century, we must stand together for the right of people everywhere to live free from fear in the 21st. And as a nuclear power – as the only nuclear power to have used a nuclear weapon – the United States has a moral responsibility to act. We cannot succeed in this endeavor alone, but we can lead it.[88]

Obama invoked a new US special responsibility claim based on giving a very different meaning to the US nuclear attacks against Hiroshima and Nagasaki in August 1945. In making this claim, Obama sought to transform the US's legal special responsibility for disarmament into a moral one as well. By establishing a moral basis that was unique to the US, he was giving it a key leadership role.

At the same time as Obama articulated a new responsibility claim, he also restated the importance of the NWSs and the NNWSs living

---

[88] B. Obama, 'Remarks of President Barack Obama', Hradcany Square, Prague, 5 April 2009, prague.usembassy.gov/obama.html (accessed 31 July 2011).

up to their special nuclear responsibilities. After a meeting of the United Nations Security Council in September 2009 which Obama had requested, and which met for the first time to discuss nuclear non-proliferation at heads of state and government level, the US president, who chaired the meeting, repeated the basic bargain of the NPT. He declared that 'nations with nuclear weapons have the responsibility to move towards disarmament and those without them have the responsibility to forsake them'.[89] Obama recognised, in stark contrast to his predecessor, that upholding the bargain that underpinned the treaty required the US and the other recognised nuclear powers to fulfil their special responsibility for arms control and disarmament. Indeed, Ambassador Susan Burk, Special Representative of the President for Nuclear Nonproliferation, made a series of speeches in 2009 and 2010 where she invoked this very language in relation to the NPT. For example, in October 2009 she said: 'The United States and other nuclear weapon states bear a special responsibility under the NPT to pursue nuclear disarmament.'[90]

The Obama administration accepted the importance of the US being seen by the NNWSs as taking a new leadership role in the disarmament field. This reflected the administration's understanding of the mutual security dependence between the NWSs and the NNWSs which has underpinned the treaty from its inception. The logical corollary was that the fundamental security benefit that has flowed from the treaty – namely the institutionalisation and deepening of the nuclear taboo – requires both the NWSs and the NNWSs to show they are living up to their special nuclear responsibilities. Otherwise, there is always the risk that what Walker calls 'the managed system of military abstinence'[91] would collapse as some of the NNWSs decide that the NWSs are only interested in maintaining their position of nuclear supremacy.

To give substance to its rhetorical commitment to disarmament, the US was determined to finalise a new Strategic Arms Reduction Talks

---

[89] B. Obama, 'Remarks by the President at the United Nations Security Council summit on nuclear non-proliferation and nuclear disarmament, United Nations Headquarters, New York', White House press release, 24 September 2009, www.whitehouse.gov/the-press-office/remarks-president-un-security-council-summit-nuclear-non-proliferation-and-nuclear- (accessed 27 July 2011). The Security Council meeting adopted Resolution 1887 on 24 September 2009. See UN Security Council Resolution 1887 on Nuclear Nonproliferation and Nuclear Disarmament, 24 September 2009, www.acronym.org.uk/docs/0909/doc03.htm (accessed 27 July 2011).

[90] S. Burk, 'US Special Representative Susan Burk on nuclear nonproliferation challenges', Remarks to Middle Powers Initiative Event, Permanent Mission of Switzerland to the United Nations, New York, 13 October 2009, geneva.usmission.gov/2009/10/13/nptburk (accessed 27 July 2011).

[91] Walker, *A perpetual menace*, p. 154.

(START) agreement with Russia. The Obama administration pointed to the signing of the New START treaty as evidence that the US was taking seriously its special responsibility under Article VI. The New START Treaty was signed on 8 April 2010 and the US Senate ratified it in December 2010, with the Russian Duma following suit the next month. New START promises to cut US–Russian nuclear forces by a further 30 per cent from the levels agreed in the 2002 SORT.

It was no coincidence that the US and Russia concluded the New START Treaty negotiations a month before the beginning of the 2010 NPT Review Conference. Without this agreement, the prospects for the conference would have been much dimmer. Against the backdrop of the Bush administration's retreat from the thirteen steps and the failure of the 2005 NPT Review Conference, there were concerns in the run-up to the 2010 NPT Review Conference as to whether some of the NNWSs were prepared to continue to live with the inequities of the treaty. That said, it would be erroneous to think that the NNWSs were queuing up to leave the NPT in the late 2000s because they perceived the NWSs to have failed to act in good faith on nuclear disarmament. They only had to look at the challenges to the non-proliferation norm which emanated from the ambiguities as to whether Iran's nuclear programme was civilian or military in intent, as well as North Korea's decision to test nuclear devices in 2006 and 2009, to realise their security interest in the treaty. At the same time, they looked to the NWSs, crucially the US, to take the lead in reducing the inequality at the heart of the treaty by meeting their responsibilities. Consequently, they went into the 2010 NPT Review Conference looking to not only restore the gains which had been made in 1995 and 2000, but also crucially to build on these achievements after the reverses of the Bush years. It was evident to all the parties to the treaty that another failure on the scale of 2005 would deal a major, and perhaps fatal, blow to the regime.

The NNWSs, especially the New Agenda Coalition and the non-aligned state parties to the treaty, were not the only ones who went into the 2010 NPT Review Conference with a clear agenda. The US also had clear goals it wanted to secure in 2010. These related to the non-proliferation pillar of the treaty, crucially, access to the full nuclear fuel-cycle on the part of the NNWSs, and strengthened verification provisions. In this respect, there was an important element of continuity in US policy, since the Bush administration had also sought to strengthen the non-proliferation pillar of the treaty in this way.[92] US officials were

---

[92] The Bush administration had sought measures that would restrict the supply of uranium enrichment and plutonium separation facilities to states which did not

quick to point out, in Ambassador Burk's words, that the 'non-nuclear weapon states bear no less responsibility to work constructively and actively to prevent further proliferation and to help create the conditions for nuclear disarmament, and to ensure safe, secure uses of nuclear energy'.[93] Although she did not make the point explicitly, Burk seemed to be arguing, to use the language that we employ in the climate chapter, that the NWSs and NNWSs had 'common but differentiated responsibilities'.

In a highly contested move, the US sought acceptance by those NNWSs which had not yet developed enrichment and plutonium separation facilities to a new special responsibility which would limit the exercise of their sovereign rights under Article IV. It will be recalled that Article IV provides the NNWSs with a set of rightful powers (access to the peaceful uses of nuclear energy) which are conditional on them living up to their special responsibility under Article II of the NPT (not to develop nuclear weapons or receive them, or related components, from other states). The Obama administration recognised that securing agreement to a shrinking of the sovereign entitlements of the NNWSs (this would not affect those states which had already developed indigenous fuel-cycle capabilities) would only succeed if it was coupled with the US, and the other NWSs, demonstrating a serious and sustained commitment to nuclear disarmament. However, as we discuss below, what the US was offering on the disarmament front was not sufficient to compensate the NNWSs for what they saw as a move that would

possess them. Specifically, in a landmark speech in 2004, Bush had called upon the then forty nations of the NSG to 'refuse to sell enrichment and reprocessing equipment and technologies to any state that does not already possess full-scale, functioning enrichment and reprocessing plants'. For the text of his speech, see 'Bush's speech on the spread of nuclear weapons', *New York Times*, 11 February 2004, www.nytimes.com/2004/02/11/politics/10WEB-PTEX.html (accessed 27 July 2011). In addition, Bush proposed that the supply of 'equipment' for civilian nuclear programmes should be conditional on NPT parties having accepted the IAEA additional protocol. For an overview of the Bush administration's 2004 proposals on strengthening the non-proliferation pillar of the NPT, see R. Einhorn, 'President Bush's nonproliferation proposals and implications for the United Nations', UNA-USA Policy Brief No. 1, 15 March 2004, www.unausa.org/Document.Doc?id=246 (accessed 27 July 2011). On the Bush administration's approach to non-proliferation and counterproliferation in general, see G. Perkovich, 'Bush's nuclear revolution: A regime change in nonproliferation', *Foreign Affairs*, 82(2) 2003, 2–8; J. D. Ellis, 'The best defense: Counterproliferation and US national security', *Washington Quarterly*, 26(2) 2003, 115–33. On the continuity and change between Bush and Obama on US international nuclear energy policy see M. A. Pomper, 'US international nuclear energy policy: Change and continuity', Nuclear Energy Futures Paper No. 10 (Waterloo, ONT: Centre for International Governance Innovation, January 2010).

[93] Burk, 'Susan Burk on nuclear nonproliferation challenges'.

deepen still further the inequalities in the nuclear non-proliferation regime.

As noted earlier, the Bush administration had proposed a series of steps – a ban by the NSG on the sale of uranium enrichment and plutonium separation facilities – to close what Bush had called the 'loophole'[94] in Article IV. This loophole concerned the permissive nature of Article IV. The problem is that in enshrining the right of all parties to the treaty to develop the complete nuclear fuel-cycle, it permits states to develop the most proliferation sensitive technologies, whilst remaining compliant with their treaty obligations. The case which has most worried US policy-makers in this respect has been Iran, but as ElBaradei warned, the number of virtual or latent NWSs might increase by another ten or twenty in the next decade or so.[95]

Although there were elements of continuity in the Bush and Obama administration's approach to closing the loophole in Article IV, there was also one important difference. The Bush administration had sought to restrict what the NNWSs saw as their rightful powers under Article IV, by seeking an agreement restricted to the NSG. By contrast, the Obama administration sought to secure a consensus among all NPT state parties for the allocation of a new special responsibility whereby those NNWSs which had not developed indigenous fuel-cycle capabilities would voluntarily agree to refrain from doing so. Instead, parties to the treaty would be guaranteed access, at competitive prices, to nuclear fuel for power-generating purposes.[96]

Another area where the US sought to create a new special responsibility which would be allocated to the NNWSs was through securing adoption of the IAEA Additional Protocol as the precondition for supply of nuclear materials and fuel. As noted earlier, this had also been a policy goal of the Bush administration, and, as in the approach to the fuel-cycle, there were strong elements of continuity between the Bush and Obama administrations.[97] The Additional Protocol was developed in the

---

[94] 'Bush's speech on the spread of nuclear weapons'.

[95] 'Mohamed ElBaradei warns of new nuclear age'.

[96] A related approach is the development of multinational approaches to the fuel-cycle, such as the fuel bank established in 2009 on the territory of the Russian Federation as part of an agreement with the IAEA. See D. Horner, 'IAEA Board approves Russian fuel bank plan', *Arms Control Today*, January–February (2010), www.armscontrol.org/act/2010_01–02/FuelBank (accessed 27 July 2011); B. Sanders, 'IAEA safeguards and the NPT', *Disarmament Forum*, (4) 2004, 46–8, www.unidir.ch/pdf/articles/pdf-art2189.pdf (accessed 27 July 2011).

[97] T. L. Neff, 'The nuclear fuel cycle and the Bush nonproliferation initiative', paper for the World Nuclear Fuel Cycle Conference, Madrid, April 2004, www.iaea.org/newscenter/focus/fuelcycle/neff.pdf (accessed 27 July 2011).

early 1990s after the discovery of Iraq's clandestine nuclear weapons programme, and it provides the IAEA with widened powers of physical access. By increasing the transparency of a state's nuclear activities, it reduces the risk that a government might be operating a secret nuclear weapons programme, and hence reassures other treaty members that states are living up to their obligations.[98] At the time of writing, 102 states have accepted and are implementing the Additional Protocol.

How far, then, was a new equilibrium point achieved at the 2010 NPT Review Conference? The answer is less that a new point was reached than that an old one was re-established. The compromises that were thrashed out between the NWSs and the NNWSs in the Preparatory Committee meetings in the three years leading up to the 2010 NPT Review Conference itself, and during those four intense weeks of bargaining in May 2010, did not represent an agreement which fully satisfied either the NWSs or the NNWSs. Rather, the final document represented in broad terms a restatement of the consensus that had been achieved at the 2000 NPT Review Conference.[99]

The most positive achievement for the NNWSs was a reaffirmation by the NWSs in paragraph 79 of the final declaration of their 'unequivocal undertaking' to the total elimination of nuclear weapons.[100] The Bush administration had refused to make any such commitment in 2005, but given President Obama's publicly stated commitment to achieving nuclear abolition, it would have been very difficult for the US to oppose this language. The NWSs also recognised the importance of strengthening the reporting mechanism on Article VI compliance which had been agreed in 1995 and 2000, but which the Bush administration had dismissed as an encroachment on US national sovereignty. To this end, they committed themselves individually to report back on the measures they had taken to promote nuclear disarmament, including steps to reduce the role of nuclear weapons in national security policy. As in

---

[98] Sanders, 'IAEA safeguards and the NPT'.

[99] We noted earlier how it has been claimed that the indefinite extension of the NPT in 1995 only became possible because of the agreement on a Middle East resolution. Fifteen years later, a new commitment to fulfilling that promise became critical to the achievement of a consensus Final Document. Egypt's support was crucial and it was clear that this would be conditional on tangible progress towards the goal of achieving a Middle East Nuclear Weapons Free Zone (MENWFZ). To meet this Egyptian and Arab redline, diplomats proposed that a conference be co-convened by the UN secretary-general and the US, the UK and Russia (the co-sponsors of the 1995 resolution) which would be attended by 'all states of the Middle East'. It was further agreed that a 'facilitator' would be appointed by the UN secretary-general.

[100] Final Document of the 2010 Review Conference of the Parties to the Treaty on the Non-Proliferation of Nuclear Weapons (NPT), NPT/CONF.2010/50 (Vol. I), May 2010, Section I, para. 79, p. 12.

2000, the final document laid out a series of measures which all states agreed should be pursued such as a CTBT, a FMCT and other actions aimed at reducing the risks of nuclear conflict such as de-targeting missiles. It was agreed that the mechanism for this reporting would be the 2014 Preparatory Committee meeting, and the 2015 NPT Review Conference.

The key priority of the US going into the 2010 NPT Review Conference was to secure a successful outcome, and the fact that there was an agreed final document was a measure of the success of US diplomacy. However, the Obama administration failed to secure agreement from the NNWSs for what the latter viewed as a shrinking of their entitlements under Article IV. Many of the non-aligned parties to the treaty, especially Brazil, Egypt and South Africa, were anxious not to legitimise a new discrimination in fuel-cycle capabilities on top of the fundamentally discriminatory character of the NPT.[101] Egypt's ambassador, for example, opposed what he saw as 'efforts to redefine existing obligations under Article IV of the Treaty, with an aim to limit national options within the framework of the exercise of the inalienable right to the peaceful uses of nuclear energy'.[102] The non-aligned states have been prepared to accept nuclear inferiority in return for the security benefits which the NPT has afforded, but key players within the non-aligned grouping were not prepared to give up their status as nuclear equals when it came to fuel-cycle entitlements, irrespective of the security benefits this was argued by the US and others to confer on all parties to the treaty.

This resistance on the part of key players within the non-aligned grouping to legitimising new inequalities is partly a question of status, but it might also be seen as a question of hedging against an uncertain future. Just as the NWSs argue that nuclear weapons are vital to their security in an uncertain world, so some states view indigenous fuel-cycle capabilities as an insurance against potential adversaries breaking out of the restraints of the NPT. Given this political and strategic context, the most the NNWSs were prepared to do was to welcome discussions on how to multilateralise the fuel-cycle.[103] This fell well short of

[101] G. Perkovich and J. Acton, *Abolishing nuclear weapons*, Adelphi Paper 396 (Abingdon: Routledge, 2008), pp. 76–8.

[102] Statement by Egypt to Main Committee II of the 2010 Review Conference of the Treaty on the Non-Proliferation of Nuclear Weapons, New York, May 2010; Dhanapala, 'Evaluating the 2010 NPT Review Conference', 10.

[103] Final Document of the 2010 Review Conference, Section I, para. 57, p. 9. For commentary on the negotiations, see R. Johnson, 'NPT day 18: Updates, downgrading HEU and non-strategic nuclear weapons', acronyminstitute.wordpress.com/2010/05/21/day-16/ (accessed 27 July 2011).

what the US had hoped for, and prepared the ground for new rounds of political contestation over the meaning to be given Article IV.

The US was also unsuccessful in securing adherence to the Additional Protocol as the condition for NPT states exercising their rights under Article IV. Once again, it was the non-aligned states, crucially Argentina, Brazil, Egypt and South Africa which resisted this move. They rejected any proposals that weakened their 'inalienable right' under Article IV to benefit from the peaceful uses of atomic energy. Underpinning this resistance on the part of the non-aligned parties to the treaty was a sense that it was patently unfair to expect the NNWSs to take on yet more legally binding obligations to promote non-proliferation when the NWSs refused to reciprocate in relation to their nuclear disarmament responsibilities under the treaty. This refusal on the part of the non-aligned parties to accept any new erosion of their sovereign rights was well captured in Brazil's statement at the 2010 NPT Review Conference. The Brazilian ambassador reminded his fellow ambassadors that the Additional Protocol was not part of the original NPT bargain, and that:

[i]t is simply not fair to expect Non-Nuclear-Weapon States, which have already undertaken unequivocal, credible and verifiable commitments to forswear nuclear weapons ... while the international community has yet to be presented with a timeframe within which to expect the achievement of a world free of nuclear weapons.

Brazil was not denying that enhanced verification mechanisms would strengthen the regime, but it was arguing that such measures 'should be devised and grafted into a future Convention on the Prohibition of Nuclear Weapons, which would level the playing field by making zero nuclear weapons the norm for all members of the international community'.[104] As a result, the most that the non-aligned movement states would agree to in the final declaration was wording that accepted the Additional Protocol as a 'significant confidence-building measure', and encouraged 'all states parties which have not yet done so to conclude and bring into force additional protocols as soon as possible and to implement them provisionally pending their entry into force'.[105]

---

[104] Statement by Brazil to Main Committee II of the 2010 Review Conference of the Treaty on the Non-Proliferation of Nuclear Weapons, New York, 10 May 2010. See also Statement by South Africa to Main Committee II of the 2010 Review Conference of the Treaty on the Non-Proliferation of Nuclear Weapons, New York, 10 May 2010.

[105] Final Document of the 2010 Review Conference, Conclusions and Recommendations for Further Action, Section F (ii), Action 28, p. 25.

Conclusion

The NPT has provided the focal point for the allocation and acceptance of special responsibilities in the nuclear domain. As we have
shown in this chapter, the special responsibilities do not arise from the
treaty obligations alone, but crucially from the penumbra of political
expectations that surround it. The original NPT bargain can be seen
as an equilibrium point which legalised inequality in relation to the possession of nuclear weapons. Although the categorisation of the NWSs
and the NNWSs has remained stable in so far as (with the exception
of North Korea) no party to the treaty has left it, the legitimacy of
an unequal nuclear order remains deeply problematic for many of the
NNWSs. They have held on to the idea that a hierarchical nuclear order
was a temporary arrangement, necessary for coping with the challenge
of proliferation, before the principle of juridical equality could be
re-established as the ordering principle of the nuclear sphere.

The non-nuclear state parties to the treaty, especially members of
the non-aligned movement, have sought from the NPT's inception to
hold the NWSs accountable for what has been viewed as the special
responsibility of the NWSs to take the steps that would eventually lead
to nuclear disarmament. To this end, they have used the vehicle of the
NPT Review Conferences to press for greater commitments on disarmament and the de-legitimisation of nuclear weapons as the price for
their continued support for the treaty. They have also secured in this
ongoing process of contestation a strengthened review process which
has not only increased the ability of the NNWSs to hold the NWSs to
account, but also opened the door to civil society NGOs who play an
increasingly important role in holding all states accountable for their
actions in relation to both their general and special responsibilities in
the nuclear domain.

Article VI, inserted at the initiative of the NNWSs, has been the
weapon which the NNWSs have mobilised to keep the NWSs honest to the spirit – if not the letter – of the treaty. As we saw, the US
did not attribute much significance to Article VI when the treaty was
drafted, reflecting the fact that it did not impose upon Washington, or
the other nuclear powers, specific disarmament commitments. Yet as the
example of the concessions secured by the New Agenda Coalition at
the 2000 NPT Review Conference showed, the NNWSs have been able
to use the legitimating power of Article VI to secure important gains
on the disarmament front. The significance of the 2000 NPT Review
Conference lies in the acknowledgement by the NWSs that they have
a special responsibility to disarm their nuclear arsenals, coupled with

an unprecedented interpretation of that responsibility in terms of their agreement to specific actions to promote this goal (for example, the thirteen steps).

Despite the new responsibilities which the NWSs accepted in 2000, it is important to understand how much freedom the NWSs continued to have regarding their nuclear strategies. Whatever the legal basis of the thirteen steps (and this is contested by lawyers), it is evident that what was agreed in 2000 by the parties to the treaty represented a form of collective authority. But what the NPT Review Conference process lacks is sovereignty, in the sense that the power of sovereign decisions remains with the individual states.[106] The problem has been that the NNWSs have wanted to invest such sovereign powers in the review process, seeing it as the vehicle for leveraging the NWSs on the question of disarmament. As a consequence, when conference decisions are not subsequently lived up to by the NWSs, this has led to increased frustration and disillusionment on the part of the NNWSs.

Accepting this key limitation of the NPT review process, the failure of the Bush administration to legitimate its marginalisation of the disarmament pillar of the treaty supports our key contention that power is socially constituted: the US has not been able to control the terms of legitimacy in the nuclear domain through the exercise of its preponderant power. The Bush administration was prepared to ride roughshod over the other parties to the treaty, including close allies like the UK, who accepted the legitimacy of the thirteen steps. However, *contra* Brooks and Wohlforth, the US was not successful in persuading the vast majority of NPT state parties that it did not have a special responsibility for nuclear disarmament. The return of the Obama administration to the NPT fold, by regarding the treaty as a balance of responsibilities in relation to both disarmament and non-proliferation, shows that even the most powerful of nuclear actors was not able to bend the NPT membership to its will.

The Bush administration's revisionism on the NPT stemmed from the core conviction of US policy-makers that the treaty was not fit for purpose, in that it was not stopping determined proliferators (Iran, Iraq and North Korea). The US argument that the parties to the treaty should recognise and accept their general responsibility to promote the goal of non-proliferation by giving the US a free hand to enforce non-proliferation norms was an explicit criticism of how the existing NPT bargain was working out. This perception of the sub-optimality of the original bargain is shared, albeit for very different reasons, by many of

---

[106] We are grateful to William Walker for suggesting this point.

the NNWSs who increasingly worry that the treaty is setting in stone the inequalities of the global nuclear weapons order.

Despite these concerns about the NPT institutionalising a system of legalised inequality, the NNWSs have also accepted, in John Simpson's words, that 'hard headed considerations of national security [should] dominate more intellectual and emotional concerns over unfairness, hypocrisy, discrimination and the interests of mankind'.[107] Thus, despite the oscillations between power and equality, and perceptions of unfairness and discrimination which have shaped the contours of successive NPT Review Conferences, neither grouping – NWSs or NNWSs – has ever seriously contemplated abandoning their general and special responsibilities in the nuclear domain. There have been arguments over the meaning of these responsibilities, and the balance to be struck between the goals of non-proliferation and disarmament in the treaty, but at no point has anyone seriously challenged the idea that there are no responsibilities in the nuclear domain. The NWSs and NNWSs understand that they are better off with the treaty as a barrier against possession – and ultimately nuclear use – than any of the alternatives which pull towards either pole of material power politics or a system built solely on the principle of sovereign equality.

The fundamental retreat from the principle of juridical equality in the NPT, in relation to the most powerful weapons that humanity has invented, bears testimony to international society's conviction that neither material power politics nor sovereign equality can provide an adequate basis on which to address the challenges of coexistence and cooperation in the nuclear domain: in their absence, special responsibilities have occupied the middle ground.

Acknowledgements

We would like to thank Ken Berry, Molly Cochran, Justin Morris, Tristan Price, Jan Ruzicka and William Walker for their comments on earlier versions of this chapter. We are also grateful to Tristan Price for the research assistance he provided during the preparation of this chapter.

---

[107] Simpson, 'The Non-Proliferation Treaty at its Half-Life', p. 5.

4 Climate change

Environmental problems arrived relatively late on the agenda of international relations but they are now persistent and ubiquitous, having crept up, as it were, on a rapidly modernising world as the unintended and in many cases unforeseen side-effects of otherwise acceptable practices. These special features of environmental problems make the allocation of responsibility especially difficult and troublesome, and explain why they are often characterised as 'wicked problems'. In this chapter, we focus on the wickedest of them all – the problem of human-induced climate change – which is destined to remain a permanent item on the international agenda for the foreseeable future.

The debate over who should take responsibility for climate change has become more urgent as the successive reports of the Intergovernmental Panel on Climate Change (IPCC) have become more confident about the seriousness of the problem and the window of opportunity for preventative action diminishes. The development of a low carbon global economy requires a massive transformation of social purpose and social practices at multiple levels of social aggregation. Few would deny that everyone should 'play a role' and share in the general responsibility to address such a major collective action challenge. Yet it does not follow that everyone should play the same role or take on the same responsibility, given the vast differences among individuals, households, communities, firms, organisations and states in terms of their historical contribution to the problem, capacities to respond and adapt, levels of income, development needs and vulnerability. The problem of climate change is especially pernicious from an ethical point of view because the impacts cannot be geographically quarantined to ensure that the big greenhouse gas emitters suffer impacts in proportion to their causal responsibility, or that the least culpable and most vulnerable are protected. Indeed, in many (though not all) cases, there is an inverse relationship between causal responsibility and capacity to respond, on the one hand, and vulnerability and under-development, on the other. These features suggest that the collective task of preventing dangerous climate change can be more fairly and effectively fulfilled by differentiating social roles and responsibilities among different social agents. Our task in this chapter is to examine how states have negotiated different roles and responsibilities to address climate change, with a particular emphasis on the roles and responsibilities of the US. Our principal focus is the history and fate of the principles of 'common but differentiated responsibilities' (CBDR) in the United Nations Framework Convention on Climate Change (UNFCCC) 1992, which confer special responsibilities on developed countries to take the lead in addressing climate change.[1]

The chapter unfolds in three parts. First, we identify the source, meaning and allocation of the special responsibilities, beginning with the Stockholm Conference on the Human Environment in 1972 and culminating in the Rio Declaration and UNFCCC signed at the 1992 Earth Summit, which introduced the specific language of CBDR. We also explore to what extent the US's special responsibilities are quantitatively and/or qualitatively different from those of other developed countries.

Next, we examine the dynamics of the evolution and contestation of special responsibilities in the negotiation of the Kyoto Protocol, debates over ratification of the Kyoto Protocol, the negotiations for a second commitment period under the Kyoto Protocol and the negotiations for a new 'post-Kyoto' treaty on Long-term Cooperative Action (hereafter the LCA treaty).[2] The negotiations for this latter treaty were launched in 2007 in an effort to re-engage the US following its repudiation of the Kyoto Protocol in 2001. After tracking the evolution and contestation of special responsibilities in the international negotiations, we identify the key continuities and changes in the US posture towards them since 1992, with a special focus on the Barack Obama administration's efforts to re-engage with the international negotiations. We also set this re-engagement in the context of the changing international landscape, particularly the rising aggregate emissions of China, and explore to what extent special responsibilities have been, or are likely to be, internationally renegotiated to accommodate these developments. Here we draw out two crucial differences between this case study and the case studies on nuclear proliferation and global finance.

---

[1] United Nations Framework Convention on Climate Change, FCCC/INFORMAL/84 GE.05–62220 (E) 200705, adopted 9 May 1992.
[2] The negotiations for this treaty are formally conducted by the Ad Hoc Working Group on Long-Term Cooperative Action under the Convention (AWG-LCA).

First, special leadership responsibilities for climate change entail major positive obligations on the part of developed countries, but no corresponding rights or privileges, merely flexibility mechanisms (such as emissions trading) which enable developed countries to discharge their responsibilities in a cost-effective manner. Second, climate leadership responsibilities seek to narrow (or prevent the widening of) the development gap between developed and developing countries and therefore rest on an egalitarian understanding of the international order that challenges the existing hierarchy of privilege and prestige. This understanding impinges upon traditional constructions of not only the US's domestic interests but also key elements of its foreign policy in the economic and security domains. In this sense, the case study of climate change exposes a 'clash of responsibilities' for the US, some of which are general and others special, and this is set to continue until such time as the US is able to recalibrate its understanding of its economic, energy and security responsibilities to accommodate climate leadership responsibilities, reshape their meaning under the climate regime, or both.[3]

In the final part of the chapter, we reflect on how the politics of special responsibilities have played out since 1992, and explore the implications for the constitution of power in international climate governance and the functionality of the climate regime. Here we respond to Stephen Brooks and William Wohlforth's challenge to constructivists, which is that hegemonic states are less constrained by legitimacy than constructivists aver because they have a disproportionate power to shape the social environment not only through coercion and bribery but also through persuasion, framing and argument.[4] One might therefore expect the US to be in a stronger position than any other state to define and secure the social sanctioning of responsibilities in the climate regime in terms that are concordant with its identity and favourable to its interests and *other* special and general responsibilities. However, we show that over most of the twenty-year negotiating history of the climate regime, the US has made very little headway in reshaping the formal meaning of special responsibilities for developed countries

---

[3] By 'climate regime' we are referring to the UNFCCC, the Kyoto Protocol and the negotiations for the LCA treaty, which are conducted by the parties to the UNFCCC. All of these agreements seek to further the basic goals of the UNFCCC and therefore may be considered part of the one regime, in the same way as the various World Trade Organization agreements are all considered part of the one multilateral trading regime.

[4] S. G. Brooks and W. C. Wohlforth, *World out of balance: International relations and the challenge of American primacy* (Princeton, NJ: Princeton University Press, 2008), especially p. 180.

in ways that reduce expectations about the proper responsibilities that belong to the US (or other developed countries), although its shirking of these responsibilities has weakened the collective effort by developed countries to discharge theirs. The US has therefore not been able to convert its superior communicative capacity into persuasive communicative power.

We also show that US participation has become increasingly important to the functionality of the climate regime, and that the sheer size of its 'emissions power' has overshadowed the European Union's (EU) 'normative power' in shaping the Copenhagen Accord, and the ongoing negotiations for an LCA treaty. The US is also gradually gaining support for the construction of a new set of special responsibilities for major emitters in the developing world in the light of China's rapid economic growth and energy appetite over the past decade and a half, although these arguments are far from officially recognised and are vehemently rejected by China. China's rising aggregate emissions have also given it more bargaining power in the negotiations, which it has used to block efforts to ascribe any international (as distinct from voluntary) commitments on developing countries. The irony is that China has done more to discharge the new set of responsibilities conferred on it by the US than the US has done in meeting its formally recognised special responsibilities.

In terms of future prospects, we see little likelihood of an equilibrium point being reached in the near future over the ascription and acceptance of old special responsibilities by the US or new ones by China. This may change in the medium term if the US is able to re-evaluate its traditional special and general responsibilities to accommodate climate concerns and/or if China is able to fulfil the ambitious low-carbon growth revolution envisaged in its latest five year plan. Each of these developments would considerably enhance the political and institutional capacity of the US and China to accept their respective special responsibilities. This would reinvigorate the social status of traditional special responsibilities under the UNFCCC and provide a basis for the collective negotiation of a new set for a new category of states: major emitters in the developing world. Over the longer term, the old division between developed and developing countries may be overshadowed by the new division between major emitters and the rest.

The allocation of special responsibilities

The notion of differentiated environmental responsibilities has numerous antecedents, and can be traced to the UN Conference on the Human

Environment held at Stockholm in 1972, where the special circumstances and difficulties experienced by developing countries in managing environmental demands in the face of unmet development needs were acknowledged.[5] The notion of differentiated environmental responsibilities has since evolved to include differentiated substantive obligations, differentiated compliance with common obligations and differentiated support to enable developing countries to comply with their (common or differentiated) obligations, or for general capacity-building.[6] The Basel Convention 1989 provides a clear example of differentiated obligations. The past practice of rich countries dumping hazardous waste in poor countries led to the complete prohibition of hazardous waste exports from developed to developing countries while allowing developed countries to export hazardous waste to other developed countries on the basis of prior informed consent. The 1987 Montreal Protocol on Substances that Deplete the Ozone Layer provides a clear example of differential compliance and support. Article 5 of the Montreal Protocol enabled developing countries consuming less than a specified amount of chlorofluorocarbons to delay compliance for ten years under certain conditions (the differential compliance dimension) while developed countries were obliged to contribute to a Multilateral Fund for the Implementation of the Montreal Protocol which was used to pay the full incremental costs of developing countries fulfilling their obligations (the special responsibility and differential support dimension). As Matthew Hoffman explains, the Montreal Protocol 'enshrined the common but differentiated responsibility principle and solidified an altered set of expectations about the appropriate way to address global environmental problems'.[7]

However, it was not until the Earth Summit at Rio de Janeiro in 1992 that differentiated environmental responsibilities were consolidated in the language of 'common but differentiated responsibilities'. This was forcefully expressed in Principle 7 of the Rio Declaration, which provides, inter alia, that:

[5] See, for example, P. G. Harris, 'Common but differentiated responsibility: The Kyoto Protocol and United States policy', *New York University Environmental Law Journal*, 7(1) 1999, 27–48; C. D. Stone, 'Common but differentiated responsibilities in international law', *American Journal of International Law*, 98(2) 2004, 276–301; and C. Okereke, 'Equity norms in global environmental governance', *Global Environmental Politics*, 8(3) 2008, 25–50.

[6] The practice of allowing developing countries more generous compliance timetables, and the acknowledgement of the need for capacity-building for developing countries, have also emerged in other policy domains. For example, the principle of 'special and differential treatment' is now considered a core principle of the multilateral trading system.

[7] M. J. Hoffman, *Ozone depletion and climate change: Constructing a global response* (Albany, NY: State University of New York Press, 2005), p. 120.

In view of the different contributions to global environmental degradation, States have common but differentiated responsibilities. The developed countries acknowledge the responsibility that they bear in the international pursuit [of] sustainable development in view of the pressures their societies place on the global environment and of the technologies and financial resources they command.[8]

The UNFCCC likewise enlists CBDR in Article 3(1) but adds 'equity' and differentiated capabilities to the mix:

The Parties should protect the climate system for the benefit of present and future generations of humankind, on the basis of equity and in accordance with their common but differentiated responsibilities and capabilities. Accordingly, the developed country parties should take the lead in combating climate change and the adverse effects thereof.[9]

The special responsibilities under the UNFCCC are *leadership* responsibilities, which arise from the principles of CBDR. These principles are not explicitly defined, but the UNFCCC preamble sets the interpretive context by noting, inter alia, 'that the largest share of historical and current global emissions of greenhouse gases has originated in developed countries, that per capita emissions in developing countries are still relatively low and that the share of global emissions originating in developing countries will grow to meet their social and development needs'.[10] Article 4(2)(a) requires developed countries to undertake policies and measures that demonstrate that they are taking the lead in reducing emissions while Article 4(3) requires developed countries to provide the financial resources (including technology transfer) to enable developing countries to meet their commitments.

CBDR represents an alternative to the more generalised polluter pays principle (PPP), which never found its way into the UNFCCC, despite its presence in the Rio Declaration and its obvious relevance to climate change. The Organisation for Economic Co-operation and Development (OECD) formulation of the PPP in the early 1970s had recognised exceptions for developing countries in the form of assistance to reduce the costs faced by local polluters in conforming to harmonised environmental regulations.[11] However, the idea that all polluters, rich

---

[8] United Nations Environment Programme, Rio Declaration on Environment and Development, 1992, www.unep.org/Documents.Multilingual/Default.asp?documen tid=78&articleid=1163 (accessed 8 August 2011).

[9] United Nations Framework Convention on Climate Change.

[10] Provisions in the body of the Convention also make special mention of the development needs, and the special vulnerability to climate change, of developing countries, such as Articles 3(2), 3(3) and 4(5).

[11] OECD, Joint Working Party on Trade and Environment, 'The polluter-pays principle as it relates to international trade', COM/ENV/TD(2001)44/FINAL, 23 December 2002, pp. 31–2.

and poor, should accept their common responsibility for climate change made no headway at the Rio Earth Summit. Despite lone efforts by the Alliance of Small Island States (AOSIS) to include PPP,[12] developed countries rejected the PPP because of worries over legal liability and the likely costs they would incur while developing countries preferred CBDR because it acknowledged the greater historical responsibility of developed countries as carbon polluters and provided headroom for developing countries to pursue their development needs.

The UNFCCC requirement that developed countries take the lead in mitigation provides both an *ethical and functional* division of labour between developed and developing countries. The developed countries are not only the most causally responsible, as a group, for cumulative emissions to date but also the most capable in terms of their ability to pursue mitigation and adaptation, and thereby ensure regime functionality. These special responsibilities are owed to the international community as a whole, but particularly to its most vulnerable members, who are the least responsible for climate change, the most exposed to the risks of climate change and the least capable of adapting.

The developed countries' leadership responsibilities under the climate regime provide a fundamental deviation from the traditional liberal contractual norms of multilateralism based on generalised principles of conduct, diffuse reciprocity and a rough equivalence of benefits over time.[13] Indeed, CBDR has been described and defended as a version of 'international affirmative action' for developing countries.[14] As Adil Najam has explained, 'developing countries have consistently contextualised environmental issues as being part of the larger complex of North-South concerns, particularly concerns about an iniquitous international order and their desire to bring about structural change in that order'.[15] Although developing countries failed in their efforts to create a New International Economic Order in the 1970s, closing the yawning gap between wealth, income and opportunities between North and South has remained an overriding priority of China and the Group of 77 (G77). Developing countries' support for the UNFCCC therefore depended on

[12] J. W. Ashe, R. Van Lierop and A. Cherian, 'The role of the Alliance of Small Island States (AOSIS) in the negotiation of the United Nations Framework Convention on Climate Change (UNFCCC)', *Natural Resources Forum*, 23(3) 1999, 215.

[13] J. G. Ruggie, 'Multilateralism: The anatomy of an institution', *International Organisation*, 46(3) 1992, 571.

[14] P. Cullet, 'Differential treatment in international law: Towards a new paradigm of interstate relations', *European Journal of International Law*, 10(3) 1999, 549–82.

[15] A. Najam, 'The view from the South: developing countries in global environmental politics', in R. S. Axelrod, D. L. Downie and N. J. Vig (eds.), *The global environment: Institutions, law and policy* (Washington, DC: CQ Press, 2005), p. 232.

general acceptance of the principle that their development aspirations would not be sacrificed at the altar of climate protection. From the perspective of developing countries, requiring tit-for-tat emissions reductions between North and South would have enabled the North to 'kick the ladder down', and freeze-frame structural global inequalities.[16]

The principles of CBDR, and the leadership responsibilities to which they give rise, also serve as moral touchstones for wider international debates about climate justice, burden-sharing and the adequacy of individual country commitments among the thousands of non-state stakeholders that are admitted as observers to the annual Conferences of the Parties (COP) and other meetings.[17] Aid, environmental, development and humanitarian non-governmental organisations (NGOs) have been in the forefront of calling for climate leadership by developed countries, particularly the US, on the basis of their significantly greater responsibility and capacity. Key examples include Climate Action Network, which is a worldwide network of over 450 NGOs campaigning to promote strong action to prevent dangerous climate change,[18] Oxfam International and Friends of the Earth, which is the world's largest grassroots environmental and social network.[19]

The developed countries' special responsibilities under the UNFCCC are *positive* obligations that require them to lead the way in mitigation and to provide financial and other forms of assistance to developing countries to enable them to pursue both mitigation and adaptation. However, they provide no corresponding rights or privileges that might be seen to compensate for, or enable the performance of, these obligations.[20] It could be argued that the so-called 'flexibility mechanisms' in the Kyoto

[16] See, for example, Harris, 'Common but differentiated responsibility'; and Najam, 'The view from the South'.

[17] These include intergovernmental organisations (IGOs), non-governmental organisations (NGOs), research and independent NGOs (RINGOs) and business and industry NGOs (BINGOs).

[18] Climate Action Network-International has endorsed CBDR, called for developed countries to commit to reduction targets of more than 40 per cent by 2020, and argued that '[r]eductions for individual countries should be assigned based on historic and present responsibility for emissions as well as current capacity to reduce emissions'. Climate Action Network-International, 'Fair, ambitious and binding: Essentials for a successful climate deal' (Climate Action Network-International, 2007), pp. 3–4, www.climatenetwork.org/sites/default/files/CAN_FAB_Essentials_1.pdf (accessed 27 July 2011).

[19] Oxfam International, 'Climate shame: Get back to the table', Oxfam Briefing Note, 21 December 2009, www.oxfam.org/sites/www.oxfam.org/files/briefing-note-climate-shame-get-back-to-the-table.pdf (accessed 27 July 2011); Friends of the Earth International, 'Our climate demands', 2009, www.foei.org/en/what-we-do/un-climate-talks/global/2009/our-demands-in-copenhagen (accessed 27 July 2011).

[20] The language of rights is generally avoided in the UNFCCC. According to Article 3(4) of the UNFCCC, all parties have a right to, and should promote, sustainable

Protocol – emissions trading, joint implementation and the clean development mechanism (CDM) – constitute special rights or privileges. These mechanisms formed part of the grand bargain upon which the Kyoto Protocol was based: the Bill Clinton–Al Gore US negotiating team reluctantly accepted that developing countries would not be required to commit to mandatory targets in return for considerable flexibility for developed countries in meeting their targets. The EU, which had initially opposed carbon trading, later emerged as its biggest champion by pioneering a regional emissions trading scheme.[21]

However, these flexibility mechanisms were negotiated in 1997, not 1992 when special responsibilities were originally negotiated, so they do not form part of the original special responsibilities package and therefore cannot be seen as essential for their performance. Rather, they simply make performance easier and cheaper than it would otherwise have been. Indeed, many environmental movement critics of carbon trading have claimed that they have made performance too easy, and have effectively enabled many developed countries to shirk their special leadership responsibilities by postponing domestic action in mitigation and achieving emissions reductions via the international carbon market through carbon trading and/or offsetting under the CDM. Moreover, in theory at least, developing countries are also free to embark upon international carbon trading once they decide to impose a national cap on emissions, so this particular flexibility mechanism cannot be said to be uniquely attached to developed countries as the holders of special leadership responsibilities.

We saw in Chapter 2 that negative special responsibilities with empowering rights are more attractive than positive ones without such rights, and this is certainly borne out in this case study given the distance that many developed countries have yet to travel to fulfil them. Indeed, only a minority of developed states have positively embraced their special responsibilities. Germany (from the outset) and the United Kingdom (since the mid-2000s) have actively sought to fulfil their leadership responsibilities by setting an example in terms of policy output and future commitments, and taking on a disproportionate share of mitigation within the EU. Most developed states, however, have displayed much lower levels of commitment and implementation and have

development, but there is no specific right to development, or a right to receive assistance, by developing countries despite the acknowledgement of their development needs, and strong expectation that assistance should be provided.

[21] L. Cass, 'Norm entrapment and preference change: The evolution of the European Union position on international emissions trading', *Global Environmental Politics*, 5(2) 2005, 38–60.

found their leadership responsibilities to be rather burdensome – and none more so than the US.[22]

Does the US possess 'extra special responsibilities'?

Climate leadership responsibilities attach to any state that qualifies as a developed state.[23] Yet it does not necessarily follow that all developed countries parties to the UNFCCC have the same special responsibilities or that they must discharge them in exactly the same way. In debates about developed countries' leadership responsibilities, it is clear that the parties do not expect New Zealand or Portugal to fulfil the same leadership responsibilities as the US or Germany. Significant differences in national circumstances among developed countries are acknowledged but these differences have also made it difficult to reach agreement on a principled approach to the articulation and implementation of leadership responsibilities. This was demonstrated in the negotiation of quantified emissions reduction targets under the Kyoto Protocol, where the idea of uniform reduction targets quickly gave way to individually negotiated targets. During this process, many developed states enlisted arguments about differentiated responsibilities and capacities (both genuinely and disingenuously) to justify more lenient targets. This included arguments about differences in the relative effort that would be required to achieve emissions reductions. So instead of agreeing to a total carbon budget for developed countries based on scientific recommendations and allocating commitments based on a principled application of CBDR, the targets negotiated at Kyoto were based on what each individual country considered that they should or could manage. As a result, the combined developed country targets that emerged from Kyoto bore little relationship to scientific recommendations.

Nonetheless, just as CBDR provides a principled justification for a fair and functionally efficacious division of labour between developed

---

[22] For an overview of national climate policy performance, see P. Christoff and R. Eckersley, 'Comparative state responses', in J. S. Dryzek, R. B. Norgaard and D. Schlosberg (eds.), *The Oxford handbook of climate and society* (Oxford: Oxford University Press, 2011), pp. 431–48.

[23] The category 'developed state' is not as straightforward as it might first appear. The UNFCCC contains two annexes. Annex I contains a list of 'developed countries and other parties' (the 'other' being industrialised countries in Central and Eastern Europe undergoing a transition to a market economy), while Annex II contains a list of twenty-three developed countries (plus the European Economic Community), all of which were OECD members in 1992. While Article 3(1) imposes the leadership responsibility only on developed country parties, which are listed in Annex II, the countries that undertook quantified emissions reductions targets under the Kyoto Protocol are those listed in Annex I.

and developing countries, it also provides the most obvious basis for a further division of responsibility among developed countries. Indeed, the international community (both the parties as well as non-state actors such as climate scientists and environment and development NGOs) has looked to the US, more than any other state, to fulfil its climate leadership responsibilities. This is not only because the US is the most (historically) responsible and most capable state but also because the discharge of its leadership responsibilities would make the biggest single difference to the success of the climate regime.

Although China overtook the US as the world's largest aggregate emitter in 2006, the US is responsible for the largest share of cumulative emissions since the industrial revolution (around 30 per cent) and it is in the top league of per capita emitters. The US also has the largest economy and the largest financial, technological and administrative capabilities of any state. US leadership would not only produce the most significant national reduction in emissions among developed states but also galvanise action in other developed countries through the force of example as well as the sheer international pulling power of the US economy. Such leadership would also increase the moral and political pressure on the major emerging emitters in the developing world to undertake international commitments since, once climate leadership has been demonstrated by the developed world, then developing countries would be expected to follow. While the special responsibilities to lead in mitigation belong to all developed countries, the ethical and functional arguments that underpin these responsibilities have produced much higher expectations about US leadership than any other developed state.[24] In terms of the ascription of leadership responsibilities, then, it could be said that the US has 'extra special leadership responsibilities'.

The problem, as we shall see, is that the US has been very reluctant to embrace its leadership responsibilities. In effect, the UNFCCC has written a collective job description for climate leadership by developed countries based on the criteria of historical responsibility and capabilities that draws attention to the US as the number one candidate, but the US does not really want the job (and arguably cannot perform the

---

[24] This point is demonstrated by the responsibility and capacity index prepared by EcoEquity, the Stockholm Environment Institute and Christian Aid, which shows the US's obligation to be considerably higher than any other country, and greater than the combined obligation of all twenty-seven EU members. See P. Baer, T. Athanasiou, S. Kartha and E. Kemp-Benedict, *The greenhouse development rights framework: The right to development in a climate constrained world*, rev. 2nd edn (Berlin: Heinrich Böll Foundation, Christian Aid, EcoEquity and the Stockholm Environment Institute, 2008), especially p. 58.

job given domestic political constraints). The dominant view among US political elites has been that the UNFCCC has created a set of international expectations about US climate leadership that are especially burdensome and unrealistic, since the US's special responsibilities carry no compensating privileges, are likely to facilitate China's economic rise while imposing additional costs to US industry, generate significant domestic political turmoil, and clash with other foreign and domestic priorities. Not surprisingly, as we shall see, the US has played a key role in contesting special responsibilities throughout the evolution of the climate regime.

The evolution and contestation of special responsibilities

The principles of CBDR, and the leadership responsibilities of developed countries to which they give rise, have been repeatedly reaffirmed by the parties throughout the twenty-year history of climate negotiations as the official burden-sharing principles of the climate regime. At the first Conference of the Parties (COP1) to the UNFCCC held in Berlin in 1995, the parties agreed on a mandate for the negotiation of a legally binding protocol that explicitly stated that the negotiations were to be guided by CBDR. The 'Berlin mandate' acknowledged 'the legitimate needs of developing countries for the achievement of sustained economic growth and the eradication of poverty', and repeated the parts of the UNFCCC preamble 'that the largest share of historical and current global emissions of greenhouse gases has originated in developed countries, that the per capita emissions in developing countries are still relatively low and that the share of global emissions originating in developing countries will grow to meet their social and development needs'.[25] This was also the crucial stage when it was agreed that only the Annex I parties (the developed country parties and the Central and Eastern European countries undergoing a transition to a market economy) would be required to take on legally binding emission reduction targets under the new Protocol in the first commitment period. The Kyoto Protocol also explicitly reaffirmed the principle of CBDR (Article 10) and restricted the obligation to undertake legally binding, quantified emission reduction targets to Annex I countries for the commitment period 2008–12.

---

[25] UNFCCC, 'Report of the Conference of the Parties on its First Session, held at Berlin from 28 March to 7 April 1995', FCCC/CP/1995/7/Add.1, 6 June 1995, paragraphs 1(a), 1(c) and 1(d), unfccc.int/resource/docs/cop1/07a01.pdf (accessed 27 July 2011).

CBDR was also reaffirmed in the 2007 Bali Action Plan for the negotiation of the LCA treaty, which was designed to draw the US back into the regime.[26] Again, only developed countries were required to adopt 'quantified emission limitation and reduction objectives'. The Action Plan requires developing countries merely to take 'nationally appropriate mitigation actions' (NAMAs) that do not amount to mandatory targets or aggregate emissions reductions.[27] This work programme was supposed to be completed by COP15 in Copenhagen in 2009 but no legal treaty was concluded. However, the first paragraph of the short, non-binding Copenhagen Accord that emerged from this meeting reiterated the parties' 'strong political will to urgently combat climate change in accordance with the principle of common but differentiated responsibilities and respective capabilities'.[28] The report of the parties from COP16 in Cancún in 2010 repeats the principles of CBDR and calls on developed country parties to show leadership 'by undertaking ambitious emission reductions and providing technology, capacity-building and financial resources to developing country Parties, in accordance with the relevant provisions of the Convention'.[29]

Clearly, the developed countries' leadership responsibilities have maintained their formally recognised status over nearly two decades of negotiations. At the same time, these leadership responsibilities have been poorly fleshed out in terms of detail, and remain contested, particularly by many of the developed countries that are supposed to shoulder them. The signing of the Kyoto Protocol represents the parties' best efforts to implement special responsibilities to date but, as we have seen, the parties were unable to agree on a principled application of CBDR to guide the allocation of Kyoto targets *among* Annex I countries. Likewise, despite the radical differences between the least developed countries and the rapidly growing economies in the developing world, there was no agreement on a formula as to how

---

[26] UNFCCC/CP, Bali Action Plan (Decision 1/CP.13), FCCC/CP/2007/6/Add.1, paragraphs 1(b)(i) and 1(b)(ii)(b). Virtually all the country delegates interviewed by Steven Bernstein at the annual conferences between 2005 and 2007 'emphasized that the legitimacy of the KP depended on developed countries taking the lead and differentiation of commitments, although views diverged on timing, scope, distribution, and financing of those commitments'. S. Bernstein, 'Legitimacy in intergovernmental and non-state global governance', *Review of International Political Economy*, 18(1) 2011, 33.

[27] UNFCCC/CP, Bali Action Plan, paragraphs 1(b)(i) and 1(b)(ii)(b).

[28] UNFCCC/CP, Copenhagen Accord, 18 December 2009, FCCC/CP/2009/L.7/CP.15, paragraph 1.

[29] UNFCCC, 'Report of the Conference of the Parties on its Sixteenth Session, held in Cancún from 29 November to 10 December 2010', FCCC/CP/2010/7/Add.1, 15 March 2011, paragraphs 1 and 2.

the latter might 'graduate' to Annex I, and thereby assume special responsibilities.

The significant differences in responsibility, capability and vulnerability on either side of the Annex I/non-Annex I divide continue to serve as a bone of contention. Indeed, if we return to each of the key words in Article 3(1) of the UNFCCC – 'equity', 'responsibilities' and 'capabilities' – it is clear that there is considerable scope for different interpretations which have been exploited by both developed and developing countries. For example, equity has been interpreted to include a right of developing countries to develop, an equal right of individuals to a sustainable livelihood or a right to a certain sustainable portion of atmospheric space.[30] Some members of the Umbrella Group[31] have suggested a principle of 'equality of effort' in mitigation and adaptation by developed countries (for example, New Zealand). The principle of responsibility has been interpreted to mean historical responsibility for cumulative emissions since the industrial revolution (a strict application of the PPP), responsibility for benefits derived from cumulative emissions (the beneficiary pays principle),[32] responsibility for high aggregate and per capita emissions and responsibility for rapidly growing future emissions. The latter has been a key claim of the US. Likewise, capabilities have been interpreted to mean economic and institutional capacity to take action (using gross domestic product as a simple proxy measure) or simply relative opportunity to take action based on different national circumstances, such as differences in energy resources endowments and energy and policy histories, population growth, extra heating or cooling costs in hot or cold climates, and national transport infrastructure.[33] So, for example, those developed countries that had already committed to efficiency measures prior to the UNFCCC have

---

[30] The latter is reflected in the popular model of contraction and convergence. See A. Meyer, *Contraction and convergence: The global solution to climate change* (Dartington: Green Books, 2000).

[31] The Umbrella Group emerged during the negotiation of the Kyoto Protocol out of the pre-Kyoto JUSSCANNZ group which represented Japan, the US, Switzerland, Canada, Australia, Norway and New Zealand. Switzerland now belongs to the small Environmental Integrity Group, with Mexico and South Korea, neither of which are Annex I parties. The Umbrella Group is now made up of Australia, Canada, Iceland, Japan, New Zealand, Norway, the Russian Federation, Ukraine and the US.

[32] It is often pointed out that developed countries were not aware that their emissions were causing harm until at least the late 1980s, and therefore should only be required to take responsibility for emissions after then.

[33] For a fuller discussion of these and other interpretations, see M. Heywood, 'Equity and international climate change negotiations: A matter of perspective', *Climate Policy*, 7(6) 2007, 518–34 and E. Page, 'Distributing the burdens of climate change', *Environmental Politics*, 17(4) 2008, 556–75.

less opportunity to improve energy efficiency at low marginal cost than countries that are currently relatively inefficient.

These examples by no means exhaust the range of ethical and political disagreements over the range of possible interpretations of CBDR, and concomitant meaning of leadership responsibilities, but they are sufficient to highlight the scope for disagreement. Nonetheless, CBDR have been routinely invoked by both state and non-state actors to *judge the adequacy* of individual developed country commitments and performance under the Kyoto Protocol, as well as the more recent Copenhagen pledges. The principles of CBDR continue to provide the yardstick by which successful climate leaders have been identified and praised, and failed climate leaders or laggards have been 'named and shamed' for reinterpreting or shirking their special responsibilities. Predictably, developing countries, particularly the more vulnerable ones, are in the forefront of ascribing these leadership responsibilities and calling on developed countries to account for their actions. Although these are positive special responsibilities with no corresponding rights or privileges, no developed country has engaged in outright denial of them, although there are plenty of instances of shirking and/or reinterpreting the responsibilities, for which the US is the chief example.

The political dynamics of the negotiating blocs

China and the G77, but especially its most vulnerable sub-groupings such as AOSIS (which represents small island countries as well as low-lying countries), the African Group and the least developed countries, have been the strongest proponents of leadership responsibilities for developed countries. Indeed, China and the G77's ongoing participation in the negotiations have been dependent upon an ongoing commitment to developed country leadership. China and the G77 have played key roles in upholding the Annex I/non-Annex I division and insisting on developed country leadership, including 2020 targets at the upper end of the range recommended by the IPCC (that is, emissions reductions of minus 25 to 40 per cent from a 1990 baseline). They have also staunchly rejected the idea of aggregate emissions cuts for developing countries in view of their development needs, rejected the imposition of any international obligations (as distinct from undertaking voluntary NAMAs), and rejected the argument that these national measures should be subject to external review. For China and the G77, developed countries must fulfil their leadership responsibilities by *demonstrating* leadership before developing countries can be expected to take on any major international commitments.

Among the developed countries, the members of the EU have more or less embraced their leadership responsibilities. The EU has also led the developed world in climate policy commitments and policy output, despite considerable unevenness in domestic implementation among member states and ongoing criticisms about loopholes in the European emissions trading scheme.[34] In contrast, the enthusiasm for climate leadership responsibilities among the members of the loose coalition known as the Umbrella Group has been much more reserved, with the exception of Norway and Japan. Among the members of this group, the US (supported for a period by Australia) has mounted the strongest critique of both CBDR and the special responsibilities to which they give rise under the Kyoto Protocol, culminating in the George W. Bush administration's repudiation of the Kyoto Protocol in 2001.[35] Despite playing a major role in shaping many of its key provisions (such as the flexibility mechanisms mentioned above), the US has rejected the bifurcated structure of the Kyoto Protocol precisely because it imposes special responsibilities to pursue mandatory emission reduction targets on the Annex I parties while absolving non-Annex I parties of any international commitments to reduce emissions. Highlighting the trans-Atlantic divide on this issue, the US has rejected the Kyoto Protocol as Eurocentric and, by implication, unAmerican.[36] This repudiation has enabled the EU to emerge as the recognised 'climate leader' in the developed country group as much by default as by exemplary policy performance on the EU's part, with the US serving as the significant 'other' against which EU policies and future commitments are compared.[37]

[34] See, for example, J. Gupta and M. Grubb (eds.), *Climate change and European leadership: A sustainable role for Europe* (Boston, MA: Kluwer Academic Publishers, 2000); O. Elgström, 'The European Union as a leader in international multilateral negotiations – A problematic aspiration?', *International Relations*, 21(4) 2007, 445–58; S. Oberthür, 'The European Union in international climate policy: The prospect for leadership', *Intereconomics – Review of European Economic Policy*, 42(2) 2007, 77–83; M. Schreurs and Y. Tiberghien, 'Multi-level reinforcement: Explaining European Union leadership in climate change mitigation', *Global Environmental Politics*, 7(4) 2007, 19–46; J. Vogler and H. R. Stephan, 'The European Union in global environmental governance: Leadership in the making?', *International Environmental Agreements*, 7(4) 2007, 389–413.

[35] Australia ratified the Kyoto Protocol in 2007. Canada also ratified the Kyoto Protocol, but has effectively abandoned its Kyoto target and aligned its policies with the US.

[36] M. Paterson, 'Post-hegemonic climate change?', *British Journal of Politics and International Relations*, 11(1) 2009, 145.

[37] J. Vogler, 'In the absence of the hegemon: EU actorness and the global climate change regime', paper presented to the conference 'The European Union in International Affairs', National Europe Centre, Australian National University, Canberra, 3–4 July 2002, p. 20.

However, as we shall see, the US's critique of special responsibilities has never amounted to a total rejection. Rather, it has sought to reinterpret special responsibilities in ways that require more robust, but still differentiated, commitments by developing countries, and within the *same* commitment period rather than at some future unspecified period. While *formal* special responsibilities have successfully weathered a major US assault, the US has sought to construct an alternative, *informal* and more pragmatic interpretation of special responsibilities which is becoming increasingly influential in the negotiations for the LCA treaty. We shall now track this process from the George H. W. Bush administration through to the Obama administration.

The US response to special responsibilities

The George H. W. Bush administration was generally opposed to the inclusion of core burden-sharing principles in the body of the UNFCCC, and argued that they should be located in the preamble.[38] While the US was eventually persuaded to accept the inclusion of such principles in the UNFCCC legal text, it insisted on language that limited their 'scope, legal implications and precedent value'.[39] The upshot was that the main operative provisions of the UNFCCC reflected the objectives of the US Senate, which was for the US to conclude a treaty 'without targets or timetables for emissions reduction'.[40] The provision in Article 4 that required parties to reduce their emissions to 1990 levels by 2000 was widely regarded as a non-binding, aspirational requirement that was full of qualifications, and the details of how developed countries would fulfil their leadership responsibilities were left open for future negotiations.

However, hints of what was to come were already provided in the interpretive statement lodged by the US delegation at the Earth Summit in relation to the Rio Declaration. First, the US registered its objection to the idea that development is a 'right' as distinct from a goal in relation to Principle 3. Second, in relation to Principle 7, the US accepted the special leadership role of the developed countries based on their industrial development, environmental policy experience and capabilities, but rejected any interpretation that implied 'a recognition or acceptance

---

[38] D. Bodansky, 'The United Nations Framework Convention on Climate Change: A commentary', *Yale Journal of International Law*, 18(2) 1993, 501.

[39] F. Yamin and J. Depledge, *The international climate change regimes: A guide to rules, institutions and procedures* (Cambridge: Cambridge University Press, 2004), p. 67.

[40] Hoffman, *Ozone depletion and climate change*, p. 157.

by the United States of any international obligations or liabilities, or any diminution in the responsibilities of developing countries'.[41] Any acknowledgement of the US's historical responsibility for emissions or damage to third parties, or differences in per capita emissions, was conspicuously absent. This written statement effectively sought to head off any attempt by developing countries to use the climate regime as a vehicle for reviving the push for a New International Economic Order, and to quash any expectations on the part of developing countries that they should enjoy specific legal rights and entitlements flowing from the Rio Declaration and, by implication, the UNFCCC. In sum, the George H. W. Bush administration and Congress acknowledged the US's special *capabilities* to address climate change but rejected the idea that the US had any special *responsibilities* based on its past or present emissions, or the benefits derived from these emissions.

In contrast, the Clinton administration generally affirmed special responsibilities, gave its support to the Berlin Mandate in 1995, and signed the Kyoto Protocol in 1997. Nonetheless, as is well known, the Clinton administration was unable to follow through on any of its key climate commitments owing to strong opposition in Congress. Indeed, the gap between President Clinton's climate aspirations, and the views of Congress, increasingly widened from the time of his inauguration to the Kyoto meeting in 1997 and beyond. Even before the Republicans gained control of both Houses in 1994, Clinton suffered a major Congressional defeat over his attempt to introduce a broad-based tax on fuels, which was his major initiative for fulfilling his pre-election pledge to return US carbon dioxide emissions to 1990 levels by 2000.[42] The Clinton administration's Climate Change Action Plan, which relied on voluntary measures, bore little relationship to the president's climate pledge. The initiative was eventually replaced with a much more modest tax on gasoline.

Since the Berlin COP in 1995, the G77, led by China (and supported by the EU), has resolutely insisted that developing countries should not be expected to undertake any mandatory emissions reductions in the first commitment period. Indeed, at the second COP in Geneva in 1996, developing countries insisted that the Annex I countries should fulfil their leadership commitments *before* the developing

---

[41] UNCED, 'Report of the United Nations Conference on Environment and Development, Rio de Janeiro, 3–14 June 1992', A/CONF.151/26/Rev.1, Vol. II, Proceedings of the Conference, Chapter III, p. 18.

[42] N. Vig, 'Presidential leadership and the environment', in N. J. Vig and M. E. Kraft (eds.), *Environmental policy: New directions for the twenty-first century* (Washington, DC: Congressional Quarterly, 2006), p. 108.

countries would consider undertaking *any* commitments.[43] By the time of the meeting at Kyoto in 1997, the G77 position had hardened to the point of rejecting any language whatsoever in the Protocol that hinted at even *voluntary* commitments by developing countries to limit their emissions. Meanwhile, in the lead up to the Kyoto negotiations, there was also growing disquiet within the Department of State, the Department of Energy and in Congress about the whole concept of the US acting first, and the lack of developing-country commitments in the climate regime.[44] Following the Geneva COP in 1996, Senator Jesse Helms (R-NC) expressed the sentiments of most sceptics in declaring that the Clinton administration's 'position turns basic principles of sound economic policy on its head since it directs industrialized countries to subsidize developing countries by polluting less while incurring higher costs so that developing countries can pollute more without incurring costs'.[45] Many industry groups, including the US Chamber of Commerce, also waged campaigns against the treaty.

However, most observers have singled out as the most decisive event in shaping the US's climate policy future to be the unanimous adoption of the Byrd-Hagel Resolution by the US Senate in July 1997, five months prior to the Kyoto COP. In this resolution the Senate announced that it would not ratify the Protocol if developing countries did not undertake to limit or reduce emissions 'within the same compliance period' *or* if the agreement 'would result in serious harm to the US economy'.[46] A key concern of the senators was that developing countries were being given an *unfair* advantage or 'free ride', that the US economy and employment would suffer and that the treaty would not be effective without the participation of major emitters such as China and India. But this was not an outright rejection of special responsibilities. Most senators accepted that developing countries should not be required to make the same commitments as developed countries, that developed countries had a greater historical responsibility for emissions and greater capabilities to pursue mitigation, that there should be flexibility for developing countries, and that the least developed countries should have the most lenient commitments.[47] However, for the US Senate in 1997, 'taking

---

[43] Hoffman, *Ozone depletion and climate change*, p. 175.

[44] *Ibid.*, pp. 170–1.

[45] J. Helms (R-NC), 'Global climate change', *Congressional Record-Senate* S11490, 27 September 1996, p. 11490, frwebgate.access.gpo.gov/cgi-bin/getpage.cgi?position= all&page=S11490&dbname=1996_record (accessed 27 July 2011).

[46] United States Senate, Byrd-Hagel Resolution, 105th Congress, First Session; S Res 98, Sponsored by Senator Robert Byrd (D-WV) and Senator Chuck Hagel (R-NE), 25 July 1997, www.nationalcenter.org/KyotoSenate.html (accessed 27 July 2011).

[47] Harris, 'Common but differentiated responsibility', 38–42.

the lead' in combating climate change should not mean that the US or other developed countries should 'go it alone'.

The Byrd-Hagel Resolution also made it clear to the Clinton administration that it would not ratify a treaty that committed the US to anything more than a zero increase in emissions from 1990 levels by 2012 *and* only if developing countries also undertook commitments. In an effort to appease the Senate, Clinton's negotiators at Kyoto asked merely for *voluntary* commitments from developing countries (excluding the least developed countries) in the same time period to 'abate the increase' in emissions but not so as to impede economic development.[48] However, these proposals were flatly rejected by the G77, led by China. In the end, under pressure particularly from the EU and as a result of late hour interventions by Vice-President Al Gore at Kyoto, the US negotiators agreed to a target of a 7 per cent reduction in emissions, which was only 1 per cent lower than the European's collective target of an 8 per cent reduction. Instead of insisting on developing-country commitments in the same time period, the quid pro quo for the US was to insist on greater flexibility for parties to meet their commitments – in the form of international carbon trading, joint implementation with other Annex I countries and international carbon offsetting through the CDM. Predictably, the negotiated outcome attracted strong condemnation from the US Congress, and President Clinton avoided any domestic showdown by declining to submit the Kyoto Protocol for Senate approval. Nonetheless, during subsequent COPs, where the parties sought to negotiate the finer legal details of the Kyoto Protocol, the Clinton administration continued to push, unsuccessfully, for more 'meaningful participation' by key developing countries in the hope of selling the treaty domestically.

The inauguration of President George W. Bush junior saw a significant shift in the US's international posture towards special responsibilities. His letter to the Senate in March 2001, which explained his repudiation of the Kyoto Protocol, set the scene for the remainder of his tenure: 'As you know, I oppose the Kyoto Protocol because it exempts 80 percent of the world, including major population centers such as China and India, from compliance, and would cause serious harm to the US economy.'[49] The Bush administration also highlighted the uncertainty of climate change science and called upon the National

---

[48] *Ibid.*, 44–5.
[49] G. W. Bush, 'Text of a Letter from the President to Senators Hagel, Helms, Craig, and Roberts', 13 March 2001, www.gcrio.org/OnLnDoc/pdf/bush_letter010313.pdf (accessed 1 August 2011).

Academy of Sciences to review the state of climate science. However, the Bush administration subsequently excised the climate change chapter before the report was released because it had affirmed the findings of the second IPCC assessment report.[50]

Although the Bush administration had withdrawn from the Kyoto Protocol, it remained a party to the UNFCCC and therefore, in principle at least, committed to special responsibilities. However, the Bush administration went to considerable lengths to reinterpret these responsibilities in ways that required no real sacrifice or burden to the US. In formally announcing the administration's 'Clear Skies Initiative and Global Climate Change Initiative' in 2002, President Bush declared:

> As President of the United States, charged with safeguarding the welfare of the American people and American workers, I will not commit our nation to an unsound international treaty that will throw millions of our citizens out of work. Yet, we recognize our international responsibilities. So in addition to acting here at home, the United States will actively help developing nations grow along a more efficient, more environmentally responsible path.[51]

Bush's solution to taking action without sacrificing economic growth (for both the US *and* for developing countries) was to pursue a reduction in greenhouse gas (GHG) emission intensity (the amount of emissions per unit of gross domestic product), rather than aggregate emissions reductions from an historical baseline. This approach was disingenuously defended by Bush as superior to absolute emissions reductions for developing countries because it 'recognizes their right to economic development'. As he explained:

> It would be unfair – indeed, counterproductive – to condemn developing nations to slow growth or no growth by insisting that they take on impractical and unrealistic greenhouse gas targets. Yet, developing nations such as China and India already account for a majority of the world's greenhouse gas emissions, and it would be irresponsible to absolve them from shouldering some of the shared obligations.[52]

The Bush administration's response was effectively to replace the idea of differentiated responsibilities with 'mutual burden-sharing' based on its own 'pro-growth' emissions intensity approach. This was defended

[50] K. Harrison, 'The road not taken: Climate change policy in Canada and the United States', *Global Environmental Politics*, 7(4) 2007, 105; National Academy of Science, *Climate change science: An analysis of some key questions* (Washington, DC: National Academy Press, 2001).

[51] White House, 'President announces clear skies and global climate change initiatives', Silver Spring, Maryland, 14 February 2002, georgewbush-whitehouse.archives.gov/news/releases/2002/02/20020214–5.html (accessed 27 July 2011).

[52] *Ibid.*

as 'fairer' than the Kyoto Protocol's 'anti-growth' approach because it protected the legitimate development aspirations of developing countries. However, it did not require any additional obligations on the part of the US. Reducing emissions intensity via technological innovation is hardly a 'burden' or responsibility given that improvements in energy efficiency *increase* rather than reduce economic productivity. Indeed, emissions intensity has been in gradual decline in most economies, including in the US, owing to general efficiency improvements. The Bush administration's own target of improving the emissions intensity of the US economy by 18 per cent by 2012 largely through voluntary measures and technology development was only slightly above forecasts based on a business-as-usual scenario and therefore provided only a modest 'stretch' target.[53] In effect, 'mutual burden-sharing' enabled the US to avoid any costs of adjustment, and effectively place the economic and development interests of the US and developing countries on an equal moral footing. Yet the Bush administration's climate policy initiatives failed to put a price on carbon or impose any regulatory limits on the use of fossil fuels and therefore were not able to reduce the US's aggregate emissions. Indeed, these initiatives were largely overshadowed by its National Energy Strategy, which focused primarily on increasing the domestic and foreign supply of (mainly fossil fuel) energy, rather than reducing domestic demand.

On the international front, the Bush administration sought to undermine the Kyoto Protocol by developing 'environmental coalitions of the willing', in the form of voluntary partnerships for clean technology development that cut across the developed/developing country divide. The most significant of these partnerships was the Asia-Pacific Partnership on Clean Development and Climate 2006 (APP), although the US has negotiated voluntary partnerships with a total of fifteen countries and regional organisations.[54] While the APP prompted no defections from the Kyoto Protocol, and enjoyed the support of China and India, it rested on a radically different understanding of responsibilities than the Kyoto Protocol. Instead of focusing on equity, historical responsibility, capabilities, or the ethical implications of cumulative

[53] J. Depledge, 'Against the grain: The United States and the global climate change regime', *Global Change, Peace and Security*, 17(1) 2005, 23.

[54] These include Australia, Brazil, Canada, China, CONCAUSA (an organisation of seven Central American countries), EU, Germany, India, Italy, Japan, Mexico, New Zealand, South Korea, the Russian Federation and South Africa. See J. McGee and R. Taplin, 'The Asia-Pacific Partnership on Clean Development and Climate: A Complement or Competitor to the Kyoto Protocol?', *Global Change, Peace and Security*, 18(3) 2006, 173–92.

per capita emissions, the APP effectively erased the past and focused on reducing emissions intensity in the future through technological innovation and transfer. The APP was based on market-friendly procedural norms of equality of commercial opportunity.[55] It was intended as a 'win-win' partnership that imposed no sacrifices or significant costs on any of the partners, but nor did it address the fundamental problem of rising aggregate emissions or responsibility for cumulative emissions. China and India had nothing to lose in joining the partnership, but reiterated their commitment to the Kyoto Protocol.

In his last year of office, President Bush sought to pre-empt the post-Kyoto negotiations by announcing a more ambitious framework for cooperation that included the fifteen biggest energy consumers and GHG emitters in the developed and developing world. Described as a 'post-Kyoto' framework on climate change, this initiative, like the APP, sought to cut across the developed/developing country division of responsibility by focusing on technological solutions based on the twin goals of energy security and economic growth. The Bush administration remained opposed to a national emissions trading scheme for the US, although in its final year of office it announced plans to cap US carbon dioxide emissions by 2025.

In sum, the George W. Bush administration sought to supplant CBDR with an alternative framing of 'mutual burden-sharing' that effectively denied the issue of historical responsibility and focused instead on reducing the rate of increase of future emissions through technological innovation. The intent was clearly to widen the holders of special responsibilities and dilute the obligations, conceding the US's special technological capabilities but denying its special historical responsibilities. This approach was also consistent with US domestic climate policy and provided no challenge to cognate policies in the domains of energy, security, finance and macroeconomics. Nonetheless, the 110th Congress saw a significant increase in the number of climate change bills and debates within Senate and House Committees, although the active supporters of these bills remained a minority. This period also saw the growth in climate initiatives at the sub-state level, including the Regional Greenhouse Gas Initiative involving northeastern states and the enactment of stricter standards for motor vehicle emissions and enforceable GHG reduction targets in California.[56]

[55] McGee and Taplin, 'The Asia-Pacific Partnership', 188; P. Christoff and R. Eckersley, 'Kyoto and the Asia Pacific Partnership on Clean Development and Climate', in T. Bonyhady and P. Christoff (eds.), *Climate law in Australia* (Sydney: Federation Press, 2007), pp. 32–45.
[56] C. Fogel, 'Constructing progressive climate change norms: The US in the early 2000s', in M. Pettenger (ed.), *The social construction of climate change: Power, knowledge,*

The Obama administration: a new era?

The election of Obama in November 2008 marked an important shift towards re-engagement in the multilateral climate negotiations, a broad reaffirmation of CBDR and the US's leadership responsibilities (with some important qualifications) and a general shift in direction in domestic climate policy, including support for national cap-and-trade legislation that imposed an aggregate limit on US emissions. Unlike its predecessor, the Obama administration has acknowledged the US's responsibility to lead based on both historical responsibilities and capabilities. In a pre-election interview, Obama had already indicated that the US should not look for a single tit-for-tat exchange with China and India in emissions reductions but rather that the US, as the largest economy and emitter, has the responsibility 'to take the first step'.[57] Yet he went on to declare:

We cannot expect China and India, with a billion people each, to take the lead on this if we do not – but we can expect them to join us if we demonstrate leadership. If we must take the first step, our second and third steps must be conditioned on meaningful participation by all countries. This is also an enormous opportunity for us to provide our technological expertise to these nations so they can leapfrog to cleaner technologies.[58]

However, the fall-out from the global financial crisis combined with the legacy of the Clinton administration's failure to win domestic support for the international commitments made at Kyoto in 1997, have stalled the Obama administration, muted its domestic advocacy for strong economy-wide mitigation targets, constrained its international leadership and led to efforts to reinterpret special responsibilities in ways that are more compatible with Congressional concerns. The Obama administration and the Democrat's leading sponsor of climate legislation in Congress, Senator John Kerry, have tried to manage these tensions by redefining China's responsibilities and linking progress on the fulfilment of the US's responsibilities to meaningful action by China and other major emitters in the developing world. At no stage has President Obama made any effort to revive and sell

---

norms, discourse (Aldershot: Ashgate, 2007), pp. 99–120; and W. M. Hanemann, 'How California came to pass AB 32, the Global Warming Solutions Act of 2006', Working Paper 1040 (Berkeley, CA: Department of Agricultural and Resource Economics, University of California, 2007).

[57] A. Little, 'Obama on the record: An interview with Barack Obama about his presidential platform on energy and the environment', *Grist: Environmental News and Commentary*, 30 July 2007, grist.org/feature/2007/07/30/obama (accessed 27 July 2011).

[58] *Ibid.*

domestically the US's Kyoto obligation, which would be a Herculean task given the lack of any concerted emissions reduction strategy by his predecessors and the fact that US emissions had risen by 16.8 per cent between 1990 and 2007 even before President Obama had assumed office.[59] However, the president has given his political support for long-term targets through the Group of Eight (G8) decision in July 2009 to support a halving of global emissions by 2050, which requires an 80 per cent reduction in emissions from developed countries during the same time period to allow for growth on the part of developing countries.

The Copenhagen meeting in December 2009 proved to be a significant turning point in the international climate negotiations. The presidential election of Obama had raised international expectations of US leadership that went well beyond the sorts of voluntary partnerships that had been the signature of the previous administration. Indeed, the Copenhagen meeting proved to be one of the most anticipated COPs in the negotiating history of the regime because it was scheduled to deliver a comprehensive new treaty on long-term cooperative action that would include the US, and the new administration had made it clear that it wished to re-engage with the international negotiations. However, expectations were progressively lowered as the conference approached and it became clear that the new administration would not be in a position to commit to targets and policies that were robust enough to fulfil the expectations of the EU, China, the G77 and international civil society. In the end, no binding treaty was delivered, only a short, non-legally binding political accord (the Copenhagen Accord) and a decision to continue the negotiations.

Caught between a reluctant Congress and high international expectations, the Obama administration had to walk a tightrope at Copenhagen, keenly aware that the passage of domestic climate and energy legislation would be dependent upon commitments from China to reduce its growth in emissions and just as keenly aware that China would require strong US domestic climate legislation before it was prepared to undertake any future international commitments. The administration responded by drawing attention to the new 'post-Kyoto environment' and China's rapid emissions growth trajectory as a backdrop for a recalibrated understanding of special responsibilities, one that requires commitments from the major emerging emitters in the

---

[59] This data represents total aggregate GHG emissions for 1990–2007, excluding Land Use, Land-Use Change and Forestry. See UNFCCC, 'GHG data from UNFCCC', unfccc.int/ghg_data/ghg_data_unfccc/items/4146.php (accessed 27 July 2011).

developing world in the same commitment period, rather than at some future, unspecified time *after* the US has demonstrated leadership. The administration has also emphasised that the commitments of the major emerging emitters in the developing world should be transparent.

For example, in a much-anticipated speech delivered at the Opening Plenary Session of the UN Summit on Climate Change in September 2009, in the countdown to the Copenhagen COP15, Obama urged his audience to 'move beyond old divisions'. While acknowledging the special needs of the poorest and most vulnerable developing countries, and the developed countries' responsibility to provide financial and technology transfer to developing countries, he argued that the major emerging emitters in the developing world should shoulder more of the burden. As he explained:

> Yes, the developed nations that caused much of the damage to our climate over the last century still have a responsibility to lead – and that includes the United States. And we will continue to do so – by investing in renewable energy and promoting greater efficiency and slashing our emissions to reach the targets we set for 2020 and our long-term goal for 2050.
>
> But those rapidly growing developing nations that will produce nearly all the growth in global carbon emissions in the decades ahead must do their part, as well ... they need to commit to strong measures at home and agree to stand behind those commitments just as the developed nations must stand behind their own. We cannot meet this challenge unless all the largest emitters of greenhouse gas pollution act together. There's no other way.[60]

Obama's deputy special envoy for climate change, Jonathan Pershing, put the matter even more forcefully during the Bangkok talks in October 2009, declaring that '[t]hings have changed since Kyoto. Where countries were in 1990 and today is very different. We cannot be stuck with an agreement 20 years old. We want action from all countries.'[61] On day three of COP15, Obama's Chief Special Climate Change Envoy Todd Stern was even blunter, declaring to reporters that '[i]t's not a matter of politics or morality or anything else. It's just math. And you cannot get the kind of reductions you need globally if China is not a major player in this.'[62]

---

[60] 'Remarks of the President at United Nations Secretary General Ban Ki-Moon's Climate Change Summit', United Nations Headquarters, New York, 22 September 2009, www.whitehouse.gov/the_press_office/Remarks-by-the-President-at-UN-Secretary-General-Ban-Ki-moons-Climate-Change-Summit (accessed 27 July 2011).

[61] J. Vidal, 'US threatens to derail climate talks by refusing to include targets', *Guardian*, 7 October 2009.

[62] D. Samuelsohn, 'No "pass" for developing countries in next climate treaty, says US envoy', *New York Times*, 9 December 2009.

Senator Kerry's speech at Copenhagen provided a rare acknowledge-ment of the US's historical contribution to aggregate emissions, noting that while the US was not aware of the climate damage it was caus-ing for most of this period, it has known for the last twenty years and that this 'only adds to our responsibility'. However, he also reinforced the president's 'future conditional' affirmation of the US's special responsibilities:

Let me be clear: America will continue to honor the bedrock principles of common but differentiated responsibility. 'Differentiated' means less devel-oped countries can adopt different reduction targets at different rates reflect-ing their economic and energy realities. But let's be honest here: our common responsibility demands that if we're serious about solving climate change, then every country that contributes significantly to the problem today or will con-tribute in the future, must be a part of the solution in a way that is transparent and accountable.[63]

Senator Kerry went on to single out 'rising emissions from others' as 'one of the last barriers to bold American leadership', noting that China's emissions will be 40 per cent larger than America's by 2020.[64]

Making the fulfilment of the US's special (historical) responsibilities conditional on mitigation of *future* emissions by China represents a sig-nificant reframing of CBDR that effectively *produces two sets of special responsibilities* – one for developed countries and another for the major emitters in the developing world. The former arise primarily from past emissions while the latter arise primarily from projected future emis-sions. While the mitigation obligations are not the same in terms of level and rate, the developed countries' commitment to their special responsibilities is made conditional on an international commitment by major developing countries to address their rising future emissions. This not only downplays the independent ethical significance of respon-sibility for cumulative emissions since the mid-nineteenth century, but also erases the significance of differences in per capita emissions and capabilities.

President Obama's much-anticipated address to the plenary session at the Copenhagen conference pursued a similar theme, particularly in pointedly describing the US 'as the world's largest economy and as the world's *second* largest emitter' (emphasis added). He also called upon *all* major economies to 'put forward decisive national actions that will

---

[63] J. Kerry, 'Text of Sen. Kerry's speech at COP15', boston.com, 16 December 2009, www.boston.com/news/world/europe/articles/2009/12/16/text_of_sen_kerrys_speech_at_cop15 (accessed 27 July 2011).

[64] *Ibid.*

reduce their emissions' and underscored the importance of 'transparency' of commitments.[65]

One of the significant new developments at Copenhagen in 2009 was the emergence of the new BASIC group made up of the most significant emitters in the developing world, namely, Brazil, South Africa, India and China. The US and the BASIC group played a key role in brokering the political accord that emerged in the last twenty-four hours of the Copenhagen conference when it looked as though a stalemate would emerge. Developed countries had not been able to agree on a binding 2020 interim target to fulfil their special responsibilities – the distance between the EU's proposal of minus 30 per cent and the more modest targets of the key members of the Umbrella Group (particularly Australia, Canada and the US) was simply too great. Nor were key developing countries, particularly China and India, prepared to turn their national climate policy commitments into international obligations of a kind that would ease the passage of cap-and-trade bills that were before Congress. Whereas at the 1997 Kyoto meeting the key division between the US and the developing world was over whether developing countries might undertake voluntary commitments, at the 2009 Copenhagen meeting the debate was over what form developing countries' commitments would take and how they would be verified. At Bali in 2007 it was agreed that developing countries would undertake NAMAs that would be 'measurable, reportable and verifiable' (MRV). At Copenhagen, however, developing countries argued that MRV should only apply to internationally supported actions (to satisfy donors) but not those national actions that were undertaken voluntarily and independently of financing. Since China declared that its measures would not be internationally supported, this meant that its Copenhagen pledges would not be subject to external review. On this issue, China was insistent that its sovereignty should be respected. The compromise that was brokered in the Copenhagen Accord deftly side-stepped this highly sensitive issue but has remained a point of contention.[66]

The opening paragraph of the Copenhagen Accord reaffirms CBDR, and acknowledges the need to prevent an increase in global temperature

---

[65] 'Obama in Copenhagen speech: Full text', *Huffington Post*, posted 18 December 2009, www.huffingtonpost.com/2009/12/18/obama-in-copenhagen-speec_n_396836.html (accessed 27 July 2011).

[66] The compromise was that only national actions that are internationally supported shall be subject to MRV and that other actions would be the subject of their national communications to the UNFCCC 'with provisions for international consultations and analysis under clearly defined guidelines that will ensure that national sovereignty is respected'. See UNFCCC/CP, Copenhagen Accord, paragraph 5.

below 2 degrees, the need for deep cuts in emissions and the need to achieve the peaking of global emission as soon as possible (albeit over a longer timeframe for developing countries). However, the Accord contains no targets or timetables for developed countries. Instead, it invited Annex I parties to submit their self-chosen, quantified, economy-wide reduction targets for 2020 to the UNFCCC Secretariat by the end of January 2010. Non-Annex I parties were likewise required to submit their national actions by the same date. In return for 'meaningful mitigation actions and transparency on implementation' by developing countries, developed countries agree to mobilise US$100 billion by 2020 to address the needs of developing countries.[67]

However, it was China and not the US that resisted the inclusion in the Accord of a global emissions reduction target for 2050 and a specific timetable for the peaking of global emissions.[68] In the aftermath of the conference, China's leading climate negotiator declared that China had no intention of capping its emissions for the time being because the Chinese economy was still developing, that China would focus instead on reducing its emissions intensity and that it never accepted the idea of external reviews of its national climate policies.[69] Nonetheless, China, India and South Africa have all undertaken significant voluntary national commitments to reduce the rate of future emissions growth by 2020, and China's latest five-year plan has stepped up these commitments.[70] The EU, the US, China and India have all duly submitted information to the UNFCCC on their quantified targets and voluntary national strategies respectively which seek to improve emissions intensity or reduce emissions growth from business-as-usual projections. The EU has pledged a 20 per cent cut from a 1990 baseline while the US pledged its pre-Copenhagen promise to reduce emissions by 17 per cent from a 2005 baseline, which translates to around 3 to 4 per cent from a 1990 baseline. However, the combined pledges of all parties remain well below what is required to reduce the risk of dangerous climate change.[71]

---

[67] UNFCCC/CP, Copenhagen Accord, paragraph 8.

[68] P. Christoff, 'Cold climate in Copenhagen: China and the United States at COP15', *Environmental Politics*, 19(4) 2010, 637–56.

[69] Both China and India have also resisted reviews of their national commitments and have declared they will not accept assistance from the green funds pledged at Copenhagen, which requires recipients to ensure their climate measures are MRV.

[70] UNFCCC, 'Appendix II: Nationally appropriate mitigation actions of developing country parties', unfccc.int/home/items/5265.php (accessed 27 July 2011); Climate Group, 'Delivering low carbon growth: A guide to China's 12th Five Year Plan: Executive summary', March 2011, Commissioned by HSBC, www.theclimategroup.org/_assets/files/China-Five-Year-Plan-EXECUTIVE-SUMMARY.pdf (accessed 27 July 2011).

[71] Researchers at the Potsdam Institute for Climate Impact Research concluded that the Copenhagen pledges would commit the Earth to more than a 50 per cent chance

Despite the significant strains that emerged at Copenhagen, President Obama acquitted himself well from the standpoint of his domestic audience, as distinct from his international audience. He followed previous administrations in drawing attention to the issue of future growth in emissions in the major economies in the developing world and introduced a new emphasis on the importance of trust, transparency and accountability of differentiated commitments by parties on either side of the Annex I divide. He was careful to commit to targets that were in step with the bills before Congress and he played a key diplomatic role in the closing days of the meeting in brokering a political accord with the newly formed BASIC group that prevented the meeting from being a diplomatic failure. The Copenhagen Accord was noted but not formally endorsed at the plenary on the last day of COP15 because of lack of consensus. Given that the Accord has no formal legal status, President Obama was not obliged to submit it for Senate approval.

At the following meeting in Cancún in 2010, the Copenhagen Accord was officially endorsed as a decision of the COP, since no other agreement appeared on the horizon. This effectively vindicated the US's preferred model of a bottom-up 'pledge and review' process over the so-called top down, Kyoto model. As one seasoned observer from the Third World Network put it:

Cancún may be remembered in the future as the place where the UNFCCC's climate regime was changed significantly, with developed countries being treated more and more leniently, reaching a level like that (of) developing countries, while the developing countries are asked to increase their obligations to be more and more like developed countries.[72]

Despite its success in narrowing the differences in the responsibilities of developed countries and the major developing countries, the Obama administration's task of domestically implementing its Copenhagen pledge has been made much more difficult following the 2010 mid-term Congressional elections, where the Republicans gained control of the House of Representatives (242–193) and the Democrats majority in the Senate was reduced to fifty-three. Moreover, a majority of the House Republicans (128 or 53 per cent) publicly question climate change

of warming of more than 3 degrees, which is well above what is required to reduce the risk of dangerous climate change. See J. Rogelj, J. Nabel, C. Chen, W. Hare, K. Markmann, M. Meinshausen, M. Schaeffer, K. Macey and N. Höhne, 'Copenhagen Accord pledges are paltry', *Nature*, 464(7292) 22 April 2010, 1126–8.

[72] M. Khor, 'Spotlight Cancún: Strange outcome of Cancún conference', *TripleCrisis*, 14 December 2010, triplecrisis.com/spotlight-cancun-strange-outcome-of-cancun-conference (accessed 27 July 2011).

science.[73] These results may be attributed, in part, to unrest over high unemployment following the global financial crisis, strong lobbying by fossil fuel interests against a price on carbon, and the aggressive anti-climate change campaigning by the Tea Party movement, which converted climate change denial or scepticism into a litmus test of 'true conservativism'.[74] The scale of the Democrat losses is so large that any significant domestic action on climate change is unlikely until after the next mid-term elections in 2014 given the advantages of incumbency in the 2012 elections. The Democrats and pro-climate action Independents are unlikely to regain a two-thirds majority in the Senate in 2012.[75]

Still, the Obama administration does have another card to play. Unlike his predecessor, President Obama has welcomed the Supreme Court ruling that allows the Environmental Protection Agency (EPA) to regulate GHGs as a pollutant under the Clean Air Act following an 'endangerment finding'. This ruling effectively gives the executive branch power to regulate emissions from sources such as light vehicles and new coal plants. President Obama initially indicated his strong preference for Congress to enact national cap-and-trade legislation rather than rely on EPA regulations. Before the mid-term Congressional elections, this looked like a real possibility following the passage of the Waxman-Markey bill in the House of Representatives on 26 June 2009 (219 votes for, 212 against), which included a national cap-and-trade scheme. However, efforts to enact similar legislation in the Senate – beginning with the Kerry-Boxer bill introduced into the Senate in October 2009 and followed by the draft of the Kerry-Lieberman bill introduced on 12 May 2010 – failed due to lack of an effective majority. Both bills had sought a 17 per cent reduction in US emissions by 2020 from a 2005 base through a cap-and-trade scheme, albeit with significant qualifications. However, none of these bills had provided any explicit acknowledgement of CBDR or leadership responsibilities. Moreover, to shore up domestic political support, all of the bills contained provisions for border adjustment measures to prevent the migration of

---

[73] B. Johnson, 'The climate zombie caucus of the 112th congress', *ThinkProgress*, updated 23 November 2010, wonkroom.thinkprogress.org/climate-zombie-caucus (accessed 27 July 2011).

[74] M. T. Boykoff and J. M. Boykoff, 'Balance as bias: Global warming and the US prestige press', *Global Environmental Change*, 14(2) 2004, 125–36; A. M. McCright and R. E. Dunlap, 'Anti-reflexivity: The American conservative movement's success in undermining climate science and policy', *Theory, Culture and Society*, 27(2–3) 2010, 100–33.

[75] One reason is that more Democratic Senators will be up for re-election in 2012 than Republican Senators.

energy intensive industries and jobs to countries without comparable emissions regulation and to protect US industry from unfair competition from imports produced in such countries (most notably China and India). Such measures, which seek to level the commercial playing field, pose a significant challenge to the basic idea of differentiated responsibilities between developed and developing countries and undermine the very idea of special responsibilities. Both China and India reacted angrily to such measures as 'backdoor targets'.[76]

However, once it became clear that a carbon tax or cap-and-trade bill was off the table following the mid-term Congressional elections, the EPA, with the Obama administration's support, moved to regulate emissions from cars and light trucks, and new and modified stationary sources through new performance standards (rather than a cap-and-trade scheme). This has drawn strong opposition from Republicans and many Democrats from so-called coal states, and prompted the passage of a bill in the House of Representatives designed to strip the EPA of power to regulate GHGs. In response to strong pressure from key environment organisations, President Obama made it clear that he would veto the bill. The EPA's regulatory powers have also become entangled in the brinkmanship over passing the budget.

While President Obama has declared his administration's commitment to climate change, it has never been a top priority, and he has not been prepared to stake his presidency on the issue. Nor has he chosen to emphasise the US's international responsibilities when addressing his domestic audience. Instead, he has highlighted the domestic economic and employment benefits of a diversification of the US's energy profile. The Obama administration has made significant budget allocations for the advancement of renewable energy, and the inclusion of clean energy provisions and environmental infrastructure expenditure in the so-called green economic stimulus package in response to the financial crisis. The massive oil explosion from BP's Deepwater Horizon rig in the Gulf of Mexico on 20 April 2010 also provided a basis for both Obama and the Congressional supporters of the American Power Act to highlight the dangers of the US's excessive dependence on oil and has prompted the president to halt deepwater drilling, but the disaster did little to change public opinion on climate change. Indeed, in the face of increasingly fierce domestic opposition to a climate bill, the Obama administration has shifted its policy narrative by avoiding any

[76] International Centre for Trade and Sustainable Development, 'China, India lash out at talk of "carbon tariffs"', *Bridges Weekly Trade New Digest*, 13(25) 8 July 2009, ictsd. net/i/news/bridgesweekly/50301 (accessed 27 July 2011).

mention of climate change altogether, focusing instead on the general advantages of removing US dependency on imported oil and increasing energy efficiency.

On the international front, Obama has mobilised his senior diplomats, including Secretary of State Hillary Clinton and special climate envoy Stern, in bilateral negotiations with China and India which have resulted in joint projects on clean coal and electric cars. The administration has also continued the George W. Bush administration's major economies initiative, which was renamed and launched in March 2009 as the Major Economies Forum on Energy and Climate. The Forum, made up of seventeen economies responsible for around 75 per cent of global emissions, launched a Global Partnership for low-carbon and climate-friendly technologies in July 2009.[77] However, the category 'major economies' cuts across the developed/developing country binary and is consistent with the Obama administration's reconstruction of special responsibilities.

The US's role in reshaping special responsibilities

Although the parties to the UNFCCC have reaffirmed their commitment to CBDR and the developed countries' responsibilities for climate leadership, the US has nonetheless succeeded in gradually reshaping the post-Kyoto game in four significant respects.

First, the US's ongoing rejection of the Kyoto Protocol has led other countries in the Umbrella Group (Canada, Japan and Russia) to argue that there is no point in negotiating a second commitment period to the Kyoto Protocol and that the negotiations should concentrate on the LCA treaty. However, China and the G77 insist on the continuation of the Kyoto Protocol, especially given that it is not clear whether a formal LCA treaty will be concluded. Much will therefore turn on how the EU responds. If it decides to abandon its commitment to the Protocol in the light of the defections by significant emitters in Annex I, then it will seal the demise of the Kyoto Protocol, and the demise of a clear bifurcation in the responsibilities of the developed and developing countries. If the EU holds out, and a second commitment period is negotiated, then the legitimacy of the Kyoto Protocol will diminish in accordance with its shrunken constituency of support.

Second, the political form of the Copenhagen Accord, along with the final process by which it was produced, sidelined the EU, which has

---

[77] Major Economies Forum on Energy and Climate, www.majoreconomiesforum.org (accessed 27 July 2011).

been widely recognised as the climate leader that has pushed strongly for a legally binding LCA treaty with strong 2020 targets for developed countries. This has not only exacerbated ongoing trans-Atlantic tensions but also introduced new tensions in the G77 between the major developing countries, on the one hand, and the smaller and more vulnerable sub-groupings, on the other, such as the African Group, AOSIS and the less developed countries. Although the political agreement forged between the US and the BASIC group saved the meeting from total failure, it also demonstrated that 'emissions power' rather than the EU's normative power, or the special vulnerability of many members of the G77, had become increasingly influential in driving the negotiations. If this trend continues then the division between the major emitters and the rest will increasingly rival the division between developed and developing countries as the key division determining special responsibilities.

Third, the endorsement of the Copenhagen Accord at COP16 in Cancún signals a general lowering of expectations about what developed countries are likely to deliver based on a resignation to the fact that the US is not politically capable of discharging the special responsibilities that have been conferred upon it by the international community, including the kinds of mitigation commitments that the IPCC recommends for developed countries as necessary to prevent dangerous climate change. Just as flexibility instruments were included in the Kyoto Protocol to buy US support for the treaty in 1997, a flexible pledge and review approach was accepted in the Copenhagen Accord to buy ongoing participation by the US in 2009. This replaces the Kyoto model of a common baseline and common methodology for measuring emissions reductions with what might be called a do-it-yourself approach to national climate policy based on different, nationally chosen targets, baselines and national accounting systems. In effect, all parties were free to choose what kind of responsibility they would seek to discharge, with the only rider being that developed countries would pursue aggregate reductions that would be labelled 'international commitments' while developing countries' responsibilities were to reduce the rate of growth in their emissions that would be called 'nationally appropriate mitigation actions'. Despite the additional proviso of transparency (to enable judging of national performance) the absence of a common metric will make performance comparison among countries harder rather than easier.

Finally, China's rapid economic growth over the past ten years has generated increasing acknowledgement that, even if developed countries were to pursue mitigation targets recommended by the IPCC, dangerous climate change may still not be averted without significant action from China. Addressing climate change is now looking more like a collective responsibility of great and emerging powers (insofar as they are big emitters) than a special responsibility of developed countries or an extra special responsibility of the US. Indeed a growing number of commentators are now arguing that climate multilateralism has become too cumbersome and slow, and that it should be replaced or at least augmented with 'minilateralism' by the major emitters in forums such as the Major Economies Forum on Energy and Climate and/or the Group of Twenty (G20).[78] This argument does not necessarily lessen the special leadership responsibilities of developed countries but it does provide a basis for acknowledging a new set of special responsibilities for states that belong to the category 'major emitter in the developing world'. The idea of two sets of special responsibilities can be expected to gain increasing traction over time if the Chinese economy continues to grow at predicted rates. However, as we have seen, the US has sought to push this argument even further in making commitment to its responsibilities *conditional* on China committing to its responsibilities. China, for its part, has rejected this argument and reminded all developed countries that they must demonstrate leadership before developing countries take action. Nonetheless, at the national level, China has pursued increasingly aggressive targets in emissions intensity and energy efficiency and it has placed the idea of a clean industrial revolution at the heart of its next five-year plan (2011–15).[79] Curiously, if the US's Copenhagen pledge is converted to the same emissions intensity metric as China's, then it is in the same range (around 40 per cent).[80]

We therefore reach an ironic conclusion about the contestation and evolution of special responsibilities. On the one hand, the US has not succeeded in reshaping the formal meaning of special responsibilities for developed countries – it has merely lowered political expectations about whether those responsibilities will be effectively discharged. On the other hand, the sheer size of the US's historical, per capita and

---

[78] M. Naim, 'Minilateralism: The magic number to get real international action', *Foreign Policy*, 173 (July/August) 2009, 135–6; A. Light, 'Showdown among the leaders at Copenhagen', Center for American Progress, 18 December 2009, www. americanprogress.org/issues/2009/12/showdown_copenhagen.html (accessed 27 July 2011).

[79] Climate Group, 'Delivering low carbon growth'.

[80] F. Jotzo, 'Comparing the Copenhagen emissions targets', CCEP Working Paper 1.10 (Canberra: Centre for Climate Economics & Policy, Australian National University, October 2010, rev. 16 November 2010), p. 14. As Jotzo notes, '[t]his is a potent comparison that could receive significant attention in the policy debate in years to come' (p. 14).

aggregate emissions makes its participation essential to regime functionality. This 'emissions power' has given the US enormous bargaining power in the climate negotiations. Non-participation by the US in the Kyoto Protocol has impeded the practical implementation of climate leadership responsibilities by the developed states as a group, and the future of the Kyoto Protocol is now uncertain. Moreover, the US's bargaining power has strengthened as the window of opportunity for effective action diminishes, which has placed it in an increasingly influential position to 'change the game' in the negotiation of the LCA treaty. Indeed, since 2009, the US has succeeded in shaping a new, informal understanding among certain key states that special responsibilities must extend to major developing countries, most notably China. While the idea of a different set of special responsibilities for major developing countries is gaining momentum, it is far from officially recognised. From the standpoint of China, there is too much unfinished business to agree to such a step. Developed countries, as a group, have yet to discharge their leadership responsibilities, which China and the G77 have always regarded as a condition precedent to taking on any international commitments, as distinct from voluntary domestic actions. Further, China's development needs, and its associated thirst for energy, remain considerable, and it does not appear ready to tie its hands by accepting international commitments despite its considerable efforts to pursue a low carbon growth strategy. To bolster its case, China has drawn attention to the trend in 'offshoring emissions', which has meant that developing countries 'have to bear a large amount of transferred emissions as they are placed at the lower end of the international industrial chain in the process of economic globalization'.[81] Starkly contrasting understandings of fairness, which cannot simply be reduced to strategic assessments of relative gains, have framed the responses of the world's two largest emitters and fundamentally shaped their international commitments, national responses, multilateral partnerships and bilateral negotiations.

It is therefore difficult to envisage an equilibrium point on special responsibilities emerging in the near future, whether between the international community's allocation of special responsibilities to the US, and the US's acceptance, or between the US's bestowal of formal special responsibilities on China, and China's acceptance. This does not augur well for the future of the regime. Indeed, the closest the parties

---

[81] Hu Jintao, 'Join hands to address climate challenge', President Hu Jintao's Speech at the Opening Plenary Session of the United Nations Summit on Climate Change, 23 September 2009, www.china-un.org/eng/gdxw/t606111.htm (accessed 27 July 2011).

came to such an equilibrium point in the allocation and acceptance of special responsibilities was the signing of the Kyoto Protocol, but that gradually fell away as it became clear that the US would never ratify. It was, in any event, a precarious equilibrium point because the parties were unable to reach any principled agreement over how to differentiate special responsibilities among developed countries, or how developing countries might one day graduate to the category of developed country. These differences continue to plague the negotiations.

Conclusion

It should be clear from our analysis of the allocation, contestation and evolution of special responsibilities in the climate regime, that this is a story of sub-optimality, rather than failure.

On the one hand, it is possible to show that the allocation of special responsibilities has indeed made a difference. It is difficult to see how any agreement would have been reached with China and the G77 in 1992 and in subsequent climate negotiations if the responsibility to mitigate emissions had been defined as a general responsibility rather than a special responsibility of those who were most responsible and most capable. Special responsibilities may therefore be seen as playing a major role in securing agreement, and global emissions are now much lower than they would otherwise have been were it not for such an agreement. While our focus has been on the US, the EU – spearheaded by leading members such as Germany and the UK – has embraced and sought to discharge its leadership responsibilities. While the EU's climate performance is far from perfect, it is nonetheless on track to achieve its Kyoto target of a reduction in its aggregate emissions by 8 per cent below 1990 levels, and it is on track to achieve its 2020 target of a 20 per cent reduction.[82] Had the EU also chosen to join the US and resist the allocation of special responsibilities, then the story of special responsibilities would be one of failure. Instead, the EU has put the US on the defensive. Moreover, special responsibilities do not simply mirror the distribution of material capabilities or aggregate emissions among states but rather rest on moral arguments concerning the obligations of the most responsible and most capable towards the global community, but especially towards its most vulnerable members. The allocation of special responsibilities has defined the realm of legitimate

---

[82] European Environment Agency, 'Tracking progress towards Kyoto and 2020 targets in Europe', EEA Report No 7/2010 (Copenhagen: European Environment Agency, 2010), p. 6.

action in response to climate change by differently situated states. Instead of merely reflecting material capabilities, special responsibilities have shaped the moral and social meaning of capabilities in this particular domain.

On the other hand, not all of the holders of special responsibilities have accepted or discharged their responsibilities in ways that will ensure the provision of the collective good of climate protection. Indeed, there are good reasons to be concerned about whether the climate regime will succeed in achieving its basic purpose, which is to prevent dangerous climate change. If, as we claim, special responsibilities provide both an ethical and functional division of labour in response to complex collective problems, then it should come as no surprise that contestation by the US over the meaning and scope of special responsibilities has been a major (although not the only) reason why the regime has been sub-optimal.

What, then, does this story of sub-optimality tell us about the constitution of power and, in particular, US power, in this particular social domain? Brooks and Wohlforth have argued that power and legitimacy form a 'two-way street', and that powerful states have a disproportionate power not only to bribe or coerce others, or exit negotiations, but also to shape social meaning through persuasion, and they are therefore less likely to be constrained by legitimacy than less powerful states.[83] However, this case study shows that, despite the US's significant diplomatic and intellectual resources, it has largely failed to shape the social meaning of developed country special leadership responsibilities in terms that are less onerous, and more favourable to its interests. The administration's efforts to 'update' special responsibilities to the new 'post-Kyoto' context may have helped to raise expectations about China's future responsibilities, but they have not served to lower expectations about the US's special responsibilities. Indeed, Brooks and Wohlforth acknowledge that the Kyoto Protocol, in particular, is a good illustration of the constructivist argument that power does not always translate into legitimacy.[84] We agree, since it is clear that the US has not been able to persuade the EU, developing countries or global civil society that either the special leadership responsibilities of the US in particular, or those of developed countries as a whole, should be lessened. However, Brooks and Wohlforth also maintain that the larger body of evidence across key security and economic domains shows that the legitimacy constraints arising from US rule-breaking or non-cooperation is weak, that the

---

[83] Brooks and Wohlforth, *World out of balance*, p. 180.
[84] *Ibid.*, p. 204.

US – even under the George W. Bush administration – has succeeded in weathering significant criticisms of its foreign policies and that the US's global role and the institutional order have been upheld.

Our argument, though, is that it is necessary to disaggregate the global order into different domains if we want to understand the constitution of US power. Against realist sceptics, we have shown that special responsibilities have remained a persistent feature of the international climate debates and shaped social understandings and judgements about what ought to be done and by whom. The US, in particular, has not been able to brush off criticisms of its climate leadership performance, or draw support for alternative formulations such as 'mutual burden-sharing', since it has not only failed to lead, but also failed to make any significant headway in reducing emissions on the scale recommended by the IPCC. If the US continues to fail in discharging its responsibilities for climate leadership, and the consequences of climate change prove to be as globally disruptive and dangerous as scientists warn, then international resentment is destined to grow over time with potentially serious repercussions for the US, which may spill over into other domains. Indeed, if CBDR, rather than pure emissions power, remains the international benchmark for determining special responsibilities, then there is a real risk that the US may suffer a permanent stigma as not simply a failed climate leader but also the chief climate spoiler. China will also have to take on increasing international responsibility as its annual aggregate and cumulative emissions continue to grow. However, its cumulative emissions are not expected to overtake those of the US until well after the window of opportunity for effective action has closed.[85]

Even if the US succeeds, through its own defection and the defection of others, in bringing about the demise of the Kyoto Protocol and an end to the rigid distinction between industrialised and developing countries that defined that agreement, the negotiations on the LCA treaty are still framed by CBDR. The pledges made by developed and developing countries under the Copenhagen Accord are still qualitatively and quantitatively different, and those differences arise from an ongoing commitment by the parties to the principles of CBDR. Any reconstruction of special responsibilities by the US or others to include the major emerging emitters in the developing world will have to work with, rather than against, the grain of these principles.

---

[85] See, for example, W. J. W. Botzen, J. M. Gowdy and J. C. J. M. van den Bergh, 'Cumulative CO_2 emissions: Shifting international responsibilities for climate debt', *Climate Policy*, 8(6) 2008, 569–76.

Finally, this case study highlights the role of the US Constitution and US national identity in shaping and constraining how the US responds to the conferral of special responsibilities. This has both an internal and external aspect. Just as it is necessary to disaggregate the global order into different domains, it is also necessary to disaggregate US political power internally into different branches and levels of government to understand where and why resistance to climate leadership has occurred. While Congress has yet to enact any major climate change legislation, we have seen that the allocation of special responsibilities has nonetheless made a difference to climate governance at the executive level and at the sub-national level in the US. The Obama administration has made significant budget allocations for the advancement of renewable energy, and the EPA has developed new performance standards covering emissions from cars, light trucks and new and modified stationary sources. Many local governments have embraced the US's Kyoto target and many states, including the economic powerhouse of California, have adopted mitigation targets and embarked upon emissions trading schemes. The net effect of these initiatives, when combined with the slower economic growth following the financial crash and the expansion of lower emission gas reserves, is that the US is on track to meet its Copenhagen pledge.[86] A key obstacle in the way of more ambitious emissions reductions, however, has been Congress. The procedural rules of Congress, combined with strong polarisation between Democrats and Republicans over climate change and regulatory styles,[87] create a strong bias in favour of the status quo in US policy-making by enabling well-organised minorities to thwart the passage of new bills and/or prevent treaty ratification. The Senate's oversight of the President's treaty power provides the most significant institutional expression of US civic nationalism, which is resistant to the domestic imposition of externally generated, treaty-based norms and asserts the US's right to author its own laws on its own terms in accordance with the US Constitution.

Turning to the external aspect, special responsibilities to take the lead in climate mitigation fundamentally challenge the US's status and identity as an exceptional (liberal) state, which has always carried with it a basic sense of entitlement, and access, to the necessary energy resources (and consequent emissions) at home and abroad that are required to uphold US pre-eminence and maintain the American

---

[86] R. Garnaut, *The Garnaut review 2011: Australia in the global response to climate change* (Cambridge: Cambridge University Press, 2011), p. 61.

[87] See, for example, R. E. Dunlap and A. McCright, 'A widening gap: Republican and Democratic views on climate change', *Environment*, 50(5) 2008, 26–35.

way of life.[88] The idea that the US should drastically restrict its emissions in order to provide room for developing countries, including rapidly growing China, to expand their emissions in the short to medium term is generally regarded as the equivalent to unilateral disarmament. It is completely foreign to US political elites' understanding of fair play as well as the US's traditional strategic interests. A robust enactment of special responsibilities would therefore stand in direct conflict with many of the US's traditional special responsibilities in the security and economic domains – responsibilities that have been actively claimed and exercised by the US political executive ever since it emerged as a great power. The interesting question, however, is whether a superpower like the US, with global military reach and the world's biggest economy, is able to move towards a low-carbon economy, and a low-carbon footprint and military bootprint, and still retain its social identity as a superpower and its self-identity as an exceptional state.

Postscript

This chapter was finalised before COP17 held at Durban in late 2011, where the parties agreed, after a marathon end-game negotiating session, to launch a fresh round of negotiations to conclude a new treaty by 2015, to come into effect by 2020 and to include all major emitters. In return, the EU agreed to a second commitment period under the Kyoto Protocol notwithstanding the lack of support from the US, Canada, Japan and Russia. The Durban decision more or less reflects the EU's negotiating bid at the start of the conference, and signals a reassertion of the EU's climate leadership following the dominance of the US and the BASIC group at COP15 in Copenhagen in 2009. What is most noteworthy about the Durban Platform for Enhanced Action (the name of the COP decision that launched the new negotiations) is that, unlike all previous negotiating mandates for a new treaty, it does not include the hallowed language of CBDR. This portends a potentially significant shift in the burden-sharing responsibilities of the major emitters. However, Durban Platform merely represents a nonbinding commitment to commit to a binding treaty, and it is expected that some version of the language of CBDR will find its way into the negotiating text – although in exactly what form and to what effect remains to be seen.

---

[88] R. Eckersley, 'Climate leadership and US exceptionalism', paper presented to the Australian Political Studies Association Conference, University of Melbourne, 27–29 September 2010. Henry Nau has defined national identity as 'the principal idea on which a nation accumulates and legitimates the use of lethal force. This idea may be a creed or ideology, as in the case of the identity of the United States.' H. R. Nau, *At home abroad: Identity and power in American foreign policy* (Ithaca, NY: Cornell University Press, 2002), p. 5.

5   Global finance

The financial crisis of 2007–9 severely shook global confidence in the regulatory approach and capacities of the United States. Is the country which, since the end of the Second World War has been the presumed lynchpin of the global financial order, still capable of exercising special responsibilities in the domain of global finance? Has the US been consistent in exercising special financial responsibilities, or has its faith in the ability of market forces to be self-regulating undermined the exercise of special responsibilities? Since special responsibilities are 'socially sanctioned' powers,[1] the answers to these questions depend not only on our assessment of US material power, interests and will to lead, but also on how US authority is viewed by other important actors in the domain of global finance.

In keeping with the overall orientation of this volume, our primary focus in this chapter is on how special responsibilities have been articulated by states and in international institutions. However, we cannot neglect the responsibilities of market players in global finance, especially now that many have grown so large, and the amount of capital they command is so voluminous. The interplay between private firm and market responsibilities on the one hand and political responsibilities on the other, is thus an important theme explored in this chapter. In the political realm, we highlight and analyse the tension between formal articulations of responsibility embedded in institutions such as those negotiated at Bretton Woods, and more informal tacit arrangements which have at times replaced and supplemented the formal agreements. We find a pervasive tension between the institutionalised expression of *general* responsibilities of all states on the one hand, and informal or tacit articulations and claims of *special* responsibilities of specific states on the other. This tension can at least partly be understood as an aspect of the gap between formal equality and actual differentiation of capability so often faced in international society, as laid out

---

[1] See Chapter 2 in this volume.

in the introductory chapter of this volume. The broader normative context of sovereign equality, and concerns of narrow national self-interest, condition and in some cases limit the articulation of special responsibilities, rendering certain forms of special responsibility more tacit than explicit, and others the source of contention and conflict. And yet, the influence of claims of special responsibilities is discernible in shaping developments that cannot be adequately accounted for in terms of material power politics.

The term 'global finance' covers a large domain, and we have narrowed down the field of inquiry to focus on two centrally important aspects of the governance of global finance: (1) responsibility for management of sustained global imbalances, and in particular the allocation of responsibility for adjustment in light of such imbalances ('the adjustment problem'); and (2) responsibility for systemic financial stability. As should become clear, these two focal points can be quite closely related, but are nevertheless distinct in the problems they pose and the solutions that have been crafted to deal with them.[2] Moreover, how the problems of adjustment and stability are framed and understood has changed over time. That is, the problems in global finance for which responsibility – special or otherwise – ought to be exercised are themselves socially constructed.

This chapter begins by reviewing the responsibilities outlined in the Bretton Woods institutions, with a particular focus on the International Monetary Fund (IMF). We also discuss the more informal practices that emerged alongside these institutions, before turning to the contestation that arose as the US federal deficit grew and balance of payments on current account shifted from surplus to deficit during the late 1960s, and the final unravelling of the Bretton Woods agreements that accompanied the Nixon shocks of 1971. The Cold War and considerations of security and defence spending loom large beginning in the late Dwight Eisenhower administration, and the US increasingly framed its position on global finance within a broader discourse on special US security responsibilities. The narrative trajectory from Bretton Woods to the Nixon shocks is roughly one of *contested diffusion* of US financial responsibility.

The primary 'contestants' in this period were the US and its European allies, especially Britain, France and West Germany. Each of these actors interpreted US responsibilities differently, despite their formal

---

[2] On the relatively recent vintage of the term financial stability, see H. Davies and D. Green, *Global financial regulation: The essential guide* (Cambridge: Polity Press, 2008), p. 24.

alliance and common commitments to multilateral financial institutions. The scope of their disagreement was perhaps kept narrower than it might have been by their common commitment to checking Soviet power and by their commitment to sustaining open trade, but disagreement and conflict within the alliance was nevertheless significant.[3] The differentiated and even de-coupled sense of special responsibility in the realm of finance, on the one hand, and security, on the other, became especially clear during the John F. Kennedy administration, which was the first to seriously grapple with the structural weakening of the US balance of payments position.[4] In the domain of global finance and monetary affairs, the US began a process of what realists might call retrenchment far earlier than in the security realm. This should lead us already to question the extent to which it is appropriate to treat power as a monolithic concept.

Despite the diffusion away from special towards general responsibility in finance, special responsibilities reappear periodically after the decline of the Bretton Woods exchange rate regime, most significantly alongside the acceleration of financial globalisation in the 1980s. But they appear in a rather different guise than in the Bretton Woods era, because the world economy had changed significantly. Fixed exchange rates, at least among the major economic powers, were no more, and financial globalisation had far exceeded anything previously seen, or probably even imagined. The period of financial globalisation and the crises of the 1990s and 2007–9 was characterised by contestation about how to articulate responsibilities for payments imbalances and global financial stability, with the outcome being continued, threefold diffusion of responsibility: diffusion among states; diffusion into a networked mix of global and national regulators and major market players; and diffusion away from states and public institutions and towards markets.

In this more recent period, states have more consistently articulated generalised or shared responsibilities rather than special responsibilities attributable to a single great power. This seriously disrupts the common narrative of unipolarity. On the adjustment problem, we find the re-emergence of a discourse about special responsibilities of surplus versus deficit powers, this time centred on the relationship between the US and China. Moreover, because of the perceived collective action

---

[3] On conflict within the alliance, see especially F. J. Gavin, *Gold, dollars, and power: The politics of international monetary relations, 1958–1971* (Chapel Hill, NC: University of North Carolina Press, 2004).

[4] F. J. Gavin, 'The gold battles within the Cold War: American monetary policy and the defense of Europe', *Diplomatic History*, 26(1) 2002, 61–94; Gavin, *Gold, dollars, and power*.

problems posed by the volume, depth and dynamism of the global financial markets, states have at times articulated and allocated special responsibilities as a way to try and solve collective action problems when those generalised responsibilities have either remained unimplemented, or have failed to produce the desirable outcomes of financial stability and smooth adjustment. The twin problems of adjustment and financial stability thus remain important focal points in the post-Cold War period, and especially from the late 1990s onward, although as already noted their character as problems has changed somewhat from the Bretton Woods era.

A focus on special responsibilities allows us to fine-tune our understanding of the social and discursive construction and contestation of power. Although in general terms the material preponderance of the US throughout the postwar period and on through today cannot be plausibly denied, this does not mean that the US has been able unilaterally to set the terms of its special responsibilities, which in turn means that the US does not set the terms of its own legitimacy. Material power has not consistently translated into an ability to create a global order that can be read as a mere reflection of US interests and dominance. By exploring the articulations and contestations of differential allocation of responsibility in specific issue areas, we can more clearly see how and why this is so. If we treat power monolithically as hegemonic stability theories often do, we risk missing the crucial point that the US retrenched in key issue areas far earlier than is normally acknowledged. One of the consequences of this retrenchment in the case of global finance has been to reinforce the trend, presciently identified by Susan Strange,[5] that exhibits a shift in the global balance of social power between states and markets, away from states and towards markets. The question of whether markets or major market players can be vested with special responsibilities for governing themselves seems, in the wake of the crisis of 2007–9, to warrant a sceptical answer.

Moreover, focus on special responsibilities shows us that the contours of a rule-based regime do not neatly co-vary with US power and preferences. At times, the US has used the notion of special responsibilities and their accompanying prerogatives to try to get its unilateral way in global monetary and financial affairs. But it has at times been inhibited in these efforts by more diffuse and generalised understandings of political responsibility in the face of market forces, as well as by market forces themselves.

---

[5] S. Strange, 'The Westfailure system', *Review of International* Studies, 25(3) 1999, 345–54.

Special responsibilities in the Bretton Woods agreements

United States responsibilities in the Bretton Woods regime flowed from its economically dominant position, but we must be careful about characterising what these responsibilities were, and in what sense they could be considered 'special'. On the face of it, and taken together with the negotiation of the other postwar institutions, including the United Nations and the General Agreement on Tariffs and Trade (GATT), the postwar economic order presents the textbook case of hegemonic stability.[6] Replacing Britain as the strongest economic power, the US was to bear a large share of the financial burden not only for funding the IMF, World Bank and United Nations, but also for providing direct financial aid to its allies. Can Lend-Lease and the Marshall Plan, not to mention proportionately higher contributions to the IMF and World Bank, be construed as evidence of special responsibility? And was this responsibility socially sanctioned and supported by other states in the regime? Closer scrutiny substantially undercuts the simple benign hegemony narrative of Bretton Woods. The agreement was subject to significant contestation as well as unresolved tensions regarding the allocation of responsibility; the degree to which US special responsibilities were socially sanctioned by others is something of an open question worth exploring more deeply. Arguably, the way in which the US interpreted its own special responsibilities in the domains of finance and security stretched it thin and ultimately undermined both the hegemonic position of the US, and the viability of the multilateral order it attempted to underwrite.

The Bretton Woods negotiators of 1944 articulated predominantly general or shared conceptions of responsibility for the linked goals of trade expansion and exchange rate stability. The primacy given to the principle of multilateralism in the institutions arising out of the negotiations reinforces the notion of shared responsibility. Despite the fact that the US and Britain exercised the most clout in the negotiations and indeed initially hammered out key provisions bilaterally, their commitment to multilateralism was more than mere window-dressing.[7]

---

[6] C. Kindleberger, *The world in depression, 1929–1939*, rev. edn (Berkeley, CA: University of California Press, 1986).

[7] R. N. Gardner, *Sterling-dollar diplomacy in current perspective: The origins and the prospects of our international economic order* (New York: Columbia University Press, 1980); J. G. Ruggie, 'International regimes, transactions, and change: Embedded liberalism in the postwar economic order', *International Organization*, 36(2) 1982, 379–415; H. James, *International monetary cooperation since Bretton Woods* (New York: Oxford

Fuelled by lessons from the experiences of the interwar years and the Great Depression, the negotiators at Bretton Woods nested their firm Keynesian commitments to domestic stabilisation within a broader commitment to multilateral cooperation in international economic affairs.

The intellectual consensus on Keynesian economic principles, as well as the electoral constraints generated by democratic constituencies demanding social protection, meant that in general, sovereign governments bore responsibility for taming the vagaries of markets in the interest of full employment and social stability. Responsibilities for establishing new international regimes for trade and payments would thus be shared among sovereign states. To prevent a return to the destabilising unilateralism and beggar-thy-neighbour realism of the interwar years, international institutions would ensure cooperation and coordination of trade and monetary relations. John Ruggie has characterised this postwar vision as 'embedded liberalism', since the prewar commitment to liberal economic principles – especially belief in the allocative efficiency of markets – remained but came to be tempered by twin political commitments to domestic social stability and multilateralism.[8] The underlying material foundation making it possible for governments to actually deliver on the embedded liberalism compromise was economic growth.[9] Open trade was seen as the key to providing this growth, and it is worth emphasising that the monetary and financial arrangements of the postwar period were designed to serve the purpose of open trade.

A multilateral institution, the IMF was supposed to be responsible for overseeing a return to currency convertibility, monitoring government fiscal and monetary policies, providing for a stable exchange rate regime and acting as a source of liquidity for governments experiencing short-term balance of payments problems. Its Articles of Agreement articulate the ideal purposes of the postwar economic order: expansion of trade, exchange rate stability, multilateralism, resources for easing balance of payments 'maladjustments' and promotion of equilibrium in balance of payments.[10] The Articles primarily speak the language of general or shared 'obligations' of member states for maintenance of stable exchange rates, and in fact seem to foreclose the possibility of

---

University Press, 1996), p. 42. Also see S. Berman, *The primacy of politics: Social democracy and the making of Europe's twentieth century* (Cambridge: Cambridge University Press, 2006).

[8] Ruggie, 'International regimes, transactions, and change'.

[9] James, *International monetary cooperation*, chapter 7.

[10] Note that there is no mention of financial stability, just exchange rate stability. International Monetary Fund, 'Articles of Agreement: Article I: Purposes', no date, www.imf.org/external/pubs/ft/aa/aa01.htm (accessed 28 July 2011).

special responsibility or privilege for any one member state. This is best illustrated in terms of the question of the US dollar, which was not supposed to be granted special status. Harold James, in his history of monetary cooperation, notes that: '[t]he Bretton Woods Agreements involved a recognition of the equality of all currencies. There would be no special reserve currencies'.[11]

One can further infer that responsibility for global financial stability was shared among states because of the presumption that such stability would require individual states to control the flow of capital across their borders, in order to prevent destabilising inflows or outflows of 'hot money'.[12] The immediate preoccupation at Bretton Woods had to do with how to facilitate adjustment in global balance of payments (of which more below); the main sense in which the negotiators could be said to have been concerned with financial stability was in the attempt to create a stable, and by this they meant fixed, exchange rate regime. So stability initially meant exchange rate stability, and that required rough agreement on a unit of account and global liquidity needs.

Despite the principle of equality of all currencies, two currencies served in practice as global reserve currencies (currencies held by central banks for settling international transactions) in the postwar period: the British pound sterling and the US dollar. The fact that the pound sterling continued to function as a reserve currency is often overlooked in cursory sketches of US postwar hegemony, but the war did not simply wipe the slate clean. Sterling balances held overseas were a significant postwar problem for the United Kingdom, a problem demanding the exercise of some sort of special responsibility, at least for their convertibility. But since the UK was too economically weak to exercise that responsibility, it worked politically to defer convertibility; it was unable to bear that responsibility without the assistance of the US and some forbearance on the part of Commonwealth holders of large sterling balances.[13] Thus beneath the veneer of shared responsibility, multilateralism and the equality of all currencies, special responsibilities did emerge, both explicit and tacit.

The one explicit and unquestionably special responsibility of the US was of having its currency anchor a fixed (but in principle adjustable) exchange rate regime. Since returning to the gold standard was ruled out, but no one was as yet ready to allow exchange rates to float, how

---

[11] James, *International monetary cooperation*, p. 29.
[12] *Ibid.*, p. 38; B. Eichengreen, *Globalizing capital: A history of the international monetary system* (Princeton, NJ: Princeton University Press, 1996), chapter 4.
[13] For a succinct account, see Eichengreen, *Globalizing capital*, pp. 125–8.

were countries to manage the financing of their balance of payments? What was to be the medium for clearing accounts and holding reserves? To John Maynard Keynes, the IMF seemed the appropriate institution for providing the unit of account and the liquidity needed to fuel global trade. But his negotiating partner, the US Undersecretary of Treasury Harry Dexter White, was neither willing nor able (for domestic political reasons) to sanction the existence of a truly supranational, global central bank with a generous supply of liquidity, especially since the US would be the major contributor to this global central bank – the IMF. The US negotiators rightly feared that the generous system envisioned by Keynes would put the US, as largest contributor to the Fund, in a position of having unlimited liability and, since it was the sole significant creditor, of being consistently outvoted on policy matters by debtor countries.[14]

The initial difference between Keynes and White as to the amount of liquidity the IMF would make available to its members was rather large, with Keynes proposing a facility of $23 billion, and White, constrained by Congress, proposing a much more modest $5 billion, of which the US obligation would be $2 billion.[15] The US came closer to winning the day with a total facility of $8.5 billion, of which the US contribution was $3.175 billion; the IMF never took on the liquidity provision role envisioned by Keynes. Moreover, negotiations on a new unit of account (Keynes's 'bancor') did not produce results. As is well known, rather than a multilateral unit of account centred on the IMF, the US dollar became the international reserve currency, convertible to gold at $35 an ounce, thus imparting to the US the special responsibility of maintaining a fixed exchange rate and providing central banks around the world with their key reserve currency.

This special responsibility emerged as a pragmatic compromise born of the lack of a viable alternative, rather than as a result of reasoned and principled negotiation. As early as 1947, the economist Robert Triffin warned of its unsustainability.[16] However, the dollar's position as key international reserve currency was formally institutionalised in the IMF's Article IV, section 1(a) which stated: '[t]he par value of the currency of each member shall be expressed in terms of gold as a common denominator or in terms of the United States dollar of the weight and fineness in effect on July 1, 1944'.[17] Historical accounts of

---

[14] James, *International monetary cooperation*, p. 42.

[15] Eichengreen, *Globalizing capital*, pp. 96–7.

[16] B. Eichengreen, *Exorbitant privilege: The rise and fall of the dollar and the future of the international monetary system* (Oxford: Oxford University Press, 2011), p. 50.

[17] As quoted in James, *International monetary cooperation*, p. 50.

this decision suggest that it was born of a rather last minute, ad hoc compromise.[18] It also contradicts the Bretton Woods principle of equality of all currencies.

The formal recognition of the dollar's status was not accompanied by ringing endorsement from the US's negotiating partners. The gold-dollar exchange standard gave the US a special privilege, and this made others uneasy and in some cases (notably that of Charles de Gaulle) downright hostile. As Barry Eichengreen puts it:

American consumers and investors could acquire foreign goods and companies without their government having to worry that the dollars used in their purchases would be presented for conversion into gold. Instead those dollars were hoarded by central banks, for which they were the only significant source of additional international reserves. America was able to run a balance-of-payments deficit 'without tears,' in the words of the French economist Jacques Rueff. This ability to purchase foreign goods and companies using resources conjured out of thin air was the exorbitant privilege of which French Finance Minister Valéry Giscard d'Estaing so vociferously complained.[19]

Liquidity was needed to fulfil the liberal vision for the revival of world trade, and thereby to generate the growth engine that would sustain the embedded liberalism compromise. But as Richard Gardner has noted, the ratio of gold to world imports 'dropped ominously in the years after Bretton Woods ... Since it could not be borne by the Fund, the responsibility for filling this gap in reserve growth was assumed by the United States.'[20] Yes, the US took on a special responsibility by having the dollar serve as international reserve currency. But it did so because it had denied the alternative supranational unit of account governed by a multilateral institution, and because no other country on its own had the means to step into the role (although again, sterling remained an important reserve currency as a hangover from the previous era). And from the very beginning, this special responsibility looked to some observers more like an 'exorbitant privilege' than a responsibility. As Eichengreen notes, countries buying into the Bretton Woods regime were from the beginning preoccupied with 'how to limit the ability of the United States to manipulate that system to its advantage'.[21]

The fact that initial negotiations on IMF and World Bank contributions explicitly linked contribution size to power and prestige, and involved contention about the US contributing *too much*, suggests

---

[18] *Ibid.*; Gardner, *Sterling-dollar diplomacy*.
[19] Eichengreen, *Exorbitant privilege*, p. 40.
[20] Gardner, *Sterling-dollar diplomacy*, p. xxxv.
[21] Eichengreen, *Exorbitant privilege*, p. 45.

that the desire to make the US less special and more responsible in a *collective* sense was an important political issue at Bretton Woods.[22] The negotiators were from the beginning clearly attuned to the difference between the US exercising preponderant power and influence by virtue of its wealth, on the one hand, and the US committing itself to share responsibility for sustaining a multilateral system, on the other. Most of its negotiating partners worked to *limit* US influence by attempting to diffuse responsibility in the face of US preponderance. For example, James notes that the chair of the Soviet delegation to the Bretton Woods negotiations 'presented the demand to raise the Soviet quota from $800 million to $1,200 million', in the context of debate about the US quota being too large.[23] Yes, in this we can see jostling for influence and prestige (the Soviets soon opted out of the organisation altogether), but this example also suggests that we cannot simply infer that larger contributions imply larger responsibility. The greater decision-making clout claimed by the largest contributor to the Fund was actually a source of concern to other participants in the regime, who sought to dilute that clout by more generalised articulations of responsibility.

The non-US negotiators feared that the US's larger contributions to the IMF could dilute the sense of shared responsibility, and the US actually made concessions to these concerns by bringing its initial 61 per cent of the quota proposal down to under 30 per cent.[24] From this aspect of the negotiations we can infer that one major concern was for the US to agree to bind itself to the *shared* responsibilities implicit in multilateralism. The other negotiators could not deny that the US would have a *bigger* responsibility based on its economic might, but they worked to make that responsibility quantitatively smaller, with the understanding that greater contributions brought greater clout, and that the issue was therefore one of limiting the exercise of US privileges, rather than acquiescing to US special responsibilities. The social character of special responsibility conditions our interpretation of power, even when it is being exercised in an apparently benign and charitable manner.

There are other features of the Bretton Woods agreements which suggest a qualitatively special responsibility (in contrast to simply bigger responsibility), but these arise *despite rather than because of* the text and intent of the agreements establishing the institutions. As indicated above, a key preoccupation of the negotiators was how to bring about adjustments in case of global imbalances: if a member state experienced

[22] James, *International monetary cooperation*, p. 49.
[23] *Ibid.*   [24] *Ibid.*

balance of payments surpluses or deficits, what sorts of adjustment burdens should or could be imposed upon it by the Bretton Woods institutions? The negotiators had rejected a return to the gold standard – an automatic adjustment mechanism that triggered austerity in deficit countries and demand stimulation in surplus countries by virtue of gold outflows from or inflows to a country's reserves.[25] But they remained committed to fixed (albeit adjustable, via multilateral consultations) exchange rates. In this they sought to avoid a system where states could exercise sovereign discretion without considering the broader effects of their actions: the interwar experience of aggressive unilateral policies (competitive currency devaluations, sky high tariffs and so on) seeking to rectify imbalances was fresh in their memory.

Thus, adjustment came to be seen as a multilateral problem involving coordinated action. Even so, it was a problem subject to different interpretations. The IMF's Articles of Agreement are vague about the responsibility for adjustment, although the basic underlying economic logic of what countries have to do to adjust to payments imbalances remains roughly as it was during the gold standard: a country's overall spending should contract if it is in deficit, and expand if it is in surplus. But how and according to what criteria are such decisions to be made and executed if there is no automaticity to them?

The IMF's lending facilities, its surveillance function, and its status as a forum within which to negotiate changes in exchange rates suggest that it should have some authority over member state policies, but in terms of its leverage over sovereigns it clearly had (and still has) more leverage over countries experiencing deficits and needing to borrow, than over those experiencing surpluses.[26] Still, the institutional language is one of *reciprocal* obligations to adjust to imbalances; that is, obligations fall on both surplus and deficit countries. The responsibilities for adjustment are differentiated between surplus and deficit countries but theoretically should be shared among all countries. The system of obligation has a symmetry to it, appropriate both to the economic notion of equilibrium and to the functional requirements of double entry bookkeeping.

The 'scarce currency' clause in the IMF Articles of Agreement implied that the US, as the dominant surplus and creditor country it initially was, would be willing to take on a significant burden of adjustment in case of global payments imbalances, by allowing discrimination

---

[25] Eichengreen, *Globalizing capital*, chapter 2 provides a fuller explanation and commentary.

[26] R. Foot and A. Walter, *China, the United States, and global order* (Cambridge: Cambridge University Press, 2011), chapter 3.

against it through exchange and trade restrictions should the dollar be deemed a scarce currency.[27] The immediate postwar fear of a 'dollar shortage' conditions our interpretation of the scarce currency clause: it was designed with the US specifically in mind. By agreeing to the clause, the US appeared to acquiesce to the Keynesian idea that adjustment should not just be the burden of countries in deficit and debt who had to curtail their spending and imports, but also of those running surpluses and extending credit, who would have to rectify the imbalance by boosting domestic demand and allowing others to apply exchange restrictions and possibly trade barriers to help rectify the imbalance. Since the US was the *only* globally significant surplus country and creditor at the time of the negotiation, this implied that it would bear a de facto special responsibility for adjustment via the mechanism of the scarce currency clause.[28]

According to the contemporary interpretation of the British economist Roy Harrod, commenting on the drafting negotiations, the scarce currency clause meant that the Americans 'would come in and accept their full share of responsibility when there was a fundamental disequilibrium of trade'.[29] Perhaps this can be interpreted as a tacit special responsibility insofar as the US was the specific target of the clause. However, as a principle it simply connotes recognition of differentiated but symmetrical responsibilities between surplus and deficit countries. In any case, the scare currency clause never quite played out as Harrod had hoped; it proved much weaker in practice than in theory.

Despite the language of the Articles, the US (at least while it was a net creditor) did *not* accept that a surplus and creditor country bore as much responsibility for adjustment as did deficit and debtor countries. Rather, it expected that the burden of adjustment would fall mostly on deficit countries. Since the most significant deficit countries were its allies, the US then decided to take on a different sort of special responsibility – not exactly the responsibility entailed by the scare currency clause, but rather that of assisting allies with *their* adjustment problems via aid and loans:

In immediate terms, Marshall Plan assistance appeared to solve the European balance of payments problem. In 1946, the Western European trade deficit with

---

[27] International Monetary Fund, 'Articles of Agreement: Article VII – Replenishment and scarce currencies', no date, www.imf.org/external/pubs/ft/aa/aa07.htm (accessed 28 July 2011); see also Eichengreen, *Globalizing capital*, p. 115; James, *International monetary cooperation*, pp. 45–6.

[28] This was despite the fact that the British pound sterling continued to be held as a reserve currency. There were no fears of shortage of sterling, but rather fears about convertibility leading to a run on sterling.

[29] Quoted in James, *International monetary cooperation*, p. 46.

the United States had been $2,356 million, and in 1947 it rose to $4,742 million. In its first year of operation (April 1948–June 1949), the ERP [European Recovery Program] made $6,221 million available, and then $4,060 million in 1949–50 and $2,254 million in 1950–51.[30]

Instead of addressing the initial postwar adjustment problem using the IMF's mechanisms, then, the US dealt with it via direct aid to Europe. It did so in order to facilitate not only economic recovery but West European integration. The US viewed economic integration as the path to a strong and prosperous Western Europe, making those countries lucrative trading partners and more capable allies. Arguably, this can be read as a self-allocation of special financial responsibility for the broader purposes of nurturing a multilateral system of embedded liberalism and an alliance to contain Soviet expansion. However, the choice of how to allocate this responsibility was, if not nakedly unilateral, then at least not formally multilateral, and this had consequences for the sustainability of an economic regime requiring the exercise of generalised and shared responsibilities amongst its members. In particular, the choice set the US up to evade IMF surveillance, and undermined the symmetry of a regime designed to trigger more automatic forms of adjustment in both deficit and surplus countries.

Francis Gavin has noted that, although the designers of Bretton Woods tried to insulate the monetary system from international power politics, 'in fact, postwar monetary relations were highly politicized and required constant political intervention to keep the system functioning smoothly'. The biggest design flaw, as Gavin sees it, was 'lack of an effective, automatic mechanism to adjust and settle the payments imbalances that inevitably arose between surplus and deficit countries'.[31] The initial postwar adjustment problem was European deficits; these were addressed 'by a series of political interventions: the Europeans imposed trade and exchange controls, undertook a round of devaluations vis-à-vis the dollar in 1949, and received large amounts of American aid to close their deficits'.[32]

But the problem was not deficits in themselves; it was the lack of an effective adjustment mechanism. In a dynamic world economy, countries' economic circumstances and resulting balance of payments positions inevitably change. At any given time, there will be differences in countries' rates of inflation and savings. The lack of an automatic adjustment mechanism in a system committed to stable exchange rates was a recipe for monetary instability.[33] According to Gavin, 'exchange

[30] *Ibid.*, p. 74.   [31] Gavin, 'Gold battles', 64–5.
[32] *Ibid.*, 67.   [33] Gavin, *Gold, dollars, and power*, pp. 21–3, 27.

rate stability can only be sustained when there is comparable price stability between countries – a near impossibility. If prices change markedly because of inflation or deflation in a given domestic economy, then currency exchange rates must shift accordingly or else their initial par rates will quickly be rendered meaningless.'[34] But countries were reluctant to utilise the IMF's rules on changing par values. Such changes could make them vulnerable to speculation, which would exacerbate the pressure on the value of the currency. Adjusting via deflation was politically difficult, and long-held fears of inflation in West Germany made expansionary policies especially difficult there. The most common recourse for dealing with imbalances was thus to deploy trade and capital controls – thereby endangering one of the core purposes of the Bretton Woods regime, which was to liberalise trade (although not necessarily to liberalise the capital account).[35]

With regard to adjustment in the immediate postwar period, then, the US as the economically strongest power took on what appears to be a special responsibility for the problem of adjustment by allowing Europeans to violate (temporarily, it was hoped) free trade norms very dear to the US and inhibit capital mobility (a norm to which the US aspired but upon which it could not yet insist) by channelling large amounts of US aid to Europe. Does this constitute a tacit, but special, US responsibility with respect to the adjustment issue? We argue in the affirmative but, like the dollar's role as anchor of a fixed exchange rate regime, it was an unsustainable responsibility in the longer term, and it undermined the theoretical, institutionalised symmetry of a rule-based system of generalised and reciprocal responsibilities. Gardner has summarised the issue as follows:

The inadequacies of the Bretton Woods adjustment mechanism were camouflaged in the early postwar years when the United States was in surplus and the rest of the world was in deficit. Nobody paid much attention to the problem of how the Fund would 'police' surplus and deficit nations ... In effect, the United States 'policed' the economic policies of deficit countries unilaterally, using the leverage of postwar aid to encourage the adoption of internal and external policies it regarded as appropriate. It also, in a sense, 'policed' itself – adopting liberal aid and trade policies appropriate to a surplus nation because it quickly recognized that if it failed to do so the rest of the world would go broke ... The United States was the economic giant among nations; there was no one with whom to *share responsibility*; it alone had the power to save the wartime multilateral dream and assure the survival of freedom in the West.[36]

---

[34] *Ibid.*, p. 21.   [35] *Ibid.*, p. 22.
[36] Gardner, *Sterling-dollar diplomacy*, p. xl, emphasis added.

It is worth emphasising how Gardner's text moves from a recognition that the US had undermined the IMF's surveillance mechanism to a phrase about saving the wartime dream and 'survival of freedom in the West'. This is characteristic of many writers who use the narrative of hegemonic stability as benign leadership to paint in broad brush strokes what was in its details a far more contentious struggle over the nature of power and responsibility in the postwar era. The hegemonic stability narrative itself seems very much a product of the US self-understanding of its postwar role. That said, it would be difficult to argue that US special responsibilities were *not* sanctioned by its allies, especially if one considers the big picture which includes security guarantees. But the specific character of those responsibilities was indeed contested, and many were (and still remain) unreconciled to other developments, such as the reserve status of the US dollar.

The Bretton Woods agreements formally articulated a system of generalised, shared and reciprocal responsibilities anchoring a multilateral rule-based regime governing trade and foreign exchange. Surplus and deficit countries were to submit themselves to surveillance and adjustment pressure from the IMF. The de facto assumption and self-allocation by the US of special responsibilities in that regime helped make what may have been an unworkable system work. It helped to spur what in retrospect looks like a 'golden age', over a decade of steady economic growth, soaring international trade levels and rising prosperity in the countries linked into the regime. But the US assumption of special responsibilities in the form of aid, loans, capital investment and the practice of running balance of payments deficits also undermined the core norms and symmetry of the regime, thus setting it up for eventual failure.

Reallocation of responsibility in the breakdown of Bretton Woods

As Robert Triffin had predicted, the special responsibility attached to having the US dollar anchor a fixed exchange rate regime was unsustainable; its unravelling, and the emergence of the order which replaced it, is a study in the contestation and reallocation of responsibility in the international financial system. Foreign dollar liabilities exceeded US gold reserves by about 1960.[37] In the late 1960s and early 1970s, any

---

[37] Eichengreen, *Exorbitant privilege*, p. 50.

remaining pretence of US special responsibility for exchange rate stability faded away, while responsibilities for adjustment had to be renegotiated in the face of new economic realities. The new economic realities meant that the initial, largely tacit postwar solution to the adjustment problem no longer held. Since the US was no longer the overwhelming surplus country and creditor, but rather faced the threat of chronic deficits, American policy-makers began to rethink the issue of how to allocate responsibility for adjustment, especially in light of the emergence of Japan and Germany as export powerhouses and substantial surplus countries.

The US postwar economic position exempted it from *external* adjustment pressure. James observes that 'the system required the imposition of fiscal restraint or deflation for balance of payments purposes in circumstances that might be difficult politically. For the largest economy and the major "key currency," the United States and the dollar, such discipline could not be imposed from the outside: it had to be self-generated.'[38] He further observes that the manner in which Bretton Woods operated during its supposed heyday was by *delaying* adjustment in the major reserve centres, the US and Britain.[39] What seemed like a special responsibility in the days of a 'dollar shortage', and then in the period of sustained growth in the 1950s and early 1960s, came to be seen as an unfair privilege and irresponsibility as doubts grew about the sustainability of the US commitment to dollar convertibility into gold at $35 an ounce. The breakdown of the Bretton Woods exchange rate regime signalled a breakdown in policy cooperation and coordination, and a unilateral abdication of US responsibility for exchange rate stability.

But the breakdown of Bretton Woods was not only the inevitable playing out of economic realities. Both James and Eichengreen, among the best historians of the Bretton Woods period and its aftermath, suggest that the regime might have been given a longer lease on life by political cooperation and policy coordination. Many efforts were made in this direction, including the establishment of the Gold Pool,[40] the creation of a 'special drawing right' in the IMF, and various temporary US schemes to alleviate pressure on the dollar, such as 'Roosa Bonds',

---

[38] James, *International monetary cooperation*, p. 175.
[39] *Ibid.*, p. 152.
[40] The Gold Pool was initiated in 1961 as a cooperative agreement between Belgium, France, Italy, West Germany, the Netherlands, Switzerland, the UK and the US to 'regulate the London price of gold and to share responsibility for stabilizing the market'. See B. Eichengreen, *Global imbalances and the lessons of Bretton Woods* (Cambridge, MA: MIT Press, 2010), p. 35.

named after the Undersecretary of Treasury in the Kennedy administration, or the attempt to decouple official central bank gold prices from private market gold prices. Attempts to generate institutionalised surveillance and cooperation centred on the IMF, the OECD, the Bank for International Settlements and the Group of Ten (G10). All of these were attempts to cope with the unsustainability of the dollar's link to gold, given the US unwillingness to adjust its fiscal and monetary policies to account for its changing balance of payments position. All these attempts at 'cooperation' involved efforts by the US to shift onto others some of the burdens it felt it was bearing for the good of the Western world.

The economic developments that posed the greatest challenge to sustaining the Bretton Woods regime were the emergence of the Euromarkets, the rise of West Germany and Japan as strong surplus countries and the growth of US budget deficits. Payments crises in Britain and economic turmoil in France in the late 1960s also played their part.

The Euromarkets consisted of US dollars being held abroad, initially by central banks but eventually by commercial banks as well. 'After exchange controls on current account transactions were lifted in 1958, Swiss and British commercial banks were free to accept foreign currency deposits and could offer more favorable rates than those on the US domestic market.'[41] As the deposits grew, so did the size of the market. 'Once the market had reached a certain size, it generated transactions no longer necessarily limited to outflows from the United States.'[42] The Eurodollar market grew in size from $1,500 million in 1959 to $46,000 million in 1970.[43]

The growth of the Euromarkets (which included currencies other than dollars, although the dollar was predominant) exponentially increased the power of market players to put speculative pressure on currencies. But it also provided new borrowing opportunities to governments. As we explain in the following paragraphs, the emergence of the Euromarkets can be seen as an important step toward a 'vertical' diffusion of responsibility for adjustment and stability away from states and towards markets, even as the dominant discussion at the turn of the decade was about reallocating responsibilities 'horizontally' among states.[44]

---

[41] James, *International monetary cooperation*, p. 179.
[42] *Ibid.*, pp. 179–80. [43] *Ibid.*, p. 180.
[44] We are indebted to Andrew Walter for suggesting the vertical and horizontal terminology.

As a result of the growth of the Euromarkets, exchange rates 'hardened'.[45] That is, states grew increasingly unwilling to contemplate changes in par values of their currencies (allowed under IMF rules with IMF surveillance and advice) because such changes – or even the news that such changes were being contemplated – would send signals to market players who now had the capacity to exacerbate or even bring on the very crises that the changes in par value would be designed to avert. Speculators could bet against a currency on the mere expectation of devaluation. For countries facing deficits, the option to devalue in order to improve their export position was made less attractive not only by fear that speculative attacks would bring the currency down further than desirable, but also by the idea that devaluation was a sign of weakness, thus affecting overall confidence in a country's economic position.

Countries in surplus – and West Germany was the prime example in the 1960s – were also reluctant to change the value of their currencies (revaluation in this case) for both ideological and pragmatic reasons. The ideological reasons were that a strong currency was considered a 'healthy' currency, thus not needing adjustment; it was the weak or 'sick' currencies that needed adjustment.[46] The pragmatic reasons were that revaluation would hurt the country's export position, often seen as the source of the 'healthy' surplus in any case. Germany faced repeated pressures to revalue, and speculators who anticipated such revaluation periodically rushed into German marks: '[a] massive rush into the German mark in November 1968 called international attention to the problem. Defying the combined pressure of Britain, France, and the United States, the government in Bonn belligerently refused to peg the D-mark higher – a decision that defused the immediate crisis but ultimately redoubled expectations of some future parity change.'[47] West Germany did revalue eventually, but the whole issue was highly contentious.

The domestic politics of these issues were more complex than this brief review indicates, because different constituencies within the same country had different preferences on currency values, and also because not only trade balances but capital flows were affected by changes in currency values. But the overall message here is that the growth of Euromarkets and financial speculation made the adjustment problem

---

[45] James, *International monetary cooperation*, p. 205 and chapter 7.
[46] The terminology of healthy and sick was used at the time and is documented in W. G. Gray, 'Floating the system: Germany, the United States, and the breakdown of Bretton Woods, 1969–1973', *Diplomatic History*, 31(2) 2007, 295–323.
[47] *Ibid.*, 299.

more difficult for governments because it constrained them from using changes in par values as a tool for economic management – something that was technically part of the IMF regime. On the other hand, with a growing pool of available private capital, governments began to realise that they could put off adjustment via fiscal constraints by instead turning to global capital markets. If a country's balance of payments position threatened to undermine full employment policies, instead of cutting back on spending they could try to attract foreign capital by floating bonds, for example. This was one stepping stone on the path to the inflation which began in the late 1960s and took off in the 1970s.[48]

German and Japanese recovery and transformation into export powerhouses produced new adjustment pressures in the system as well. These countries found themselves in a difficult position in relation to the US as it slipped into a deficit position, and they became important actors determining the fate of the Bretton Woods regime. William Glenn Gray presents a nuanced picture of US responsibility and the limits of US capability in governing international economic relations purely according to its preferences:

The United States occupied a 'pivotal position' within Bretton Woods, for it was uniquely responsible for guaranteeing convertibility of dollars into gold at the ratio of $35 per ounce. But historians would do well to recall the systemic character of monetary relations. American and British economists had conceptualized and framed the world of Bretton Woods; but precisely because of their success in promoting an expansive, liberal world economy, neither the dollar nor the pound completely determined the fate of the international monetary system. Set against these two currencies in decline were two emerging forces, the Japanese yen and the German mark. It was the interplay among all of these currencies that generated intolerable strains on the system of fixed exchange rates.[49]

Because of their experience with hyperinflation in the 1920s and financial collapse in the 1930s, West German voters were especially committed to price stability. Both government officials and central bankers 'shared this inflation-fighting zeal, but the central bankers always suspected that, given a choice, politicians would sacrifice stability for the sake of growth'.[50] However, West Germany could not ignore the pressure from its allies regarding the adjustment issue.

Since 1962, the Bonn government had been making 'offset' purchases – mainly American military hardware and Treasury bonds – in order to counterbalance the immense foreign exchange costs of hundreds of thousands of American

---

[48] James, *International monetary cooperation*, p. 200.
[49] Gray, 'Floating the system', 296.   [50] *Ibid.*, 297.

soldiers in Germany. In the years 1966–1968, the Bundesbank repeatedly came to the aid of the Bank of England and the Bank of France, helping those institutions to weather the punishing rounds of speculation that had depleted their reserves.[51]

Whereas once US dollar outflows helped to cushion the fact that the adjustment burden would fall primarily on deficit countries rather than surplus countries, the US now began to advocate adjustment by surplus countries such as West Germany and Japan. The US had significant leverage over West Germany due to the US troop presence on its soil. The threat to withdraw those troops was explicitly used by the Kennedy administration to get the Germans to bear more of the costs of adjustment to global imbalances. As early as the second Eisenhower administration, the issue of US troops in Europe became central to the discussion of the vulnerability of the dollar. The Eisenhower administration rejected capital and trade controls as solutions to the problem.

Instead, it began to scrutinize balance-of-payments cost-of-government expenditures overseas, particularly troop deployment costs, an account the administration could control without reversing the cherished goal of trade and currency liberalization. US foreign exchange expenditures in NATO Europe were roughly the size of the national deficit, a fact few found coincidental.[52]

Although both Eisenhower and Kennedy after him faced significant domestic resistance (by some of their own advisers) to American troop withdrawals from Europe, the threat of such withdrawals became part of the bargaining process involved in trying to save the Bretton Woods exchange rate regime. That process only succeeded in delaying the regime's demise, but in it we can clearly see the US attempting to get others to share the burden of the responsibility that it, in its immediate postwar economic superpower status, had allocated to itself. By singling out West Germany – both out of strategic opportunity and because of the material fact of West German economic strength – the US set in motion a process whereby West Germany began to assume a greater share of responsibility for European financial stability, a process that plays itself out in the history of European economic and monetary integration.

West Germany unilaterally let the Deutschmark float three times before the complete unravelling of the Bretton Woods regime of fixed exchange rates: in 1969, 1971 and 1973. Gray argues that 'the stability and attractiveness of the German currency helped to accentuate the imbalances across the monetary system. The dollar's weakness is only

---

[51] Gray, 'Floating the system', 301.   [52] Gavin, 'Gold battles', 68.

part of the story.'[53] But the Germans learned important lessons from their experiences in this period, as Gray notes:

[R]ecognizing that German unilateral action only exacerbated political tensions, they strove to articulate their interests within a European framework. The nascent plans for monetary union provided a focal point for European attentions during the transition from Bretton Woods to the 'non-system' that still prevails. In other words, Bonn's moderating influence helped to rally Europeans around a new point of reference, thus allowing the Nixon adminis- tration to back away from its Bretton Woods responsibilities with more grace than it was likely to muster on its own.[54]

The Germans also faced large inflows of capital as money fled the US and sought sounder investments in Germany. They feared the inflation- ary consequences of such inflows, but were reluctant to deploy capital controls.

The French position with respect to global imbalances had been to defend the franc with capital controls and other restrictions, and to pressure the US to devalue the dollar by raising the dollar price of gold. The strategic context was one of French attempts to limit US hegemony in Western Europe and to form a common European political front as a counterweight. French policy of insisting on exchanging dollar holdings for gold was part of a broader stance that included the development of an independent nuclear deterrent and exit from the North Atlantic Treaty Organisation (NATO) command structure.[55] The French also worked to enhance their global economic clout through West European cooperation, although their vision for an integrated Europe differed from that of their German and British allies – as is clear from de Gaulle's refusal to let the UK enter the Common Market, and from the history of Franco-German tension on economic and currency policies.

Britain experienced a different set of issues due to the role of sterling as reserve currency. Its troubles foreshadowed what was to happen to the US with the dollar. Spending on overseas commitments appropriate to an imperial power had over-extended the UK, but the pace of retrench- ment was too slow to bring balance of payments into line, especially since successive governments were unwilling to pursue harsh austerity measures. US aid, IMF loans and eventual devaluation of the pound sterling did not resolve British balance of payments troubles. The UK thus experienced problems analogous to those of the US, although on

---

[53] Gray, 'Floating the system', 323.   [54] *Ibid.*
[55] K. Schwabe, 'Three grand designs: The USA, Great Britain, and the Gaullist con- cept of Atlantic partnership and European unity', *Journal of Transatlantic Studies*, 3(1) 2005, 7–30.

a smaller scale. Moreover, in the late 1960s, as the dollar came under increased pressure, speculative attacks on the pound sterling translated directly into further stress on the dollar, insofar as central banks holding sterling reserves sought to convert them into dollars, which the US then feared they would try to convert into gold on concerns about the ability of the US to maintain the dollar peg.[56]

Government spending played a major role in the deterioration of the relative economic position of the US in the 1960s. Already large US military expenditures were increased by escalation of the war in Vietnam. Gross military outflows of dollars to Asia, 'which had averaged less than $1 billion a year between 1960 and 1964, rose to an average of $2.7 billion in 1969 and 1970'.[57] Lyndon Johnson's administration coupled this with a 'Great Society' reform agenda, which involved increased spending at home. The federal deficit rose from $5,922 million in 1964 to $25,161 million in 1968.[58] All this affected the trade balance and the current account balance, which became negative in 1968. This shift led the US to draw on IMF funds for the first time in 1968, and then again in 1970 and 1971.[59] In addition, capital began to flow out of the US and into Germany in 1970 and 1971. These developments cast further doubt on the ability of the US to continue to exercise its special responsibility in the Bretton Woods regime.

By 1970, the chorus of criticism faced by the US regarding the dollar's position was overwhelming, and it was often couched in the language of responsibility. In a speech to the IMF Annual Meeting in 1970, French Finance Minister d'Estaing chided: 'Nations whose currency is widely used in the world thereby have *increased responsibilities*, a natural counterpart to the advantages they derive from the dissemination of their currency.' But the remainder of that speech reaffirmed faith in a fixed exchange rate regime as the key to global financial stability: 'A currency that aims to play an international role as an accounting unit must obviously be of a highly fixed nature, since the other currencies cannot be permanently determined in relation to a standard that is no longer fixed but variable. None of you would agree to set his watch by a clock that was out of order.'[60]

The fact that it was Richard Nixon's administration which had to face the culmination of the crisis definitively coloured the US response to the adjustment problem brought on by the dollar overhang. Nixon's

---

[56] Gavin, *Gold, dollars, and power*, chapter 7.
[57] James, *International monetary cooperation*, p. 208.
[58] *Ibid.*   [59] *Ibid.*, p. 209.
[60] Quoted in *ibid.*, p. 212, emphasis added.

Treasury Secretary, John Connally, said to the Europeans: 'The dollar may be our currency but it's your problem.' To his home audience he was even blunter: 'Foreigners are out to screw us. Our job is to screw them first.'[61] As the dollar crisis crested, the Nixon administration abandoned all pretence to special responsibility: 'President Richard Nixon spoke exclusively the language of national power and national advantage. International cooperation appeared to be suspect; international agencies futile.'[62]

On Sunday 15 August 1971, Nixon delivered a speech on his 'New Economic Policy' to the American public. The programme he introduced included tax cuts; a ninety-day freeze on wages and prices; the suspension of the Federal Reserve swap network; a (temporary) 10 per cent surcharge on imports; limitation on the use of gold as a reserve asset; and 'a notification to the IMF that there would no longer be free buying and selling of gold in the United States'. James notes: 'It was a decision in which international institutions had no role.'[63] This move became known as the 'Nixon shock': the closing of the gold window and the formal end of Bretton Woods as a fixed exchange rate regime.

In what borders on Orwellian double-speak, Nixon referred to the threat of attack from 'international money speculators', and insisted that '[w]e must protect the position of the American dollar as a pillar of monetary stability around the world'. He announced that he was 'temporarily suspending convertibility of the dollar into gold'. He added that:

The United States has always been, and will continue to be, a forward-looking and trustworthy trading partner. In full cooperation with the International Monetary Fund and those who trade with us, we will press for the necessary reforms to set up an urgently needed new international monetary system. Stability and equal treatment is in everybody's best interest. I am determined that the American dollar must never again be a hostage in the hands of international speculators.[64]

Most European countries responded to the Nixon shocks by allowing their exchange rates to float, as the Germans and also the Dutch had already begun doing. The Japanese attempted to sustain the dollar parity of the yen but eventually gave in and allowed it to float.[65] The move to floating exchange rates, managed or not, changed the character of

---

[61] Connally, quoted in *ibid.*, p. 210.
[62] *Ibid.*, p. 209.   [63] *Ibid.*, p. 291.
[64] R. Nixon, 'Address to the nation outlining a new economic policy: "The challenge of peace"', 15 August 1971, in J. T. Woolley and G. Peters, *The American presidency project* [online], Santa Barbara, CA, www.presidency.ucsb.edu/ws/index.php?pid=3115 (accessed 28 July 2011).
[65] James, *International monetary cooperation*, pp. 220–1.

the twin problems of adjustment and financial stability. First, the adjustment problem could be to some extent depoliticised, because as already foreshadowed by the Euromarkets, market pressures would be brought to bear on the currencies of countries whose accounts were out of balance: deficit countries would face downward pressure, surplus countries upward pressure, and theoretically this should facilitate something approximating automatic adjustment in the balance of payments.

The qualitative character of the stability problem changed, because stability would no longer simply mean exchange rate stability. Concerns with global financial stability would become focused on capital flows and the potential power of speculative market movements to cause economic damage to sovereign states and their domestic economic conditions and social objectives. The consequences of the US abrogation of special responsibility for the Bretton Woods system, combined with the weakness of the European attempts to coordinate a common response to the shocks of the 1970s and of attempts to institute new forms of monetary cooperation in the IMF and the G10, set the stage for a global financial regime where political responsibility appeared weak and diffuse. In the absence of strong leadership, questions of adjustment and stability were increasingly left to the allocative 'wisdom' of market forces.

Horizontal and vertical diffusion of responsibility in the post-Bretton Woods era

Harold James writes that '[t]he general evolution of the international monetary system since the Bretton Woods conference has been a movement away from rules and toward cooperation'.[66] Ruggie has argued that the cooperative arrangements following the breakdown of the Bretton Woods regime remained within the principled scope of the embedded liberalism compromise, while Robert Keohane argued that the period after 1971 shows that cooperation can occur 'after hegemony'.[67] International relations theorists of a more liberal and constructivist bent have tended to see rule-following as evidence for cooperation; they do not distinguish, as James does, between a rule-based system and one grounded in political cooperation. Yet there is an important insight in the distinction drawn by James. Regulation of global finance

---

[66] James, *International monetary cooperation*, p. 586.
[67] Ruggie, 'International regimes, transactions, and change'; R. O. Keohane, *After hegemony: Cooperation and discord in the world political economy* (Princeton, NJ: Princeton University Press, 1984).

in the post-Bretton Woods era has been the purview not of the rule-based, universal membership multilateral IMF, but rather of a mix of national regulators and various more limited membership cooperative groupings of states. Dan Drezner characterises the regulation of global finance as an arena of 'club standards', or looser, less formal arrangements where greater play is given to political power than to rules and norms. Drezner's realist account thus reinforces James's distinction.[68]

Looking at the case through the lens of special responsibilities, their allocation and their acceptance allows us to acknowledge the distinction between a rule-based regime and one based on political power and bargaining, without necessarily ceding all ground to realist assertions that political cooperation is based purely on the preferences of the powerful. Social power and social roles get constituted through the negotiation and allocation of special responsibilities, but capabilities to perform the responsibilities vary and change over time, and the capabilities can themselves be transformed because of the social allocation of roles and responsibilities.[69] The demise of Bretton Woods shows that the US lost the ability to contribute to global financial stability by underpinning a fixed exchange rate regime with its currency. Yet it did not entirely lose its power preponderance in the global system as a whole. Preponderance does not automatically translate into capability to perform specific social responsibilities. Moreover, after the demise of Bretton Woods, the character of the domains for which responsibilities were to be exercised was transformed. Adjustment became a somewhat different problem given the increased importance of financial markets for countries' balance sheets and central bank reserves, and stability became a different problem altogether in a world with globalised capital markets and without fixed exchange rates.

What does embedded liberalism mean in a world where its multi-lateral component is substantially weakened due to the turn to 'club standards'? And what does it mean when wealthy states begin to consistently 'disembed' the market from political control, as Mark Blyth has written was the trend by the end of the twentieth century?[70] The post-Bretton Woods era is characterised by a horizontal diffusion away from special and towards general responsibilities, as well as a vertical diffusion of responsibility away from states and toward markets.

[68] D. W. Drezner, *All politics is global: Explaining international regulatory regimes* (Princeton, NJ: Princeton University Press, 2008), chapter 5.

[69] See Chapter 2 in this volume.

[70] M. Blyth, *Great transformations: Economic ideas and institutional change in the twentieth century* (Cambridge: Cambridge University Press, 2002).

The story of capital account liberalisation, which significantly accelerated after the decline of the Bretton Woods exchange rate regime, shows not only the horizontal diffusion of responsibility among states and networks of club organisations, but the vertical diffusion of responsibility away from states and towards markets. It also shows a change in the character of the collective action problems facing governments. On the issue of adjustment, in an age where finance is such an integral part of fiscal policy and of the world economy as a whole, market forces exert increasing pressure on states through capital flows and foreign exchange trading. Adjustment is thus less a problem of political cooperation, surveillance and bargaining between states than it once was (although these aspects are still important), and more of a problem of governments adopting policies to make themselves attractive to financiers, institutional investors and bond rating agencies.

On the issue of stability, rather than focusing primarily on misaligned exchange rates and central bank reserve positions (though these factors are still important), attention now also focuses on high volumes of private capital flows, complex financial instruments and extremely large financial institutions that transcend the definitions and regulatory regimes that apply to traditional banks and investment houses. In a world of liberalised capital accounts, these developments bring with them the threat of contagion where shock or institutional failure in one area can lead to a widespread crisis in credit and finance. The term that has emerged to describe the new stability threats is 'systemic risk'; there are a variety of definitions of this term, but the gist of it is that, as Steven Schwarcz puts it, 'a trigger event, such as an economic shock or institutional failure, causes a chain of bad economic consequences – sometimes referred to as a domino effect. These consequences could include (a chain of) financial institution and/or market failures.'[71]

The responsibility regime that has emerged to try to cope with this form of instability is at present highly fragmented and complex.[72] It is fragmented in that it is grounded in national legal systems and differentiated between different sectors of finance (banking, investment, insurance, accounting, currency trading, money laundering and so on). It is complex because a wealth of bodies has emerged to try to coordinate national regulations, although in most cases these bodies have little to no actual power to enforce rules or even impose rough guidelines.[73]

---

[71] S. L. Schwarcz, 'Systemic risk', *Georgetown Law Journal*, 97(1) 2008, 198.
[72] A. G. Haldane and R. M. May, 'Systemic risk in banking ecosystems', *Nature*, 469 (20 January) 2011, 351–5.
[73] Davies and Green, *Global financial regulation*.

The fragmentation and complexity of the global financial regulatory architecture has not rendered it a force for producing financial stability in the current system.[74] But the story of how this came to be, rooted in the globalisation of finance, is not simply a story of US abrogation of responsibility and push toward neoliberalism. That is part of the story, but other countries have played important roles as well, as have innovations in financial practice and ideas about how markets work.

Western Europe's initial response to the closing of the gold window was to try and manage floating rates by keeping them within a certain band, with the objective of moving towards a stable European monetary system and ultimately a single currency. Efforts at currency stabilisation propelled the dismantling of capital controls within the European Community (EC), and the eventual transmission of the capital account liberalisation imperative to the OECD. Rawi Abdelal tells the story of these developments with persuasive evidence and clarity.[75] Ironically, it was the French socialists under François Mitterand who ultimately acquiesced to UK and German pressures for capital account liberalisation in the EC, thus removing the key obstacle to making such liberalisation official policy. In the early 1980s, French socialists came to see that capital controls only constrained the middle classes; the wealthiest financiers had already found ways around them. So the socialists saw their *tournant* towards capital liberalisation as a way of balancing the power of the rich and acting in favour of the middle class. French Socialist policy-maker Henri Chavranski recounted in an interview:

Our capital controls failed not in the sense that everyone was able to elude their grasp; they failed in the sense that those who were less well connected bore their burden most. We recognized, at last, that in an age of interdependence capital would find a way to free itself, and we were obliged to liberate the rest.[76]

The Europeans then liberalised capital accounts within the EC and between the EC and the rest of the world. According to Abdelal, they did this *before* the US began pushing its neoliberal 'Washington consensus'. Abdelal also argues that it was the European policy-makers who were instrumental in prioritising capital account liberalisation in the OECD's Committee on Capital Movements and Invisible Transactions,

---

[74] Haldane and May, 'Systemic risk in banking ecosystems'; also see A. G. Haldane, 'Capital discipline', based on a speech given at the American Economic Association, Denver, 9 January 2011, www.bankofengland.co.uk/publications/speeches/2011/speech484.pdf (accessed 28 July 2011).

[75] R. Abdelal, *Capital rules: The construction of global finance* (Cambridge, MA: Harvard University Press, 2007).

[76] Interview with Henri Chavranski conducted by Rawi Abdelal, Paris, 2 April 2004, quoted in *ibid.*, pp. 58–9.

turning the OECD into a peer group club which, through its Code of Liberalisation of Capital Movements, socialised its members into favouring capital account liberalisation.[77]

IMF staff began to discuss the potential virtues of capital account liberalisation arguably as far back as the 1950s and definitely by the mid-1960s, despite the absence of a capital account liberalisation imperative in the Articles of Agreement.[78] Although the Articles were never amended to include a capital account liberalisation clause, the manner in which the world changed as capital became liberalised pushed IMF staff to reorient their positions. IMF staff became more neoliberal in orientation due to the changing intellectual climate of economics education, and began to advise capital account liberalisation in some of their bilateral country talks. But when IMF staff began to advocate for a change in the Articles of Agreement to include a capital account liberalisation clause, they failed to push it through. Abdelal emphasises European political leadership in supporting new capital account liberalisation rules in the IMF, and recounts that the US actually ended up being responsible for the death of the proposal, which the private financial community strongly opposed due to their suspicions of the Fund's management.[79]

The US was content to have its powerful financial firms exploit open capital markets, but it did not lead the drive for liberalisation via the key universal multilateral organisation, the IMF. Abdelal's interpretation of the US position provides an apt example of an instance where power in the domain of finance does not necessarily entail the exercise of special responsibility:

Because of the overwhelming dominance of the United States in international financial markets, neither Wall Street nor the US Treasury has perceived any need to write rules that might ultimately constrain them as well. Ad hoc globalization befits the United States' hyperpower and its narrow economic ambitions. Managed globalization, on the other hand, befits France, a middle power with ambitions to influence international politics and economics by putting rules and organizations, rather than American power, at the center of the system.[80]

This point seems to place the US outside of a social domain of responsibility being articulated and spearheaded by the Europeans. It might be possible to interpret this as an instance of US 'great irresponsibility' in

[77] Abdelal, *Capital rules*, chapter 5.
[78] *Ibid.*, chapter 6; J. Best, *The limits of transparency: Ambiguity and the history of international finance* (Ithaca, NY: Cornell University Press, 2005), p. 109.
[79] Abdelal, *Capital rules*, pp. 160–1.   [80] *Ibid.*, p. 220.

the sense meant by Hedley Bull:[81] the Europeans form an international society to govern global finance, while the US stands outside that society and offers a competing vision based on its preponderant power. But since the parties involved experience high levels of economic interdependence, this characterisation is not quite accurate. Neither the Europeans nor the US acting alone can shape the global financial order to their specifications and preferences. The understanding of the domain of global finance and what exactly should be done to govern it, and the allocation of responsibilities for such governance, have to be negotiated among a multitude of parties – not only the US and Europeans, now, but also the big emerging market economies of China, India, Brazil, Russia and others.

The liberalisation of financial flows was not simply the result of a process of deregulation; it was accompanied by the evolution of standards and best practices for the private finance sector, an approach Andrew Walter terms 'regulatory neoliberalism'.[82] The institutional loci of these standards are not only – or even primarily – formal multilateral institutions with legal treaty status like the IMF, but rather bodies such as the Basel Committee on Banking Supervision and the International Accounting Standards Board. These organisations do not so much govern as coordinate and pressure national regulators and private firms towards 'best practices'. National regulations and institutional frameworks of the major Western powers, especially the US, the UK and increasingly the EU as an entity,[83] have been central to global financial governance since the financial liberalisation and globalisation of the 1980s onward. These national regulations include such things as capital adequacy requirements for financial institutions, exposure limits and limits on lending; national institutional functions include such things as deposit insurance and lender of last resort functions of the central bank. Institutions such as the Basel Committee work to harmonise and set common standards for things such as bank capitalisation, but they are far from having strong regulatory authority over the global financial system as a whole. And the IMF has been very much on the sidelines when it comes to the major financial centres despite its potential importance.[84]

---

[81] See Introduction and Chapter 1 in this volume.

[82] A. Walter, *Governing finance: East Asia's adoption of international standards* (Ithaca, NY: Cornell University Press, 2008).

[83] On the regulatory clout of the EU see E. Posner, 'Making rules for global finance: Transatlantic regulatory cooperation at the turn of the millennium', *International Organization*, 63(4) 2009, 665–99.

[84] Davies and Green, *Global financial regulation*.

Private credit rating agencies such as Moody's, Fitch's and Standard & Poor's have become central to global financial regulation as well.[85] Since the 1970s these agencies' credit ratings, that is, ratings of the risk of lending to a firm or government, have been incorporated into the US regulatory framework via the Securities and Exchange Commission's designation of key ratings agencies as 'nationally recognized statistical ratings organizations' (NRSROs).[86] The US government then incorporated the risk ratings of these NRSROs into its financial regulations, particularly those 'designed to limit the exposure of investment funds to risky securities, a quite understandable public policy concern'.[87] Ratings agencies have been able to move markets with their estimation of the risk of lending to a particular firm or sovereign. This is a crucial example of the US government deferral of responsibility to a private actor. As Abdelal notes, 'the [national] regulators increasingly *ceded their responsibility* to limit the public's exposure to risk to the rating agencies' analysts'.[88]

Credit risk ratings have influenced all sorts of firms around the globe, but since the agencies also rate sovereign debt risk, they have had direct impact on government borrowing costs and on general perceptions of the investment climate in a given country. And the ratings agencies, like the European Commission, the leadership of the OECD and the staff of the IMF and World Bank, have (until the global financial crisis of 2007–9) all adopted the view that capital controls are ineffective, inefficient and inappropriate to the new era of financial globalisation.[89] Thus, for example, when the Malaysian government imposed capital controls as a temporary measure during the Asian financial crisis in the late 1990s, its sovereign debt rating was downgraded by the ratings agencies, which increased its borrowing costs and exacerbated its economic crisis. But when it turned out that those controls did not after all lead to disaster, its rating went back up again, and some analysts began, in the wake of the Asian crisis, to rethink the orthodoxy on capital controls.[90]

An important piece of the global regulatory architecture emanates from the Bank for International Settlements in the form of the Basel Committee on Banking Supervision. The Committee was established

---

[85] T. J. Sinclair, *The new masters of capital: American bond rating agencies and the politics of creditworthiness* (Ithaca, NY: Cornell University Press, 2005).
[86] Abdelal, *Capital rules*, p. 168 and chapter 7.
[87] *Ibid.*, p. 168.   [88] *Ibid.*, p. 171, emphasis added.
[89] *Ibid.*; Sinclair, *New masters of capital*; Best, *Limits of transparency*; Blyth, *Great transformations*.
[90] Abdelal, *Capital rules*, pp. 185–9.

by the central bank governors of the G10 in 1974, and now brings together central bankers and regulators from twenty-seven different countries.[91] The Basel Committee sets international bank capital standards, or how much reserves a bank must hold to buffer against the risk of losses. In 1988 the Basel Committee introduced the first Basel Capital Accord, which established a formula for a minimum capital standard of 8 per cent. In 2004, the Accord was revised into the form known as Basel II. Andrew Haldane notes that 'Basel I regulatory rules were arbitraged due to their risk insensitivity. This gave rise to Basel II.'[92] The Basel II approach went beyond capital adequacy (now considered the first 'pillar' of an international regulatory system for banks) to include two further pillars: supervisory review and market discipline. Although the minimum capital standard was retained from Basel I, according to Howard Davies and David Green the 'main innovation is the greater use of assessment of risks provided by banks' own internal systems as an input to capital calculation'.[93] Basel II provided a standardised approach to risk assessment for those banks lacking the sophisticated in-house models of the global financial giants. But in the global financial crisis of 2007–9, the supposedly sophisticated risk-assessment models of the giant financial holding companies emerged as important pieces of a network of culprits leading to the crisis. Haldane argues that because of their emphasis on risk calibration, Basel II rules 'caused regulatory complexity and opacity to blossom. This may have inhibited the effectiveness of supervisory discretion and market discipline.'[94]

In the wake of the crisis it was widely agreed among policy-makers and commentators that the Basel II framework was inadequate for delineating capital adequacy standards, although in the acrimony that followed the crisis the Europeans took pains to point out that the US had failed to fully implement Basel II in the first place.[95] The inadequacy of Basel II did not come as a surprise, though, to those who studied these issues before the crisis.[96] Financial innovation, regulatory

---

[91] See Bank for International Settlements, 'History of the Basel Committee and its membership', August 2009, www.bis.org/bcbs/history.htm (accessed 28 July 2011).

[92] Haldane, 'Capital discipline', p. 2.

[93] Davies and Green, *Global financial regulation*, p. 44.

[94] Haldane, 'Capital discipline', p. 2.

[95] See T. Braithwaite and P. Spiegel, 'US defends its banking reforms', *Financial Times*, 2 June 2011; 'Risk weightings: Let's standardise', *Financial Times*, 25 May 2011; P. Jenkins, 'Time to work out the real odds in the weighting game', *Financial Times*, 2 May 2011. For a US perspective arguing why the US should not adopt Basel II, see D. K. Tarullo, *Banking on Basel: The future of international financial regulation* (Washington, DC: Peterson Institute for International Economics, 2008).

[96] See Davies and Green, *Global financial regulation*.

arbitrage and complexity all conspired to elude the capacity of regulators to stem systemic risk. The new Basel III framework has attempted to redress the perceived failures of Basel II, but it has done so not by radical innovation but rather, as Haldane puts it (ironically), 'more of the same – and better'.[97] Basel III has increased capital adequacy standards for banks, but still has not addressed all the entities which do not call themselves banks at all – the so-called 'shadow banking system' – but which have great influence on the financial sector overall.[98] Another criticism of Basel III is that it attempts to deal with the complexity of the financial system with still more regulatory complexity, which according to Haldane is 'to fight fire with fire'.[99] Haldane argues instead that the role of regulators is to provide 'over-arching rules of the game', which should be simple, robust and timely.[100] Clearly he and others do not believe that Basel III will do the job in addressing the systemic risk problem. Although much discussion about Basel III has taken place in the Group of Twenty (G20, of which more below), considerable regulatory debate and innovation after the crisis of 2007–9 remains within national governments. The international institutions and club forums provide a venue for debate and some semblance of coordination, but national governments continue to have a great deal of discretion in how to interpret and apply global standards.

In considering the evolution of special responsibilities in global finance since the 1970s and especially from the mid-1980s onward, it is clear that hegemonic stability theory is no longer adequate not only because of growing economic multipolarity, but also because so much authority has been delegated or deferred to the private sector, including to financial firms, giant institutional investors, and ratings agencies. More critical analyses speak of regulatory capture and collusion between the giant financial firms which have become too big to fail, central bankers and treasury officials.[101]

The highly technical nature of international finance and monetary relations and the staggering complexity of the piecemeal regulatory structure that has developed since the demise of Bretton Woods, when combined with the sheer magnitude of the numbers involved in global finance, conspire to sustain a condition wherein there seems to be no

---

[97] Haldane, 'Capital discipline', p. 2.
[98] 'Unfinished business', *Economist*, 14 May 2011, 10–13.
[99] Haldane, 'Capital discipline', p. 13.   [100] *Ibid.*
[101] One of the best essays expressing this view is S. Johnson, 'The quiet coup', *The Atlantic*, May 2009, www.theatlantic.com/doc/200905/imf-advice (accessed 28 July 2011). See also S. Johnson and J. Kwak, *13 bankers: The Wall Street takeover and the next financial meltdown* (New York: Pantheon, 2010).

way to really allocate or claim special responsibility anymore. The problems seem just too big and complex and technical for 'mere politicians' to handle. There appears to be little alternative but to leave them to a technocratic elite. As Rodney Hall observed quite some time before the latest crisis, central banking is a form of global governance,[102] but it is a form which few really understand. This helps to some extent to insulate this domain from the types of political control that are implied by the concept of special responsibility conceived as political leadership. And when central bankers are closely networked with giant private financial players, as well as the economic modellers and analysts who facilitate financial innovation, the technocratic character of this domain of governance stands out even more starkly.

The United States has been a central player in a global shift of responsibility from universal membership intergovernmental organisations such as the IMF (which never functioned as intended in regulating the global payments system in any case), to networks of national regulators, private market players, international regulatory 'clubs' and multilateral institutions. But it has not been alone in this; other powerful countries have supported this trend.[103] Moreover, it would not be accurate to say that authority and responsibility have been completely privatised. Rather, the locus of authority and responsibility seems to have become diffused into complex networks of regulators, experts and market actors.

In a recent work on global regulatory regimes, Miles Kahler and David Lake have articulated a 'network governance' model to contrast with a hegemony or hierarchy model of regulation.[104] In the network approach, 'states, private actors, or both share regulatory authority through coordinated and repeated interaction'.[105] While hegemonic states figure as important actors in this model, they interact in complex ways with private and non-governmental actors, such that it becomes impossible to argue that the preferences or ideas of the dominant state alone determine regulatory outcomes. For example, in his study of the politics of regulating sovereign debt restructuring, Eric Helleiner concludes that the US played a background role and used informal mechanisms of influence, while sovereign debtors and private creditors 'played

---

[102] R. B. Hall, *Central banking as global governance: Constructing financial credibility* (Cambridge: Cambridge University Press, 2008).

[103] Drezner, *All politics is global*, chapter 5.

[104] M. Kahler and D. A. Lake, 'Economic integration and global governance', in W. Mattli and N. Woods (eds.), *The politics of global regulation* (Princeton, NJ: Princeton University Press, 2009), pp. 242–75.

[105] *Ibid.*, p. 242.

a much more significant role than the United States in developing the Principles',[106] that is, a 'new set of standard legal clauses – "collective action clauses" (CACs) – designed to facilitate a more orderly restructuring of unsustainable sovereign bond debt owed to foreign private creditors'.[107]

Although network governance can be viewed in a positive light in issue areas such as human rights, in some domains of governance it can be prone to 'capture' by less virtuous private interests.[108] This is particularly evident in the case of global finance, and many commentators have argued that the US has taken a rentier turn; that a financial oligarchy (in Simon Johnson's words), or a 'Wall Street-Treasury Complex' (Jagdish Baghwati's term) have collaborated to generate the sort of regulatory network that facilitated financial innovations such as collatoralised debt obligations, credit default swaps, over-the-counter trade in derivatives and all the rest, that helped fuel the housing bubble in the US and ultimately undermined the stability of the global financial system.[109]

Issues of 'state capture' and regulatory failure – in the form of accusations of corruption and crony capitalism – ironically constituted a part of the US Treasury and IMF discourses regarding the Mexican peso crisis of 1994 and the Asian financial crisis of 1997–8.[110] Such accusations were, in the late 1990s, accompanied by technocratic advice that touted the virtues of regulatory neoliberalism, and the need for Asian governments to improve their information, disclosure and transparency. As Jacqueline Best argues, 'it was assumed that the problem lay with emerging market economies' excessive reliance on the state and underdeveloped regulatory systems; the problem was their lack of fit with the global financial system rather than with the system itself'.[111] Now that the source of the latest crisis was presumably the most advanced economy with the most sophisticated financial institutions and regulatory framework, such allocation of blame rings rather hollow. As scholars

---

[106] E. Helleiner, 'Filling a hole in global financial governance? The politics of regulating sovereign debt restructuring', in Mattli and Woods, *Politics of global regulation*, p. 120.

[107] *Ibid.*, p. 90.

[108] W. Mattli and N. Woods, 'In whose benefit? Explaining regulatory change in global politics', in Mattli and Woods, *Politics of global regulation*, pp. 1–43; Helleiner, 'Filling a hole'; Kahler and Lake, 'Economic integration and global governance'.

[109] Johnson, 'Quiet coup'; J. Bhagwati, 'The capital myth: The difference between trade in widgets and dollars', *Foreign Affairs*, 77(3) 1998, 7–12; M. Blyth, 'Bouncy castle finance', *Foreign Policy Online*, 14 September 2009, www.foreignpolicy.com/articles/2009/09/14/bouncy_castle_finance (accessed 28 July 2011).

[110] See R. B. Hall, 'The discursive demolition of the Asian development model', *International Studies Quarterly*, 47(1) 2003, 71–99.

[111] J. Best, 'The limits of financial risk management: or, what we didn't learn from the Asian crisis', *New Political Economy*, 15(1) 2010, 30.

such as Best, Blyth, Helleiner and others have been arguing for some time now, calls for 'transparency' are not going to solve the systemic risk problem – that is, the problem that failures in one market or institution rapidly transmit and cascade to cause collapse and crisis in many other markets and sectors.[112] And it is the systemic risk problem that has emerged as the crux of global financial governance in the present era.

In the evolution – or perhaps devolution – of responsibility for stabilising global finance, the US has partnered with the EU, the OECD membership and now increasingly the G20 group of finance ministers and central bank governors. Since its inception in 1999, the G20 has replaced the G7/G8 by including emerging market economies in the 'club' of finance ministers and central bank governors meeting to discuss issues pertaining to global financial stability. The G20 was formed in the wake of the Asian financial crisis of 1997, but the global financial crisis of 2007–9 brought about significant contestation and renegotiation about who and what should bear special responsibility in stabilising global finance.

This has taken place in a context where the balance of economic power in the world, if measured in terms of market size, continues to trend toward multipolarity, and not just the traditional multipolarity of the European-Atlantic system, but a multipolarity that includes countries once relegated to the economic 'periphery'.[113] According to Davies and Green:

as concentration in the financial industry has grown, the global economy itself has become multipolar. Economic activity is no longer dominated by the United States and Europe, but is spread more broadly, including across markets once described as emerging. Thus there have been fundamental changes in both financial architecture and in the real economy, but no alignment between the two.[114]

This lack of alignment between a concentrated global financial industry and a world economy where the most dynamic growth is in emerging markets is one of the issues which preoccupy the reform proposals for the IMF and World Bank, and now also the G20. This point also lends credence to our call to disaggregate power according to different domains of governance and economic or social activity. Finance has shown itself to be a domain where the exercise of governmental power

[112] For a very interesting take on systemic risk in banking, see Haldane and May, 'Systemic risk in banking ecosystems'.
[113] J. Y. Lin and M. Dailami, 'Are we prepared for a multipolar world economy?', Project Syndicate, 2 June 2011, www.project-syndicate.org/commentary/lin3/English (accessed 28 July 2011).
[114] Davies and Green, *Global financial regulation*, pp. 9–10.

is proving increasingly problematic, because of the ability of the private sector to assert its interests in the political sphere and to create a climate whereby attempts at governance can be arbitraged, circumvented, or overwhelmed.

The global financial crisis of 2007–9, which resulted in taxpayer-financed government bailouts of over-leveraged institutions in the order of $14 trillion, or nearly one-quarter of the world's gross domestic product,[115] at the very least produced extreme wariness about, and desire to curb, the 'structural power' of large segments of the financial sector. The innovations of that sector helped to produce the conditions of the crisis, and this cast doubt on the neoliberal faith in the self-regulating capacity of markets, and in the risk-assessment models of the large financial institutions as well as the adequacy of their capitalisation. Since then, no clear consensus on the allocation of special responsibilities for financial stability or, for that matter, adjustment of structural imbalances, has emerged. Rather, there has been a reassertion of the notion of general and shared responsibilities which characterised the early days of the Bretton Woods negotiations. But this time, this generalised responsibility talk is not accompanied by a self-allocation of special responsibility by a hegemonic power. If anything, the US has been cast by others as the 'great irresponsible' and chastised for its failings, while in the US the culprit has been 'Wall Street'. The rhetoric of blame is worth reviewing, in that it shows the failure to come to some consensus on the allocation of responsibility for global financial stability.

US President Barack Obama, in a speech at Cooper Union, admitted that 'crisis was born of a failure of responsibility – from Wall Street to Washington – that brought down many of the world's largest financial firms and nearly dragged our economy into a second Great Depression'.[116] President Obama and other politicians denouncing 'Wall Street' obviously allude to the irresponsibility of private market players, and the push for such measures as curbing bankers' bonuses reflects populist anger at corporate greed. On the other hand, Ben Bernanke, Chairman of the US Federal Reserve Board, concluded that regulatory policy more than monetary policy was to blame for the US housing bubble, thus arguably attempting to shift responsibility away

---

[115] P. Alessandri and A. G. Haldane, 'Banking on the state', speech, Bank of England, November 2009, www.bankofengland.co.uk/publications/speeches/2009/speech409. pdf (accessed 28 July 2011).

[116] B. Obama, 'Remarks by the president on Wall Street reform', Cooper Union, New York, 22 April 2010, www.whitehouse.gov/the-press-office/remarks-president-wall-street-reform (accessed 28 July 2011).

from the US Federal Reserve technocrats and towards those who are ultimately responsible for regulation: legislatures.[117]

Expert commentaries in the immediate wake of the crisis assigned responsibility to the US in a variety of ways. Jacques de Larosière chaired the High-Level Group on Financial Supervision in the EU, which issued a widely respected and cited report in February 2009.[118] The report stated that the crisis originated "primarily" in the US, and refers to the US Federal Reserve's permissive monetary policy, the housing bubble, insufficient regulation of financial techniques, insufficient oversight of government-sponsored enterprises Fannie Mae and Freddie Mac, low personal savings and high indebtedness in the US, as key factors in helping to create the 'global imbalances' which fuelled and spread the crisis. Roger Altman, who was a partner at Lehman Brothers before he become Deputy Treasury Secretary under Bill Clinton and is now back in the private sector, wrote in mid-2009: '[t]he Ango-Saxon financial system is seen as having failed. The global downturn, and all its human devastation, is being attributed to that failure.' Further, '[t]he United States has turned inward, preoccupied with severe unemployment and fiscal pressures. Its economic model also is now out of favor.'[119] Jeffrey Garten was particularly harsh in the *Wall Street Journal*:

given that the global rot started in the US with egregiously irresponsible lending, borrowing and regulation, America's brand of capitalism is in serious disrepute around the world. Even if President Obama had the mental bandwidth to become a cheerleader for globalization, America's do-as-I-say-and-not-as-I-do leadership has been badly compromised.[120]

The financial crisis certainly struck a blow at the moral authority of the US, but that is nothing really new. Anglo-Saxon capitalism has been in the French crosshairs ever since de Gaulle. But the hostility and scepticism is now more widespread, and given the rise of the emerging market economies, has at times morphed into a broader critique of 'the West'. For example, a *Financial Times* commentary by Ronnie Chan, Chair of Hang Lung Properties in Hong Kong, extends the indictment of the US to a broader indictment of the moral authority of the West:

---

[117] B. S. Bernanke, 'Monetary policy and the housing bubble', paper presented at the Annual Meeting of the American Economics Association, Atlanta, Georgia, 3 January 2010.

[118] J. de Larosière (chair), 'High-Level Group on Financial Supervision in the EU: Report', Brussels, 25 February 2009, ec.europa.eu/internal_market/finances/docs/de_larosiere_report_en.pdf (accessed 28 July 2011).

[119] R. C. Altman, 'Globalization in retreat: Further geopolitical consequences of the financial crisis', *Foreign Affairs*, 88(4) 2009, 6.

[120] J. E. Garten, 'The dangers of turning inward', *Wall Street Journal*, 5 March 2009.

The system that the west has touted as superior has failed. Why should developing countries blindly follow its model now? Remember the moral high ground that western leaders took during the Asian financial crisis? Hong Kong was bashed when its government intervened in August 1998 in the stock market to fend off the western investment banks and hedge funds bent on destroying the city's currency. Yet only a month later, the US government intervened in the market to bail out Long-Term Capital Management, a move that proved to be the harbinger of the western bail-outs of financial institutions in the past year. Hong Kong's government was not allowed to save its citizens, yet by a double-standard the US could save its companies.[121]

When reviewing the post-global financial crisis commentary it becomes evident that blaming the US is not the only game in town; in many commentaries the US is only a proxy for something both more sinister and more diffuse: a type of capitalism – neoliberalism or Anglo-Saxon capitalism, underpinned by apparently mistaken ideas about the efficiency of financial markets and the price signals therein.

In an influential and much-cited speech at the Economist's Inaugural City Lecture on 21 January 2009, Lord Turner, the Chair of the British-based Financial Service Authority, cited worldwide macroeconomic imbalances and financial innovation as causes of the crisis; he certainly refers to US markets and macroeconomic policies, but diffuses blame more broadly to a failure in perception or mindset:

The far bigger failure – shared by bankers, regulators, central banks, finance ministers and academics across the world – was the failure to identify that the whole system was fraught with market-wide, systemic risk. The key problem was not that the supervision of Northern Rock was insufficient, but that we failed to piece together the jigsaw puzzle of a large UK current account deficit, rapid credit extension and house price rises, the purchase of UK mortgage-backed securities by institutions in the US performing a new form of maturity transformation, and the potential for irrational exuberance in the market price of credit. We failed to realize that there was an increase in total system risk to which financial regulators overall – authorities, central banks and fiscal authorities – needed to respond.[122]

In a commentary for the *Guardian*, Andrew Walter stated the point most succinctly in a headline: 'Intellectual laziness caused the economic crisis.' Denying that blame can be placed solely on the US, he notes the misreading of signals from the Asian financial crisis and the willful ignoring of warnings by the Bank for International Settlements

---

[121] R. Chan, 'The West's preaching to the East must stop', *Financial Times*, 3 January 2010.

[122] A. Turner, 'The financial crisis and the future of financial regulation', speech, Economist's Inaugural City Lecture, 21 January 2009, www.fsa.gov.uk/pages/Library/Communication/Speeches/2009/0121_at.shtml (accessed 28 July 2011).

and other institutions about the systemic risks 'posed by the rapid growth of derivatives markets, house prices, and financial sector leverage'.[123] The broader mindset that is being discredited in these and many other commentaries is neoliberalism, at least as applied to the financial sector. Academics – many of them working in the field of political economy rather than economics 'proper' – have been expressing doubts about the market rationality of the financial sector for decades now, and in this they follow and expand on the ideas of Keynes. But now doubts about the ability of financial markets to police themselves and to generate optimal outcomes are much more broadly articulated in policy circles and public media. In this view, while the vertical diffusion of responsibility away from states and toward markets has not eliminated regulation altogether, it has produced a complex and anarchic regulatory structure ill-suited to the task of taming 'Anglo-Saxon capitalism'.

Among scholarly and expert commentators there seems to be general agreement that effective reform of the global financial architecture requires harmonisation and cooperation at the international level in order to prevent regulatory arbitrage, that is, the exploitation by firms of differences in national regulatory systems in order to evade regulation. In a book published before the global financial crisis took hold, but which certainly seems to have anticipated the problem, Kern Alexander, Rahul Dhumale and John Eatwell state concisely that 'the domain of the regulator should be the same as the domain of the financial market'.[124] By this they mean that given the size, complexity and global integration of financial markets, only a global public institution will have the capacity to regulate them. Davies and Green in a more conservative vein suggest that the appropriate institutional leadership should come from the G7 finance ministers, and in an updated commentary Davies extended the membership of that group to include the G20.[125] The general recommendation is institutionalised cooperation at the international level, although the appropriate forum remains a point of contention. And although the formation of the Financial Stability Board and the negotiation of Basel III suggest some movement in the multilateral direction, so far the primary activity has been at the national level, with an overlay of coordination and information-sharing in various international fora. This suggests that we are still in what

---

[123] A. Walter, 'Intellectual laziness caused the economic crisis', *Guardian*, 27 March 2009.
[124] K. Alexander, R. Dhumale and J. Eatwell, *Global governance of financial systems: The international regulation of systemic risk* (Oxford: Oxford University Press, 2006), p. 15.
[125] Davies and Green, *Global financial regulation*; and H. Davies, 'Global financial regulation after the credit crisis', *Global Policy*, 1(2) 2010, 185–90.

James has called a system based on political cooperation rather than one based on strong and clear rules.

In addition to the denunciations of Anglo-Saxon capitalism, the long-standing issue of adjustment has become more acute in the aftermath of the financial crisis. The Obama administration has consistently articulated the need to correct 'global imbalances' – its pressure on China to revalue its currency is only one prong in this drive. For example, on the eve of the Toronto Summit of the G20 leaders held in June 2010, Obama was quoted as saying: 'No nation should assume its path to prosperity is paved with exports to America.'[126] Tim Geithner actually introduced this line of thought at the finance ministers' meeting prior to the leaders' meeting, and the *Wall Street Journal* summed up his remarks to G20 finance ministers as follows: 'US Treasury Secretary Timothy Geithner told his foreign counterparts that they can no longer count on the American consumer to absorb the world's exports and lift the global economy.'[127]

As in the era of German and Japanese surpluses and US deficits, the US is seeking to share the burden of adjustment in the era of the rising power of Brazil, China, India and others. And again as in that era, the status of the dollar as reserve currency is facilitating the ability of the US to defer its own adjustment via fiscal constraint. Now that credit-fuelled consumption has revealed itself to be unsustainable, the US is seeking 'recalibration' in the form of stimulus for consumption in the surplus countries, notably China but also Germany and others. This point bears mentioning in the context of special responsibilities because what was once arguably a privilege – the ability to put off adjustment and run seemingly permanent deficits – is now being cast as having been a responsibility which the US can no longer bear! However that may be, the discourse on the need to correct global imbalances suggests that the US is once again deploying the rhetoric of burden-sharing in global economic leadership; here it follows a pattern established as early as the Kennedy inaugural speech.[128]

The communiqués of the G20 provide evidence that rather than special responsibility of the US or any other major power, global financial governance should be conceived of as a collective enterprise. Commenting on the Washington DC Summit in November 2008, which was the

---

[126] Barack Obama, commenting on the G20 Summit in Toronto, June 2010, quoted in C. Giles and A. Beattie, 'G20 backs drive for crackdown on banks', *Financial Times*, 28 June 2010.

[127] M. M. Phillips, A. Frangos, S. Fidler and M. Walker, 'Geithner urges G-20 to step up consumption', *Wall Street Journal*, 4 June 2010.

[128] Gavin, *Gold, dollars, and power.*

first time that the G20 met at the level of national leaders (rather than finance ministers and central bank governors), Helleiner and Stefano Pagliari drew a parallel between that summit and the Bretton Woods meetings. Both were held in the wake of a massive global financial crisis, but there is another parallel having to do with broadening the legitimacy of the global financial order:

A parallel can also be drawn between Bretton Woods and the Washington meeting's objective of widening global financial governance to be more inclusive of poorer countries by widening the G7/8 to a G20 for the first time at the leaders' level. It is often forgotten today that over half of the countries invited to Bretton Woods were from what is now called the South and that some were assigned a significant role at the conference. US policymakers explicitly saw the conference as a way to shift post-war planning away from a strictly US–British focus (as the British initially preferred) in order to build a new multilateral financial order that had wider legitimacy.[129]

This attempt to broaden the participation in global financial governance to include so-called emerging market countries provides evidence of emerging new conceptions of special responsibility in the sense that it opens up to new membership the club of what were once called 'great powers'.

Responsibility talk was evident in the G20 summits that took place in the midst of and immediately after the financial crisis, but it centred on shared responsibilities. To the extent that responsibilities could be thought of as 'special', the specialness came from their being allocated not to a single power but to a group of leading states, which was now constituted as the G20. The 2008 Washington G20 summit articulated responsibility in a diffuse manner, as belonging to national regulators, while at the same time acknowledging the need for shared standards:

Regulation is first and foremost the responsibility of national regulators who constitute the first line of defense against market instability. However, our financial markets are global in scope, therefore, intensified international cooperation among regulators and strengthening of international standards, where necessary, and their consistent implementation is necessary to protect against adverse cross-border, regional and global developments affecting international financial stability.[130]

---

[129] E. Helleiner and S. Pagliari, 'Towards a new Bretton Woods? The first G20 leaders summit and the regulation of global finance', *New Political Economy*, 14(2) 2009, 275–6.

[130] G20, 'Declaration: Summit on financial markets and the world economy', Washington, DC, 15 November 2008, www.g20.org/Documents/g20_summit_declaration.pdf (accessed 28 July 2011).

Summit participants endorsed and pushed to expand the work of the Financial Stability Forum (FSF) on bank regulation and better oversight of over-the-counter trade in credit default swaps, a form of financial derivative that Warren Buffet famously termed 'weapons of mass destruction'.[131]

The final communiqué of the London Summit of 2009 made two references to responsibility: the leaders pledged 'to endorse and implement the FSF's tough new principles on pay and compensation and to support sustainable compensation schemes and the corporate social responsibility of all firms', and also noted that: 'We recognise that the current crisis has a disproportionate impact on the vulnerable in the poorest countries and recognise our collective responsibility to mitigate the social impact of the crisis to minimise long-lasting damage to global potential.'[132]

The Pittsburgh Summit of September 2009 produced somewhat more robust statements and aspirations.[133] The preamble stated: 'We meet in the midst of a critical transition from crisis to recovery to turn the page on an era of irresponsibility, and to adopt a set of regulations, policies, and reforms to meet the needs of the 21st century global economy.' Amidst promises of a return to fiscal responsibility once the crisis ebbs, the notion of 'irresponsible' behaviour by banks is referred to twice. Also, like the London Summit, the idea of collective responsibility (the collective being the G20) is reiterated thus: 'We share a collective responsibility to mitigate the social impact of the crisis and to assure that all parts of the globe participate in the recovery.' And again: 'Each G-20 member bears primary responsibility for the sound management of its economy. The G-20 members also have a responsibility to the community of nations to assure the overall health of the global economy.'[134] The Pittsburgh Summit also launched a 'Framework for Strong, Sustainable, and Balanced Growth', which again emphasises 'shared responsibility'.

The idea, then, is that each sovereign state has responsibility for sound management of its economy, and that such responsibility helps to support a more stable and continued open world economy (this is echoed in IMF texts as well); that moreover the G20 countries have

---

[131] Quoted in Helleiner and Pagliari, 'Towards a new Bretton Woods?', 279.

[132] G20, 'The global plan for recovery and reform', 2 April 2009, www.g20.org/Documents/final-communique.pdf (accessed 28 July 2011).

[133] G20, 'Leaders' statement, The Pittsburgh Summit', 24–25 September 2009, www.g20.org/Documents/pittsburgh_summit_leaders_statement_250909.pdf (accessed 28 July 2011).

[134] *Ibid.*

a shared responsibility to cushion the poorest and weakest from the vagaries of economic crisis (this is also shared by the IMF in its conception of solidarity); and that the G20 have a general responsibility to keep the global economy 'healthy'.[135]

But as the crisis has eased, the G20 appears to have lost some of its momentum in producing regulatory cooperation. The Toronto Summit Declaration formally articulated the commitment to treat the G20 as 'the premier forum for our international economic cooperation'. It repeated the G20 'responsibility to the community of nations', and emphasised the responsibility of 'the financial sector' for paying more of the costs of risk gone bad.[136] But the consensus underpinning the Toronto Summit and subsequent meetings has been much weaker than that evident in Pittsburgh. The fact that the global financial crisis seemed to be over, that many economies were back on a growth path (albeit anaemic and possibly unsustainable) and that the EU was facing its own sovereign debt crisis all seemed to have conspired to undercut further substantive cooperation on creating a strong regulatory framework of a scope capable of dealing with the size and scope, as well as the concentration, of the financial sector.

Conclusion

The global financial governance problems of adjustment and stability have undergone redefinition with the shift from fixed to flexible exchange rates, the shift in status of the US from primarily a surplus and creditor country to deficit and debtor country, and with the advent of capital account liberalisation, the concomitant surge in volume and volatility of financial flows, and structural changes in the financial sector itself. Traditional multilateral rule-based governance regimes have to some extent given way to more informal, politicised bargaining within various clubs. In finance, the complexity of the issues has to some extent enabled technocratic elites to evade broader public scrutiny of their policies, although this is hardly a new development. Still, the range of innovation in developing new financial instruments and the complexity of the models used in sophisticated financial decisions has certainly posed new challenges for regulators, not to mention the publics to whom those regulators are ultimately accountable.

---

[135] On the IMF discourse that parallels these aspirations, see J. Best, 'Co-opting cosmopolitanism? The International Monetary Fund's new global ethics', *Global Society*, 20(3) 2006, 307–27.
[136] G20, 'The G-20 Toronto Summit Declaration', 26–27 June 2010, www.g20.org/pub_communiques.aspx (accessed 2 August 2011).

In the post-Bretton Woods era of liberalised capital accounts and floating exchange rates, it has become more common for those states who are able to borrow on private markets to defer adjustment and finance their deficits rather than to drastically contract their overall spending, while those countries who must rely on IMF and World Bank funds continue to face more 'traditional' adjustment pressures. Even for those latter countries, and certainly for those routinely borrowing in the private sector, adjustment has come more and more to mean making oneself look good to globalised financial market players. This is not exactly the same thing as exercising fiscal responsibility and seeking to bring spending into line with productivity growth and domestic savings rates. Even for those countries that are not wealthy and powerful, financial markets have offered more and more ways to defer 'real' adjustment. It is hard to know what the limits of such developments are, but surely there are limits.

The old adjustment problem of how to deal with sustained imbalances between countries in surplus and those in deficit has led to much talk about reallocation of responsibility now that the US is the biggest deficit country, but such talk has yet to lead to sustained, coordinated action. Deferring adjustment – often by courting financiers – remains a common practice, although there is also intergovernmental bargaining geared towards getting countries with large current account surpluses such as China and Germany to bear more responsibility for adjustment by stimulating their domestic demand and, in the case of China, revaluing their currency. Thus, although the world is trending toward economic multipolarity, as evidenced by the relative weakening of the US's global economic position vis-à-vis China, the EU and others, there has not been a clear accompanying shift in the allocation of special responsibility for adjustment. Ever since the US began to shed its special responsibility for adjustment, which was quite early on in the Bretton Woods era, the trend has been towards diffusion rather than concentration of responsibility for adjustment in the domain of global finance.

But we should be careful about distinguishing between diffusion and shirking of responsibility for adjustment. At times diffusion has not simply been a 'sharing out' of the burden, but rather a shirking or denial of the burden, a process of passing the burden on to others without their consent. This was the case with the Nixon shock, for example, though in the eyes of the Nixon administration and some of its successors the US 'paid' for this abrogation of responsibility with its defence of freedom in the West. But in order for diffusion of responsibility to be seen as burden-sharing, others must buy into that interpretation; otherwise it is mere buck-passing (literally, in the Nixon case)! In any event, the adjustment problem cannot be deferred indefinitely; sovereign debt crises, the drying up of credit, and the increased burdens on taxpayers as governments have to step in to bail-out endangered sectors of the economy all point to the sub-optimal character of deferring and shirking rather than coming up with a new responsibility regime for adjustment. It is clear that, given the more multipolar distribution of global economic power, such a regime will require articulation of mutual responsibilities and symmetrical obligations shared amongst surplus and deficit countries, in the knowledge that the status of being either a surplus or deficit country can hardly be considered permanent. These were of course some of the founding ideas of the Bretton Woods regime which, although never fully implemented (because of the US assertion of special responsibility), deserve some reconsideration and reconfiguration for the present circumstances.

With respect to the issue of stability in global finance, the very character of the issue has been transformed with the abandonment of the Bretton Woods exchange rate regime and the liberalisation of capital flows. Rather than exchange rate stability and the fear of speculative attacks on a country's currency, the size, concentration and networked global reach of the financial sector has spawned concerns about systemic risk, or the risk that a failure or downturn in one area will spread and cascade such that it can lead to a breakdown of the whole, or significant parts, of the financial system, leading to a drying up of credit, stifling 'real' economic activity. There is little international political consensus as yet on how to allocate responsibility for dealing with systemic risk, although there is much talk about the death of neo-liberalism. Perhaps 'Anglo-Saxon capitalism' has lost moral authority and governments have begun to attempt to develop new regulations for a financial sector widely perceived to have run wild – a development which the US and the EU, at least, once encouraged through their permissive regulatory stances. However, no global regulatory architecture of a scope capable of dealing with the financial sector has yet emerged, nor is it clear that such architecture that is emerging (Basel III in particular) will be more heavy-handed than in the past. National regulatory efforts are only partially coordinated in multilateral institutions, despite the observation that a global regulatory architecture would need to be in place to effectively regulate a globalised financial market.

Few have suggested, since the global financial crisis of 2007–9, that special responsibilities ought to be reallocated to a hegemonic state in order to provide for financial stability; rather, the emphasis is on collective or shared responsibility, for states to cooperate in order to tame the vagaries of markets. The one possible exception to this generalised character of responsibility is that wealthier states as a group are acknowledged to bear a larger responsibility as befitting their economic strength; this can perhaps be construed as a special responsibility, especially to protect those most vulnerable to severe market downturns. Membership in this group of wealthier states has grown to include emerging market countries, and the advent of the G20 is representative of the move towards a multipolar world economy. Even the dominant status of the US dollar as reserve currency, which has long been used as evidence for the premature nature of reports of US decline, appears finally to be reaching its limit. At least according to a survey of central bank reserve managers polled by UBS, the dollar 'will lose its status as the global reserve currency over the next 25 years'.[137] Thus, there is a good deal of evidence for the waning of any last vestige of special US responsibility in global finance.

Does this chapter then simply tell a story of the waning of US power and the rise of a new international power grouping in the G20, centred perhaps on China? There are some glimmers of hope that the G20 could constitute the core of a new international society with a concomitant responsibility regime, but to herald its arrival now would be premature. In any event, reducing the developments recounted here to a simple shift in the distribution of material power would offer scant insight into, and would indeed distract us from, the core governance problems and developments generated by the globalisation of finance. The story told here has been one of the US not only exercising leadership, but also of shedding responsibility and redirecting the locus of authority away from itself. It is a story of frequent misalignment of responsibilities and capabilities. Moreover, it is a story involving far more than states. Markets and private market players have increased in power, but this is not simply material power in the sense thought of by political realists. This is social power, constituted, constrained and enabled by regulatory networks (which include states, private actors and international institutions) and contingent on shared ideas not only about responsibility, but also about what constitutes 'banking', for example, or 'risk', or even 'capital'. This chapter has attempted to show that tracking the evolution and devolution of responsibility in finance means far more than tracking shifts in

---

[137] J. Farchy, 'Dollar seen losing global reserve status', *Financial Times*, 27 June 2011.

the distribution of material capability. This is especially true since the constitution of that 'material' capability is itself increasingly the product of the distinctly *immaterial* machinations of money and finance.

Acknowledgement

We are especially indebted to Andrew Walter for his insightful and constructive comments on an early version of this chapter.

Part III

Ethical dimensions

6   The ethics of special responsibilities

The previous chapters have worked through the history and theory of special responsibilities and provided an empirical analysis in three different domains of global governance. It now remains to explore the ethics of special responsibilities.[1] We offer an initial, and tentative, account that we consider both ethically compelling, and also largely consistent with the preceding sociological history. Here our primary task is to elucidate and defend the ethical basis for the assignment of special responsibilities to particular states or other actors. What claims to special responsibilities are justified? Given that one of our core sociological arguments has been that special responsibilities are domain specific, then we might expect that the ethical justification for the allocation of special responsibilities would be similarly so. We certainly show this to be the case when we explore the specific content and application of ethical principles in the domains of nuclear weapons, climate change and global finance. It nonetheless remains an open, and interesting, question whether there are some core or common principles, a recognisable family of arguments, or at least a common moral grammar that would apply to all the cases.

There are two possible methodological routes to exploring this possibility. The first is to develop specific ethical arguments for each of our three case studies, and then see if there are sufficient commonalities to allow development of universal ethical claims. The second is to begin by developing general ethical arguments for the allocation of special responsibilities in world politics, and then applying them to each of the case studies. Both routes would enable an exploration of the extent to which our ethical arguments formed part of the actual allocation, or subsequent contestation, of special responsibilities in the three cases. We opt for the second route because it is more interesting and challenging, and likely to be of broader interest to normative International

---

[1] In this discussion, we use the term ethics and morality, and ethical and moral, interchangeably.

Relations (IR) theorists. Either way, it is revealing to see if there is any rough convergence between our ethical arguments and those that actually arise in the political discourses of at least some of the prominent parties engaged in real world debates concerning the allocation, contestation and evolution of special responsibilities in different domains of global governance: we could then claim that special responsibilities in world politics do offer a distinctive type of functionalist cosmopolitan ethic that provides a potentially viable response to an increasingly interdependent world, characterised by both formal equality and inequality of material capability among states, as well as other actors.

The chapter unfolds as follows. We begin by briefly revisiting our basic theory of special responsibilities in order to draw out the conceptual building blocks that are relevant to the development of an ethics of special responsibilities. We then identify the moral referents and holders of special responsibilities (that is, on whose behalf such claims should be made and upon whom such responsibilities should fall). As we show, identifying the holders of special responsibilities has to start with capabilities (rather than causal responsibility or culpability per se), since this is presupposed in our basic definition of special responsibilities. However, we also demonstrate that the justifiable assignment of special responsibilities is not a straightforward function of capabilities alone, and this is consistent with our general argument that special responsibilities represent a unique fusion of both functional and ethical arguments. We introduce, explain and defend our core ethical cosmopolitan claim, which assigns special responsibilities to those capable agents upon whose actions or inactions vulnerable constituencies are largely or entirely dependent for the alleviation of their plight. We also identify the circumstances where the holders of special responsibilities might make reasonable claims to place limits upon them. We then turn to the case studies, and flesh out our ethical arguments in relation to them, and also reveal to what extent there is convergence or divergence with the real world arguments that have been deployed in support of special responsibilities. Finally, we turn to the special case of the US, and critically examine the claim of exceptionalism in order to clarify the circumstances under which the US might, by virtue of its preponderance or status, have a unique authority to decide which special responsibilities it should assume.

Assigning special responsibilities

It is frequently observed in ethical discussions about the multiple meanings of responsibility that there is no necessary connection between causal responsibility, moral responsibility (in the sense of culpability or fault) and those with the social role and/or requisite capacity to prevent or remedy harm.[2] The agent who caused harm may not have intended or foreseen harm; the agent who is clearly at fault may not have the capacity to redress the harm; and the agent with the capacity to prevent or remedy the harm may be entirely free of blame. This means that the decision regarding who should ultimately 'take responsibility', in the sense of addressing harm, is never a straightforward matter. If we restrict taking responsibility only to those who are directly causally responsible and/or culpable, then some harms suffered by innocent victims may never be addressed at all. In situations of complex interdependence, where causes and effects are increasingly dispersed and agency is fragmented, this means that there will be many situations when no one would take responsibility. As Andrew Linklater has put it, 'large-scale social systems are unusually vulnerable to the crippling effects of "diffuse responsibility", the condition in which specific duties are not clearly assigned to particular people'.[3] This seems intuitively problematic when there may nonetheless be agents with the capacity to prevent or ameliorate such harm.

In Chapter 2, we argued that taking responsibility (whether special or general) necessarily entails accountability or answerability. This accountability is normally *to* the broad community that makes judgements about the discharge of those responsibilities. However, in this ethical discussion that follows, we will place particular emphasis on accountability *for* vulnerabilities inflicted upon an affected constituency. This is not the only possible form of responsibility, but in the absence of vulnerable constituencies already able to speak for themselves (for example, future generations), responsibility encompasses the guardianship role that the international community must play. Responsibility also assumes certain prerequisites. First, the responsible agent (which we argued includes states) must have both the discretion and capacity to act or refrain from acting in certain ways in relation to that constituency. Second, it is assumed that the responsible agent can be held accountable for the rational and moral exercise of discretionary power in the performance or non-performance of the obligations that define

[2] R. E. Goodin, 'Vulnerabilities and responsibilities: An ethical defence of the welfare state', *American Political Science Review*, 79(3) 1985, 775–87; R. E. Goodin, *Protecting the vulnerable: A reanalysis of our social responsibilities* (Chicago, IL: University of Chicago Press, 1985); and D. Miller, 'Distributing responsibilities', *Journal of Political Philosophy*, 9(4) 2001, 453–71.

[3] A. Linklater, *The problem of harm in world politics: Theoretical investigations* (Cambridge: Cambridge University Press, 2011), p. 225.

the responsibility. The task of this chapter is to explore and defend ethical arguments that might give rise to responsibility qua accountability for affected constituencies. Clearly, determining the ethically relevant meaning of responsibility in this sense cannot be determined wholly in the abstract; rather, it arises from the nature of the social relationship between the responsible agent and those who suffer harm or are put at risk, by the actions or inactions of the responsible agent.

Responsibility – in this context understood as answerability for vulnerable constituencies – can be general, in the sense of applying to all members of a particular community, or special in the sense of applying only to certain members with particular capabilities or attributes. Although our primary task is to defend ethical principles for the assignment of special responsibilities, we acknowledge that special responsibilities in a particular domain may sometimes conflict with general responsibilities, or indeed with special responsibilities in another domain. Our account of special responsibilities must also address such tensions, particularly in relation to the US, which is arguably now overburdened with responsibilities of various sorts.

Our first task, however, is to elaborate the ethically relevant capabilities and relationships that ought to give rise to the just assignment of special responsibilities in world politics. Capabilities are clearly a necessary ingredient of any ethics of special responsibilities, but they do not answer all the ethical questions that need to be addressed. The general maxim, made famous by the Spiderman films, that 'with great power comes great responsibility' might appear to offer an intuitively appealing and simple basis upon which to assign special responsibilities: those with superior capabilities have greater, and therefore a 'special', responsibility to tackle global problems. Jean Elshtain, for example, has argued that the US should embrace precisely such a 'Spiderman ethic'.[4] For Elshtain, while all states have a stake in the system, 'the more powerful have greater responsibilities'.[5] We explore the uses and abuses of a Spiderman ethic later in our discussion of US exceptionalism. For now, we merely note that a Spiderman ethic is ultimately question-begging, since it provides no guidance on which capabilities are ethically relevant, how such responsibilities should be properly discharged, and to whom special responsibilities might be owed. These questions can be expected to yield different answers in different domains of global governance, so

---

[4] J. B. Elshtain, 'International justice as equal regard and the use of force', *Ethics and International Affairs*, 17(2) 2003, 63–75. See also C. Brown, 'Do great powers have great responsibilities? Great powers and moral agency', *Global Society*, 18(1) 2004, 6.
[5] Elshtain, 'International justice', 73.

we reject any notion of a generic special responsibility on behalf of all preponderant powers. Since responsibility entails accountability to particular constituencies (rather than simply a vindication of the interests or values of importance to powerful states), capable agents must be ethically linked to the constituencies that are harmed by, or put at risk or made vulnerable by, the actions or inactions of such agents. This helps also to distinguish the ethics of special responsibilities from the general responsibilities flowing from ideal cosmopolitan ethics.

To which constituencies, then, should capable agents be linked? Given that our focus is on global problems involving systemic risk, it might seem plausible to argue that special responsibilities are owed to the entire global community, by those states and non-state actors that possess the relevant capability to reduce the global community's exposure and vulnerability to such risk. While we have no objection to this argument, we consider that there is an even stronger basis for the assignment of special responsibilities on behalf of those who are most vulnerable to such risks. Here it is helpful to distinguish between impacts or potential impacts (risks), on the one hand, and vulnerability, on the other. Vulnerability refers to the ability of an individual, community or state to anticipate and prepare for particular risks, to manage and withstand impacts when they occur and to recover. For example, two countries may experience the same exposure to the impacts of a pandemic, but country A may be much more vulnerable to those impacts than country B because of a lack of communication facilities, hospitals, trained medical staff and medicines. Indeed, all global problems that entail systemic risk typically have variable impacts due to significant differences in vulnerability across social classes, communities and nations due to differences in wealth, income, education, state capacity and the like. We say 'typically' since there are sometimes exceptions. Ulrich Beck once quipped that 'poverty is hierarchical, while smog is democratic'.[6] However, smog is a local risk and environmental justice advocates have been quick to respond to Beck by pointing to the significant maldistribution of both environmental benefits and environmental burdens around the world. Nonetheless, there are some vulnerabilities and impacts from which no amount of wealth can insulate individuals, communities or nations from exposure. The most notable example here would be an attack by nuclear weapons. It is often the case that capable agents also form part of the constituency of the vulnerable, but there is a crucial difference: they have the greater capability to address

---

[6] U. Beck, *Ecological enlightenment: Essays on the politics of the risk society* (Atlantic Highlands, NJ: Humanities Press, 1995), p. 60.

their vulnerability. That is why we focus our ethical attention on those vulnerable who are dependent on action or inaction by the capable agent. Our particular ethics of special responsibilities – with harm and vulnerability as the key criteria – is necessarily cosmopolitan since it addresses the plight of the (dependent) vulnerable, wherever they may reside. This is not the only way one could attempt to formulate an ethic of special responsibilities for global governance challenges, although we seek to begin the debate with this cosmopolitan point of departure as our sense is that the likely alternatives, such as a pluralist ethic priv-ileging the order of the society of states, are manifestly inadequate and indeed themselves a source of the problems.

Yet acknowledging that there are differences in the scope or degree of vulnerability of different social classes, communities and nations in many, if not all, cases does not challenge our basic argument con-cerning the ethical significance of vulnerability. Our ethical argument focuses on vulnerability in the context of asymmetric capabilities, 'the power hierarchies that explain unequal vulnerabilities to harm and the uneven distribution of security, and which invariably lead to percep-tions of injustice'.[7] Those who are most vulnerable are those who are unable to protect themselves from particular risks or impacts. However, instead of singling out all those 'others' who may be able to contribute in some way to the alleviation of the plight of the vulnerable, for the purposes of determining whether there are special responsibilities, we single out instead those upon whom the vulnerable are most depend-ent; these are the agents with the requisite capabilities whose actions or inactions will most determine their degree of exposure and vulnerabil-ity. Here we follow Robert Goodin's formulation: 'A is vulnerable to B if and only if B's actions and choices have a great impact on A's interests' (understood as welfare).[8] He goes on to argue that '[t]hose to whom one is relatively more vulnerable have relatively greater responsibilities. Anyone to whom A is uniquely vulnerable (no one else will help if that person does not) has the greatest responsibilities of all.'[9] Vulnerability, dependency and relevant capabilities are therefore ethically co-related in the assignment of special responsibilities.

Now it may be asked, as David Miller does, what if the vulnerable, like the grasshopper in the fable that refused to plan for the winter, made themselves vulnerable through their own irresponsible neglect?[10] These can certainly constitute complicated cases. We know of no general rule

---

[7] Linklater, *Problem of harm*, p. 6.
[8] Goodin, 'Vulnerabilities and responsibilities', 779.
[9] *Ibid.*   [10] Miller, 'Distributing responsibilities', 461.

that can resolve the issue; rather, the extent to which an agent's own culpability in their vulnerability undermines claims they may make to be the beneficiaries of other's special responsibilities to address their plight, is something that can only be determined on a case-by-case basis. What can be said here is the converse, that we find arguments for special responsibilities at their most powerful when they rest on vulnerabilities brought about by past action of the would-be responsible(s) *and* necessary future action or forbearance to prevent or minimise future risks and vulnerabilities. Moreover, in at least some of the cases we consider, the most vulnerable are among the least causally responsible and the least culpable for generating global risks, although the case of nuclear weapons in particular is quite complex in this regard.

However, if we return to the responsibility qua accountability side of the moral equation, there are several objections that might be raised against the assignment of special responsibilities towards the most vulnerable based purely on capabilities, without regard for causal responsibility or culpability of the capable agent, or the cost of discharging such responsibilities. It would seem intuitively problematic to demand that a state with the requisite capabilities ought to alleviate the plight of the most vulnerable by expending all their relevant capabilities, even though they may not be causally responsible, or in any way morally culpable for the plight of the vulnerable. Yet, for those who want to address global collective action problems that defy solution by communitarian commitments, it would be equally problematic simply to conclude that such a state should take no responsibility at all. Some kind of ethical calibration is needed here.

A cosmopolitan ethic enjoins the especially capable to take responsibility wherever possible to reduce vulnerabilities. Nonetheless, if we are to be tempered by a practical sensibility, we recognise that for those capable agents who are relatively blameless other competing demands reasonably gain more weight as their own culpability lessens. That does not, however, lessen the rightness of taking up the moral opportunity to assume special responsibilities wherever possible. We propose that capable agents who are blameless, or relatively blameless vis-à-vis other capable agents, should be entitled to appeal to competing ethical responsibilities to limit the extent of their own special responsibilities, such as the moral harm that may be caused to their own communities if they were to have to meet unending demands by others.[11] Of course,

---

[11] Bashshar Haydar has suggested that the idea of a special responsibility to alleviate harm should be understood in terms of the discount on the weight of an agent's appeal to cost in obtaining moral permission not to alleviate the harm in question; we

not all moral theories give weight to the appeal to costs to absolve agents of responsibility (for example, some versions of consequentialism), while those that do may assign different weight to different arguments. Nonetheless, even capable agents who are blameless should still have a prima facie special responsibility towards those vulnerable who are dependent on their action. This is so because there may be some situations where it is difficult to identify any capable agent who is also clearly culpable, in which case the vulnerable would be simply left to suffer through no fault of their own. However, the special responsibility would need to be calibrated in response to requisite capacity and competing responsibilities (special and general). We would expect that practical appeals for limits to special responsibilities in the face of endless demands would be unconvincing in situations where the cost to the capable agent is relatively low and the vulnerability is very high, but such appeals become more persuasive as the costs rise. Conversely, capable agents who may be considered culpable or have benefited from the plight of the vulnerable would have minimal or no opportunities to limit their responsibility in this way.

So, for example, an agent who deliberately, recklessly or negligently causes harm is in most societies held legally answerable through criminal sanction or compensation to those who suffer, irrespective of the costs. This is a principle of general responsibility that is widely recognised in legal systems around the world and in international law, as in the customary law principle of state responsibility for environmental harm, the just war principle of unnecessary suffering, and fraud in finance. It would therefore seem reasonable that capable agents who are otherwise liable for a special responsibility to alleviate the plight of the vulnerable should not be entitled to successful appeal to undue costs in those situations where they deliberately, recklessly or negligently created the situation of vulnerability.

However, wrongful intention is not the only basis upon which the appeal to cost, or competing considerations, should be limited. There may be situations where a capable agent did not intend and could not have foreseen that their actions would make others vulnerable, but they nonetheless derive benefits from the activity that created the relevant vulnerability. If A accepts a free meal, not knowing that it was intended for B who was impoverished and malnourished, then A would be expected to purchase B a replacement meal or provide compensation

emphasise that legitimate costs to make such appeals should be understood as moral ones. See B. Haydar, 'Special responsibility and the appeal to cost', *Journal of Political Philosophy*, 17(2) 2009, 129–45.

because the benefits derived by A may be directly linked to the unmet needs of B. Indeed, climate justice theorists have invoked precisely this argument in addressing the special responsibility for historical emissions by developed countries who claim that responsibility under the polluter pays principle should not apply, because they did not know they were causing harm to others when they decided to pursue a path of industrialisation based on fossil fuels.[12] The same can be said for using something to which others ought to have been entitled, such as receiving stolen property. Climate justice theorists have invoked a similar argument in defending the 'beneficiary pays principle', as one basis for assigning special responsibilities to states with capacity (that is, developed countries) to take the lead in mitigation since they have acquired considerable benefits from unknowingly polluting the atmosphere, and these same benefits have placed them in a situation where they are also much more capable of responding, and therefore much less vulnerable, to the impacts of climate change than developing countries.[13]

Capabilities, then, are clearly necessary to the assignment of special responsibilities in world politics, but there is more to this ethical story. Much depends on the nature of the link between the agents with the relevant capability and the vulnerable constituency, including how the relevant capability is derived. This is consistent with our sociological argument that special responsibilities cannot simply be reduced to capabilities. It should also be clear that the assignment of special responsibilities in global politics is much more than an administrative device for discharging general duties more efficiently and effectively.[14] Of course, there may be situations where vulnerability cannot be traced to any particular agent whose actions will have a greater impact on alleviating it. In such circumstances, there is no basis for assigning special responsibilities, even though the problem may be a global collective action problem. Here we concur with Goodin that in such a situation, all morally competent agents would have a general responsibility to push for a general scheme of coordinated action to protect the vulnerable.[15]

---

[12] However, as Simon Caney argues, much depends on whether we are seeking to attribute responsibility to individuals or collectives. If the individual polluters are dead, we cannot make them pay. But if they are collectives or corporate identities then they still exist and may take responsibility. See S. Caney, 'Cosmopolitan justice, responsibility, and global climate change', *Leiden Journal of International Law*, 18(4) 2005, 747–75.

[13] See, for example, E. Page, 'Distributing the burdens of climate change', *Environmental Politics*, 17(4) 2008, 556–75.

[14] R. E. Goodin, 'What is so special about our fellow countrymen?', *Ethics*, 98(4) 1988, 663–86.

[15] Goodin, 'Vulnerabilities and responsibilities', 781.

In light of the foregoing, it is now possible to draw together and restate our core ethical claims. Recall that our working definition of special responsibilities is that they are *a differentiated set of obligations, the allocation of which is collectively agreed, and provide a principle of social differentiation for managing collective problems in a world characterised by both formal equality and inequality of material capability.* Our concern here is to put forward an ethical argument for the assignment of special responsibilities that we consider *ought* to be collectively agreed (whether such arguments are actually agreed in our three case studies is a separate question that we explore later). Accordingly, we offer as a prima facie ethical claim that *special responsibilities ought to be assigned to those states and non-state actors with the relevant capability to make the biggest difference to alleviating the plight of those who are most vulnerable to particular global or transboundary risks, and who are therefore entirely or largely dependent on action or inaction by the capable agents.* We propose that claims to special responsibilities upon an agent with the relevant capability are at their strongest when the alleviation of vulnerability is wholly or largely dependent upon their action. While the claim may be weaker in cases where no causality and/or benefits are at play, we see precious little scope for how capable agents could provide a defensible moral justification either to the most vulnerable in the sense we have defined, or to the international community in general, for doing nothing and not availing themselves of the moral opportunity to ameliorate global vulnerabilities. However, we do recognise that the obligations that attach to special responsibility are weaker in certain situations, particularly where the capable agent has neither caused, nor benefited from, the vulnerability of others. We also weigh the adequacy of other possible grounds limiting claims in particular cases, assessing how they address what we argue to be the overriding and defensible moral purpose of the domain. In doing so, we seek to be sensitive to the practical liabilities of an overly demanding ethic that would place limitless demands upon the preponderantly capable, not all of which they could be reasonably expected to discharge.

For example, Germany, as the strongest economy in the European Union (EU), has the greatest financial capability to bail out the Greek economy, and therefore has a special responsibility to alleviate the vulnerability of those living and working in Greece whose welfare and livelihoods are most at risk, and therefore most dependent on action by Germany. However, while it would be unethical for Germany completely to walk away from its special responsibility, neither should it be expected to write a blank cheque: it has not caused or benefited from the Greek financial crisis, and it does have other legitimate claims on its financial resources. Likewise, the US cannot be expected to be responsible across the globe for dealing with every natural disaster or atrocity in civil war, simply because it has the most substantial and advanced technical capacity for preventing further suffering and loss of life. Under such circumstances, the US should be entitled to appeal to other competing responsibilities to limit its special responsibilities, and to spread responsibility and costs to other capable agents. Thus we propose the merits of applying a practical sliding scale between unlimited demands and easily met special responsibilities: this has to be measured in each given case, on the understanding that the sliding scale applies only when the capable agent is not culpable in any way.

However, in those situations where the most capable agents have knowingly exposed particular constituencies to harm or risk of harm, and have also derived benefits from such actions at the expense of those who are made vulnerable, then they should be required to do all that they can, within the full limits of their capability, to prevent risk of harm or alleviate harm. Between these two extremes, there is doubtless a range of ethical arguments that might be advanced to add to, or subtract from, the weight and extent of the special responsibilities borne by the most capable agents, vis-à-vis the most vulnerable constituencies in different contexts. These arguments should form part of the process whereby the especially capable must answer to those who are vulnerable to their actions or inactions. However, we would expect these arguments to represent qualifications to our core claim that special responsibility arises from a relationship between the most vulnerable and the most capable, whereby the former is wholly or largely dependent on actions by the latter for the alleviation of their plight. We consider this an ethically compelling cosmopolitan claim for assigning differentiated obligations in a globalised world of asymmetrical capacity.

We can anticipate objections to our assignment of special responsibilities by communitarians, who would claim that special responsibilities should be based on special ties towards family, fellow citizens, those with whom ethnic or religious identities are shared, or other grounds of particularistic community. Indeed, that is how the notion of 'special responsibilities' is often treated in the philosophical literature: those special ties provide the grounds for special responsibilities, and justify giving some persons and communities priority over others when resources are scarce. Yet our argument is structurally no different: the ethically relevant ties that bind in this particular relationship are ties of vulnerability and dependency. These are also the ties that communitarians sometimes invoke to justify the responsibilities of states to defend their citizens, or parents to protect their children.

Communitarians might nonetheless claim that it is precisely the absence of thick constitutive ties of identity or community at the global level that undermines the case for the assignment of special responsibilities to those agents who are most capable. Yet an ethical analysis of which special responsibilities *ought* to be undertaken does not necessarily reduce to what is empirically present here and now; indeed, this objection betrays the conservative face of communitarianism, which is prone to conflate 'is' with 'ought'. Communitarians cannot deny that the processes of globalisation have reshaped and expanded social relations and the idea of moral and political community, along with the expansion of obligations to others and the spread of a range of cosmopolitan norms, such as human rights (if typically thinly and unevenly). In any event, our ethical argument for the assignment of special responsibilities is sensitive to particularistic ties and communitarian concerns. As Linklater has pointed out, '[s]eldom does the intellectual retreat from cosmopolitanism and the wider project of the Enlightenment lead to a celebration of ethnic particularism or patriotic loyalties which disavow all forms of answerability to others'.[16] Our stance recognises that states with greater relevant capabilities also have duties to their own citizens which must be weighed alongside the needs of other vulnerable communities, and the latter only become overriding to the extent that the state in question has both caused and profited from that vulnerability. In these ways, we affirm general ethical principles underpinning the assignment of special responsibilities. However, the acceptable qualifications that may be attached to their discharge cannot be articulated fully in advance, but rather must be worked through in particular domains of global governance in specific contexts. This follows from our core claim that special responsibilities are domain specific.

We now turn to the case studies of nuclear weapons, climate change and global finance in order to apply our core ethical claim (and subsidiary ethical qualifications) concerning the assignment and discharge of special responsibilities. In each case, we identify the relevant vulnerabilities, explore to what extent the alleviation of these vulnerabilities is dependent on actions by certain capable agents such as to justify the assignment of special responsibilities, and whether the capable agents might have a basis for appealing to cost or to competing ethical claims to reduce their responsibility. Our primary concern is to flesh out our ethical arguments for the assignment of special responsibilities in each of the domains, and also use them as a basis for evaluating how capable

---

[16] A. Linklater, *The transformation of political community: Ethical foundations of the post-Westphalian era* (Cambridge: Polity Press, 1998), p. 47.

agents, including the US, have responded or ought to respond. We explore whether there is any convergence between the special responsibilities that we believe ought to be assigned in our ethical theory, and those that have actually been conferred, claimed and/or accepted, in practice.

Nuclear proliferation

The invention of nuclear weapons has undoubtedly made the world and its peoples more vulnerable to catastrophic violence than at any time in history. Nuclear weapons present an unprecedented global risk, and therefore perhaps are the notable exception to our earlier argument that there is typically a greater variation in vulnerability to the impacts of systemic risk, than there is exposure to such risks. Even as the possession of nuclear weapons is believed by some to have stabilising effects in preventing nuclear and/or conventional wars, the extent to which that may be the case is bought at the price of making populations more vulnerable, in the sense of the heightened risk entailed by the magnitude of potential destruction resulting from any use of nuclear weapons. That risk is a function of magnitude and probability. Hence, even if we think the taboo against using nuclear weapons is fairly robust, it is the enormity of destruction that could be wrought by nuclear weapons that means even a chance of use entails for us (and most non-nuclear weapon states (NNWSs) in the world as parties to the Nuclear Non-Proliferation Treaty (NPT)) an unacceptable moral risk.

We are primarily interested in the risks and vulnerabilities suffered by those who are dependent on action by those who possess nuclear weapons. The latter are the most immediately relevant capable agents in terms of our ethical argument for the assignment of special responsibilities, since they are the ones who actually have nuclear weapons. Yet the assignment of special responsibilities is not quite as straightforward as this because, as we discussed in Chapter 3, the NNWSs have their own responsibilities too. Moreover, the willingness of the nuclear-armed states (the NPT nuclear weapon states (NWSs), along with the possessors of nuclear weapons outside the treaty) to eliminate their arsenals will surely depend upon how confident they are that others are not going to declare themselves as nuclear possessors: preventing this outcome (for example, by strengthening verification provisions and controlling the transfer of proliferation sensitive technologies) depends upon collective action by *all* states. Of course, populations in those NWSs are also at risk and vulnerable to action by their own governments, and by others who possess nuclear weapons or who may seek to acquire them. However, unlike those who do not possess such weapons, the peoples in the NWSs are in a position to take some action (albeit to varying degrees, depending on the openness and responsiveness of their individual political systems) to reduce their risk of exposure and vulnerability by pressuring their governments not to acquire more weapons and, ultimately, to disarm. While realists may not consider this a prudent strategy for nuclear-armed states, from our standpoint, and that of the majority of states who do not possess nuclear weapons,[17] this is indeed the most morally justifiable strategy. Prima facie, then, we have a clear ethical basis for the assignment of special responsibilities, and for articulating the substance of those responsibilities. That is, states in possession of nuclear weapons have, arguably, a greater special responsibility towards NNWSs to reduce their arsenal to zero. On the other side, the NNWSs are likewise answerable to the NWSs for the discharge of their own responsibilities, but the responsibilities of the nuclear-armed states are the most important from the standpoint of the vulnerable: that is, existing nuclear weapons produce greater vulnerability than do potential ones.

While the assignment of special responsibilities in this case is relatively straightforward, determining whether the relevant capable agents may have grounds to limit their special responsibility is less so. Indeed, the realist objection that we have already raised would constitute the primary candidate here. That is, a state with nuclear weapons would argue that if it were to rid itself of its entire nuclear arsenal, it might make those who did not possess such weapons less vulnerable, but only at the cost of making itself more so. This argument leads to the conclusion that the safest path lies in reduction, not elimination. Accordingly, if it is accepted that a state's first duty is to protect its territory and citizens from external attack (a classic communitarian ethic), this principle comes into direct conflict with our cosmopolitan ethic of special responsibilities. Why would Pakistan, for example, yield all its nuclear weapons so long as India continues to possess such weapons and dominant conventional forces? Why would Iran not pursue a nuclear weapons programme so long as it feels threatened by Israel and the US? The possession of nuclear weapons is considered by proponents of deterrence, including the NWSs themselves, as the best defence against a possible nuclear attack.

The obvious response to this objection, presaged in our argument that in such cases all morally competent agents have a general responsibility

---

[17] We acknowledge that those governments who benefit from extended deterrence might also disagree – Canada, Japan and Taiwan present such possible cases, although there are vital differences between them.

to push for a general scheme of coordinated action, is to require all those who possess nuclear weapons to enter into a collective agreement not to encourage proliferation, and collectively to reduce and ultimately eliminate their nuclear arsenals.[18] As it happens, of course, just such a collective promise forms part of the grand bargain that lies at the heart of the NPT, as we saw in Chapter 3. The NWSs under the treaty promised (albeit in somewhat vague rather than actively specified terms) to pursue negotiations in 'good faith' to bring the nuclear arms race to an end, to move towards nuclear disarmament and to negotiate a general treaty on complete disarmament. In return, the NNWSs agreed not to acquire nuclear weapons, in return for the right to pursue a civilian nuclear programme under strict safeguards, and with the support of the NWSs. In short, what was agreed, in broad terms, more or less conforms to what we consider ought to be agreed, according to our ethics of special responsibilities. To this extent, there is broad consistency between our ethical theory and the sociological history reviewed in Chapter 3. Moreover, the NWSs remain answerable to the NNWSs for the performance of their special responsibilities in terms of their crucial nuclear disarmament side of the bargain, and as such are the relevant capable agents in this particular context. At one level, the near universal participation in the NPT represents a most impressive consensus on the assignment of special responsibilities. It is, of course, much less impressive on their discharge. As we saw in Chapter 3, commitment to implementation of the key disarmament provision has been hotly contested for decades, while the regime has been subject to slow erosion on the proliferation front.

Without at all denying the responsibilities upon all states who possess nuclear weapons, the US and Russia – as the states that have had and continue to possess by far the two largest nuclear arsenals, 96 per cent of the world's total warheads[19] – clearly have the most to answer for vis-à-vis vulnerable constituencies. Nevertheless, there are solid grounds for assigning an even greater responsibility to the focus of our book, namely the US, to take on a leadership role in getting to zero. The US was the first to acquire such a capability, which spurred the nuclear arms race, and the US is the only state ever to have used nuclear weapons. While

---

[18] We do not enter into the technical and practical questions here of what exactly that could look like, given that NWSs and threshold NWSs would remain 'virtual' nuclear powers in the sense of having the knowledge to (re-)constitute nuclear weapons, but confine ourselves to articulating the basic responsibility as such.

[19] R. S. Norris and H. M. Kristensen, 'Nuclear notebook: Worldwide deployments of nuclear weapons, 2009', *Bulletin of the Atomic Scientists*, bos.sagepub.com/content/65/6/86.full (accessed 31 July 2011).

there is room to debate the degree of culpability that should attach to the US for developing and using nuclear weapons, the US must nonetheless answer to vulnerable peoples for the consequences of those decisions. In a remarkable statement in 2009, President Barack Obama accepted a special responsibility for nuclear disarmament on precisely that latter ground, in acknowledging that 'as the only nuclear power to have used a nuclear weapon, the United States has a moral responsibility to act. We cannot succeed in this endeavor alone, but we can lead it.'[20] The US would have limited grounds upon which to appeal to other competing ethical considerations to justify reducing its responsibility to disarm from the standpoint of the vulnerable. That is, the acquisition of nuclear weapons by the US has directly and knowingly contributed to the vulnerability experienced by those who do not possess nuclear weapons, and it has derived security benefits at the expense of the vulnerable. Accordingly, the US should be fully held to account for discharging its special responsibilities to reduce and eventually eliminate its nuclear arsenal.

While the George W. Bush administration did considerable damage to the symmetry of the original bargain on nuclear non-proliferation and disarmament, the Obama administration's rhetorical embrace of an agenda of global leadership in the nuclear domain has been aimed at rebuilding that consensus. As Obama stated so explicitly in Prague:

So today, I state clearly and with conviction America's commitment to seek the peace and security of a world without nuclear weapons. This goal will not be reached quickly – perhaps not in my lifetime. It will take patience and persistence. But now we, too, must ignore the voices who tell us that the world cannot change ... the United States will take concrete steps toward a world without nuclear weapons.[21]

As we have seen in the previous chapters, this contrasts sharply with the failures of the US to acknowledge a special lead in addressing global financial stability or climate change (including under Obama). On the nuclear front, however, Obama has acknowledged the logic that many others share – that for meaningful movement towards zero, the US would have to take leadership as the world's foremost nuclear power. In Obama's words, '[w]hen the United States fulfills our responsibilities as a nuclear power committed to the NPT, we strengthen our global efforts to ensure that other nations fulfill their responsibilities'.[22]

[20] B. Obama, 'Remarks of President Barack Obama', Hradcany Square, Prague, 5 April 2009, prague.usembassy.gov/obama.html (accessed 31 July 2011).
[21] Ibid.
[22] White House, Office of the Press Secretary, 'Press conference by the President at the nuclear security summit', Washington Convention Center, Washington, DC,

There is, however, an interesting irony here. For decades the US and other NWSs have been criticised for not moving adequately towards disarmament in keeping their part of the NPT bargain. And yet, as President Obama acknowledges for the US the fundamental disarmament part of the NPT as a special moral responsibility, such a move will no doubt provoke its own share of scepticism, as nothing more than yet another policy suiting US national interests. Given the US's overwhelming advantage in conventional force projection capability, a world without nuclear weapons would more effectively restore US predominance, than a world armed with the 'great equaliser'. In other words, a US leadership role will only be acceptable to the other NWSs if nuclear disarmament is accompanied by effective and verifiable restraints on current and future US conventional capabilities.

Vulnerability may be an incidental byproduct of the activities associated with climate change and the pursuit of wealth through global finance. In the case of nuclear weapons, vulnerability is more deeply embedded, and is intrinsic to the very nature of the weapons, and to the military strategies that have been developed around them. For that reason, vulnerability must be placed at the heart of the ethics of special nuclear responsibilities. Since most of the world's population is dependent on the actions of others, it is the decisions of the most capable nuclear states that are of most immediate ethical relevance, and key to the allocation of special responsibilities in this domain. However, since nuclear weapons are but one dimension of a wider security problem, there are also special responsibilities for non-proliferation that fall on other states, as well as general responsibilities for arms control and disarmament that belong properly to all states.

Climate change

Just as nuclear weapons have made the world more vulnerable, so too has human-induced climate change. However, in this case, the differences in exposure and vulnerability to the impacts of climate change are much more striking. For example, the US and Australia are expected to experience quite severe impacts, but their vulnerability is much lower than many developing countries experiencing the same impact.[23] Differences in causal responsibility, culpability and capacity

---

13 April 2010, www.whitehouse.gov/the-press-office/press-conference-president-nuclear-security-summit (accessed 31 July 2011).

[23] J. Gulledge, 'Three plausible scenarios of future climate change', in K. M. Campbell (ed.), *Climate cataclysm: The foreign policy and national security implications of climate change* (Washington, DC: Brookings Institution Press, 2008), p. 53.

also abound, and contribute to what Stephen Gardiner has called a perfect moral storm.[24] The most affluent nations seek to pass on the risks of climate change to the least affluent nations, while present generations seek to pass on the risks of climate change to future generations (and to nonhuman species). But this is ultimately a self-deceit, made possible by the generally poor grasp of science and ecological relationships, and the inattention to international justice that threatens to usher in an ethical tragedy of potentially enormous proportions that will swell the ranks of the vulnerable over time.

While no class, community or country can be expected to escape the impacts of climate change, we are interested in identifying those who are most vulnerable because they lack the capacity to prepare and adapt, and are therefore destined to suffer the most unless those who have the capability to reduce emissions take the necessary action within the rapidly diminishing window of opportunity for effective action (roughly one decade). The most vulnerable are easy to identify: the least developed countries, low-lying island states and developing countries with low-lying coastal areas. It is also widely acknowledged that developing countries are also more vulnerable as a group than developed countries. However, in terms of our understanding of vulnerability, future generations and nonhuman species are extremely vulnerable, since they are entirely dependent on mitigation action by present capable agents.

In line with our core ethical argument, the relevant capable agents for the purposes of assigning special responsibilities are the major emitters, above all the US and China, which together account for over 40 per cent of total carbon dioxide emissions. The top ten carbon dioxide emitters are responsible for around two-thirds of total emissions, while the top twenty account for around three-quarters.[25] Indeed, Barry Carin and Alan Mehlenbacher have argued that 'the G20 [Group of Twenty] is as good as it gets' whatever criteria one chooses to determine capability and responsibility.[26] There is, of course, a degree of arbitrariness in settling on the number of capable agents: should it be ten, or twenty? While the collective capacity to produce emissions reductions increases as the number of capable agents grows, our purpose here is simply to make the general point that the plight of those who are most vulnerable

[24] S. Gardiner, *A perfect moral storm: The ethical tragedy of climate change* (New York: Oxford University Press, 2011).

[25] UNFCCC, 'GHG data from UNFCCC', unfccc.int/ghg_data/ghg_data_unfccc/items/4146.php (accessed 31 July 2011).

[26] B. Carin and A. Mehlenbacher, 'Constituting global leadership: Which countries need to be around the summit table for climate change and energy security?', *Global Governance*, 16(1) 2010, 33.

to the impacts of climate change is largely in the hands of decisions made by the biggest emitters.

However, as we made clear, this is merely our prima facie ethical claim for the assignment of special responsibilities. We allowed room also for ethical arguments that might add to, or subtract from, the weight and extent of the special responsibilities borne by the major emitters. In particular, we would allow major emitters to appeal to cost, or to other competing ethical arguments, to limit their special responsibility in situations where they were blameless or less blameworthy than other major emitters. Conversely, major emitters would be less entitled to appeal to costs or competing ethical considerations, to the degree to which they knowingly or recklessly brought about the relevant vulnerability and/or benefited from it. We accept that there are ethical grounds for differentiating responsibility among major emitters, and not simply in proportion to emissions power.

As we noted in Chapter 4, no country, whether developed or developing, can be said to have set out with the deliberate intention of producing climate change, and scientific understanding of human-induced climate change developed in fits and starts and did not evolve into a general consensus until the late 1980s. From this time, no state can reasonably claim to be unaware of the foreseeable risks flowing from exploiting fossil fuels. Accordingly, neither of these arguments provides any basis for differentiating the special responsibilities to be assigned among the major emitters.

However, the major emitters who have exploited fossil fuels over a longer period, and who have therefore produced greater cumulative emissions over time, have derived much greater benefits than those who have exploited fossil fuels more recently, according to the beneficiary pays principle. This has been at the expense of the vulnerable. Greater cumulative emissions also correlate strongly with greater per capita carbon footprints. In both cases, these benefits include much greater wealth and income, and greater general economic and technological capacity to reduce emissions and to adapt to climate change. These two arguments provide a compelling basis for differentiating the special responsibilities of major emitters in the developed and developing world.

Aggregate emissions and projected growth in future emissions are highly relevant from the standpoint of the most vulnerable. We noted in Chapter 4 that China has recently overtaken the US to become the world's biggest aggregate emitter, and that its future emissions are expected to grow significantly and at a faster rate than developed countries' business as usual projections. Moreover, all states – including

China – have been aware for nearly two decades of the climatic consequences of the continued exploitation of fossil fuels, and China (like other major and minor emitters) has derived considerable economic benefits from this exploitation. So no major emitter can avoid the beneficiary pays rule although it is clear that early developers have derived considerably more benefits, and capacity, than late developers and that this should be reflected in their relative responsibilities.

Yet there are strong grounds for differentiating the degree of special responsibility among major emitters on the basis of not simply differences in per capita emissions, but also development needs. While major emitters in the developing world cannot be completely absolved of special responsibility toward what might be called 'the global vulnerable', they should be entitled to draw attention to their responsibilities towards their own citizens who are suffering other kinds of vulnerabilities (such as those arising from poverty) in order to limit their global special responsibilities. These are, of course, painful trade-offs here, especially given that 'the local vulnerable' in developing countries are typically also among the global vulnerable. However, the difference between subsistence and luxury emissions is more ethically discriminating than the simple binary between developed and developing.[27] There is a growing middle class in many developing countries and there are still pockets of serious poverty in many developed countries. This has given rise to proposals to allocate responsibility to countries in terms of their proportionate share of middle class or luxury emissions, or to their emissions beyond a subsistence threshold.[28] It is not our concern here to evaluate the finer points of these proposals. Our main purpose is simply to highlight ethically relevant arguments that would justify differentiation among major emitters.

To recapitulate, our core ethical argument requires us to identify all major emitters as relevant capable agents from the standpoint of those most vulnerable to the impacts of climate change. However we have identified at least three arguments that would justify conferring considerably greater special responsibilities on the shoulders of developed countries and limiting their appeal to costs: a greater cumulative

---

[27] H. Shue, 'Subsistence emissions and luxury emissions', *Law and Policy*, 15(1) 1993, 39–59.

[28] See, for example, P. Baer, T. Athanasiou, S. Kartha and E. Kemp-Benedict, *The greenhouse development rights framework: The right to development in a climate constrained world*, rev. 2nd edn (Berlin: Heinrich Böll Foundation, Christian Aid, EcoEquity and the Stockholm Environment Institute, 2008); S. Chakravarty, A. Chikkatur, H. de Conink, S. Pacala, R. Socolow and M. Tavoni, 'Sharing CO_2 emission reductions among one billion high emitters: A rule for among all nations', *PNAS*, 106(29) 21 July 2009, 11884–8.

contribution to global emissions and consequently greater benefits derived from past emissions; greater economic and technical capacity to reduce emissions and to adapt to climate change; and no significant and widespread poverty or unmet development needs that might justify any significant restriction of this responsibility.

When we turn to the case study, we find that our ethical arguments have a strong resonance with the arguments that have been advanced to justify the climate leadership responsibilities of developed countries according to the United Nations Framework Convention on Climate Change (UNFCCC) principles of common but differentiated responsibilities (CBDR), but there is also an important difference. The UNFCCC principles have been interpreted and enacted by the parties in the Kyoto Protocol in terms of a rigid binary between developed and developing countries that confers no prima facie special responsibilities on the major emitters in the developing countries. However, the logic of our core ethic, which draws a link between vulnerability, dependency and capability, would reject the rigid binary and require that we include all major emitters as capable agents, while acknowledging differentiated responsibilities and capabilities among them. In effect, our ethics of special responsibilities provides a more nuanced understanding of CBDR that still leaves the onus on developed countries to take the lead, while also requiring major emitters in the developing world to take action to stem their projected growth in future emissions.

Our ethics of special responsibility should therefore *not* be misinterpreted as supporting the US's particular case for a reinterpretation of CBDR and the rejection of the Kyoto Protocol. We do not see the division between the major emitters and the rest as the only significant division of ethical or practical consequence. In contrast to Todd Stern's claim that responsibility should be allocated on the basis of mathematics (that is, raw aggregate emissions), not morality,[29] our ethics of special responsibility represents a fusion of both ethical and functional arguments. Unlike the US, we do not focus exclusively or primarily on future growth in aggregate emission; we also acknowledge the ethical significance of radical differences in cumulative emissions, per capita emissions, capacity and unmet development need. The view, prominent among many political elites in Washington, is that what is past is past ('just let bygones be bygones'), and in any event the US 'deserves' the advantages it derived from the exploitation of fossil fuel and to expropriate these advantages would be unjust. This claim does not wash with

---

[29] T. Stern quoted in D. Samuelsohn, 'No "pass" for developing countries in next climate treaty, says US envoy', *New York Times*, 9 December 2009.

our ethics of special responsibilities, and neither has it convinced the EU, developing countries and climate justice advocates.

That said, we consider that the parties missed an important opportunity at Kyoto and Copenhagen to develop principles for applying CBDR across either side of the Annex I versus non-Annex I divide. Of course, these were not considerations that were uppermost in the mind of the Bush administration when it chose to repudiate the Kyoto Protocol in 2001. The Bali Action Plan in 2007 represented a modest breakthrough, however, since this was the first time that developing countries acknowledged a commitment to pursue nationally appropriate mitigation action. They did not, however, go quite so far as to express these in the form of binding international commitments, and this has been a sticking point for the US. Nonetheless, as we saw in Chapter 4, China has taken considerable steps to reduce its emissions growth, particularly in its twelfth five-year plan. This has partially undercut the US's argument that it should not be required to take action in the absence of commitments from China. In any event, China and other major developing countries have been able to argue that the US and other major developed countries must demonstrate their leadership under the terms of Article 3(1) of the UNFCCC before developing countries should undertake international commitments, as distinct from voluntary national action.

In Chapter 4, we showed that CBDR has become entrenched in the climate regime and has structured the normative discourse among both parties and civil society actors, but there has not been effective agreement among states on precisely how these principles might be interpreted, configured and operationalised. While China's rising emissions are the subject of increasing attention, and therefore its capacity to make a difference is increasingly acknowledged, the majority of states still continue to attach a different meaning to the emissions of the US and the emissions of China (along with other big developing country emitters like India). The reasons for this vary among different states and negotiating coalitions, which may give different emphasis to cumulative emissions, per capita emissions, development need and capacity. However, what is interesting for our purposes is that these arguments represent, more or less, the dominant repertoire of arguments enlisted by the parties for the assignment of special responsibilities on developed countries. The US, sometimes supported by other members of the Umbrella Group, has sought to lessen its responsibility by appealing to cost (that is, harm to the US economy, and the possible migration of industry), or by seeking to spread the burden more widely to include major emitters by focusing on aggregate emissions and future growth in emissions. The latter argument has gained some traction in the recent negotiations, but the US has been unable to deflect the parties' attention to differences in historical responsibility (encapsulated in cumulative and per capita emissions), capacity and development needs. Still, despite persistent and often deep resistance to the principles animating the Kyoto Protocol's approach to climate change in the US Congress, Chapter 4 noted that even the Senators who passed the Byrd-Hagel Resolution in 1997 did not reject the idea of differentiated responsibilities among developed and developing countries out of hand. Moreover, agreement would not have been reached at Rio, Kyoto or Copenhagen were it not for the collective acknowledgement of differences in responsibility, capacity and development needs.

Nonetheless, the full implementation of the principles of CBDR has been frustrated, due in no small part to the US' difficulty in accepting and shouldering its special responsibilities for the reasons outlined in Chapter 4. What is interesting for present purposes is that the efforts to redefine CBDR by the George W. Bush administration were ineffective. It is difficult to know whether this was because they were genuine but found to be simply unconvincing, or because they were seen as disingenuous, as a fig-leaf for US economic interests. However, a decade on from the Bush administration's repudiation of Kyoto, the ground has shifted and the Obama administration's case for the major emitters to take on at least some responsibility is no longer quite so easily dismissed. The more serious ethical objection to the US position is its insistence that its own action should be conditional on action by major emitters in the developing world.

Indeed, the question of leadership remains one of the key sticking points in the negotiations, particularly between the US and China. The US cannot escape the charge that whatever ethical criteria one chooses – historical responsibility, per capita emissions, capacity or development needs – the US emerges with the biggest obligation to reduce emissions, and by enough as to reasonably constitute its responsibilities as 'extra special'. It is this convergence of ethical demands that places the US in the spotlight with nowhere to hide. This is not to deny that the costs to the US would be considerable, but the US's accusations that other states are free riders cannot be solved by the US becoming a free rider itself. Here we give the last ethical word on this problem to Henry Shue:

> It is one thing to refuse to do more than one's own share until others have done, or have agreed to do, at least their fair shares. However, it is an entirely different matter to refuse to do even one's own share – that is, to refuse to do anything at all – until others have done or have agreed to do so as well. Ethically,

one's minimum obligation is to do at least one's own fair share, irrespective of whether one should ever do more than one's fair share to compensate for the noncompliance of others. This minimum obligation is especially compelling when, as in the instance of climate change, one's share includes ceasing destructive activity that creates a danger for vulnerable others now and in the future.[30]

Shue goes on to argue that:

[t]he need for global leadership is so desperate that the duty to provide it falls on anyone who has the capacity to lead ... Whichever nation is capable of leading a change in direction away from fossil fuels has a duty to do so before our carbon emissions send us into our own climatic ditch, and this certainly includes the United States.[31]

Global finance

The vulnerabilities that arise from sustained global imbalances are not necessarily the same as those arising from financial crises, although they are not unconnected. We shall focus here mainly on the vulnerabilities that flow from financial crises in the post-Bretton Woods world we now inhabit, since they are typically more extreme, and increasingly more widespread in the wake of the removal of restrictions on capital controls. In any event, we noted in Chapter 5 that the fiscal responsibilities of deficit/debtor and surplus/creditor states are best understood as reciprocal obligations, rather than as special responsibilities. However, different considerations arise for the one state that has been able to enjoy the 'exorbitant privilege' of having its currency serve as the reserve currency – a situation that would not have arisen had the US accepted a supra-national unit of account managed by a multilateral institution during the Bretton Woods negotiations.

Who are most vulnerable to financial crises and upon which capable agents are they dependent for the maintenance and/or restoration of financial stability, such as to justify the assignment of special responsibilities? While very few are immune from the pain of financial crashes, those who are most acutely vulnerable are typically those on low incomes, with low or no savings, who are already committed to servicing large loans. But the ripple effects of financial crashes can be far and wide, so both vulnerability and dependency are likewise widespread. Given the considerable disparities in the financial resources among states, we

---

[30] H. Shue, 'Face reality? After you! – A call for leadership on climate change', *Ethics and International Affairs*, 25(1) 2011, 22–3.
[31] *Ibid.*, 24.

would ordinarily expect, prima facie, those who command the lion's share of such resources (along with those who possess the expertise to manage financial resources) to be assigned special responsibilities to protect the vulnerable from financial instability. The range of potential candidates for capable agents would therefore include the states with the biggest financial resources, the International Monetary Fund (IMF) and major market players, but the degree of that responsibility, and hence answerability, would vary according to culpability (including benefits derived). 'The market' – through its so-called invisible hand – would not qualify as a capable agent since it lacks the moral capacity and discretion to take responsibility and therefore answer to vulnerable constituencies. However, those who write the rules for market actors would qualify, and such actors are increasingly found in networks of global and national financial regulators.

Of course, we must be open also to the possibility that, in some cases, vulnerability may not be traceable to any particular capable agent or group of capable agents whose actions will have a greater impact on alleviating vulnerability than those of any other agent. Under such circumstances, we must look to a coordinated multilateral response, rather than to an assignment of special responsibilities to protect the vulnerable. The threefold diffusion of responsibility (among states, into a networked mix of global and national regulators and major market players, and away from states and public institutions and toward markets) chronicled in Chapter 5 is more suggestive of such a situation in global finance than in the other domains we examine. Still, given the significant disparities in the distribution of financial resources, we are not in a situation of complete dispersal of accountability away from any special responsibilities.

Consistent with our ethical criteria, only those capable agents who are not culpable should be entitled to make appeals to limit their responsibility. This makes things difficult for the US in relation to the global financial crisis of 2007–9. In contrast to the neoliberal strictures that had accompanied the 1997 Asian economic crisis, many proponents of neoliberal finance find themselves on the defensive after this latter crisis. And far from making claims of special responsibilities and perhaps rights to accompany them, or making claims for exceptional exemptions from general financial responsibilities, the US finds itself instead on the receiving end of criticisms similar to those it, and other actors like the IMF, had levelled at governments beset by earlier crises: charges include insufficiently developed financial sectors, the corruption of 'crony capitalism', and regulatory capture. In terms of our ethics of assigning special responsibilities, the US can be identified as not only the most significant capable agent in terms of its financial resources, but also as one that is blameworthy, and should therefore be held accountable for the crisis. This is not in particularly great dispute even in the US itself. But somewhat more contested is precisely whom to hold accountable: the administration; Congress; regulatory oversight bodies; or Wall Street? It is clear that there is plenty of blame to go around in the US for a retrospective accounting of the latest global financial crisis arising from decisions made with reckless disregard of the consequences for vulnerable constituencies. Indeed, the complexity of actors involved belies simple attributions of responsibility that might make more sense in other domains where one can speak, for example, of 'the US' as the key state agent in nuclear non-proliferation.

While such accounting of one particular episode of crisis is no doubt very helpful in diagnosing what prescriptions may be needed, our chief concern here is formulating more prospective judgements of what claims for assigning responsibilities (including special ones) for adjustment and systemic financial stability more generally are in order, which takes us beyond this one particular crisis and requires us to look at the broader constituencies of global finance. Here we need to consider the defensible moral purposes of this domain, what, if any, allocations of responsibility including special ones might follow, upon what criteria, and to what agents.

As the characteristics of the domain of financial governance where responsibilities are to be exercised have changed, so too the constituencies to which governments might be deemed especially responsible vary. For example, the private financial sector has emerged as both a lobbyist and a constituency for whose 'health' and stability governments might be deemed responsible by forbearance (that is, refraining from 'excessive' regulation), for the sake of finance itself. We would argue that this (the interests and needs of finance) should not be the primary focus of financial regulation, since it directs attention away from the vulnerable and towards those who are likely to put at risk the needs of the vulnerable. However, redirecting responsibility towards the vulnerable is no easy matter given the degree to which states are captive to finance, and the degree to which financial governance involves closely articulated, technocratic elite networks of private actors and regulators (with a revolving door between the public and private sectors). Nonetheless, questions are now being asked, even by the previously faithful defenders of the neoliberal market such as Alan Greenspan.[32]

---

[32] As Greenspan admitted, '[t]hose of us who have looked to the self-interest of lending institutions to protect shareholders' equity, myself included, are in a state of shocked

Without wading in depth into the debates about whether the contemporary global economy produces net gains overall, and for whom, even as it may exacerbate inequalities, we do take as a central moral point of reference that global financial crises (and the national ones that typically ignite them) are not a desired byproduct of a globalised financial system from the perspective of not only the most vulnerable constituencies, but also governments and the vast majority of their citizens more broadly. Systemic instability has emerged as a core global financial governance problem in the present era, and avoiding financial crises that produce system-wide contagion ought to be included as the overriding moral purpose in assigning special responsibilities. The gains to be had from such crises are primarily by a rather circumscribed group of private financial actors who get bailed out by being deemed 'too big to fail', or those in a position to buy up at bargain rates the casualties of such crises. While the arguments for global financial stability may be many and varied (employment, poverty reduction, human security, prosperity, redistribution, growth, control of inflation, to name prominent ones), mitigating the most adverse consequences of financial crises, such as mass bankruptcies and unemployment, would seem to be an end worthy of commanding widespread agreement, even among those whose voices are not represented at the negotiating tables of the G20. Chapter 5 chronicles that the G20 has rhetorically accepted such a moral purpose, as evidenced for example in its final communiqué of the 2009 London Summit: '[w]e recognise that the current crisis has a disproportionate impact on the vulnerable in the poorest countries and recognise our collective responsibility to mitigate the social impact of the crisis to minimise long-lasting damage to global potential'.[33] From both a practical cosmopolitan perspective and a pluralist position embracing the comity of the society of states, then, there seem to be good reasons to embrace as morally worthwhile the avoidance of global financial crises. This might well be a perilously thin consensus (which may seem to be the order of the day for special responsibilities at the global level), insofar as the devil is of course in the details: namely, whether tinkering with reforms of neoliberal financial globalisation is sufficient, and if so which ones, or whether much more far-reaching restructuring of the global economy and its regulatory oversight are required. Such considerations can produce very different proposals for

disbelief'. E. L. Andrews, 'Greenspan concedes error on regulation', *New York Times*, 23 October 2008.

[33] G20, 'The global plan for recovery and reform', 2 April 2009, www.g20.org/Documents/final-communique.pdf (accessed 28 July 2011).

how to approach long-term financial stability, and who ought to bear responsibilities including special ones.

We have argued on theoretical and ethical grounds, and also demonstrated empirically, that capacity is powerfully associated with claims to special responsibilities. But it should be clear from the empirical case study of global finance that the possession of capabilities and the exercise of responsibilities are not always in alignment. In finance the US has been, at various times, simultaneously capable and responsible (early Bretton Woods), responsible without being capable (late Bretton Woods) and capable without being responsible (1990s onward). Since the late 1990s, the US has had a lot of capacity to draw capital but has not been taking responsibility for the financial regulatory regime except to promote liberalisation (on which it did not even take the lead). The dollar remains the safe-haven currency of choice, giving the US something of a special role, but the US has not been leading particularly strongly on reforming the global financial architecture in the interests of stability, nor has it really faced the harsh adjustment pressures that continue to loom. US capability still remains strong in some areas, as evidenced by the confidence in the dollar. However, with the horizontal and vertical diffusion of responsibility for the global governance goals of adjustment and stability described in our empirical analysis, there seems now to be no way exactly to correlate special responsibility with capacity, due to the complexity of agents and the fragmentation of authority in the domain of global finance. As noted in Chapter 5, the diffusion of responsibility both horizontally (from special to general among states), and vertically (into a networked mix of global and national regulators and major market players), helps to some extent to insulate this domain from the types of political control that are implied by the concept of special responsibility when it is conceived as political leadership. Fragmentation of agency may amount to an abrogation of special responsibility, but we would still maintain that *diffusion* of more generalised responsibilities among multiple actors need not amount to complete *dissipation* of responsibility.

The dominant idea emerging among the G20 and the IMF in the aftermath of contemporary financial crises is that each sovereign state has responsibility for sound management of its economy, and that such responsibility helps to support a more stable and open world economy which is the surest path to growth and prosperity. While the reduction of poverty has recently been cited by the IMF as an ethical goal, accompanying the economic pillars of growth and stability, as Jacqueline Best notes, 'even here, the emphasis is on states' responsibility for alleviating their own poverty – rather than one another's – in order to ensure global financial stability ... the term "self-responsibility", which is more clearly individualist, thus better captures the logic of the concept'.[34] Thus, the lowest common denominator at present is agreement on a more communitarian focus on the sovereign prerogative of keeping one's own house in order, rather than a cosmopolitan ethic of special responsibility of the kind we have defended. The analysis in Chapter 5 provides plenty of reasons for questioning the adequacy of such a general allocation of responsibility-cum-thin pluralist solidarity, as opposed to a more centralised and thickly institutionalised assumption of either special or collective responsibility. If the US has done too little to mitigate the costs of globalisation to those most vulnerable, it has done this not just to other citizens, but arguably also to its own who have suffered as much as anyone as a result of the financial malfeasance spurring the global financial crisis. Given this, and the train of preceding and subsequent national crises, there are, not surprisingly, some emergent elements of greater internationalised and globalised responsibility, such as the recognition of the need for collective responsibility by the G20 as the new forum for global economic governance. The G20, in turn, has legitimised the regulatory power of other actors such as the Basel Committee, the Financial Stability Board and the IMF more generally. But recent IMF and G20 discourses also re-emphasise sovereignty and governance at the national level, and this embodiment of sovereign equality seems manifestly inadequate to the task of global financial regulatory coordination. Best puts it well when pointing out that if the causes of economic deprivation are far more complex than simply assuming each country is responsible for its own economic success or failure, 'then so too are the ties of international responsibility. Self-responsibility must be tempered by a different kind of responsibility – that of those who have gained from global inequalities towards those who have suffered from them.'[35] Our analysis certainly supports such a sentiment.

What we see instead, however, are developments such as a rise in the role of credit ratings agencies, which amounts to state deferral of responsibilities to private actors, and voluntary assumptions of responsibilities such as the 'Principles for Stable Capital Flows and Fair Debt Restructuring in Emerging Markets', agreed upon between private creditors and sovereign debtors.[36] The resulting diffusion of any former

---

[34] J. Best, 'Co-opting cosmopolitanism? The International Monetary Fund's new global ethics', *Global Society*, 20(3) 2006, 313.

[35] *Ibid.*, 320.

[36] On the latter, see R. Ritter, 'Transnational governance in global finance: The principles for stable capital flows and fair debt restructuring in emerging markets', *International Studies Perspectives*, 11(3) 2010, 222–41.

or potential special responsibilities claimed by, or ascribed to, the US has been abetted by 'the staggering complexity of the piecemeal regulatory structure that has developed since the demise of Bretton Woods', which, 'when combined with the sheer magnitude of the numbers involved in global finance, conspire to sustain a condition wherein there seems to be no way to really allocate or claim special responsibility anymore', as was noted in Chapter 5. This is not simply a story of US abrogation of responsibility, and it may be unfair morally to indict some of these developments as such, as with some of the failures to recognise early enough the concatenation of practices producing an increase in total systemic risk. Still, there are clear moments of hypocrisy in the shirking and denying of special responsibilities for global financial stability. With respect to adjustment, as we noted in Chapter 5, what began as privilege (the capacity to defer adjustment and run a permanent deficit) is now being cast by the US as a responsibility it can no longer bear.

The US has been called to account by a range of actors, including even by US President Obama himself, for its inciting role in the most recent global financial crisis, thus incurring responsibility for that crisis and to avert a future such crisis. We concur. But full accountability seems to have been evaded, and the diagnosis of why might present a moral dilemma. State capture by private financial interests has proven morally abhorrent in the global financial crisis, but it is in no small part a product of institutions of democracy, at least a particular version of it. If it is too much to expect the US government to shoulder the burden of acting in the interests of the rest of the world, it should not be too much to ask that those engaging in irresponsible practices that brought so much harm even to its own vulnerable citizens be held accountable. The former includes the agents of private finance, but importantly also those who abetted the structural failures of inadequate oversight within which capital operated, failures that by the time of the crisis were inexcusable in light of the lessons from previous crises. Surely the practice of socialising risk and privatising profits that emerged so clearly in the latest crisis deserves moral condemnation on the grounds outlined in this chapter.

Ironically, a healthy dose of populist domestic agitation in the US and elsewhere *might* bring about a certain amount of accountability and checks on the power of the financial sector, as it has in the past.[37] This would be consistent with our ethical argument that the US and the member states of the EU ought to shed their responsibility

---

[37] This is part of the argument in S. Johnson and J. Kwak, *13 bankers: The Wall Street takeover and the next financial meltdown* (New York: Pantheon, 2010).

to finance as a constituency, and reorient their responsibility to those more vulnerable to the vagaries of finance. But in the US and probably in other countries, the constituency that will emerge as of primary importance in that move will be the domestic public, and this could be to the detriment of the society of states and multilateral institutions, since domestic politics, especially of the populist variety, has not lately been entirely sympathetic to cosmopolitan principles or, in the US at least, to multilateralism in general. Even in resolutely multilateral Germany, public support for exercising special German capabilities in the wake of the European sovereign debt crisis has not been forthcoming. Therefore, from an ethical standpoint, it will be crucial to recover that element of the embedded liberalism compromise which entailed a commitment to cooperation through rule-based multilateral institutions and regimes. That in turn means abandoning a stance that asks a preponderant power to perform special responsibilities, which ended up undermining Bretton Woods in the first place, and instead reviving a more diffuse, society-of-great-powers approach to the problem of governing global finance, where that society includes emerging market countries previously excluded, but now such central players in the game of global economic growth.

US exceptionalism

So far, we have defended an ethical argument for the assignment of special responsibilities, and applied it to our case studies. Given that the US has considerable capacity on a range of different fronts, it is not surprising that the US often finds itself in the frontline when special responsibilities are assigned, and therefore ends up with a larger burden of special responsibilities than other states. We have already offered principles for addressing this problem: particularly insofar as the US is not culpable, it may legitimately appeal to competing ethical responsibilities (including responsibilities to its own citizens) to limit its obligations. However, here we address the question of US superior capacity from another angle: are there any ethical grounds upon which it could be argued that the US has a unique authority to determine the meaning and content of the special responsibilities it should assume by virtue of its preponderance and/or status?

It has been taken for granted in numerous accounts of IR from Kissinger to the English School that great powers constitute a distinctive set of actors whose claims are of special significance, and ought to be of predominant weight in the establishment of international order: it is not the claims of all persons nor all states, but especially the claims of great powers, that ought to matter in this context. In such a formulation, there is an ontological presumption about the nature of the relevant claiming agents that carries with it an ethical prescription: it is *right* that the claims of great powers matter more or even exclusively. Here the theoretical problem of thinking about the rise of special responsibilities for a single great power, as discussed in Chapter 1, can be seen to constitute an acute ethical problem: is a preponderant power to be understood as a distinctive moral agent, a category apart from other states, with attendant unique moral standards that we ought to accept as applying to it, and it alone? If so, then does it matter so much for an ethic of international order what other states think, and whether there is validation of the special responsibilities claimed by the predominant power? If special responsibilities are regarded as flowing from capacities, might it not in fact be morally logical to ascribe a distinctive moral status to those agents with such unique capacity? Or, conversely, would a satisfactory moral account still have to look to social approval for such special responsibilities of a particular category of agents, even by those who themselves might not occupy the same role in executing those responsibilities?

Those concerns raise the spectre of moral exceptionalism. This can be addressed in two ways: the first is an exception based on the nature of the circumstances, and the second based on the nature of the agent. Claims to exceptions to moral rules in general usually depend upon *special circumstances* that require overriding what should otherwise be held to be obligatory rules; for instance, claims about the suspension of a moral responsibility for civilian casualties in war may rest upon their co-mingling with legitimate military targets, the difficulty in determining who actually counts as a civilian, the taking advantage of such norms by non-regular forces, and the resulting extremity of the circumstances. But these are only plausible as claims of special responsibilities in the case of a *particular agent*, if the situations are uniquely encountered by that agent, in our case, the predominant power. The reason here is that agent is in fact doing things that others simply are not engaged in doing.

To sharpen the significance of agent-based claims to exceptionality, let us consider the role that circumstance rather than the alleged exceptional nature of the agent as such can play in assigning special responsibilities. Most of us would sympathise with the claim to exception of a parent driving in considerable excess of the speed limit to the hospital to get care for their child in life-threatening distress: here it is not a claim that such an agent is of a special nature as such that creates a claim for a special moral responsibility, as it is the nature of the pressing circumstance. But is there an alternative analogue where the case can instead be made on the uniqueness of the agent's role? Can the US plausibly claim that it is the only agent confronting various situations, and is thus due special consideration on the grounds of that role? Part of the US resistance to the International Criminal Court has been couched in comparable terms: the US should not be held to standards formulated by those states that are not involved in forceful external interventions, requiring the reach and depth of global power projection possessed by the US alone.

Here we need to distinguish further between two types of claims to special responsibility that might be made by a preponderant power: those that attempt to seek exemptions from global moral expectations and standards, and thus cultivate states of amoral exception, as against those based on legitimate moral rules for exceptional states as actors in international society, but which differ enough in kind to warrant the replacement of normal mores by exceptional ethics. It is famously common at least since Machiavelli, if hardly uncontroversial, to consider politicians as having special obligations distinct from, and not to be assessed by the rules of, personal morality; indeed, Max Weber argued along just such lines in formulating his ethic of responsibility.[38] Is a great power similarly to be held as beyond the regular mores of inter-state politics, even as that realm is already often depicted as one of 'dirty hands', but additionally subject to the suspension of normal private morality? That is, are special responsibilities to be understood as a moral standard only for the predominant, that follows from the fact that only such states face the kind of choices that simply do not confront ordinary states? The point is that there is a serious potential argument that pre-eminence does not mean exception in the sense of exemption from the moral standards that are to apply, but rather exception in the sense of a different moral standard that we could ask and expect only the exceptional to meet. Can any of the claims made by the US be so regarded? And what is the status of such claims?

Such claims have resonated in the academy in recent years with an explosion of interest in the politics of the states of exception in the writings of Carl Schmitt, and explored by such contemporary thinkers as Giorgio Agamben, spurred in no small part by the apparent politics of exception particularly in the 'war on terror', as practised and pronounced rather acutely by the Bush administration. Some commentators have pointed out that it is one thing to claim a state of exception as a way to escape the moral realm, and define the politics of exception in

---

[38] M. Weber, *Politics as a vocation* (Philadelphia, PA : Fortress Press, 1965).

just that way, and quite another to claim exception as a necessary way to re-establish a moral and political order.[39] Without engaging in a lengthy treatment of the relationship of morality to politics, we would similarly submit that claims to exception that are made in the name of the very accepted standards from which temporary exemption is being claimed in exceptional circumstances are indeed of a different, and potentially more acceptable, moral character than those that represent little more than a veiled attempt to secure free licence.[40]

In contrast, state claims to exceptionalism lack legitimacy, when simply asserted rather than socially validated. We have shown that some special responsibilities carry with them special privileges to enable their discharge, but that both responsibilities and rights must be socially conferred. In any case, claims to exceptional status are of a different character, and are hotly contested, even *within* the US: witness the disagreement even among American realists as to whether the US even is, or has been, a genuinely unipolar power. Our rejection of monolithic treatments of power tends to undercut the ontological basis for such claims, although with our move to domain-specific accounts of special responsibilities, in principle it is still conceivable for an actor to be dominant in any given domain. Thus, we need to consider carefully whether the preponderant power is claiming exception due to its engaging in activities that others cannot, the extent to which that is in fact the case and whether such assessments justify a delegation of not just special privileges but also special exemptions.

The Spiderman ethics discussed earlier – that 'with great power comes great responsibility' – seem to have significant appeal within the rhetoric of practitioners, as we have seen with US President Obama, as well as with a number of political theorists. Jean Elshtain, whose defence of Spiderman ethics has already been noted, has argued the case for differentiated moral responsibilities among morally like agents, by way of degree due to capacity and role, rather than as a morally distinct kind of agent as such. In that we are in agreement. Elshtain is perfectly aware that '[i]t is extraordinarily difficult to articulate a strong universal justice claim and to assign a particular state and its people a disproportionate burden to enforce that claim'.[41] Since in the case of interventions for

---

[39] See the discussion in J. Ralph, 'The laws of war and the state of the American exception', *Review of International Studies*, 35(3) 2009, 631–49.
[40] For an argument about how one might tell the difference, see M. Bukovansky, 'Cynical rascals or conscientious objectors? Interpreting non-compliance with international norms', in O. Kessler, R. Hall, C. Lynch and N. Onuf (eds.), *On rules, politics, and knowledge: Friedrich Kratochwill, international relations, and domestic affairs* (New York: Palgrave, 2010), pp. 158–77.
[41] Elshtain, 'International justice', 75.

those who cannot defend themselves, '[t]he burden of this responsibility will be borne disproportionately by the United States, given its unique capability to project power', she explicitly recognises

that some will argue that the kinds of interventions I call for in this essay amount to imperialism. I believe, however, that we simply must get past the almost inevitable initial negative reaction to views that call on the United States to exercise robust powers of intervention.[42]

But her case here is a very truncated one, and for us, this is the key point: upon what basis exactly could both the US and others accept the fairness of such claims of special responsibilities, without such suspicions getting in the way? Elshtain for her part simply posits as self-evident that 'with great power comes great responsibility', as if the responsibilities hoped for by others will be taken on unproblematically by the US, on the one hand, and on the other that '[t]he United States is itself premised on a set of universal propositions concerning human dignity and equality. There is no conflict in principle between our national identity and universal claims and commitments.'[43] A similar kind of claim has been made by Robert Kagan:

The United States can neither appear to be acting, nor in fact act, as if only its self-interest mattered. It must act in ways that benefit all humanity or, at the very least, the part of humanity that shares its liberal principles. Even in times of dire emergency, and perhaps especially then, the world's sole superpower needs to demonstrate that it wields its great strengths on behalf of its principles and those who share them.[44]

Here then are normative claims, made by Americans, that the US as a predominant power or sole superpower *ought* to be taking on special responsibilities on behalf of all humanity. Chris Brown has noted that despite debates between 'unilateralists' and their critics during the Bush administration, both camps have been

driven by a strong sense that the power of the United States brings with it great moral responsibility, and both of whom believe that the United States should act in the world as the agent of something other than simply US national interests ... both multilateralists and unilateralists believe that the United States has special (moral) responsibilities by virtue of the power it wields in the world; both hold that this power must be deployed in the service of a higher good.[45]

The problem, however, is that even within the US, what those responsibilities entail is contested. In accounts such as Elshtain's, the usual

---

[42] *Ibid.,* 64.   [43] *Ibid.,* 74.
[44] R. Kagan, 'America's crisis of legitimacy', *Foreign Affairs*, 83(2) 2004, 85.
[45] Brown, 'Do great powers have great responsibilities?', 6.

expected tension between the interests of a unipolar power and cosmopolitan principles is erased with an empirical assumption that they are coterminous. If and when that happens, a good part of our ethical problem would seem to be solved, to the extent to which the US discharges special responsibilities towards those who are most vulnerable and dependent on its action or inaction, because it has the requisite capacity to make a difference. The discharge of such responsibilities usually brings with it significant common benefits; there is certainly a common interest in avoiding a cataclysmic nuclear war, catastrophic climate change and a breakdown of the global financial system. To the extent that these global problems are also US problems, and vice versa, the paradigmatic threshold between (national) interests and (more universal) ethics can potentially assume less significance. But it is manifest that a sufficiently robust and happy coincidence of the US and others' standards of justice is lacking in our domains. Thus any argument like Elshtain's does not provide a sufficient response to the abundant evidence of rejection by others: there has been widespread resistance to various US operationalisations of key principles like freedom and its purported political requirements, or to Kagan's liberal values, not to mention frequent US failure itself to live up to those values.

Conclusion

We have placed the links between vulnerability, dependency and capacity at the heart of our ethics of special responsibilities. The idea of vulnerability driving morality is not new. Adam Smith maintained that empathy issuing from a shared sense of vulnerability is the bond keeping social structures intact. From Immanuel Kant's Categorical Imperative, to Jürgen Habermas's requirement of consent in his communicative ethics, to the capability approach of Amartya Sen, many international ethical prescriptions seek to guard against the imposition of unelected risks on the innocent, and all the more so when they have no capacity to insulate themselves from such risks. These ideas animate Linklater's development of a harm principle in contemporary international normative theory.[46] Needs-based ethics and human rights discourses would also lean towards the moral injunction against ignoring the plight of persons made vulnerable due to the actions of others.

[46] See Linklater, *The problem of harm*, as well as A. Linklater, 'Towards a sociology of global morals with an emancipatory intent', *Review of International Studies*, 33(S1) 2007, 135–50; and A. Linklater, 'The harm principle and global ethics', *Global Society*, 20(3) 2006, 329–43.

The ethics of special responsibilities that we have outlined assigns responsibilities to those capable agents upon whose actions or inactions vulnerable constituencies are largely or entirely dependent for the alleviation of their plight. These ethics represent a distinctive type of cosmopolitan ethics that are fashioned as a response to a world characterised by both formal equality of states and inequality of material capability. This unique fusion of both functional and ethical arguments that underpins the assignment of special responsibilities seeks to avoid the problem of no-one having moral responsibility for the plight of the vulnerable. Our three case studies provide pertinent examples of vulnerability that is dependent on the actions or inactions of those with the requisite capacity to make a difference: the plethora of threats to human and other life by the variety of processes unleashed by the threat of victimisation by nuclear weapons, climate change and widespread poverty wrought by financial crises.

Of course, there is no perfect match between the ethical arguments we defend, and the arguments that have largely supported real world assignments of special responsibility, and we would not expect to see such a complete match. Our purpose was merely to offer ethical arguments that we consider ought to form the basis for assigning special responsibilities. Sociologically speaking, special responsibilities determine the realm of legitimate action when they are actually agreed by those affected. Nonetheless, the case studies reveal a host of cosmopolitan ethical claims that resonate with our own, even if some of these come from the sidelines, or from unsuccessful coalitions, rather than the centre of power. This lends further force to our broader sociological claim that special responsibilities represent a distinctive ethical and functionalist response to an ever more deeply interdependent world, characterised by both formal equality and inequality of material capability, among both states and persons. This chapter highlights also the various ways in which ethical arguments conspire to place the US in the frontline of shouldering special responsibilities in our three case studies. Specifically in the cases of nuclear weapons and climate change, this responsibility must take the form of a leadership obligation, if the vulnerabilities in question are to be addressed in anything approaching an adequate form.

Conclusion

> 'President Obama and I believe that despite the budget pressures, it would be a grave mistake for the US to withdraw from its global responsibilities.'[1]

> 'US leaders have understood that to claim authority over others would force their counterparts in subordinate states to deny this fact and thus undermine the legitimacy of US rule. As a result, US authority has been cloaked in euphemisms.'[2]

The term 'special responsibility' is more than a euphemism for US authority or 'soft power'. The language of responsibility and special responsibility is routinely used in the practice of international relations, often to delimit specific collective action problems and to articulate guidelines for the exercise of legitimate, accountable authority in addressing those problems. The above epigraph from former US Secretary of Defense Robert Gates's speech to the North Atlantic Treaty Organisation (NATO) allies was part of an exhortation to the Europeans to bear more of the burden of NATO responsibilities in Afghanistan, Iraq, Libya and elsewhere. Rather than cloaking US power in euphemism, Gates seems instead to be acknowledging US special responsibility, while also asking that the burden of responsibility be shared among capable allies. In doing so he must evoke shared notions of legitimacy – not to cloak US power, but to enlist cooperation in achieving common goals.

This book has attempted systematically to analyse the practice of evoking special responsibility, explicating with theory and evidence how special responsibilities have been allocated and contested in the face of three important global problems: nuclear non-proliferation, climate change and financial regulation. We have also developed a way of

---

[1] R. M. Gates, 'The security and defense agenda (future of NATO)', speech delivered in Brussels, Belgium, 10 June 2011, www.defense.gov/speeches/speech.aspx?speechid=1581 (accessed 3 August 2011).
[2] D. A. Lake, 'Making America safe for the world: Multilateralism and the rehabilitation of US authority', *Global Governance*, 16(4) 2010, 471–2.

reasoning through the ethical issues surrounding special responsibilities, and suggested how such ethical reasoning may be applied in the specific case studies. In this conclusion, we consider special responsibilities as a form of social power, their relationship to international orders, the global role of the US and the consequences of the diffusion of responsibility in world affairs.

Contemporary debates about the US position in the world focus both on the question of whether US primacy will endure, and whether the international order presumably underpinned by that primacy will survive.[3] Often the concepts of primacy and order are presented as being so intertwined as to be inseparable. Yet it would be a mistake to reduce international order to US preponderance.[4] The contours of international order are shaped by norms and ideas allocating responsibility as much as by material capability. These responsibility regimes are not mere reflections of US preponderance. Although the US has often enough contributed disproportionate resources to the solution of global governance problems, and has in its own policy discourse often claimed 'ownership' of the international institutional manifestations of the post-Second World War global order, in the final analysis, preponderance and order cannot be conflated.

It is a long-standing tradition in International Relations (IR) theorising to treat order as if it had some intrinsic content – for Hedley Bull it meant a society of states with basic rules of coexistence, whereas for Kenneth Waltz it meant the distribution of material power, for example – but this book has instead sought to cast the problem of international order more concretely as the governance of global problems. We have thus remained open to the idea of a multiplicity of international orders, depending on which governance issue we are considering. Our choice of cases was not meant to provide an exhaustive and complete account of 'the' international order, or even of the most important international regimes (although we do think our chosen cases are particularly important in our time), but rather to illustrate how international order is shaped by the allocation of responsibility in specific domains and in specific ways, and how these allocations help to constitute social power. In this sense, the book opens up an agenda

---

[3] S. G. Brooks and W. C. Wohlforth, *World out of balance: International relations and the challenge of American primacy* (Princeton, NJ: Princeton University Press, 2008); F. Zakaria, *The post-American world* (New York: W. W. Norton, 2008); D. Deudney and G. J. Ikenberry, 'The myth of the autocratic revival: Why liberal democracy will prevail', *Foreign Affairs*, 88(1) 2009, 77–93; Lake, 'Making America safe for the world'.

[4] This point is also made in G. J. Ikenberry, 'The future of the liberal world order', *Foreign Affairs*, 90(3) 2011, 56–68.

for further exploration of the allocation of special responsibilities to tackle other global issues such as humanitarian crises, trade, ecological challenges beyond climate change, immigration, the containment of infectious diseases and so on.

Perceptions of global problems, and the assignment of responsibility for their management, are products of communication (arguing and bargaining), which in turn are conducted through the medium of shared and contested ideas about how to frame, address and solve those problems. Although differences in material capability strongly influence this process, the cases presented in this volume demonstrate that material power alone determines neither the perception of global problems, nor the allocation of responsibility for their solutions. Moreover, although the US has served and continues to serve as a strong voice in the articulation of global governance norms, it is not now, nor has it ever been, the only voice. Increasingly, we find as well that states, and international organisations conceived of as tools of states, no longer have a monopoly on the articulation and management of global problems.[5] An ethical point that parallels this development is that communitarian ethics which privilege the state as a bounded moral community no longer hold sway in many global governance domains, and it becomes possible to defend more cosmopolitan principles as plausible criteria for moral judgements about special responsibilities in global governance (see Chapter 6 in this volume).

Different governance domains further exhibit different criteria of legitimacy and of ethical judgement about legitimacy, so how a leading state is viewed by others, and the willingness of others to comply with or contribute to the solution of governance problems, will also vary across different issue areas. This explains why the US may still appear as the sole superpower in the military sphere, while many of those who follow international political economy have already heralded the advent of a multipolar world, and those concerned with global environmental problems bemoan the abject lack of leadership available from all but a very few of the most materially capable developed states.

Despite its material preponderance in the military sphere, the US nevertheless relies on the cooperation of many other actors in stemming the tide of nuclear proliferation, and that cooperation is conditioned by perceptions of responsibility and legitimacy. Thus the social power to achieve a desired outcome – non-proliferation – is shaped by shared understandings of responsibility and special responsibility. Should the

---

[5] L. Van Langenhove, 'The transformation of multilateralism mode 1.0 to mode 2.0', *Global Policy*, 1(3) 2010, 263–70.

willingness of the non-nuclear weapon states (NNWSs) to accept their status and responsibilities falter, then it is hard to see how any amount of material preponderance could stem proliferation. Indeed, such a situation has been used by the US and other nuclear weapon states (NWSs) as justification for keeping their weapons, and for investing in new types of capabilities such as missile defences and space-based weapons systems. The allocation of special responsibility for addressing climate change has been constituted by the concerted effort of a collection of actors notably missing, and in some senses working against the will of, the preponderant power of the US. And in governing global finance it has at least partly been the willful dispersion of authority and responsibility away from states and towards markets which has served to undercut the capability of the US to continue to impose its regulatory neoliberalism on others. There is perhaps no clearer example of the social constitution of power than what has emerged in the financial markets since the capital account liberalisation process took off in earnest in the 1980s. One need only consider the panicked responses of the wealthiest states when facing the prospect of a downgrade of their credit rating to see the import of this.

Despite our analytical resistance to conflating social order and material power, a focus on special responsibilities also entails a moral judgement about the appropriate exercise of material capacity by those who possess relatively more of such capacity. As the preceding chapter has shown, we often expect those actors with the greatest capacity to step up to the plate, contribute resources to the solution of global problems and address the plight of those most vulnerable to such problems – this takes the form of an ethical imperative rather than a causal prediction. Even as our case studies have shown variation in the willingness of the most capable agent to take on and exercise special responsibilities, as well as variation in the capacity of the US in different governance domains, we nevertheless want to retain and emphasise the ethical force of the concept of special responsibility, especially as it links together capability, accountability and vulnerability. We have, in this volume, addressed both sets of questions: whether and how special responsibilities *have actually been* exercised to address problems of nuclear proliferation, climate change and global finance, and whether and how special responsibilities *should* be exercised to address those issues. We have been struck by the extent of the overlap (albeit imperfect) between the principles appealed to in the former, and the ethics we have elaborated in the latter.

Analysing leadership and governance of global problems in terms of the language of special responsibilities brings into focus that which is often assumed but not made explicit: social order hinges on the concept of responsibility (even in the anarchic realm of international relations). Responsibility in turn entails accountability to specific constituencies, and tracking the evolution of special responsibilities enhances our understanding of legitimacy and authority in world politics. Although the concept of special responsibilities has long been an aspect of the international society approach to IR, as we have shown in Chapter 1, it has rarely found a place in analyses of a single great power world, as opposed to a world of multiple great powers.

Perhaps because in a unipolar world it seems natural to associate order with a single authority, the post-Cold War international context tempts us to consider all questions regarding governance of global problems by looking first to the dominant power in the system. This then invites us to blame the US for failures of governance, and to assign it credit for successes. While there may be moral reasons to do so (although even this is contestable in some cases), there are strong empirical reasons to resist expecting the materially strongest state to be the lynchpin of global governance in every issue area. The arguments and case studies of this book have sought to balance necessary attention to US leadership and special responsibilities, with sensitivity to diversity in the array of actors and their problem-solving capabilities in different issue domains. By disaggregating the international system into different issue areas representing different governance challenges, a more nuanced picture emerges of the character and challenges of US primacy, the future of multilateralism and the changing contours of international society.

As a preponderant power, the US has clearly asserted and been asked to exercise special responsibilities in many domains of governance. Our study cannot evade, but also cannot be reduced to, the question of the durability of US primacy; it leaves open the possibility of other actors taking on special responsibilities according to new configurations of capacity, such as China in climate change, or networks of public institutions and private companies in the governance of finance. Even so, the US is clearly a major player in all the cases presented here, and this invites further reflection on US leadership in the governance of global problems. What then does this book tell us about the character and durability of US primacy? Is the story we tell here one of US decline and failure to address some of the most pressing global problems, or does it add support to the more optimistic readings about the durability of a liberal internationalist order – and how closely linked to US preponderance is such durability? Is any US decline simply consequent on material shifts in the distribution of power, or can we associate US decline with its failure to harness its power to socially productive and socially licensed ends? If great power brings great responsibility (the 'Spiderman ethics' evoked in Chapter 6), is it the failure to discharge that responsibility that is now making the US less of a great power? Our case studies do suggest that legitimate social power has been slipping out of the grip of the US, diffusing not only to other states but also to non-state actors. But this is not simply the result of exogenously sourced changes in the global distribution of material power; it is also the product of the social dynamics involved in the allocation and contestation of responsibilities in multiple issue areas. When different responsibilities pull in different directions, a great power may find itself losing authority on at least some fronts.

A key problem revealed by the case studies is that special responsibilities may clash with other responsibilities, special or not. This problem has at least two dimensions: first, the exercise of special responsibilities in one governance domain may clash with their exercise in another, and second, the US – or indeed any democratic 'great responsible' – may face significant difficulties and tensions in discharging international responsibilities, when these clash with political pressures to focus primarily on domestic concerns. In short, international special responsibilities may conflict with each other, as well as with domestic responsibilities. This 'clash of responsibilities' does not simply mean that states must make choices and rationally decide on trade-offs between distinct options. Certainly, some instances can be interpreted as trade-offs, such as the US abandonment of its special economic responsibilities during the 'Nixon shocks', which can be read as the price paid for continued exercise of special responsibility in the security realm. But in other instances, policy-makers have attempted to downplay or deny the tensions between different responsibilities (as further discussed below). Because special responsibilities are articulated and negotiated in a social realm, replete with ideas about legitimacy and right conduct, as well as ideas about how to understand and frame governance problems, they cannot be understood solely in terms of rational calculations of cost and benefit, nor in terms of trade-offs between clearly demarcated alternatives. Moreover, clashes of responsibility may themselves be a source of change in the governance of global problems and in how such problems are perceived.

When the US has experienced tensions and clashes between its international responsibilities, it has at times attempted to deny the inconsistency, and elsewhere has had to face the necessity of favouring one over the other. For example, in the Bretton Woods era the US interpreted its global economic responsibilities in terms of a commitment to encouraging economic openness and growth. That interpretation shaped and limited the type of responsibilities it was willing to exercise for the adjustment of global accounts and ensuring financial stability. But the commitment to economic openness has, over time, come into tension with the special responsibility for nuclear non-proliferation in that non-proliferation requires restraint and closure of certain types of economic exchange – namely that of proliferation-sensitive technologies (uranium enrichment and plutonium separation facilities) that could contribute to the development of nuclear weapons (as opposed to peaceful nuclear energy). On the face of it, though, the tension between free economic exchange and restraints on nuclear materials has not necessitated a clear trade-off between responsibilities (although it has come close with the case of India); it has instead been papered over. Further, the social identity assumed by the US as 'defender and leader of the free world' has, to some extent, allowed it to gloss over the tensions between its economic and security responsibilities, although the consequences of this elision for the US financial position are still working themselves out.

Perhaps because the United States' other commitments – to economic openness and growth, and security guarantees to its allies nested within a broader regime of peace and security centred on the United Nations – have been of a much longer standing than its still contested and partial awareness of the dangers of climate change, it has had difficulty reorienting itself to the sort of restraint and redirection that would be truly required to address the latter issue. While the US may, over time, recalibrate its special responsibilities in the security and economic domains in ways that allow for the discharge of its climate leadership responsibilities, this is unlikely to happen quickly or easily. If it does eventually come to pass, then the world's attention may have already shifted to China and the US's special leadership responsibilities may no longer be quite so special.[6]

When special responsibilities become institutionalised and constitutive of broader social roles and identities, such as 'defender of the free world', this creates a form of path dependency which may foreclose or make more difficult a reorientation of policy based on relatively later articulations of global problems, and the responsibilities required to address them. As Robert Falkner has observed, 'unlike trade and monetary policy, environmental policy has never been central to the US

---

[6] See, for example, W. J. W. Botzen, J. M. Gowdy and J. C. J. M. van den Bergh, 'Cumulative CO_2 emissions: Shifting international responsibilities for climate debt', *Climate Policy*, 8(6) 2008, 569–76.

effort to create international order'.[7] Yet it is precisely because climate protection has not formed part of the US's vision of the international order that it raises new and interesting questions about possible future changes in the international order. As shown in our chapter on climate change, the developed countries' climate leadership responsibilities rest on a new, more egalitarian understanding of international order, one which seeks to close the development gap by providing space for developing countries to grow, while requiring developed countries to undertake aggregate cuts in emissions. Similarly, emerging conceptions of responsibility for global finance in the Group of Twenty (G20) also articulate a more egalitarian approach to order, in that the 'club' of 'great responsibles' has grown to include countries previously consigned to 'developing country' status. In the nuclear realm, by contrast, the formal club of great responsibles remains (somewhat anachronistically) frozen, and thus rather than include new developing country nuclear powers into the club on the basis of their material qualifications, the effort continues to freeze the gap between NWSs and NNWSs. At the same time, the willingness of the US to cut a deal with India, despite its status as a non-signatory to the Nuclear Non-Proliferation Treaty (NPT), may threaten the equilibrium achieved by the treaty insofar as India may be seen to have profited from breaking the non-proliferation norm.[8]

Tensions between different responsibilities also serve to highlight our key theoretical point that the concept of special responsibility is a manifestation of the attempt to reconcile the reality of material power differentials with the norm of sovereign equality. Rather than adopting a monolithic view of power, looking at social power in terms of various governance problems and domains reinforces the observation that even a preponderant state will experience variations in its capacity to achieve its desired outcomes. Power is never perfectly fungible, then, and in fact success in promoting one set of social objectives, such as economic liberalisation, may undercut the capacity to promote another set, such as averting climate change. Even in cases where the predominant power believes that different domains of governance can be harmonised according to a singular vision of global order, as was the case in the Bretton Woods era, when the US saw economic liberalisation and maintenance of global peace and security as part and parcel of the same

---

[7] R. Falkner, 'American hegemony and the global environment', *International Studies Review*, 7(4) 2005, 586.

[8] W. Walker, *A perpetual menace: Nuclear weapons and international order* (London: Routledge, 2011).

ideology, the practical consequences of attempting to realise the different governance goals simultaneously may reveal unanticipated (and ultimately unbearable) costs and trade-offs: as a result, the vision may no longer appear coherent, and its elements no longer harmonious. In the wake of a great recession, the US executive branch finds itself hard-pressed to sell to Congress and the American public the notion that free trade is essential to the US vision of a better world. The Doha Round of trade negotiations is effectively dead, and the leadership to push ahead with further liberalisation in the multilateral forum of the World Trade Organization is clearly absent. Does this mean that US primacy is on the wane, or that the coherence of the post-Second World War vision of order has unravelled because of the practical difficulties of sustaining that vision?

During the early Bretton Woods era, the US put forth the dollar as the anchor of a global payments system, and this was part and parcel of a vision of sustaining a strong Western alliance against communism. With the end of the Bretton Woods exchange rate regime, the US gave up on the idea that global financial stability would be based on linking the dollar to gold in order to sustain its militarily preponderant role as defender of the West. The two governance domains could no longer be so easily harmonised, although the dollar, and US Treasuries, retained a central position in the global financial system, even as the link to gold was abandoned. Will the nuclear non-proliferation regime experience a similar crisis and transformation in the face of irreconcilable imperatives and a mismatch between aspirations and capabilities? How long can the legalised inequality of the NPT remain a central governing norm in the face of demonstrated non-compliance on the part of 'rogue' states, both outside and inside the regime? How long before the long-standing observation that the promise of nuclear disarmament by the NWSs is nothing but a hypocritical way to freeze the status quo ends up sapping it of any remaining legitimacy? Or with respect to climate change, will the imperative of curbing emissions push a further de-coupling of the idea of economic growth from that of survival and flourishing of the global ecosystem, including the human species?

The idea that there is such a thing as one 'international order' is contingent on such an order being pulled together, not just by the leading state but by many states, and surely non-state actors as well, whose cooperation is needed to make the vision of order into a practical, working reality. Although the narrative of US post-Second World War leadership is often constructed so as to make it appear as though there was a singular and coherent character to the postwar order, our case studies cast doubt on that view. It is true that the US worked very hard to put forth a coherent vision of order, but the coherence was unsustainable because of the variety of sometimes clashing responsibilities required to implement it. The fact that the requirements of exercising responsibility in one issue area can lead to conflict with the exercise of responsibilities in other issue areas is not simply a matter of having to deal with trade-offs and choices, although it is of course partly that. Rather than claim that the US rationally chose to abandon its financial responsibilities in exchange for maintaining its security responsibilities, for example, our approach suggests that different problems (or governance domains) have different responsibilities associated with them, as well as different capacities to exercise such responsibilities. Resolution of the tensions between these different responsibilities is not simply determined by rational decisions about how to allocate material resources; a deeper social process of cobbling together shared visions of legitimate authority and responsibility is central to either the sustenance or the unravelling of the conglomeration of responsibility regimes that constitutes international order at any given time. The challenges of exercising responsibility in a variety of domains can lead not only to resource depletion and trade-offs, but to the unravelling of the very notion of international order as a unitary concept.

The role of US domestic politics – both the institutional structure of such politics, and the interest groups and political processes at work within that structure – emerges as an important dimension of US special responsibilities. Perhaps one of the reasons the story of US special responsibilities in averting nuclear proliferation is somewhat more hopeful than the other two cases is that US decisions in this area rest primarily on executive power and can therefore avoid at least some of the entanglements of Congress (although the Senate non-ratification in 1999 of the Comprehensive Nuclear-Test-Ban Treaty is a notable counter-example). In the climate and finance domains, Congressional support is more routinely crucial to the successful discharge of special responsibilities, but political polarisation, policy gridlock and a distinct lack of any cosmopolitan orientation or preoccupation with the rest of the world make it extremely difficult to build an effective majority to accept and discharge special responsibilities, especially in times of economic turmoil; perhaps this is why we see, in the climate and finance cases, 'a return to sovereign responsibility'.

Of course, the US is not alone in its domestic preoccupations; this is a characteristic of many states, and not just democracies. It is not that the US has greater concerns about domestic responsibilities than other governments; it is just that the gap between those responsibilities can become more acute as more is demanded of the US globally due to its greater capacity in key areas. The gap, in turn, is exacerbated by the institution of divided government in the US, which makes bold international leadership extremely difficult in all but the most acute circumstances, such as post-Second World War recovery, or after 11 September 2001. So there is a twofold problem with expecting the US to take on special responsibilities ascribed to it, one generic to those with great capacity, one more specific to the US, or at least to any state with a deeply institutionalised system of checks and balances. Further research might reveal more about how leading states other than the US, including historical empires, have internalised conceptions of international special responsibilities, how such states resolve the tensions and gaps between their exercise of international and domestic responsibilities, and how domestic institutional structures condition such resolution (or lack thereof).

Although as democracy spreads and deepens around the world, governments may be increasingly drawn into prioritising responsibilities to domestic constituencies, those constituencies at the same time are often linked to others around the globe through economic and cultural ties facilitated by communication and transportation technologies. Domestic constituencies are often not isolated from each other by sovereign borders, but rather interconnected with other domestic constituencies. This renders the concept of 'domestic politics' rather porous, although of course the requirements of citizenship and voting rights do pose one sort of limit, and the world is not totally borderless in that respect. Still, if domestic constituencies have a voice in articulating the character of responsibilities in specific issue areas, they exercise such a voice not in isolation from, but often in conjunction with, constituencies in other states. In some cases, domestic politics become transnational politics, as Margaret Keck and Kathryn Sikkink have shown to be the case with human rights, environmental issues and women's advocacy.[9] In the case of climate change, our book has focused on the United Nations Framework Convention on Climate Change process, but there is now increasing talk of 'a climate regime complex', involving a myriad of different regimes and looser cooperative arrangements between state and non-state actors. Those disappointed in the formal negotiations are now shifting their attention to these new fora, in the hope they might deliver what the state-centric regime has failed to do. The case of global finance may in fact be exemplary, and the case of nuclear weapons more anomalous, for understanding these emerging patterns of global order.

[9] M. E. Keck and K. Sikkink, *Activists beyond borders: Advocacy networks in international politics* (Ithaca, NY: Cornell University Press, 1998).

But even the nuclear domain – which may at first glance appear the most state-dominated – has been influenced by non-state actors, in that non-governmental organisations have, through the mechanism of NPT Review Conferences, played a key role in providing information to hold states accountable for their performance, and (perhaps to the detriment of the non-proliferation regime) the Nuclear Suppliers Group was instrumental in developing the US-India Civil Nuclear Cooperation Initiative. In this area, domestic publics have been less heavily involved (at least since the 1980s) than they are in areas such as climate change and human rights.

Although from an ethical standpoint transnational advocacy networks can often be seen as a force for good in the sense that they advocate the exercise of moral responsibility by the powerful, networks of non-state actors can in other instances be cast in a far less rosy light. This is glaringly obvious when considering terrorist networks, for example, whose connections and aims might have quite a dangerous influence on the nuclear non-proliferation regime. The case of global finance presents us with a very complex picture, neither so easy to commend as human rights advocacy, nor so easy to condemn as global terrorism. But it is clear that responsibility for governance of finance has been diffused into a complex network of private actors, credit rating agencies and various limited membership international and professional organisations, in addition to states and regional organisations, and that the sole relevant universal membership multilateral international organisation, the International Monetary Fund, is hardly at the forefront asserting authority in this domain.

The diffusion of responsibility away from state and intergovernmental actors and into networks which include non-state actors, clearly evident in two of our three case studies, and of emerging importance even in the nuclear non-proliferation regime, suggests some concluding speculations on the changing character of multilateralism.[10] It seems clear that a state-centric framework fails to capture the full array of agencies and voices contributing to the formation of collective understandings regarding the allocation of responsibility for global problems. The pessimistic view of this process of diffusion might emphasise that, as states and state-controlled intergovernmental organisations become overburdened with a diverse array of governance problems and demands on their resources, their impetus is to 'out-source' governance. Such outsourcing creates problems of accountability, simply because it becomes

---

[10] A helpful discussion can be found in Van Langenhove, 'The transformation of multilateralism'.

difficult to find a single agency or limited group of agents on whom to pin responsibility for failure to produce the 'goods' that governance is supposed to provide in a given issue area – be it curbing emissions, or coordinating adjustment of global accounts. From this perspective, we are moving away from a world where great powers exercise special responsibilities, and into a world where responsibility is viewed in such a diffuse way as to lose its meaning altogether. This is a price of globalisation not adequately highlighted in existing literature, given the lack of attention to the central role of responsibility. A diffuse entity such as 'the market' cannot plausibly bear anything like 'responsibility' for alleviating the distress of those vulnerable to a drastic cyclical downturn, because the market is not a moral agent in the sense that a human being or a state or other public institution is. So perhaps in tracking the diffusion of responsibility we are also actually tracking, in some instances, the *dissipation* of responsibility and the marginalisation of legitimate public authority for tackling collective action problems in the international sphere.

A more optimistic reading of the trend toward diffusion of responsibility would focus on the decentralisation of authority, without concluding from this that public authority in general has become marginal to the solution of global problems – that is, responsibility has become more *diffuse but not dissipated*. Rather, we can think of the process in terms of devolution as it is understood in the study of the European Union, as a transfer of authority to more diverse, often localised sources closer to the particular issues at hand, but not a neoliberal, 'virtues of unrestrained markets' sort of denial of government competency in general. Perhaps demanding that the world's sole remaining superpower assume special responsibilities for so many of the world's problems is simply a way of cultivating an unsustainable dependency on US leadership, a dependency which will continue to whittle away at both the ideological and material foundations of that leadership.

From this perspective, the task becomes a complex one of identifying competent public and private agencies in the various domains of global governance, and rethinking the allocation of responsibility in a more functionally differentiated way, taking capacities into account but not reducing capacities to a single scale of measurement of material power. For example, some agencies are competent to measure the extent of problems, others to negotiate agreements on such things as capital adequacy standards or emissions targets, still others to mobilise cooperation from the private sector using marketing, consumer advocacy and moral suasion. These dimensions of problem-solving can all entail responsibilities, and indeed some may entail special responsibilities. But we can no longer assume that there will only be one, or even only a few, bearers of special responsibilities, as was the case when international society was a society of states, or when the US held sway as the sole 'superpower' in a world of subordinate states.

From an ethical standpoint, this diffusion of responsibility may mesh quite well with the sort of cosmopolitan ethical orientation outlined in the previous chapter, in that the developments contributing to the diffusion entail rather fluid boundaries of relevant communities and constituencies. Thus, the intertwined concepts of responsibility, accountability and vulnerability resist being related to a territorially fixed constituency or group. Rather, depending on the problem, the identities of the responsible, accountable and at-risk constituencies will be defined by practical considerations of capability and vulnerability, not only by citizenship or status within a particular in-group. A more functional, cosmopolitan ethic will be appropriate to addressing the 'ought' questions regarding the exercise of responsibility and special responsibility in a globalised world of complex problems and diverse agencies.

The global problems we face today, and the intellectual, cultural, organisational and material resources we must mobilise to address them, require a much more complex and diverse network of 'great responsibles' than is envisioned by either state-centric or market-centric models of world politics. Even in the nuclear weapons domain, where statism has as strong a hold as perhaps any domain, getting to 'zero' would entail significant devolution of real authority to international organisations such as the International Atomic Energy Agency to oversee sovereign responsibility. What remains to be seen is if, and how, the circle of democratic governance at various 'domestic' levels can be squared with the demands of governance at the global level for the world's most pressing problems.

Bibliography

'266 Evatt to Deschamps for Marshall', Cablegram 69 Canberra, 20 April 1947, 9.15 p.m., www.info.dfat.gov.au/info/historical/HistDocs.nsf/12~266 (accessed 10 August 2011).

'289 Department of External Affairs to Australian Delegation, United Nations', Cablegram UNY468 Canberra, 8 December 1946, www.info.dfat.gov.au/info/historical/HistDocs.nsf/10~289 (accessed 10 August 2011).

'A nuclear-weapons-free world: The need for a new agenda', Joint Declaration by the Ministers for Foreign Affairs of Brazil, Egypt, Ireland, Mexico, New Zealand, Slovenia, South Africa and Sweden, 9 June 1998, www.acronym.org.uk/27state.htm (accessed 27 July 2011).

Abdelal, R., *Capital rules: The construction of global finance* (Cambridge, MA: Harvard University Press, 2007).

Abizadeh, A. and Gilabert, P., 'Is there a genuine tension between cosmopolitan egalitarianism and special responsibilities?', *Philosophical Studies*, 138(3) 2008, 349–65.

Acronym Institute, 'The Non-Proliferation Treaty: Challenging times', Acronym Report No. 13, February 2000, www.acronym.org.uk/acrorep/a13pt1.htm (accessed 27 July 2011).

Adler, E. and Pouliot, V. (eds.), *The practice turn in international relations* (Cambridge: Cambridge University Press, forthcoming).

Albrecht-Carrié, R., *The Concert of Europe 1815–1914* (New York: Harper and Row, 1968).

Alessandri, P. and Haldane, A. G., 'Banking on the state', speech, Bank of England, November 2009, www.bankofengland.co.uk/publications/speeches/2009/speech409.pdf (accessed 28 July 2011).

Alexander, K., Dhumale, R. and Eatwell, J., *Global governance of financial systems: The international regulation of systemic risk* (Oxford: Oxford University Press, 2006).

Allison, G. T., *Nuclear terrorism: The ultimate preventable catastrophe* (New York: Times Books, 2004).

Altman, R. C., 'Globalization in retreat: Further geopolitical consequences of the financial crisis', *Foreign Affairs*, 88(4) 2009, 2–8.

Andrews, E. L., 'Greenspan concedes error on regulation', *New York Times*, 23 October 2008.

Aristotle, *Nicomachean ethics* (New York: Bobbs-Merrill, 1962).

Aron, R., *Peace and war: A theory of international relations* (London: Weidenfeld and Nicolson, 1966).

Ashe, J. W., Van Lierop R. and Cherian A., 'The role of the Alliance of Small Island States (AOSIS) in the negotiation of the United Nations Framework Convention on Climate Change (UNFCCC)', *Natural Resources Forum*, 23(3) 1999, 209–30.

Baer, P., Athanasiou, T., Kartha, S. and Kemp-Benedict, E., *The greenhouse development rights framework: The right to development in a climate constrained world*, rev. 2nd edn (Berlin: Heinrich Böll Foundation, Christian Aid, EcoEquity and the Stockholm Environment Institute, 2008).

Bailey, E., 'The NPT and security guarantees', in D. Howlett and J. Simpson (eds.), *Nuclear non-proliferation: A reference handbook* (London: Longman, 1992), pp. 51–6.

Bain, W., *Between anarchy and society: Trusteeship and the obligations of power* (Oxford: Oxford University Press, 2003).

Bank for International Settlements, 'History of the Basel Committee and its membership', August 2009, www.bis.org/bcbs/history.htm (accessed 28 July 2011).

Barnaby, F., 'The NPT Review Conference – Much talk, few results', *Bulletin of the Atomic Scientists*, 36(9) 1980, 7–8.

Barnett, M. and Duvall, R., 'Power in global governance', in M. Barnett and R. Duvall (eds.), *Power in global governance* (Cambridge: Cambridge University Press, 2005), pp. 1–32.

Beck, U., *Ecological enlightenment: Essays on the politics of the risk society* (Atlantic Highlands, NJ: Humanities Press, 1995).

Bellamy, A. J., *Responsibility to protect: The global effort to end mass atrocities* (Cambridge: Polity Press, 2009).

Berman, S., *The primacy of politics: Social democracy and the making of Europe's twentieth century* (Cambridge: Cambridge University Press, 2006).

Bernanke, B. S., 'Monetary policy and the housing bubble', paper presented at the Annual Meeting of the American Economics Association, Atlanta, Georgia, 3 January 2010.

Bernstein, S., 'Legitimacy in intergovernmental and non-state global governance', *Review of International Political Economy*, 18(1) 2011, 17–51.

Best, J., 'Co-opting cosmopolitanism? The International Monetary Fund's new global ethics', *Global Society*, 20(3) 2006, 307–27.

'The limits of financial risk management: Or, what we didn't learn from the Asian crisis', *New Political Economy*, 15(1) 2010, 29–49.

The limits of transparency: Ambiguity and the history of international finance (Ithaca, NY: Cornell University Press, 2005).

Bhagwati, J., 'The capital myth: The difference between trade in widgets and in dollars', *Foreign Affairs*, 77(3) 1998, 7–12.

Blyth, M., 'Bouncy castle finance', *Foreign Policy Online*, 14 September 2009, www.foreignpolicy.com/articles/2009/09/14/bouncy_castle_finance (accessed 28 July 2011).

Great transformations: Economic ideas and institutional change in the twentieth century (Cambridge: Cambridge University Press, 2002).

Bodansky, D., 'The United Nations Framework Convention on Climate Change: A commentary', *Yale Journal of International Law*, 18(2) 1993, 451–558.

Bolton, J. R., 'The NPT: a crisis of non-compliance', Statement by United States Under Secretary of State for Arms Control and International Security John R. Bolton to the Third Session of the Preparatory Committee for the 2005 Review Conference of the Treaty on the Non-Proliferation of Nuclear Weapons, 27 April 2004, www.reachingcritical will.org/legal/npt/prepcom04/usa27.pdf (accessed 15 June 2011).

Borger, J., 'Mohamed ElBaradei warns of new nuclear age', *Guardian*, 14 May 2009.

Bosco, D. L., *Five to rule them all: The UN Security Council and the making of the modern world* (New York: Oxford University Press, 2009).

Botzen, W. J. W., Gowdy, J. M. and Van den Bergh, J. C. J. M., 'Cumulative CO2 emissions: Shifting international responsibilities for climate debt', *Climate Policy*, 8(6) 2008, 569–76.

Bourantonis, D., 'The negotiation of the Non-Proliferation Treaty 1965–68', Discussion Papers in Diplomacy, No. 28 (The Hague: Netherlands Institute of International Relations 'Clingendael', April 1997).

Boykoff, M. T. and Boykoff, J. M., 'Balance as bias: Global warming and the US prestige press', *Global Environmental Change*, 14(2) 2004, 125–36.

Braithwaite, T. and Spiegel, P., 'US defends its banking reforms', *Financial Times*, 2 June 2011.

Brands, H., 'Rethinking non-proliferation: LBJ, the Gilpatric Committee and US national security policy', *Journal of Cold War Studies*, 8(2) 2006, 83–113.

Breslin, S., 'Understanding China's regional rise: Interpretations, identities and implications', *International Affairs*, 85(4) 2009, 817–35.

Bridge, F. R. and Bullen, R., *The great powers and the European states system 1814–1914*, 2nd edn (Harlow: Pearson Longman, 2005).

Brooks, S. G. and Wohlforth, W. C., *World out of balance: International relations and the challenge of American primacy* (Princeton, NJ: Princeton University Press, 2008).

Brown, C., 'Do great powers have great responsibilities? Great powers and moral agency', *Global Society*, 18(1) 2004, 5–19.

Brunnee, J. and Toope, S., *Legitimacy and legality in international law: An interactional account* (Cambridge: Cambridge University Press, 2010).

Buchanan, A. and Keohane, R. O., 'Precommitment regimes for intervention: Supplementing the Security Council', *Ethics and International Affairs*, 25(1) 2011, 41–63.

Bukovansky, M., 'Cynical rascals or conscientious objectors? Interpreting non-compliance with international norms', in O. Kessler, R. Hall, C. Lynch and N. Onuf (eds.), *On rules, politics, and knowledge: Friedrich Kratochwill, international relations, and domestic affairs* (New York: Palgrave, 2010), pp. 158–77.

Legitimacy and power politics: The American and French revolutions in international political culture (Princeton, NJ: Princeton University Press, 2002).

Bull, H., 'Rethinking non-proliferation', in *Hedley Bull on arms control*, sel. and intro. R. O'Neill and D. N. Schwartz (London: Macmillan in association with the International Institute for Strategic Studies, 1987), pp. 218–34.

The Anarchical society: A study of order in world politics (London: Macmillan, 1977).

'The great irresponsibles? The United States, the Soviet Union, and world order', *International Journal*, 35(3) 1980, 437–47.

'World order and the super powers', in C. Holbraad (ed.), *The super powers and world order* (Canberra: ANU Press, 1971), pp. 140–54.

Bunn, G. and Timerbaev, R. M., 'Security assurances to non-nuclear weapon states', *Nonproliferation Review*, 2(1) 1993, 1–13.

Burk, S., 'Toward a successful NPT Review Conference', Carnegie Endowment for International Peace, Washington, DC, 31 March 2010, carnegieendowment.org/events/?fa=eventDetail&id=2841&solr_hilite=Burk+Susan (accessed 27 July 2011).

'US Special Representative Susan Burk on nuclear nonproliferation challenges', Remarks to Middle Powers Initiative Event, Permanent Mission of Switzerland to the United Nations, New York, 13 October 2009, geneva.usmission.gov/2009/10/13/nptburk (accessed 27 July 2011).

Bush, G. W., State of the Union Address, 29 January 2002.

'Text of a Letter from the President to Senators Hagel, Helms, Craig, and Roberts', 13 March 2001, www.gcrio.org/OnLnDoc/pdf/bush_letter010313.pdf (accessed 1 August 2011).

'Bush's speech on the spread of nuclear weapons', *New York Times*, 11 February 2004, www.nytimes.com/2004/02/11/politics/10WEB-PTEX. html (accessed 27 July 2011).

Butcher, M., 'What wrongs our arms may do: The role of nuclear weapons in counterproliferation' (Washington, DC: Physicians for Social Responsibility, August 2003), action.psr.org/documents/psrwhatwrong03. pdf (accessed 27 July 2011).

Cane, P., *Responsibility in law and morality* (Oxford: Hart Publishing, 2002).

Caney, S., 'Cosmopolitan justice, responsibility, and global climate change', *Leiden Journal of International Law*, 18(4) 2005, 747–75.

Carin, B. and Mehlenbacher, A., 'Constituting global leadership: Which countries need to be around the summit table for climate change and energy security?', *Global Governance*, 16(1) 2010, 21–37.

Carr, E. H., *The twenty years' crisis, 1919–1939: An introduction to the study of international relations* (London: Macmillan, 1939).

Carter, J., 'India nuclear deal puts world at risk', *International Herald Tribune*, 11 September 2008.

Cass, L., 'Norm entrapment and preference change: The evolution of the European Union position on international emissions trading', *Global Environmental Politics*, 5(2) 2005, 38–60.

Chakravarty, S., Chikkatur, A., de Conink, H., Pacala, S., Socolow, R. and Tavoni, M., 'Sharing CO_2 emission reductions among one billion high emitters: A rule for among all nations', *PNAS*, 106(29) 21 July 2009, 11884–8.

Chan, R., 'The West's preaching to the East must stop', *Financial Times*, 3 January 2010.

Christoff, P., 'Cold climate in Copenhagen: China and the United States at COP15', *Environmental Politics*, 19(4) 2010, 637–56.

Christoff, P. and Eckersley, R., 'Comparative state responses', in J. S. Dryzek, R. B. Norgaard and D. Schlosberg (eds.), *The Oxford handbook of climate and society* (Oxford: Oxford University Press, 2011), pp. 431–48.

'Kyoto and the Asia Pacific Partnership on Clean Development and Climate', in T. Bonyhady and P. Christoff (eds.), *Climate law in Australia* (Sydney: Federation Press, 2007), pp. 32–45.

Clark, I., *Hegemony in international society* (Oxford: Oxford University Press, 2011).

Legitimacy in international society (Oxford: Oxford University Press, 2005).

Clark, I. and Reus-Smit, C. (eds.), 'Resolving international crises of legitimacy', *International Politics*, 44(2/3) 2007, 153–339.

Claude, I. L., *Swords into plowshares: The problems and progress of international organization* (London: University of London Press, 1965).

'The common defense and great-power responsibilities', *Political Science Quarterly*, 101(5) 1986, 719–32.

Climate Action Network-International, 'Fair ambitious and binding: Essentials for a successful climate deal' (Climate Action Network-International, 2007), www.climatenetwork.org/sites/default/files/CAN_FAB_Essentials_1.pdf (accessed 27 July 2011).

Climate Group, 'Delivering Low Carbon Growth: A Guide to China's 12th Five Year Plan: Executive Summary', March 2011, Commissioned by HSBC, www.theclimategroup.org/_assets/files/China-Five-Year-Plan-EXECUTIVE-SUMMARY.pdf (accessed 27 July 2011).

Clinton, H., 'Implementing a nuclear arms strategy for the 21st century', 7 April 2010, malta.usembassy.gov/arms.html (accessed 27 July 2011).

Cohrs, P. O., *The unfinished peace after World War I: America, Britain and the stabilisation of Europe 1919–1932* (Cambridge: Cambridge University Press, 2006).

Coll, A. R., *The wisdom of statecraft: Sir Herbert Butterfield and the philosophy of international politics* (Durham, NC: Duke University Press, 1985).

Cullet, P., 'Differential treatment in international law: Towards a new paradigm of interstate relations', *European Journal of International Law*, 10(3) 1999, 549–82.

D'Agostino, T., 'Reducing the global nuclear threat: nuclear non-proliferation and the role of the international community', presentation to the Center for Strategic and International Studies, Washington, DC, 18 September 2008, www.nti.org/e_research/source_docs/us/department_energy/national_nuclear_security_administration/10.pdf (accessed 27 July 2011).

Daalder, I. H. and Lindsay, J. M., *America unbound: The Bush revolution in foreign policy* (Washington, DC: Brookings Institution Press, 2003).

Davies, H., 'Global financial regulation after the credit crisis', *Global Policy*, 1(2) 2010, 185–90.

Davies, H. and Green, D., *Global financial regulation: The essential guide* (Cambridge: Polity Press, 2008).

De Larosière, J. (chair), 'High-Level Group on Financial Supervision in the EU: Report', Brussels, 25 February 2009, ec.europa.eu/internal_market/finances/docs/de_larosiere_report_en.pdf (accessed 28 July 2011).

Deng, F. M., Kimaro, S., Lyons, T., Rothchild, D. and Zartman, I. W., *Sovereignty as responsibility: Conflict management in Africa* (Washington, DC: Brookings Institution, 1996).

Depledge, J., 'Against the grain: The United States and the global climate change regime', *Global Change, Peace and Security*, 17(1) 2005, 11–27.

'Deschamps to Marshall, 21 April 1947', in United States Department of State, *Foreign Relations of the United States, 1947. Council of Foreign Ministers; Germany and Austria*, Vol. II (Washington, DC: US Government Printing Office, 1947).

Deudney, D. and Ikenberry, G. J., 'The myth of the autocratic revival: Why liberal democracy will prevail', *Foreign Affairs*, 88(1) 2009, 77–93.

Dhanapala, J., 'Evaluating the 2010 NPT Review Conference', Special Report 258 (Washington, DC: United States Institute of Peace, October 2010).

Dhanapala, J. with Rydell, R., *Multilateral diplomacy and the NPT: An insider's account* (Geneva: UNIDIR, 2005).

Donnelly, J., *Realism and international relations* (Cambridge: Cambridge University Press, 2000).

Drezner, D. W., *All politics is global: Explaining international regulatory regimes* (Princeton, NJ: Princeton University Press, 2008).

du Preez, J., 'The impact of the Nuclear Posture Review on the international nuclear nonproliferation regime', *Nonproliferation Review*, 9(3) 2002, 67–81.

Dunlap, R. E. and McCright, A., 'A widening gap: Republican and Democratic views on climate change', *Environment*, 50(5) 2008, 26–35.

Eckersley, R., 'Climate leadership and US exceptionalism', paper presented to the Australian Political Studies Association Conference, University of Melbourne, 27–29 September 2010.

Eden, A., 'Secretary of State for Foreign Affairs of Great Britain, Anthony Eden's address at first plenary session of San Francisco conference', 26 April 1945, www.ibiblio.org/pha/policy/1945/450426d.html (accessed 28 July 2011).

Eichengreen, B., *Exorbitant privilege: The rise and fall of the dollar and the future of the international monetary system* (Oxford: Oxford University Press, 2011).

Global imbalances and the lessons of Bretton Woods (Cambridge, MA: MIT Press, 2010).

Globalizing capital: A history of the international monetary system (Princeton, NJ: Princeton University Press, 1996).

Einhorn, R., 'President Bush's nonproliferation proposals and implications for the United Nations', UNA-USA Policy Brief No. 1, 15 March 2004, www. unausa.org/Document.Doc?id=246 (accessed 27 July 2011).

ElBaradei, M., 'Rethinking nuclear safeguards', *Washington Post*, 14 June 2006.

Elgström, O., 'The European Union as a leader in international multilateral negotiations – A problematic aspiration?', *International Relations*, 21(4) 2007, 445–58.

Ellis, J. D., 'The best defense: Counterproliferation and US national security', *Washington Quarterly*, 26(2) 2003, 115–33.

Elshtain, J. B., 'International justice as equal regard and the use of force', *Ethics and International Affairs*, 17(2) 2003, 63–75.

Epstein, W., 'Failure at the NPT Review Conference', *Bulletin of the Atomic Scientists*, 31(7) 1975, 46–8.

Erskine, T., 'Assigning responsibilities to institutional moral agents: The case of states and "quasi-states"', in T. Erskine (ed.), *Can institutions have responsibilities?: Collective moral agency and international relations* (Basingstoke: Palgrave Macmillan, 2003), pp. 19–40.

'Introduction', in T. Erskine (ed.), *Can institutions have responsibilities?: Collective moral agency and international relations* (Basingstoke: Palgrave Macmillan, 2003), pp. 1–16.

'Locating responsibility: The problem of moral agency in international relations', in C. Reus-Smit and D. Snidal (eds.), *The Oxford handbook of international relations* (Oxford: Oxford University Press, 2008), pp. 699–707.

European Environment Agency, 'Tracking progress towards Kyoto and 2020 targets in Europe', EEA Report No 7/2010 (Copenhagen: European Environment Agency, 2010).

Falkner, R., 'American hegemony and the global environment', *International Studies Review*, 7(4) 2005, 585–99.

Farchy, J., 'Dollar seen losing global reserve status', *Financial Times*, 27 June 2011.

Farley, P. J., 'Strategic arms control, 1967–87', in A. L. George, P. J. Farley and A. Dallin (eds.), *US–Soviet security cooperation: Achievements failures, lessons* (Oxford: Oxford University Press, 1988), pp. 215–53.

Feinberg, J., *Doing and deserving: Essays in the theory of responsibility* (Princeton, NJ: Princeton University Press, 1970).

Final Document of the 1995 Review and Extension Conference of the NPT, NPT/CONF.1995/32 (Part I), 11 May 1995.

Final Document of the 2000 Review Conference of the Parties to the Treaty on the Non-Proliferation of Nuclear Weapons, NPT/CONF.2000/28 (Parts I and II), 2000.

Final Document of the 2010 Review Conference of the Parties to the Treaty on the Non-Proliferation of Nuclear Weapons (NPT), NPT/CONF.2010/50 (Vol. I), May 2010.

Fogel, C., 'Constructing progressive climate change norms: The US in the early 2000s', in M. Pettenger (ed.), *The social construction of climate change: Power, knowledge, norms, discourse* (Aldershot: Ashgate, 2007), pp. 99–120.

Foot, R. and Walter, A., *China, the United States, and global order* (Cambridge: Cambridge University Press, 2011).

Ford, C. A., 'Debating disarmament: Interpreting Article VI of the Treaty on the Non-Proliferation of Nuclear Weapons', *Nonproliferation Review*, 14(3) 2007, 401–28.

Fox, W. T. R., 'Collective enforcement of peace and security', *American Political Science Review*, 39(5) 1945, 970–81.

The super-powers: The United States, Britain, and the Soviet Union – Their responsibility for peace (New York: Harcourt, Brace & Co.: 1944).

Friends of the Earth International, 'Our climate demands', 2009, www.foei.org/en/what-we-do/un-climate-talks/global/2009/our-demands-in-copenhagen (accessed 27 July 2011).

G20, 'Declaration: Summit on financial markets and the world economy', Washington, DC, 15 November 2008, www.g20.org/Documents/g20_summit_declaration.pdf (accessed 28 July 2011).

'Leaders' Statement, The Pittsburgh Summit', 24–25 September 2009, www.g20.org/Documents/pittsburgh_summit_leaders_statement_250909.pdf (accessed 28 July 2011).

'The G-20 Toronto Summit Declaration', 26–27 June 2010, www.g20.org/pub_communiques.aspx (accessed 2 August 2011).

'The global plan for recovery and reform', 2 April 2009, www.g20.org/Documents/final-communique.pdf (accessed 28 July 2011).

Gardiner, S., *A perfect moral storm: The ethical tragedy of climate change* (New York: Oxford University Press, 2011).

Gardner, R. N., *Sterling-dollar diplomacy in current perspective: The origins and the prospects of our international economic order* (New York: Columbia University Press, 1980).

Garnaut, R., *The Garnaut review 2011: Australia in the global response to climate change* (Cambridge: Cambridge University Press, 2011).

Garten, J. E., 'The dangers of turning inward', *Wall Street Journal*, 5 March 2009.

Gates, R. M., 'The security and defense agenda (future of NATO)', speech delivered in Brussels, Belgium, 10 June 2011, www.defense.gov/speeches/speech.aspx?speechid=1581 (accessed 3 August 2011).

Gavin, F. J., 'Blasts from the past: Proliferation lessons from the 1960s', *International Security*, 29(3) 2004/5, 100–35.

Gold, dollars, and power: The politics of international monetary relations, 1958–1971 (Chapel Hill, NC: University of North Carolina Press, 2004).

'The gold battles within the Cold War: American monetary policy and the defense of Europe', *Diplomatic History*, 26(1) 2002, 61–94.

Giles, C. and Beattie, A., 'G20 Backs Drive for Crackdown on Banks', *Financial Times*, 28 June 2010.

Goodin, R. E., *Protecting the vulnerable: A reanalysis of our social responsibilities* (Chicago, IL: University of Chicago Press, 1985).

'Vulnerabilities and responsibilities: An ethical defence of the welfare state', *American Political Science Review*, 79(3) 1985, 775–87.

'What is so special about our fellow countrymen?', *Ethics*, 98(4) 1988, 663–86.

Goodrich, L. M. and Hambro, E., *Charter of the United Nations* (London: Stevens and Sons, 1949).

Gray, W. G., 'Floating the system: Germany, the United States, and the breakdown of Bretton Woods, 1969–1973', *Diplomatic History*, 31(2) 2007, 295–323.

Gulledge, J., 'Three plausible scenarios of future climate change', in K. M. Campbell (ed.), *Climate cataclysm: The foreign policy and national security implications of climate change* (Washington, DC: Brookings Institution Press, 2008), pp. 49–96.

Gupta, J. and Grubb, M. (eds.), *Climate change and European leadership: A sustainable role for Europe* (Boston, MA: Kluwer Academic Publishers, 2000).

Haldane, A. G., 'Capital discipline', based on a speech given at the American Economic Association, Denver, 9 January 2011, www.bankofengland. co.uk/publications/speeches/2011/speech484.pdf (accessed 28 July 2011).

Haldane, A. G. and May, R. M., 'Systemic risk in banking ecosystems', *Nature*, 469 (20 January) 2011, 351–5.

Hall, R. B., *Central banking as global governance: Constructing financial credibility* (Cambridge: Cambridge University Press, 2008).

'The discursive demolition of the Asian development model', *International Studies Quarterly*, 47(1) 2003, 71–99.

Hanemann, W. M., 'How California came to pass AB 32, the Global Warming Solutions Act of 2006', Working Paper 1040 (Berkeley, CA: Department of Agricultural and Resource Economics, University of California, 2007).

Harris, P. G., 'Common but differentiated responsibility: The Kyoto Protocol and United States policy', *New York University Environmental Law Journal*, 7(1) 1999, 27–48.

Harrison, K., 'The road not taken: Climate change policy in Canada and the United States', *Global Environmental Politics*, 7(4) 2007, 92–117.

Haydar, B., 'Special responsibility and the appeal to cost', *Journal of Political Philosophy*, 17(2) 2009, 129–45.

Helleiner, E., 'Filling a hole in global financial governance? The politics of regulating sovereign debt restructuring', in W. Mattli and N. Woods (eds.), *The politics of global regulation* (Princeton, NJ: Princeton University Press, 2009), pp. 89–120.

Helleiner, E. and Pagliari, S., 'Towards a new Bretton Woods? The first G20 leaders summit and the regulation of global finance', *New Political Economy*, 14(2) 2009, 275–87.

Helms, J. (R-NC), 'Global climate change', *Congressional Record-Senate* S11490, 27 September 1996, p. 11490, frwebgate.access.gpo.gov/cgi-bin/getpage.cgi?position=all&page=S11490&dbname=1996_record (accessed 27 July 2011).

Heywood, M. 'Equity and international climate change negotiations: A matter of perspective', *Climate Policy*, 7(6) 2007, 518–34.

Hinsley, F. H., *Power and the pursuit of peace* (London: Cambridge University Press, 1963).

Hoffman, M. J., *Ozone depletion and climate change: Constructing a global response* (Albany, NY: State University of New York Press, 2005).

Holsti, K. J., 'Governance without government: Polyarchy in nineteenth-century European international politics', in J. N. Rosenau and E.-O. Czempiel (eds.), *Governance without government: Order and change in world politics* (Cambridge: Cambridge University Press, 1992), pp. 30–57.

Taming the sovereigns: Institutional change in international politics (Cambridge: Cambridge University Press, 2004).

Hook, G. D., Gilson, J., Hughes, C. W. and Dobson, H., *Japan's international relations: Politics, economics, and security*, 2nd edn (Abingdon: Routledge, 2005).

Hopf, T., 'The promise of constructivism in international relations theory', *International Security*, 23(1) 1998, 170–200.

Horner, D., 'IAEA Board approves Russian fuel bank plan', *Arms Control Today*, January–February, 2010, www.armscontrol.org/act/2010_01–02/FuelBank (accessed 27 July 2011).

Hu Jintao, 'Join hands to address climate challenge', President Hu Jintao's Speech at the Opening Plenary Session of the United Nations Summit on Climate Change, 23 September 2009, www.china-un.org/eng/gdxw/t606111.htm (accessed 27 July 2011).

Hurd, I., 'Breaking and making norms: American revisionism and crises of legitimacy', in I. Clark and C. Reus-Smit (eds.), 'Resolving international crises', *International Politics*, 44(2/3) 2007, 194–213.

'Constructivism', in C. Reus-Smit and D. Snidal (eds.), *The Oxford handbook of international relations* (Oxford: Oxford University Press, 2008), pp. 298–316.

Hurrell, A., 'Power, institutions, and the production of inequality', in M. Barnett and R. Duval (eds.), *Power in global governance* (Cambridge: Cambridge University Press, 2005), pp. 33–58.

Ikenberry, G. J., *Liberal Leviathan: The origins, crisis, and transformation of the American world order* (Princeton, NJ: Princeton University Press, 2011).

'The future of the liberal world order', *Foreign Affairs*, 90(3) 2011, 56–68.

'India–US Joint Statement', Washington, DC, 18 July 2005.

International Centre for Trade and Sustainable Development, 'China, India lash out at talk of "carbon tariffs"', *Bridges Weekly Trade New Digest*, 13(25) 8 July 2009, ictsd.net/i/news/bridgesweekly/50301/ (accessed 27 July 2011).

International Commission on Intervention and State Sovereignty, *The responsibility to protect: The report of the International Commission on Intervention and State Sovereignty* (Ottawa: International Development Research Centre, 2001).

International Court of Justice, 'Legality of the Threat or Use of Nuclear Weapons', Advisory Opinion, 8 July 1996, www.icj-cij.org/docket/index.php?p1=3&p2=4&k=e1&p3=4&case=95 (accessed 27 July 2011).

International Monetary Fund, 'Articles of Agreement: Article I: Purposes', no date, www.imf.org/external/pubs/ft/aa/aa01.htm (accessed 28 July 2011).

'Articles of Agreement: Article VII – Replenishment and scarce currencies', no date, www.imf.org/external/pubs/ft/aa/aa07.htm (accessed 28 July 2011).

Jackson, R., *The global covenant: Human conduct in a world of states* (Oxford: Oxford University Press, 2000).

James, H., *International monetary cooperation since Bretton Woods* (New York: Oxford University Press, 1996).

Jenkins, P., 'Time to work out the real odds in the weighting game', *Financial Times*, 2 May 2011.

Johnson, B., 'The climate zombie caucus of the 112th congress', *ThinkProgress*, updated 23 November 2010, wonkroom.thinkprogress.org/climate-zombie-caucus (accessed 27 July 2011).

Johnson, R., 'Incentives, obligations and enforcement: Does the NPT meet its states parties' needs?', *Disarmament Diplomacy*, 70 (March–April) 2003, 3–10.

'Is the NPT up to the challenge of proliferation?', *Disarmament Forum*, (4) 2004, www.unidir.org/pdf/articles/pdf-art2186.pdf (accessed 27 July 2011).

'NPT day 18: Updates, downgrading HEU and non-strategic nuclear weapons', acronyminstitute.wordpress.com/2010/05/21/day-16 (accessed 27 July 2011).

Johnson, R. and Rauf, T., 'After the NPT's indefinite extension: The future of the global nonproliferation regime', *Nonproliferation Review*, 3(1) 1995, 28–41.

Johnson, S., 'The quiet coup', *The Atlantic*, May 2009, www.theatlantic.com/doc/200905/imf-advice (accessed 28 July 2011).

Johnson, S. and Kwak, J., *13 bankers: The Wall Street takeover and the next financial meltdown* (New York: Pantheon, 2010).

'Joint statement by US Treasury Secretary Timothy Geithner and EU Commissioner Michel Barnier on the financial reform agenda', EU/NR 22/10, 12 May 2010, www.eurunion.org/eu/2010-News-Releases/JOINT-STATEMENT-BY-UNITED-STATES-TREASURY-SECRETARY-TIMOTHY-GEITHNER-AND-EUROPEAN-UNION-COMMISSIONER-MICHEL-BARNIER-ON-THE-FINANCIAL-REFORM-AGENDA.html (accessed 27 July 2011).

Jones, B., Pascual, C. and Stedman, S. J., *Power and responsibility: Building international order in an era of transnational threats* (Washington, DC: Brookings Institution, 2009).

Jones, J. M., 'Americans see US as exceptional; 37% doubt Obama does', Gallup, 22 December 2010, www.gallup.com/poll/145358 (accessed 27 July 2011).

Jotzo, F., 'Comparing the Copenhagen emissions targets', CCEP Working Paper 1.10 (Canberra: Centre for Climate Economics & Policy, Australian National University, October 2010, rev. 16 November 2010).

Joyner, D. H., *Interpreting the Nuclear Non-Proliferation Treaty* (Oxford: Oxford University Press, 2011).

Kagan, R., 'America's crisis of legitimacy', *Foreign Affairs*, 83(2) 2004, 65–87.

Kahler, M. and Lake, D. A., 'Economic integration and global governance', in W. Mattli and N. Woods (eds.), *The politics of global regulation* (Princeton, NJ: Princeton University Press, 2009).

Kang, D. C., *China rising: Peace, power, and order in East Asia* (New York: Columbia University Press, 2007).

'Getting Asia wrong: The need for new analytical frameworks', *International Security*, 27(4) (2003), 57–85.

'Hierarchy and stability in Asian international relations', in G. J. Ikenberry and M. Mastanduno (eds.), *International relations theory and the Asia-Pacific* (New York: Columbia University Press, 2003), pp. 163–90.

Keck, M. E. and Sikkink, K., *Activists beyond borders: Advocacy networks in international politics* (Ithaca, NY: Cornell University Press, 1998).

Keeny, S. M., National Security Council Staff, Memorandum to Henry Kissinger, 24 January 1969, National Archives, Nixon Presidential Materials, NSC Files, Box 366, Subject Files, Non-Proliferation Treaty through March 1969.

'The Non-Proliferation Treaty', memorandum, 24 December 1968, NP01237, National Security Archive, Washington, DC.

Kelsen, H., *The law of the United Nations: A critical analysis of its fundamental problems* (Clark, NJ: The Lawbook Exchange, 2000).

Keohane, R. O., *After hegemony: Cooperation and discord in the world political economy* (Princeton, NJ: Princeton University Press, 1984).

'Theory of world politics: Structural realism and beyond', in R. O. Keohane (ed.), *Neorealism and its critics* (New York: Columbia University Press, 1986), pp. 158–203.

Keohane, R. O. and Nye, J. S., *Power and interdependence* (Boston, MA: Little, Brown, 1977).

Kerry, J., 'Text of Sen. Kerry's speech at COP15', boston.com, 16 December 2009, www.boston.com/news/world/europe/articles/2009/12/16/text_of_sen_kerrys_speech_at_cop15 (accessed 27 July 2011).

Khor, M., 'Spotlight Cancún: Strange outcome of Cancún conference', *TripleCrisis*, 14 December 2010, triplecrisis.com/spotlight-cancun-strange-outcome-of-cancun-conference (accessed 27 July 2011).

Kindleberger, C. P., *The world in depression, 1929–1939*, rev. edn (Berkeley, CA: University of California Press, 1986).

Kingsbury, B., 'Sovereignty and inequality', *European Journal of International Law*, 9(4) 1998, 599–625.

Krisch, N., 'More equal than the rest? Hierarchy, equality and US predominance in international law', in M. Byers and G. Nolte (eds.), *United States hegemony and the foundations of international law* (Cambridge: Cambridge University Press, 2003), pp. 135–75.

Lake, D. A., *Hierarchy in international relations* (Ithaca, NY: Cornell University Press, 2009).

'Making America safe for the world: Multilateralism and the rehabilitation of US authority', *Global Governance*, 16(4) 2010, 471–84.

Li Hongmei, 'Reflect on China's responsibility', *People's Daily Online*, 23 March 2009, english.peopledaily.com.cn/90002/96417/6619895.html (accessed 28 July 2011).

Light, A., 'Showdown among the leaders at Copenhagen', Center for American Progress, 18 December 2009, www.americanprogress.org/issues/2009/12/showdown_copenhagen.html (accessed 27 July 2011).

Lin, J. Y. and Dailami, M., 'Are we prepared for a multipolar world economy?', Project Syndicate, 2 June 2011, www.project-syndicate.org/commentary/lin3/English (accessed 28 July 2011).

Linklater, A., 'The harm principle and global ethics', *Global Society*, 20(3) 2006, 329–43.

The problem of harm in world politics: Theoretical investigations (Cambridge: Cambridge University Press, 2011).

The transformation of political community: Ethical foundations of the post-Westphalian era (Cambridge: Polity Press, 1998).

'Towards a sociology of global morals with an emancipatory intent', *Review of International Studies*, 33(S1) 2007, 135–50.

Little, A., 'Obama on the record: An interview with Barack Obama about his presidential platform on energy and the environment', *Grist: Environmental*

News and Commentary, 30 July 2007, grist.org/feature/2007/07/30/obama (accessed 27 July 2011).

Little, R., *The balance of power in international relations: metaphors, myths and models* (Cambridge: Cambridge University Press, 2007).

Lucas, J. R., *Responsibility* (Oxford: Oxford University Press, 1993).

Mahbubani, K., 'Permanent and elected council members', in D. Malone (ed.), *The UN Security Council: From the cold war to the 21st century* (Boulder, CO: Lynne Rienner, 2004), pp. 253–66.

Major Economies Forum on Energy and Climate, www.majoreconomiesforum.org (accessed 27 July 2011).

Markwell, D. J., 'Sir Alfred Zimmern revisited: Fifty years on', *Review of International Studies*, 12(4) 1986, 279–92.

Matravers, M., *Responsibility and justice* (Cambridge: Polity Press, 2007).

Mattli, W. and Woods, N., 'In whose benefit? Explaining regulatory change in global politics', in W. Mattli and N. Woods (eds.), *The politics of global regulation* (Princeton, NJ: Princeton University Press, 2009).

McCain, J., 'Remarks at the University of Denver', Denver, 27 May 2008, www.presidency.ucsb.edu/ws/index.php?pid=77369#axzz1TGGuqlhn (accessed 27 July 2011).

McCright, A. M. and Dunlap, R. E., 'Anti-reflexivity: The American conservative movement's success in undermining climate science and policy', *Theory, Culture and Society*, 27(2–3) 2010, 100–33.

McGee, J. and Taplin, R., 'The Asia-Pacific Partnership on Clean Development and Climate: A Complement or Competitor to the Kyoto Protocol?', *Global Change, Peace and Security*, 18(3) 2006, 173–92.

Medalia, J., 'Robust nuclear earth penetrator budget request and plan, FY2005-FY2009' (Washington, DC: Congressional Research Service, 24 March 2004).

Memorandum by Secretary of State for Foreign Affairs on 'Future world organisation', W. P. (44) 370, 3 July 1944, National Archives CAB/66/52/20, para. 15.

Meyer, A., *Contraction and convergence: The global solution to climate change* (Dartington: Green Books, 2000).

Miller, D., 'Distributing responsibilities', *Journal of Political Philosophy*, 9(4) 2001, 453–71.

'The responsibility to protect human rights', Working Paper SJ0007 (Oxford: Department of Politics and International Relations and Centre for the Study of Social Justice, Oxford University, May 2007).

Morgenthau, H. J., *Politics among nations: The struggle for power and peace* (New York: Knopf, 1948).

Müller, H., 'The 2005 NPT Review Conference: Reasons and consequences of failure and options for repair' (Stockholm: Weapons of Mass Destruction Commission, August 2005).

Naim, M., 'Minilateralism: The magic number to get real international action', *Foreign Policy*, 173 (July–August) 2009, 135–6.

Najam, A., 'The view from the south: developing countries in global environmental politics', in R. S. Axelrod, D. L. Downie and N. J. Vig (eds.), *The Global Environment: Institutions, Law and Policy* (Washington, DC: CQ Press, 2005), pp. 225–243.

National Academy of Science, *Climate Change Science: An Analysis of Some Key Questions* (Washington, DC: National Academy Press, 2001).

Nau, H. R., *At Home Abroad: Identity and Power in American Foreign Policy* (Ithaca, NY: Cornell University Press, 2002).

Neff, T. L., 'The nuclear fuel cycle and the Bush nonproliferation initiative', paper for the World Nuclear Fuel Cycle Conference, Madrid, April 2004, www.iaea.org/newscenter/focus/fuelcycle/neff.pdf (accessed 27 July 2011).

'New day dawns for US global warming', *Environment News Service*, 30 March 2009, www.ens-newswire.com/ens/mar2009/2009-03-30-01.asp (accessed 27 July 2011).

Nicolson, H., *The Congress of Vienna: A study in allied unity, 1812–1822* (London: Constable, 1946).

Niebuhr, R., 'Foreword', in A. Wolfers, *Discord and collaboration: Essays on international politics* (Baltimore, MD: Johns Hopkins Press, 1962), pp. vii–viii.

Nixon, R., 'Address to the nation outlining a new economic policy: "The challenge of peace"', 15 August 1971, in J. T. Woolley and G. Peters, *The American Presidency Project* [online], Santa Barbara, CA, www.presidency.ucsb.edu/ws/index.php?pid=3115 (accessed 28 July 2011).

Norris, R. S. and Kristensen, H. M., 'Nuclear notebook: Worldwide deployments of nuclear weapons, 2009', *Bulletin of the Atomic Scientists*, bos.sagepub.com/content/65/6/86.full (accessed 31 July 2011).

Norrlof, C., *America's global advantage: US hegemony and international cooperation* (Cambridge: Cambridge University Press, 2010).

O'Hanlon, M. and Mochizuki, M., *Crisis on the Korean peninsula: How to deal with a nuclear North Korea* (New York: McGraw-Hill 2003).

Obama, B., 'Obama in Copenhagen Speech: Full Text', *Huffington Post*, posted 18 December 2009, www.huffingtonpost.com/2009/12/18/obama-in-copenhagen-speec_n_396836.html (accessed 27 July 2011).

'Remarks by the President at the United Nations Security Council summit on nuclear non-proliferation and nuclear disarmament, United Nations Headquarters, New York', White House press release, 24 September 2009, www.whitehouse.gov/the-press-office/remarks-president-un-security-council-summit-nuclear-non-proliferation-and-nuclear- (accessed 27 July 2011).

'Remarks by the president on Wall Street reform', Cooper Union, New York, 22 April 2010, www.whitehouse.gov/the-press-office/remarks-president-wall-street-reform (accessed 28 July 2011).

'Remarks of President Barack Obama', Hradcany Square, Prague, 5 April 2009, prague.usembassy.gov/obama.html (accessed 31 July 2011).

'Remarks of the President at United Nations Secretary General Ban Ki-Moon's Climate Change Summit', United Nations Headquarters, New York, 22 September 2009, www.whitehouse.gov/the_press_office/Remarks-by-the-President-at-UN-Secretary-General-Ban-Ki-moons-Climate-Change-Summit/ (accessed 27 July 2011).

'Video and transcript: President Obama's remarks at the Summit of the Americas (17 April)', *EAWorldView*, 20 April 2009, www.enduringamerica.com/april-2009/2009/4/20/video-and-transcript-president-obamas-remarks-at-the-summit.html (accessed 27 July 2011).

Oberthür, S., 'The European Union in international climate policy: The prospect for leadership', *Intereconomics – Review of European Economic Policy*, 42(2) 2007, 77–83.

OECD, Joint Working Party on Trade and Environment, 'The polluter-pays principle as it relates to international trade', COM/ENV/TD(2001)44/ FINAL, 23 December 2002.

Okereke, C., 'Equity norms in global environmental governance', *Global Environmental Politics*, 8(3) 2008, 25–50.

Oppenheimer, J. R., 'Atomic weapons and American policy', *Foreign Affairs*, 31(4) 1953, 525–35.

Osiander, A., *The states system of Europe 1640–1990: Peacemaking and the condition of international stability* (Oxford: Oxford University Press, 1994).

Oxfam International, 'Climate shame: Get back to the table', Oxfam Briefing Note, 21 December 2009, www.oxfam.org/sites/www.oxfam.org/files/ briefing-note-climate-shame-get-back-to-the-table.pdf (accessed 27 July 2011).

Page, E., 'Distributing the burdens of climate change', *Environmental Politics*, 17(4) 2008, 556–75.

Paterson, M., 'Post-hegemonic climate change?', *British Journal of Politics and International Relations*, 11(1) 2009, 140–58.

Pellet, A., 'The definition of responsibility in international law', in J. Crawford, A. Pellet and Olleson S. (eds.), *The law of international responsibility* (Oxford: Oxford University Press, 2010), pp. 3–16.

Pennock, J. R., 'The problem of responsibility,' in C. J. Friedrich (ed.), *Responsibility* (New York: The Liberal Arts Press, 1960), pp. 3–27.

Perkovich, G., 'Bush's nuclear revolution: A regime change in nonproliferation', *Foreign Affairs*, 82(2) 2003, 2–8.

'"Democratic bomb": Failed strategy', Policy Brief 49 (Washington, DC: Carnegie Endowment for International Peace, November 2006).

Perkovich, G. and Acton, J., *Abolishing Nuclear Weapons*, Adelphi Paper 396 (Abingdon: Routledge, 2008).

Peterson, G., 'II: Political inequality at the Congress of Vienna', *Political Science Quarterly*, 60(4) 1945, 532–54.

Phillips, L., 'US must take responsibility for global crisis, Brussels says', *euobserver.com*, 30 September 2008, euobserver.com/9/26835 (accessed 27 July 2011).

Phillips, M. M., Frangos, A., Fidler, S. and Walker, M., 'Geithner urges G-20 to step up consumption', *Wall Street Journal*, 4 June 2010.

Philpott, D., *Revolutions in sovereignty: How ideas shaped modern international relations* (Princeton, NJ: Princeton University Press, 2001).

Pomper, M. A., 'US international nuclear energy policy: Change and continuity', Nuclear Energy Futures Paper No. 10 (Waterloo, ONT: Centre for International Governance Innovation, January 2010).

Posner, E., 'Making rules for global finance: Transatlantic regulatory cooperation at the turn of the millennium', *International Organization*, 63(4) 2009, 665–99.

Pouliot, V., *International security in practice* (Cambridge: Cambridge University Press, 2010).

'President Obama delivers joint press statement with President Hu Jintao of China', *Washington Post*, 17 November 2009, www.washingtonpost.com/wp-dyn/content/article/2009/11/17/AR2009111701090.html?sid=ST2009111700768 (accessed 27 July 2011).

Price, R., 'Nuclear weapons don't kill people, rogues do', *International Politics*, 44(2) 2007, 232–49.

Price, T., 'Reconciling the irreconcilable? British nuclear weapons and the Non-Proliferation Treaty, 1997–2007', unpublished PhD thesis, Aberystwyth University, 2010.

Ralph, J., 'The laws of war and the state of the American exception', *Review of International Studies*, 35(3) 2009, 631–49.

Reus-Smit, C., *American power and world order* (Cambridge: Polity Press, 2004).

'Politics and international legal obligation', *European Journal of International Relations*, 9(4) 2003, 591–625.

Rich, P., 'Reinventing peace: David Davies, Alfred Zimmern and liberal internationalism in interwar Britain', *International Relations*, 16(1) 2002, 117–33.

'Risk weightings: Let's standardise', *Financial Times*, 25 May 2011.

Ritter, R., 'Transnational governance in global finance: The principles for stable capital flows and fair debt restructuring in emerging markets', *International Studies Perspectives*, 11(3) 2010, 222–41.

Rogelj, J., Nabel, J., Chen, C., Hare, W., Markmann, K., Meinshausen, M., Schaeffer, M., Macey, K. and Höhne, N., 'Copenhagen Accord pledges are paltry', *Nature*, 464(7292) 22 April 2010, 1126–8.

Ruggie, J. G., *Constructing the world polity: Essays on international institutionalization* (London: Routledge, 1998).

'International regimes, transactions, and change: Embedded liberalism in the postwar economic order', *International Organization*, 36(2) 1982, 379–415.

'Multilateralism: The Anatomy of an institution', *International Organisation*, 46(3) 1992, 561–98.

Russell, R. B., *A history of the United Nations Charter: The Role of the United States 1940–1945* (Washington, DC: Brookings Institution, 1958).

Ruzicka, J. and Wheeler, N. J., 'The puzzle of trusting relationships in the Nuclear Non-Proliferation Treaty', *International Affairs*, 86(1) 2010, 69–85.

Sahlins, M., *Culture and practical reason* (Chicago, IL: University of Chicago Press, 1976).

Samuelsohn, D., 'No "pass" for developing countries in next climate treaty, says US envoy', *New York Times*, 9 December 2009.

Sanders, B., 'IAEA safeguards and the NPT', *Disarmament Forum*, (4) 2004, 46–8, www.unidir.ch/pdf/articles/pdf-art2189.pdf (accessed 27 July 2011).

'NPT Review Conferences and the role of consensus', *Programme for Promoting Nuclear Non-Proliferation Issue Review*, 4 (April) 1995, www.mcis.soton.ac.uk/PPNN/issue-reviews/ir04.pdf (accessed 27 July 2011).

Schreurs, M. and Tiberghien, Y., 'Multi-level reinforcement: Explaining European Union leadership in climate change mitigation', *Global Environmental Politics*, 7(4) 2007, 19–46.

Schwabe, K., 'Three grand designs: The USA, Great Britain, and the Gaullist concept of Atlantic partnership and European unity', *Journal of Transatlantic Studies*, 3(1) 2005, 7–30.

Schwarcz, S. L., 'Systemic risk', *Georgetown Law Journal*, 97(1) 2008, 193–249.

Shaker, M. I., *The Nuclear Non-Proliferation Treaty: Origin and implementation, 1959–1979*, 2 vols. (London: Oceana, 1980).

Shaver, K. G. and Schutte, D. A., 'Towards a broader psychological foundation for responsibilty: Who, what, how', in A. E. Auhagen and H.-W. Bierhoff (eds.), *Responsibility: The many faces of a social phenomenon* (London: Routledge, 2001), pp. 33–47.

Shue, H., 'Face reality? After you! – A call for leadership on climate change', *Ethics and International Affairs*, 25(1) 2011, 17–26.

  'Subsistence emissions and luxury emissions', *Law and Policy*, 15(1) 1993, 39–59.

Simpson, G., *Great powers and outlaw states: Unequal sovereigns in the international legal order* (Cambridge: Cambridge University Press, 2004).

Simpson, J., 'The Non-Proliferation Treaty at its half-life', in I. Bellany, C. D. Blacker and J. Gallacher (eds.), *The Nuclear Non-Proliferation Treaty* (London: Frank Cass, 1985), pp. 1–12.

Sinclair, T. J., *The new masters of capital: American bond rating agencies and the politics of creditworthiness* (Ithaca, NY: Cornell University Press, 2005).

Somerville, G., 'Geithner stresses strong dollar's global role', Reuters, 12 November 2009, www.reuters.com/article/2009/11/12/us-apec-idUS-TRE5AA0IB20091112 (accessed 27 July 2011).

Statement by Ambassador Luis Alfonso de Alba on Behalf of the New Agenda Coalition at the General Debate of the Third Session of the Preparatory Committee of the 2005 NPT Review Conference, 26 April 2004, www.reachingcriticalwill.org/legal/npt/prepcom04/mexiconac26.pdf (accessed 10 June 2010).

Statement by Brazil to Main Committee II of the 2010 Review Conference of the Treaty on the Non-Proliferation of Nuclear Weapons, New York, 10 May 2010.

Statement by Egypt to Main Committee II of the 2010 Review Conference of the Treaty on the Non-Proliferation of Nuclear Weapons, New York, May 2010.

Statement by Mr V. Dumitrescu of Romania to the 165th meeting of the Eighteen-Nation Committee on Disarmament, 11 February 1964, ENDC/PV.165.

Statement by Mr W. Foster of the United States to the 381st meeting of the Eighteen-Nation Disarmament Committee, 16 July 1968, ENDC/FPV.381.20.

Statement by South Africa to Main Committee II of the 2010 Review Conference of the Treaty on the Non-Proliferation of Nuclear Weapons, New York, 10 May 2010.

Stone, C. D., 'Common but differentiated responsibilities in international law', *American Journal of International Law*, 98(2) 2004, 276–301.

Strange, S., 'The westfailure system', *Review of International Studies*, 25(3) 1999, 345–54.

Suchman, M., 'Managing legitimacy: Strategic and institutional approaches', *Academy of Management Review*, 20(3) 1995, 571–610.

Tannenwald, N., *The nuclear taboo: The United States and the non-use of nuclear weapons since 1945* (Cambridge: Cambridge University Press, 2007).

Tarullo, D. K., *Banking on Basel: The future of international financial regulation* (Washington, DC: Peterson Institute for International Economics, 2008).

Tertrais, B., 'French perspectives on nuclear weapons and nuclear disarmament', in B. Blechman (ed.), *Unblocking the road to zero* (Washington, DC: Henry L. Stimson Center, 2009), pp. 1–22.

Treaty on the Non-Proliferation of Nuclear Weapons (NPT), 1 July 1968, www.un.org/en/conf/npt/2005/npttreaty.html (accessed 27 July 2011).

Trotter, A., *Britain and East Asia, 1933–1937* (London: Cambridge University Press, 1975).

Truman, H. S., 'Address in New York City at the opening session of the United Nations General Assembly', 23 October 1946, http://trumanlibrary.org/publicpapers/viewpapers.php?pid=914 (accessed 28 July 2011).

'Address to the United Nations Conference in San Francisco', 25 April 1945, www.presidency.ucsb.edu/ws/index.php?pid=12391 (accessed 10 August 2011).

Turner, A., 'The financial crisis and the future of financial regulation', speech, Economist's Inaugural City Lecture, 21 January 2009, www.fsa.gov.uk/pages/Library/Communication/Speeches/2009/0121_at.shtml (accessed 28 July 2011).

UN Security Council Resolution 1887 on Nuclear Nonproliferation and Nuclear Disarmament, 24 September 2009, www.acronym.org.uk/docs/0909/doc03.htm (accessed 27 July 2011).

UNCED (United Nations Conference on Environment and Development), 'Report of the United Nations Conference on Environment and Development, Rio de Janeiro, 3–14 June 1992', A/CONF.151/26/Rev.1, Vol. II, Proceedings of the Conference, Chapter III.

UNFCCC (United Nations Framework Convention on Climate Change), 'Appendix II: Nationally Appropriate Mitigation Actions of Developing Country Parties', unfccc.int/home/items/5265.php (accessed 27 July 2011).

'GHG data from UNFCCC', unfccc.int/ghg_data/ghg_data_unfccc/items/4146.php (accessed 27 July 2011).

'Report of the Conference of the Parties on its First Session, held at Berlin from 28 March to 7 April 1995', FCCC/CP/1995/7/Add.1, 6 June 1995, unfccc.int/resource/docs/cop1/07a01.pdf (accessed 27 July 2011).

'Report of the Conference of the Parties on its Sixteenth Session, held in Cancún from 29 November to 10 December 2010', FCCC/CP/2010/7/Add.1, 15 March 2011.

UNFCCC/CP (Conference of the Parties), Bali Action Plan (Decision 1/CP.13), FCCC/CP/2007/6/Add.1.

Copenhagen Accord, 18 December 2009, FCCC/CP/2009/L.7/CP.15.

'Unfinished business', *Economist*, 14 May 2011, 10–13.

United Nations, *A more secure world: Our shared responsibility: Report of the High-Level Panel on Threats, Challenges and Change* (New York: United Nations, 2004).

United Nations Environment Programme, Rio Declaration on Environment and Development, 1992, www.unep.org/Documents.Multilingual/ Default.asp?documentid=78&articleid=1163 (accessed 8 August 2011).

United Nations Framework Convention on Climate Change, FCCC/ INFORMAL/84 GE.05–62220 (E) 200705, adopted 9 May 1992.

United Nations General Assembly, *Official Records*, Second Session, Vol. I (New York: United Nations, 1947).

'Resolution adopted by the General Assembly, 60/1. 2005 World Summit outcome', A/RES/60/1, 16 September 2005.

United States Congress, *Events leading up to World War II: Chronological history of certain major international events leading up to and during World War II with the ostensible reasons advanced for their occurrence, 1931–1944* (Washington, DC: US GPO, 1944), www.ibiblio.org/pha/events/1933.html (accessed 28 July 2011).

United States Department of Defense, 'Nuclear Posture Review [Excerpts]', Submitted to Congress on 31 December 2001, www.stanford.edu/class/ polisci211z/2.6/NPR2001leaked.pdf (accessed 27 July 2011).

United States Senate, Byrd-Hagel Resolution, 105th Congress, First Session; S Res 98, Sponsored by Senator Robert Byrd (D-WV) and Senator Chuck Hagel (R-NE), 25 July 1997, www.nationalcenter.org/KyotoSenate.html (accessed 27 July 2011).

United States State Department, 'Secretary of State Madeleine K. Albright, Interview on NBC-TV "The Today Show" with Matt Lauer', Columbus, Ohio, 19 February 1998, secretary.state.gov/www/statements/1998/980219a. html (accessed 29 July 2011).

'US commerce, energy secretaries highlight cooperation with China on climate change', Xinhua News Agency, 6 July 2009, www.china.org.cn/environment/ news/2009–07/16/content_18146470.htm (accessed 27 July 2011).

'US statement', working paper submitted to the Third Session of the Preparatory Committee for the 2005 Review Conference, 7 May 2004, NPT/Conf.2005/PC.III/WP.28.

Van Langenhove, L., 'The transformation of multilateralism mode 1.0 to mode 2.0', *Global Policy*, 1(3) 2010, 263–70.

Vandenberg, A., 'Senator Vandenberg's report to the Senate on the San Francisco conference', 29 June 1945, www.ibiblio.org/pha/policy/1945/450629a.html (accessed 28 July 2011).

Vidal, J., 'US threatens to derail climate talks by refusing to include targets', *Guardian*, 7 October 2009.

Vig, N., 'Presidential leadership and the environment', in N. J. Vig and M. E. Kraft (eds.), *Environmental policy: New directions for the twenty-first century* (Washington, DC: Congressional Quarterly, 2006), pp. 100–23.

Vincent, R. J., 'Order in international politics', in J. D. B. Miller and R. J. Vincent (eds.), *Order and violence: Hedley Bull and international relations* (Oxford: Oxford University Press, 1990), pp. 38–64.

Vogler, J., 'In the absence of the hegemon: EU actorness and the global climate change regime', paper presented to the conference 'The European Union in International Affairs', National Europe Centre, Australian National University, Canberra, 3–4 July 2002.

Vogler, J. and Stephan, H. R., 'The European Union in global environmental governance: Leadership in the making?', *International Environmental Agreements*, 7(4) 2007, 389–413.

Walker, W., *A perpetual menace: Nuclear weapons and international order* (London: Routledge, 2011).

Walter, A., *Governing finance: East Asia's adoption of international standards* (Ithaca, NY: Cornell University Press, 2008).

'Intellectual laziness caused the economic crisis', *Guardian*, 27 March 2009.

Waltz, K. N., 'The spread of nuclear weapons: More may be better', *Adelphi Paper* 171 (London: International Institute for Strategic Studies, 1981).

Theory of international politics (Reading, MA: Addison-Wesley, 1979).

Walzer, M., 'The politics of rescue', *Social Research*, 62(1) 1995, 53–66.

Warner, D., *An ethic of responsibility in international relations* (Boulder, CO: Lynne Rienner, 1991).

Watson, A., *The evolution of international society* (London: Routledge, 1992).

Weber, M., *Politics as a vocation* (Philadelphia, PA : Fortress Press, 1965).

The theory of social and economic organization (New York: Free Press, 1964).

Webster, C. K. (ed.), *The Congress of Vienna, 1814–15*, 2nd edn (London: Bell, 1945).

Wendt, A., 'Collective identity formation and the international state', *American Political Science Review*, 88(2) 1994, 384–95.

Social theory of international politics (Cambridge: Cambridge University Press, 1999).

Wheeler, N. J., *Saving strangers: Humanitarian intervention in international society* (Oxford: Oxford University Press, 2002).

White House, 'President announces clear skies and global climate change initiatives', Silver Spring, Maryland, 14 February 2002, georgewbush-whitehouse. archives.gov/news/releases/2002/02/20020214–5.html (accessed 27 July 2011).

'The National Security Strategy of the United States' (Washington, DC: The White House, 20 September 2002), www.globalsecurity.org/military/ library/policy/national/nss-020920.pdf (accessed 27 July 2011).

White House, Office of the Press Secretary, 'Press conference by the President at the nuclear security summit', Washington Convention Center, Washington, DC, 13 April 2010, www.whitehouse.gov/the-press-office/press-conference-president-nuclear-security-summit (accessed 31 July 2011).

Wight, M., *Systems of states*, ed. H. Bull (Leicester: Leicester University Press, 1977).

Williams, F., *Some aspects of the covenant of the League of Nations* (London: Oxford University Press, 1934).

Williams, M. C., *The realist tradition and the limits of international relations* (Cambridge: Cambridge University Press, 2005).

Wohlstetter, A., Brown, T., Jones, G., McGarvey, D., Rowen, H., Taylor, V. and Wohlstetter, R., 'Moving toward life in a nuclear armed crowd? ACDA/PAB-263, PH76–04–389–14, final report' (Los Angeles, CA: PAN Heuristics, 4 December 1975; revised 22 April 1976).

Wolfsthal, J. B., 'The next nuclear wave: Nonproliferation in a new world', *Foreign Affairs*, 84(1) 2005, 156–61.

Wright, Q., 'The proposed termination of the Iraq mandate', *American Journal of International Law*, 25(3) 1931, 436–46.

Yamin, F. and Depledge, J., *The international climate change regimes: A guide to rules, institutions and procedures* (Cambridge: Cambridge University Press, 2004).

Yost, D., 'France's evolving nuclear strategy', *Survival*, 47(3) 2005, 117–46.

'France's new nuclear doctrine', *International Affairs*, 82(4) 2006, 701–21.

Zakaria, F., *The post-American world* (New York: W. W. Norton, 2008).

Zhang, Y., 'Understanding Chinese views of the emerging global order', in G. Wang and Y. Zheng (eds.), *China and the new international order* (London: Routledge, 2008), pp. 149–67.

Zimmern, A., *The League of Nations and the rule of law 1918–1935* (London: Macmillan, 1936).

Index